TRUE CRIME
IN THE
CIVIL WAR

0 11557 01019 0

TRUE CRIME
IN THE
CIVIL WAR

CASES OF MURDER, TREASON,
COUNTERFEITING, MASSACRE,
PLUNDER & ABUSE

TOBIN T. BUHK

STACKPOLE
BOOKS

Copyright ©2012 by Stackpole Books

Published by
STACKPOLE BOOKS
5067 Ritter Road
Mechanicsburg, PA 17055
www.stackpolebooks.com

Printed in the United States of America

10 9 8 7 6 5 4 3 2 1

FIRST EDITION

Library of Congress Cataloging-in-Publication Data

Buhk, Tobin T.
    True crime in the Civil War : cases of murder, treason, counterfeiting, massacre, plunder, and abuse / Tobin T. Buhk. — 1st ed.
        p.   cm.
    Includes bibliographical references and index.
    ISBN 978-0-8117-1019-0 (pbk.)
    1. United States—History—Civil War, 1861–1865—Social aspects.   2. Civil-military relations—United States—History—19th century.   3. United States—History—Civil War, 1861–1865—Destruction and pillage.   4. United States—History—Civil War, 1861–1865—Atrocities.   5. War crimes—United States—History—19th century.   6. Trials (Military offenses)—United States—History—19th century. I. Title.
E468.9.B887   2012
973.7'11—dc23

2011047046

Contents

Preface

—◆—

All is fair in love and war, but during every conflict there are those who go too far, those who cross an often invisible boundary between what conduct is considered appropriate and what is not. The United States Civil War was no different.

The four-year period of hostilities that began in 1861 gave rise to leaders who used their positions for personal gain; profiteers who tried to make money off of misery; generals who dueled other generals, even though they were on the same side; ruthless raids targeting civilians and their property; and bandits who used the conflict as a convenient excuse to rape, pillage, and murder. Sometimes these malefactors got away with these crimes, and sometimes they didn't.

The Great American Divorce: A Note about Voices

Whenever a divorce occurs, especially one involving custody issues, strong opinions tend to result. People take sides. Fingers are pointed. The Civil War was the biggest divorce in the nation's history. And it involved custody issues.

People took sides. Accusations, expletives, and shells flew, although not necessarily in that order. Later, many of the combatants lucky enough to survive the bullets and the grapeshot wrote about their experiences. This amazing legacy has survived in countless diaries and books.

For the writer, this material is a blessing as well as a curse. It's a blessing because there is nothing more compelling than listening to voices from the past telling their stories. Reading the archival material from the era is the next best thing to taking a time machine for a spin back to 1863. It's a curse, because as authentic as they are, these voices are not always honest. At times, they embellish or even downright lie. Sometimes, they're mistaken or inaccurate. And sometimes, they point the finger and sling accusations as if they're firing at the enemy.

Newspaper reports don't help much in sifting fact from allegation. The news reporters of the era didn't tell it like it was, but rather as they saw it.

They didn't bother with "allegedly" this or "reportedly" that. They came out and proclaimed guilt or innocence in ways that would make a twenty-first-century editor cringe.

No one, except perhaps the historian who doubles as a clairvoyant, can claim to know firsthand what happened 150 years ago. The next best thing is to find as many voices as possible from both sides and discern some middle ground between them.

The following chapters were constructed, as much as possible, using the voices of the people who lived through this turbulent era and survived to write about it. Please remember, they sometimes present myth as fact, sometimes lie, frequently exaggerate, often make mistakes, and almost always contain a bias. The author has tried, in earnest, to do none of these things.

A Brief Note about Cases

Beggars can't be choosers, except when dealing with the Civil War. There were so many Civil War–related crimes that no single volume could do it justice. Alas, choices had to be made.

The following crimes were selected because they were some of the most audacious, brutal, bodacious, or bizarre cases, representing all points on the criminal spectrum. Many contain uniquely devious twists: a riot that began with a crime that later turned out not to be a crime; an outlaw-on-paper who became so real, he was hanged; guards allegedly so sadistic from a prison so infamous, they wound up on trial; a group of terrorists whose plan went up in smoke instead of their intended targets; and a little general whose libido did him in.

And now, on to the mayhem.

The Criminal State of the Union

Two boys ambling down Pennsylvania Avenue in Washington, DC, paused at the corner of East First Street. They stared, mouths agape, at the imposing building across the street—the Old Capitol Prison—hoping to catch a glimpse of an inmate behind the barred windows. Captivated, the kids failed to hear the guard yelling at them: "You there, hurry up."

The boys were unaware as they studied the three-story edifice that they were about to get an inside look at Washington's most notorious landmark. Quick to act when the boys failed to respond to his warning, the corporal ran down the street, collared the two twelve-year-olds, and escorted them inside the prison for questioning as "suspicious persons."[1]

The entire scene, which took place on a chilly, cloudless winter afternoon in 1863, was witnessed from the arched window of Room 16, where James Williamson spent two months as a "suspicious person." Williamson, who worked for a local printing firm, was arrested on January 31, 1863, after returning from a trip to Richmond. When he refused to take the oath of allegiance to the Union, he wound up inside the Old Capitol, so named because the structure was built as a temporary capitol after the British burned down the original building during the War of 1812.

Williamson, who occupied the room with several other "suspicious persons," passed time by watching the foot traffic on the street below the window of his cell. During his brief incarceration, he witnessed many incidents in which the guards chased away or even arrested passersby on suspicion of attempting to deliver messages to the silhouettes behind the bars.

He recalled one time when a guard ran after two ladies who "bowed to our window." The guard questioned them on the street and then let them go.[2] Another person whose curiosity almost landed him in jail was an elderly man who paused, took a "spy glass" out of his pocket, and scoped out the prison. The man ignored the sentry's warning and left only after he heard the sentry ask an officer if he should invite the man inside for a better look.[3]

These curious people wanted to glimpse the hidden world of crime during the Civil War.

The epic conflict known at various times and to various people as the War Between the States, the War for Southern Independence, and the Civil War was a domestic disturbance on a nationwide scale. From the onset of hostilities in April 1861, when rebels shelled the island fortress of Fort Sumter, to the unofficial cease-fire with Lee's surrender to Grant at Appomattox Court House four years later in April 1865, the two sides fought a no-holds-barred duel to the death.

Americans were caught up in a total war that tore families apart at the seams. Emotions ran high during the four years of hostilities, and sometimes noble deeds came along with ignoble ones. Stripping away the outer layers of patriotism and cause reveals a seedy underbelly of vice, corruption, and murder.

History books don't often venture into the dark side of crime during the Civil War. They tend to stick to the splendid sacrifice of soldiers thrust into the meat grinder for the sake of the cause. To explore crime during the Civil War is to take a morbidly fascinating stroll through the dimly lit back alleys of history.

It's a necessary trip. The Civil War was such a crucial time in American history, that to fully comprehend the war and its impact on people of the era, it is necessary to examine not just the glorious moments, but also the inglorious ones.

Almost immediately, from April 12 1861, when Confederate cannon fire pounded Fort Sumter, in Charleston, South Carolina, authorities of the two governments faced the unexpected menace of war-related crime. The unique circumstances of the Civil War provided opportunities for mayhem on both sides of the Mason-Dixon Line.

War was war, but business was business, and crafty opportunists quickly realized that the war could mean big profits. From its inception, the Confederate treasury faced a major problem with counterfeiting. A shortage of precious metals forced the new government to rely entirely on paper money. Lithography and cheap paper made Southern banknotes easy to copy and reproduce, so gangs of counterfeiters immediately began to make funny money.

A brief scan of the *Richmond Dispatch*, one of the rebel capital's chief newspapers, reveals how widespread counterfeiting was in the early days of the war, before inflation caused by the Northern blockade stripped Confederate money of its value. A page-one item from September 9, 1862, reports that Robert Blossingham of Williamsburg, Virginia, went to prison for possessing $30 in counterfeit banknotes.[4]

Another counterfeiter, John Richardson, alias "Louis Napoleon," paid the ultimate price for his crime when he became the first man hanged in the Confederacy for counterfeiting. Richardson and George Elam, after imbibing a few pints at the corner tavern, strong-armed their way into the printing house of Hoyer and Ludwig, one of the firms under contract to print Confederate banknotes. They stole sheets of $10 notes and used the firm's presses to print $800 more. They then took the notes to a shopkeeper who gave them an example of an issued $10 note. Confederate notes were hand-signed by government officials for security, so Richardson and Elam forged the signatures and began passing them off as genuine in Richmond stores.[5]

These forgers were small-time compared to Sam Upham in Philadelphia and Winthrop Hilton in New York, who worked safely from printing shops beyond the reach of Confederate authorities. They sold sheaves of facsimile Confederate currency to speculators who used the banknotes to defraud ignorant cotton planters. When Federal authorities did know about these operations, they turned a blind eye, as long as the printing presses didn't go near Federal greenbacks. These two didn't, but others did.

Unlike Southern banknotes, which dropped in value as the war and the blockade took its toll on the Confederacy, Northern greenbacks maintained their value throughout the conflict, making them enticing targets. Like their Southern counterparts, Union authorities came down hard on citizens producing or passing fake money. The *Daily National Republican* of February 4, 1864, contains an item titled "A Counterfeiter 'Cooked,'" which tells the brief story of Sylvester Cook, caught passing $50 banknotes. Cook went to prison for three years.[6]

The war provided another avenue to quick wealth for the brave souls willing to take the risk. Smuggling became big business with fortunes made, or liberty lost for the ones unlucky enough to get caught. Maryland and other border states became smuggling hotspots as entrepreneurs tried to move their goods from north to south and vice versa.

Blockade runners became a constant nuisance to Federal authorities, whose "Anaconda Plan" squeezed the South of vital resources. The May 25, 1863, edition of the *Daily National Republican* ran a headline story on the arrest of some alleged blockade runners:

> Two men by the name of Frazier and Urquhart, both claiming to be British subjects, were arrested on Saturday—the former at Sigel's Hotel, and the latter at No. 527 Maryland avenue—upon the charge of being blockade

runners. Frazier, it is charged, takes goods to Richmond for others at high prices, and on his person was found papers from the Richmond authorities, dated March 3, 1863, which would procure him such business. Urquhart had employed him to take goods South. They were both sent to the Old Capitol prison.[7]

James Williamson, the Old Capitol Prison detainee, noted in his memoirs that "One of the strongest inducements for running the blockade was the enormous value of cotton outside of the Confederacy." Ships filled with medical supplies and guns would run the Federal gauntlet into Southern ports such as Wilmington, North Carolina. Once inside, they traded their supplies for cotton and made a run for it. If they managed to slip through the net of Federal ships, they could sell the cotton abroad for a huge profit. According to Williamson, this promise of instant wealth "would certainly furnish a strong incentive for other daring adventurers to take the risk of a voyage."[8] He was right, and many of them wound up behind bars in the Old Capitol, rubbing elbows with "suspicious persons," forgers, and other miscreants.

Even more troublesome to both governments were the small-scale smugglers, who played a constant game of cat and mouse with authorities. The *Richmond Dispatch* of July 31, 1862, noted that seven "citizens" were caught trying to smuggle booze into a nearby army camp. They were sent off to Castle Godwin, one in a network of former tobacco warehouses converted into makeshift prisons.[9] A hundred miles north in Washington, DC, wily cop John F. Parker collared Joseph Smith as he was trying to move a ten-gallon barrel of whiskey across the Potomac. Smith's clients on the southern side of the river, whoever they were, went thirsty; both Smith and his whiskey "were turned over to the military."[10]

A few weeks later, Richmond detectives sniffed out twenty-six boxes of tobacco on a wagon en route to the North, presumably to Washington. Patrick Reardon planned to take the load across the Potomac for sale to Northerners in exchange for Federal greenbacks or gold. Citizens of DC never got their smokes, and Reardon missed his golden payday. The detectives rerouted Reardon's wagon, sending him straight to Castle Thunder, another tobacco warehouse-turned-penitentiary in Richmond's network of prisons.[11]

During the war, hundreds of citizens on both sides also did prison stints for alleged disloyalty. In the rebel capital, they often went to Castle Godwin or Castle Thunder. The castles saw a steady stream of convicts, many of them suspected of some sort of treachery. It didn't take much to be jailed as a "disloyal citizen." A Richmond shipping merchant named Charles Palmer went to Castle Goodwin after uttering a few pro-Lincoln comments. A farmer named Stokes was thrown into the same prison as a "disloyal citizen" when he refused to take Confederate banknotes, which by then had become suspect because of the huge numbers of counterfeits in circulation.[12] Sometimes, their ticket to freedom was simply taking an oath of allegiance.

In the Federal capital, "suspicious persons" went to the Old Capitol Prison complex—the criminal capitol of the Union's first city. Many of its inmates were jailed for alleged disloyalty, and in wartime Washington—just a hundred miles from the capital of the Confederacy and surrounded by Marylanders of mixed loyalties—traffic in and out of the Old Capitol was heavy.

According to William Doster, provost marshal of Washington, DC, the prison complex suffered from one major drawback. "The great fault of this prison," Doster later recalled in his memoirs *Episodes of the Civil War*, "was that it operated like a rat trap—there was only a hole in but no hole out; in other words, plenty of provision for arresting people, but none for trying them or disposing of their cases."[13]

Just about anyone and everyone had the power to arrest, Doster notes, but no one could release a prisoner without stepping on someone's toes. As a result, "the prison was constantly crowded with people, many of whom, when their cases came to be investigated, had waited for a long time to offer a simple explanation."[14]

Some inmates of Old Capitol were jailed because they refused to take a loyalty oath. In his prison diary, James Williamson compares political prisoners like himself to the Man in the Iron Mask, with the Old Capitol as the Bastille. "Many persons confined here were arrested, robbed of everything they possessed, and kept merely on suspicion for weeks, and even months, without examination or trial, and sometimes, after an examination and no proof of charges, being still detained."[15]

The reason for the "Rat Trap" becomes a little clearer considering the cloak-and-dagger work done in Washington. Notorious Confederate spies Rose O'Neal Greenhow and Belle Boyd did stints at the Old Capitol and wreaked almost as much havoc on the inside as on the outside. Greenhow, whose eight-year-old daughter Rose lived with her in the Old Capitol, once commandeered a horse and wagon and gave the Capitol's other female prisoners a ride around the yard. Boyd, a nineteen-year-old vixen and celebrity spy, often sat at her window and sang patriotic hymns of the South.

The most troublesome of the group was one Mrs. Baxley, a Southern belle who was captured while searching the battlefields for her son and imprisoned as a "suspicious person." She wasn't as much trouble as Boyd and Greenhow on the outside, but she was a real handful on the inside.

The *New York Times* of April 15, 1862, described the forty-five-year-old as "a virulent, loquacious secesh," who often draped a "black silk apron, representing a rebel black flag," from her window. N. T. Colby, an officer who served as one of the prison's overseers, described her as "a shrewd plotter of mischief" and a fervent Southerner determined to do what she could to insult her Federal captors.[16]

On one occasion, she berated a sentinel so severely that he threatened to shoot her if she didn't leave the window. "Fire, then, you Yankee scoundrel," she screamed. "You were hired to murder women, and here is an opportunity to exercise your trade."

To scare Baxley into submission, the sentry fired a shot at the window frame. "A shot worthy of a Yankee," Baxley yelled through the window. "Load and try another," she taunted him. He didn't.[17]

While citizens traded information and goods with the enemy and detectives tried to stop them, the soldiers fought for their causes. Life in the military gave rise to other war-related crimes. Almost from the start of the conflict, Federal authorities faced the issue of criminality both in the ranks and among civilians in occupied territories where no legitimate courts existed to hear cases. To handle crimes perpetrated by soldiers, courts-martial were organized. To handle crimes committed by civilians (and Confederate soldiers accused of war crimes), the army set up military commissions. Some of the era's most infamous characters, including Andersonville commandant Henry Wirz and the Lincoln assassination conspirators, faced such panels.

These commissions—military courts consisting of officers who served as judges as well as juries—handled cases swiftly, sometimes moving from arraignment to sentencing in a matter of hours, and meted out harsh punishments, including sentences of hard labor and death by hanging. Military commissions, which initially convened in border states like Missouri, had become the legal authority in Union-occupied areas by 1863 and continued to try cases throughout the war and beyond, playing a key role during Reconstruction.

Conducting trials in chaotic war zones was tricky business, and sometimes the military courts had to wait until a lull in the action to hear cases. Their justice was swift and decisive, and their sentences, by today's standards, were severe. The curious court-martial of Thomas Wright, a private in Company B of the 7th Missouri Volunteer Infantry, is a typical example of "drumhead" justice in a war zone.

Private Wright, a heavy drinker stationed on the outskirts of occupied Vicksburg, Mississippi, tipped his spiked canteen one time too many on the evening of September 24, 1863. Inebriated, he loaded his musket and fired it at brother soldiers who, he said, had bullied him. When his superior, Sgt. John Maguire, ordered him to drop his weapon, he threatened to shoot him. Wright, possibly because he couldn't see straight, didn't shoot anyone but nevertheless wound up in front of a court-martial facing a charge of "mutinous conduct."

"What did he do?" Judge Advocate William Frohock asked Maguire.

"He took his musket out of his tent on the side of the hill, and laid down, and I heard him say that there were men on hill who were abusing him and trying to beat him," Maguire reported. "I warned him to come into the camp but he said he wanted satisfaction. I looked up the hill but could not see anyone."

Maguire, perhaps not taking Wright seriously, returned to his tent. A few minutes later, he heard the report of a rifle. He went back to Wright and ordered him to lay down his weapon. Wright, Maguire said, then threatened him: "he told me to keep away from him, or I would get into trouble."[18]

The court-martial found Private Wright guilty and sentenced him "to hard labor on the fortifications at Vicksburg, Miss., for thirty days with ball and chain attached to his leg."[19]

The case of Thomas Wright illustrates the frayed tempers sometimes caused by tensions on the battlefield. Some of the war's headline crimes resulted from feuds that developed between soldiers on the same side. In the North, the highest-profile example of internecine strife turned homicidal was the cold-blooded murder of Gen. William "Bull" Nelson in Louisville, Kentucky, by "brother soldier" Jefferson C. Davis. The South lost Gen. Lucius "Marsh" Walker in an 1863 duel with Gen. John Marmaduke—the final act in a feud that began on the battlefields of Arkansas.

The ill-defined rules of engagement, combined with strong feelings on both sides of the conflict, mixed loyalties, and the ever-present threat of irregular or guerrilla warfare, led to crimes against noncombatants. The sack of Athens, Alabama, perpetrated by troops under Union colonel J. B. Turchin in 1862, was one of the war's headline crimes. The alleged atrocities committed by the boys in blue sent Turchin to a court-martial that quickly became a referendum on proper conduct during wartime. While not everyone agreed that taking property from the enemy was wrong, just about everyone agreed that the rape of Charlotte Hine's servant girl was over the line.

Rapes by soldiers occurred occasionally during the war. Most historians, however, agree that rape during the Civil War was uncommon, although the probability that a number of rapes went unreported blurs the picture.[20] To women of the prim and proper mid-nineteenth century, forced sexual intercourse was an unspeakable atrocity and the ultimate affront to their honor. Rather than go through a public scandal, many rape victims may have instead chosen to keep their experiences hidden in diaries and locked safely away in dresser drawers, *if* they discussed them at all. Just how many women bore their humiliation and pain in silence is a question that will never be answered.

Some raiders went out of their way to prevent rape amid the violence and bloodshed. When the infamous Bushwhackers tore through Lawrence, Kansas, on the morning of August 21, 1863, they were under orders not to harm a single hair of a woman's head. As a result, when they rode out of Lawrence, they left the male population decimated but the women unharmed. There is not a single reported instance of rape, murder, or violent assault of a woman during the Lawrence Massacre. The brutal assault of the fairer sex was so distasteful to William Quantrill's men that when Kentucky bad men later raped a woman and blamed it on the Bushwhackers, Quantrill lieutenant Frank James led a group that hunted down the real offenders for a little frontier justice.

The Civil War also gave rise to racially motivated violence, some of which might today be classified as hate crimes. The 1863 national draft law, which called for conscription of troops, led to all sorts of mayhem in Northern cities as racial tensions peaked. In Detroit, the news of the draft reached the city during the trial of a dark-complexioned man named Faulkner for the crime of raping a white girl. The news, coupled with a guilty verdict, touched off a race riot in which white laborers turned on the city's black citizens. They didn't want to fight for emancipation and felt their job security would be threatened by freed slaves, and so they reacted violently. A few months later in July 1863, an epic draft riot exploded in New York City as whites again turned on blacks.

The war led to the liberation of many slaves, who lived an uneasy coexistence with their former masters throughout Union-controlled territory. This volatile situation caused other racially motivated crimes. The Kentucky Bend of the Mississippi River ran red with the blood of the Beckham family, murdered by freed slaves from nearby Island No. 10 after a dispute over a slave girl living at the Beckham place.

Two years later, even with the war officially over and the slavery question answered once and for all, crimes between Southern elite and their former property continued, and in some spots intensified. In Davie County, North Carolina, Temperance Neely shot and killed a former slave named Galina in a tussle between Galina's daughter and Temperance's mother. Race became the focal point of Neely's trial, because the prosecution's only witnesses were her mother's former slaves, who just months earlier would not have been allowed to testify against a white person.

Racially driven crimes also took place on the field of battle as freed blacks went to war for the Union Army. There were several instances in which Confederate soldiers allegedly butchered black soldiers in cold blood after they surrendered. Rebels under the command of renowned cavalryman Nathan Bedford Forrest supposedly massacred the defenders—many of them black—of Fort Pillow along the Mississippi River after the garrison threw down their weapons. The event became infamous after the US Congress conducted an investigation into the Fort Pillow Massacre.

Notorious Kentucky guerrilla Champ Ferguson was also alleged to have covered his hands in the blood of defenseless black soldiers after the Battle of Saltville, Virginia, in 1864. While Ferguson denied the charge during his ensuing war crimes trial, he freely admitted to bullying his way into a hospital and shooting a defenseless officer named Lt. Eliza Smith, who was recuperating from wounds he received at Saltville.

For those studying criminal cases of the Civil War, there are a few precautions worth noting. The twenty-first-century notion of crime and approach to law and order differs drastically from its nineteenth-century predecessor. When Dr. James Boddie Peters shot Gen. Earl Van Dorn in the back of the head in the summer of 1863, some people on both sides of the conflict would have considered the shooting a righteous kill—one done by a man protecting the sanctity and honor of his home—*if* Dr. Peters's wife and Van Dorn were engaged in an affaire d'coeur. Today, by contrast, the killing of Van Dorn would go down as premeditated murder.

Likewise, the death of Gen. Marsh Walker, although in violation of a direct order and Confederate military ethics, not to mention the ban on dueling in Arkansas, was considered not only honorable but also justified.

Court procedures have evolved significantly since the mid-nineteenth century. There is a huge gap between the way courts (both civilian and military) conducted business in 1863 and the way they do today, and it is challenging to not judge the Civil War interpretation of jurisprudence by today's rules.

For example, military courts appointed a judge advocate, who advised the court while also acting as the prosecuting attorney. The judge advocate's job was also to look after the rights of the accused, and in cases where a defendant didn't obtain an attorney, he also acted in a limited capacity as defense counsel. In today's courtroom, this dual role would be considered a conflict of interest.

Today's prosecutors don't play dual roles in court, but they often swap testimony for reduced sentences. In the 1860s, however, prosecutors didn't make such deals. The law at the time prohibited allowing a witness under indictment to testify against others, so prosecutors and judge advocates sometimes dropped charges against key witnesses altogether. This rule of law played a key role during the trial of the Lincoln conspirators; several potential coconspirators (such as Louis Weichmann) evaded a trial because the state needed their testimony.[21]

Modern-day defendants may also testify on their own behalf; during the Civil War, the practice was not legal anywhere but in the civil courts of Maine. Thus the Lincoln assassination conspirators, Henry Wirz, Champ Ferguson, and others did not take the stand during their trials.

It is also worth remembering that the victors, as the saying goes, write the history. Thus, Henry Wirz went to trial for atrocities committed inside the stockade of Andersonville, even though similar outrages took place in the Northern prison at Alton, Illinois. Guerrilla hunter extraordinaire Edwin Terrell committed crimes as bad as, if not worse than those that sent Jerome Clarke to the scaffold. But he committed them for the winning side. Terrell would have evaded punishment altogether, but he just couldn't stop killing, even after the war ended. William Quantrill, perhaps the most notorious name of the war, gets all of the infamy, even though his Northern counterparts, the Red Legs and Jayhawkers, committed ruthless acts of outrage. They just did it for the winning side.

There is another factor muddying the waters: What one side considered wrong, unethical, or downright criminal, the other side thought was justified. William Tecumseh Sherman left cinders in his wake during his 1864 March to the Sea, which many Northerners considered a viable mode of warfare; Southerners viewed it as criminal. On the other hand, rebel agents thought it justified to set fire to New York hotels in an attempt to incinerate the business district in 1864. Northerners didn't agree; would-be arsonist Robert Cobb Kennedy was captured, tried, and hanged as a criminal. Historians still argue about the criminality of what took place during the Fort Pillow Massacre and Forrest's role in the incident.

The nineteenth-century media sometimes aided and abetted crimes in a very real and direct way. The *Detroit Free Press*, according to some scholars, fueled the flames of the Detroit race riot by embellishing news of the Faulkner Outrage and running blatantly racist articles in the days leading up to the melee.[22]

George Prentice, the editor of the *Louisville Daily Journal*, went beyond embellishment when he invented guerrilla Sue Mundy, the terror of Kentucky. Union authorities bought into Prentice's rhetoric and tried a young Kentucky guerrilla named Jerome Clarke as Sue Mundy. Indeed, when reading news articles about crimes of the Civil War, it's always good to be a bit skeptical.

The cases presented in the following chapters were all considered over the line of proper conduct by one or both sides. Even rebel soldiers later spoke about atrocities during the Fort Pillow Massacre, and some of the rebel arsonists who attacked New York backed out at the last minute; they didn't see the operation as a viable act of war.

Things apparently got too out of hand inside Richmond's Castle Thunder: The Confederate Congress made Captain George W. Alexander answer for his brand of law and order during an investigative hearing, and then later gave him the hook following allegations of bribery.

On the other side of the fence, so to speak, Benjamin Butler's rule over New Orleans ruffled so many feathers that his own government reassigned him, only to later relieve him altogether after a humiliating battlefield gaffe during the siege of Fort Fisher in North Carolina.

Some of the bloody tales are told in depth here for the first time. The murder of the Beckham family evaded print for almost a century and a half. The murders were so shocking, even the audacious press of the time were reluctant to cover them in any detail. The fascinating case of Temperance Neely also slipped through the cracks of history. Until now. These and many other miscreants populate this dimly lit back alley of history.

CHAPTER 1

Inside Castle Thunder,
Notorious Richmond Prison
1862

A s soon as hostilities began in the Civil War, both sides were confronted
with a new breed of criminal created by the conflict—profiteers, traitors, spies, and deserters—and both governments created facilities to
hold them.

Many of these prisons quickly earned bad reps, but Richmond's Castle
Thunder was rumored to be so terrible that rebel lawmakers launched a
probe into the treatment of prisoners there. At the hearings, some witnesses said that the worst criminals in the joint were the men running it,
particularly Castle Thunder's version of the *Bounty*'s Captain Bligh.

Through accounts of those who spent time in these pens, it becomes possible to go behind the walls and catch a glimpse of the era's approach to law
and order, crime and punishment. Most of the time, it isn't a pretty sight.

☻ ☻ ☻

Frightened, irritated, hungry, and cold, Frank Doran and a group other
prisoners were marched down the corridor of Castle Thunder. As they
approached the large room in the former tobacco factory that housed
around one hundred prisoners, they heard a faint chant.

"Fresh fish. Fresh fish. Fresh fish."

The chanting became louder as the new prisoners approached the door.

"Fresh fish, fresh fish, fresh fish. Fresh fish."

As soon as the guards slammed the door, Doran found himself "surrounded by a pack of demoniac ruffians" who "hovered about us like hye-
nas" and began to take things from the new inmates.[1]

Such scenes occurred each time new "fish" arrived. On one occasion, a
fish was stripped to his underwear by the mob that always formed whenever

new prisoners entered. Doran lost only his hat, which he saw passed from inmate to inmate until it reached the head of a man named Charles Curtis, who Doran called "one of the worst desperadoes that ever went unhanged as long as he did."[2]

Inside Castle Thunder, Curtis led a mob that bullied and beat fellow prisoners. According to Doran, Curtis and his henchmen cut the finger off of a sleeping man to obtain his gold ring. The man had been recently captured and was exhausted, so he didn't notice them trying to pull the ring off until they began cutting.

When the man awoke from the sharp pain of his left ring finger being sliced off, Curtis's gang simply held him down while one of them sawed away until they had his ring and he had one less finger. Such accounts are sometimes spiced up with a liberal sprinkling of exaggeration, but such cruelty was not unheard of inside the prison's walls.

Later in the war, Curtis was transported to Camp Sumter (Andersonville) in Georgia, where he once again led a prison gang sometimes called "Curtis's Raiders." The group was so tyrannical to their fellow inmates that they were tried and hanged on July 11, 1864. But in 1863, Curtis and his mob helped put the "Thunder" in Castle Thunder.

Castle Thunder wasn't much of a castle. It wasn't even made of stone. It was an old tobacco warehouse of William Greanor & Sons and two smaller adjacent buildings converted to a prison complex—a move made necessary by the growing number of prisoners created by the war. To house these malefactors, Southern authorities created a system of jails in and around Richmond.

Castle Thunder, which opened in 1862, housed civilian prisoners as well as Confederate military personnel accused of crimes. So in addition to the usual suspects—thieves, murderers, and rapists—there were also traitors, spies, disloyal citizens, profiteers, counterfeiters, and others, including Federal soldiers who were sent to the castle in 1863 because of overcrowding at Libby Prison.

The "cells" consisted of rooms that ranged in size from fifteen-square-foot chambers to large, spacious galleries that sometimes held up to a hundred prisoners at a time. The inmates did not have benches or seats, because, as one guard later recalled, "they would break and burn them up if there was."[3] They didn't have beds, either; they slept on the sawdust-covered floor.

The Castle's inmates represented all points on the spectrum of crime. The prison's population was segregated according to classification. Political prisoners—spies, traitors, and those suspected of treason—occupied rooms on the second floor. Civilian criminals occupied other rooms. Men court-

A scene inside a Richmond tobacco warehouse in 1865, sketched for *Harper's Weekly*. When the need arose, some of Richmond's warehouses were converted into prisons, such as Libby and Castle Thunder. The large, spacious rooms, which were typically subdivided into "cells," made policing the prisons difficult.

martialed or awaiting court-martial occupied rooms on the third floor. The fourth floor housed the prison's infirmary.

Although it was primarily used to house males, the Castle did host several female prisoners, who were confined to a separate part of the facility. A few of these women had been caught cross-dressing in rebel gray; they had cropped their hair and suited up for the Confederacy. Later caught, they were held as suspicious characters and possibly spies. Since women were forbidden from enlisting as soldiers, their presence on the battlefield disguised as men in uniform led rebel authorities to believe they might be spying for the other side. For the women, Castle Thunder wasn't homey, but it wasn't hell, either. One woman, imprisoned as a suspected spy, gave birth inside the tobacco warehouse and immortalized her prison experience by naming her daughter Castellina Thunder Lee.[4]

One of the Castle's most famous inmates was Dr. Mary E. Walker, the renowned battlefield surgeon later decorated with the Medal of Honor. In 1864, she was captured and sent to Castle Thunder for a short time because Richmond's Libby Prison didn't have facilities for female inmates.[5] Dr. Walker kept a small knife, which she refused to relinquish, with her at all times.

During her short stint at Castle Thunder, Walker would sit and converse with the detectives, her fellow political prisoners, and reporters who came to interview the always-quotable medical marm. A Richmond newspaper editor related a colorful description of Walker: Whenever a reporter offended her, she replied, "'I am a lady, gentlemen, and I dare any man to insult me.' And her delicate fingers would tap her poignard significantly."[6]

Dr. Walker's jovial threat notwithstanding, real violence occurred inside some of the Castle's rooms. Prison personnel tried to deter violent incidents among the groups by separating dangerous felons from the general population, but they didn't always succeed. The New Orleans "wharf rats" and the Baltimore "plug uglies"—according to one guard, the most dangerous inmates in the prison—rubbed elbows with nonviolent offenders.[7]

Within months of its opening, Castle Thunder had acquired an unsavory reputation. So too did its commandant, Capt. George W. Alexander, who depending on the source is alternately described as either a true Southern gentleman forced to use an iron fist at the prison, or a ruthless, cruel tyrant with a Napoleonic complex. "He loved to command and threaten," one writer said about Alexander. "In his moods he was capable of inspiring either hatred, love, or fear."[8]

At five-foot-six, Alexander was shorter than the "Little General," but in Richmond, he was a larger-than-life character. As provost marshal of the city, he would ride about town on a horse, accompanied by a massive Russian hound named Nero. When the dog didn't obey, he would fire a shot over its head or crack a whip he always carried. An educated man, Alexander spent his free time penning plays that were performed in Richmond. On one occasion, he even played himself in a cameo, trotting onto the stage on horseback with Nero at his side.

Captain Alexander must have been quite a sight to the belles of Richmond. He may not have been tall, but he was dark and handsome; he had olive-colored skin, raven-black hair, a full mustache and beard, and a barrel chest. By the time he was placed in charge of Castle Thunder, George Alexander was considered a war hero in the South (and a pirate in the North). His military record reads like a swashbuckling adventure novel.

A native of Maryland, Alexander was a US naval engineer before the war. During his off-duty hours, he found time for romance. While stationed at Portsmouth, Virginia, he met, courted, and married the love of his life—a Virginia belle named Susie Ashby.

He resigned his naval commission on April 5, 1861, just before the rebels fired on Sumter and two months later went to work for the Confederate States of America.

One of Alexander's early missions involved leading a group to Sombrero Island (named for its hatlike shape) in the southeastern Caribbean. A 1820s geological survey of the small island found it to be rich in bat guano, otherwise known as phosphate of lime, which contained nitrates—a key ingredient of gunpowder. When the war began, the Confederacy needed all the guano it could get, so it sent George Alexander to secure the bat caves. But Alexander never got the guano. En route, his ship wrecked off the coast of Virginia.

The failed guano expedition was just a precursor to the adventure Alexander would later experience on the Potomac River. Alexander's pal Richard Thomas concocted a wild scheme to capture a merchant ship anchored in the Potomac off Alexandria, Virginia, across the river from Washington. Disguised as passengers (some of them dressed as women), Thomas, Alexander, and a small group captured the vessel and took it to Fredericksburg, Virginia.

The hijackers were lauded as heroes, and Alexander was promoted to the rank of captain. Their next mark was a ship named the *Georgeanna*. Thomas and Alexander, again in disguise, captured the ship for the Confederacy. Not long after this, both men were captured, charged as traitors and pirates, and imprisoned pending trial.

Alexander's next adventure took place inside the Federal prison at Fort McHenry in Baltimore, where he and Thomas awaited trial. The future jailor spent several months inside the Union stronghold, which sat at the end of a finger jutting into Baltimore harbor and held a variety of prisoners, including officers who served with the CSA. It wasn't easy time for the feisty captain. He and his cellmate accosted a guard for speaking "imprudently," an incident for which Alexander spent three weeks in an underground cell.

Alexander hadn't been behind bars for long before he and his wife concocted a creative escape plan. Susie visited him daily wearing the type of large hoop skirt fashionable at the time. Under the iron hoop—a place not searched by prison personnel—she smuggled into the prison a map with blue dots marking Union positions at the fort, a coat, a length of clothesline, a waistcoat-turned-life-preserver, and a Federal uniform.

During her visits, she was allowed to approach her husband's cell. She would cut the string tying the contraband to the iron hoop under her skirt; when the items dropped to the floor, she kicked them under his cot.

With the necessary items in hand, Alexander settled on September 7, 1861, a Monday night, for his escape. His cellmate agreed to run a diversion. The officers held at the prison were allowed to roam around outside of their cells as long as they were supervised, so Alexander's cellmate lured the sentinel away by striking up a conversation. Meanwhile, Alexander ruffled the bed sheets and blanket to appear that he was sleeping and slipped out of his cell.

He made his way along the parapet, but his plan soon went awry. According to one source, a sentry recognized him and fired at the escapee.[9] According to another, he forgot the clothesline he needed to get down the wall.[10] Both sources agree that whatever the cause—a bad memory or a bad aim—Alexander jumped into the bay, injuring his ankle during the fall.[11]

Despite the sprained ankle, Alexander swam to Baltimore and made his way back behind Confederate lines, where he joined the provost marshal department and became one of the men responsible for law and order in the Confederate capital.

That included oversight of the tobacco warehouse-turned-prison, which Alexander himself named "Castle Thunder" because he wanted "its very name to be a terror to all evil-doers."[12]

Castle Thunder quickly became one of the most notorious prisons in the South. Incidents of violence among the prisoners occurred often. Stronger elements of the population, like those led by Charles Curtis, preyed on the weaker ones.

"I remember when Tyree was brought to the prison," John Caphart, one of the detectives who policed the Castle, later recalled. "He was sent upstairs and put in one of the rooms. In a few minutes, I heard a tremendous noise of shouting, yelling, and hallowing mingled with cries."[13]

After hearing the screams, Caphart went to investigate and found the prisoner Tyree "all beaten and gory with blood and stripped to his drawers. He was so bloody and bruised that I could hardly recognize him." Caphart helped Tyree to his feet and walked him out of the room to the jeers of the mob. "Kill the son of the bitch," someone yelled as Tyree limped off with "nothing but his drawers on"[14]

In another incident, a prisoner was beaten so severely that he lost an eye. According to Caphart, the prisoners also pummeled a fifty-year-old man into a bloody lump of flesh; he later died of his wounds. Some inmates even made crude slingshots that they used against fellow prisoners or passersby on the street below.

Caphart, the prison's chief screw and one of only about fourteen men responsible for keeping order inside the jail, described the Castle's population as the worst he'd seen in his career. According to Caphart, the rowdies would assault visitors by throwing beef bones "large enough to knock a man down."

Going in among the prisoners was dangerous business, Caphart later recalled. "I did not feel safe unless I went with one hand on my pistol."[15] This was quite a statement from someone who had spent his life around criminals. A Norfolk cop before the war, Caphart had thirty-one years experience with law and order before he went to work for Captain Alexander.

The old flatfoot, described as a Santa Claus lookalike with a flowing white beard streaked by "a muddy rivulet of tobacco juice," was no pushover.[16] He had a bit of a reputation for manhandling. "He was never known once to let a prisoner go after the iron vice of his grasp was fairly upon him. If he [the prisoner] resisted, he [Caphart] used a peculiar heavy stick he always carried," a Richmond reporter said of Alexander's right-hand man.[17] Caphart also served as executioner when duty called, which it did three or four times during the war.

To keep law and order, Captain Alexander ran a tight ship. "He seemed to look upon the prison as a man-of-war ship," the *Richmond Dispatch* said.[18] With the aid of his detectives, Alexander meted out punishments ordered by court-martial. Brig. Gen. John Winder, the man in charge of Richmond and the overseer of the entire Confederate prison system, also gave him the go-ahead to impose corporal punishment on prison rule-breakers.

Inmates violating prison rules were sometimes shackled in irons or bucked and gagged, a common punishment throughout antebellum prisons. T. G. Bland, a steward at the prison hospital, described the punishment: "The 'gag' is effected by a stick inserted crosswise in the mouth, and the 'buck' is to tie the arms at the elbows to a cross-piece beneath the thighs"[19] One former prisoner described bucking as "in a manner of a calf going to market." The punishment was generally more humiliating than painful, and "bucked and gagged" inmates were placed somewhere in public view.

A few rowdy Castle inmates experienced another painless yet humiliating punishment: the "barrel shirt," a flour barrel with holes cut out for the head and both arms. For more serious offenses, prisoners were "punished with stripes," or whipped. Men were stripped to the waist and stung with a three-inch-thick leather band. The whipping bruised but generally didn't break the skin. Nonetheless, it wasn't a painless punishment. James McAlister, a Castle inmate who felt the bitter end of a whip, said the lash didn't cut, "but I was black and blue and was sore for a month afterwards."[20]

According to some inmates, the prison guards also strung up prisoners by their thumbs (a naval punishment called "trysting"; the prisoners called it "thumbing") and left them dangling with just their toes touching the floor. While Alexander later denounced this as a lie, several guards testified that they witnessed inmates who had been caught stealing punished this way. On occasion, men were left in this position until their hands turned black.

In November 1862, a group of prisoners detonated a quantity of gunpowder they had collected from gun cartridges by throwing it into the stove. Some said this was done to scare other prisoners, while others claimed the aim was to wreak havoc on the facility. It was a small quantity of powder, but it was loud enough to chafe Alexander, who immediately demanded the names of the ringleaders. No one wanted to snitch on the leaders of the gunpowder plot, so Alexander had the prisoners placed in the yard to cool off, literally. They remained in the yard for two days in the chill, and several of them died a few days later from pneumonia.

Erstwhile escapees and convicts were sentenced to isolation in the "sweat house," a closet-sized room about eight feet square. John Adams, a soldier confined to Castle Thunder when he deserted his regiment, said he spent two days in a sweat house cell, "the floor of which was covered with mud and water." Adams described the tiny room as "very cold" with "no dry spot in it. I could only stand up in it half bent."[21] Adams may have exaggerated a bit for dramatic effect; others testified that the Castle did not contain a room with a ceiling too low for a man to stand upright.

The sweat house didn't deter escape attempts. One group who managed to smuggle some iron from a hoop skirt into the Castle attempted to tunnel their way out by prying bricks out of the wall. They didn't make it.

A man named Webster, facing a sentence of death, also attempted a midnight run out of Castle Thunder. According to Frank Doran, Webster was kept in handcuffs at all times, although he had an uncanny ability to slip them off when he wanted. Sometime during the night, Webster slipped off the cuffs and leaped from a window, landing on the ground twenty-seven feet below. The fall broke his ankle, but he managed to crawl on top of a woodpile, where he lay writhing in agony. After a few minutes, he realized that he was going nowhere with a fractured ankle, so he hobbled back to the prison. Webster became so sick from the internal injuries sustained in the fall, according to Doran, that Caphart had to hold him upright on the scaffold when he was executed in April 1863.[22]

To keep potential escapees inside Thunder, and to prevent the rowdies from hurling objects at passersby with their homemade slingshots, Alexander ordered the guards to fire a warning shot at any man who stuck his head out of a window. On one occasion, a guard fired a warning at a convict standing by the window. The ball struck the window frame, shattering the wood casement. The convict at the window darted safely out of the way, but the shower of splinters shredded the face of an innocent bystander. This was just one of several incidents that would come back to haunt George Alexander.

By April 1863, Captain Alexander found himself embroiled in a controversy. Whispers of the goings-on at the prison reached the Confederate Congress, which ordered a hearing on the treatment of prisoners there. The committee called a variety of witnesses, including detectives and current and former prisoners. Witnesses took sides and the accusations flew. Some guards accused Alexander of overstepping his boundaries, while Alexander's allies accused the accusers of using the hearing to settle scores with the commandant. The trial transcript is an A-to-Z of allegations and finger-pointing. Some embellished the cruelties allegedly inflicted on the inmates; others downplayed them. Somewhere in the middle is the truth about what happened behind the walls of Castle Thunder.

Alexander himself questioned the witnesses, leading to some surreal scenes.

"Do you think I am unkind?" Alexander asked Marion Riggs, a warden at Castle Thunder.

"Yes," Riggs replied, "in some instances."[23]

Alexander repeated the question to others, including Dr. John De Butts, one of the prison surgeons. "Do you think I'm a cruel man?"

"I never saw any cruelty practiced in you," Dr. De Butts answered.[24]

T. G. Bland, a hospital orderly at the Castle, didn't agree with Dr. De Butts and depicted Alexander as a sadistic tyrant. Bland said that the provost marshal cheered "lay it on" as he watched a prisoner being whipped by the strongest guard under his command.[25]

One Castle inmate who felt the bitter end of the lash was Dennis O'Connor, a Confederate soldier sent to Castle Thunder for desertion. During his testimony, O'Connor said he was "taken upstairs to be flogged by order of Captain Alexander. I was ordered to take off my clothes and tied by my wrist to a post." O'Connor received several "stripes" from a man "who would spring on his toes with every lick." According to O'Connor, Alexander watched his ordeal with delight, screaming "lay it on."[26]

Bland also described the hideous scene when he discovered a mentally deranged inmate named George Wright in a heap on the floor. "I found him lying down behind a door in the prison room mired in his own filth with no clothing on but a short swallow-tailed coat," Bland said. "He was completely covered with scabs and vermin. Some of the prisoners said he had been lying there a week and more."[27]

The prison's commissary, Stephen Childrey, disagreed with Bland. He said that Wright was well cared for. Childrey claimed Wright was given clothes, but he tore them off.[28] Captain Alexander also quizzed Baldwin Allen, a warden at the Castle, about Wright's treatment. "They say you let George Wright lay for two weeks in the prison room sick without attending to his wants."

"I think there must be some mistake about this," Allen replied. "I go around every morning and call the breakfast roll, and when I find a man down by sickness I take his name and report him to the surgeon."[29]

According to Caphart, Bland's description of Wright's treatment was an attempt to give Alexander a black eye. During his testimony, Caphart recalled an incident when Alexander had Bland imprisoned for drinking on duty, implying that Bland had an axe to grind during his testimony.[30]

Caphart also defended the treatment of the prisoners, suggesting that the guards needed to wield a really big rod to keep control at Castle Thunder; another warden, Lieutenant Bossieux, seconded that opinion. Bossieux described the inmates as "some of the worst men in the world . . . I don't believe there is an hour that they are not concocting some plan to escape. I don't think they could be managed with less strictness."[31]

Some of the prisoners interviewed, however, suggested that prison personnel went too far in keeping law and order at Castle Thunder. J. T. Kirby, a Canadian imprisoned on suspicion of espionage, described Alexander as "the very opposite of kindness," although he admitted that at times, he was very kind to prisoners. This was not, according to the Canadian, true of the chief screw. Kirby claimed that Caphart was "in all respects a vile, low, inhuman person." He also described Caphart's fellow guard Baldwin Allen as a drunk who was "generally intoxicated."[32]

Such back-and-forth went on for days, sometimes becoming quite heated. At one point, Alexander locked horns with a senator from Texas, C. C. Herbert. When a witness described a flogging that occurred at Castle Thunder, Herbert exclaimed, "By God, if a man was to whip one of my sons I would kill him on sight." The senator glared at Alexander, who retorted that he would gladly whip the senator's son if he needed a whipping. The senator leaped to his feet and charged toward Alexander.

"Captain Alexander," Herbert shouted, "you must take that back." His face was cherry-red.

"Sir, I have only stated what I should have done, and I will not take it back," Alexander said as he palmed his pistol beneath the table.[33]

"Take it back," Herbert demanded.

Another senator, aware that the argument could quickly turn lethal, asked Senator Herbert to sit down. The senator reluctantly agreed and returned to his seat, glaring at Alexander as he retreated. After tempers cooled, the hearings continued.

In his defense, Alexander presented a letter from his superior, General Winder. In the note, Winder explained that as a result of violence inside Castle Thunder, such as "prisoners . . . garroting and using sling-shots upon the newly-arrived prisoners," he gave the go-ahead to "punish these ruffians severely and if necessary resort to corporal punishment."[34]

Alexander also gave a statement in which he defended the punishment at Castle Thunder as no worse than that experienced by soldiers of both sides in the field, whose commanding officers regularly used corporal punishment. "Are not soldiers in camp . . . bucked and made to ride a cannon or a wooden horse?" he asked the members.

In fact, Alexander argued, the punishment meted out inside Castle Thunder was better than what he received as a prisoner of war at Fort McHenry. He then went on to attack the credibility of several witnesses against him, including Bland, who he called "a man not fit to be about a public institution" whose "depravity was such that he was disgracefully ordered away"

Alexander added that the prisoners up north were treated no better than those at Thunder, drawing on his own experience in isolation as a prisoner of war at Fort McHenry. "I was kept in a cell seven by four for three weeks, that cell underground and no window," he recalled.

On May 1, 1863, the commission delivered its verdict. Like the combination of witnesses who testified, the commission members had mixed emotions about the punishment inflicted inside Castle Thunder. Brigadier General Winder had expressively given Alexander the right to use corporal punishment, but keeping the gunpowder plotters in the rain, according to the commission, was going too far: "This we condemn."[35]

They also considered it cruel that a sentry had fired at the man who stuck his head out of a window. "The ball struck the window and tore off some splinters, which scarred the face of another prisoner standing near. This we condemn as barbarous in the extreme." But, the commission noted, Alexander didn't order his sentry to shoot the inmate who stuck his head out of the window; he ordered him to fire a warning shot "to terrify him."

As for flogging, the commission said "This we condemn as inhuman and inconsistent with our form of government."[36] But they found overall, the "general treatment of the prisoners as humane as the circumstances would allow."[37]

When considering "the desperate and abandoned characters . . . murderers, thieves, deserters, substitutes, forgers and all manner of villains," the commission noted, Captain Alexander didn't deserve condemnation for whipping this motley crew into shape, "but on the contrary we are satisfied that he has exhibited such traits of character as in our opinion eminently fit him for such a position."[38]

Alexander, however, couldn't escape controversy. He later stood accused of taking bribes from prisoners in exchange for their release. A board of inquiry found him innocent, but to avoid further controversy, Alexander was reassigned in February 1864.

John Caphart, whom the *Richmond Whig* described as a "patriarch" of Castle Thunder, didn't survive the war. The toughest turn inside one of the Confederacy's toughest prisons died in 1864 of "gradual decay."[39]

Castle Thunder remained a prison throughout the war, and when the war ended, in an ironic twist, it was used to house Confederate war criminals. Even though some considered his actions criminal, George Alexander did not wind up in his own prison. After the war, he went to Canada and taught French for a few years. He later returned to his native Maryland, where he worked as a sanitary engineer. He died in 1895 with his beloved Susie still at his side.

CHAPTER 2

Sam Upham's Counterfeiting Scheme 1862

According to Sam Upham, his "facsimile" banknotes may have been the Union's most effective piece of artillery, doing more damage to the Confederacy than all of the bullets and batteries of Federal troops.

When Upham read a newspaper article about currency of the Confederate states, the Philadelphia businessman recognized an opportunity for a tidy profit: printing facsimiles of Southern banknotes and selling them as curios. Upham's moneymaking scheme netted him a lot of cash; it also became one of the most—if not the most—audacious counterfeiting operations in history.

☻ ☻ ☻

When the Southern states seceded from the Union, people in both the North and the South began to hoard coins for their metal content. First gold and silver vanished, followed by copper, leading to a shortage of coinage in both the United States and the newly formed Confederate States. Due to a general lack of specie caused in part by such hoarding, the Confederate States of America became one of the first entities to rely almost completely on paper money for commerce.

Almost as soon as they seceded, individual states and the CSA government began issuing currency. The sheer number of note designs, combined with the low-grade paper and inks used to print them, made this new money an easy target for counterfeiters. Since the cash-strapped CSA relied on the cheaper method of lithographic printing for its currency, its banknotes fell victim to counterfeiters as soon as they hit the streets.

Enter Samuel C. Upham, Philadelphia impresario and promoter extraordinaire. When the war began, Upham was a middle-aged veteran of the

US Navy. Born in 1817 in Vermont, Upham had traveled west and joined the 1849 Gold Rush. Failing to find his fortune in California, Upham came back east and eventually settled in Philadelphia, where he opened a general store.

An entrepreneur, Upham sold a combination of things, including stationery and newspapers, from his drugstore. When the war began, he tried to take advantage of the patriotism sweeping throughout the North by printing a caricature of CSA president Jefferson Davis as a jackass.

Then one day, Upham discovered a surefire way to make a small fortune from the war. His get-rich scheme began with a newspaper. The February 24, 1862, edition of the *Philadelphia Inquirer* contained a facsimile of a CSA $5 note. The red-and-black beauty featured an intricate design of five women who represented Agriculture, Commerce, Industry, Justice, and Liberty. Curious about the rebel government's money, people flocked to drugstores to buy the newspaper.

Upham wondered what caused that particular issue to fly off his shelves, so he asked around and discovered that people wanted a copy of the banknote as a curio. Never one to miss a moneymaker, Upham made a trip to the *Inquirer* and managed to purchase the electrotype the newspaper used to produce the facsimile. He then took the plate to a printer who whipped out three thousand copies that Upham sold at a penny apiece. Upham's first issue of facsimiles sold out in a matter of days.

Realizing that he had hit on something, Upham decided to have another issue made. *Leslie's Illustrated* had printed a facsimile of a CSA $10 note in its January 11, 1862, edition. Upham purchased the electrotype from Leslie's and began mass-producing the tens, which featured the design of a woman representing Liberty holding a shield containing the Stars and Bars.

Upham's "facsimiles" were near-perfect knockoffs of the originals with one exception: Upham's "signature," or imprint, in tiny letters along the bottom margin. The imprint varies depending on the issue, but the print leaves little doubt as to the note's originator: FAC-SIMILE CONFEDERATE NOTE—SOLD WHOLESALE AND RETAIL BY S.C. UPHAM, 403 CHESTNUT ST. PHILADELPHIA.[1]

By March 1862, the war had begun to pick up momentum. In the West, the two armies tangled in a large battle at Pea Ridge, Arkansas; in the East, the ironclads USS *Monitor* and the CSS *Virginia* dueled in the epic sea battle at Hampton Roads.

As Federal and rebel forces traded lead, Sam Upham's business took off. He put out a circular advertising MEMENTOES OF THE REBELLION. After his success with his $5 and $10 Confederate knockoffs, Upham had developed an entire line of facsimiles. In the advertisement, dated March 1862, he offers both a $10 and a $5 note issued by the CSA, as well as five different

An exact copy of a genuine Confederate banknote issued by Samuel Upham in 1861. Note Upham's "signature" at the bottom margin. Enterprising profiteers trimmed off this statement and used the notes to purchase cotton in Tennessee. Upham later offered them for sale without his imprint, saving users the trouble. HERITAGE AUCTIONS, WWW.HA.COM

"shinplasters"—period slang for fractional (in amounts less than or a fraction of a dollar) notes—issued by Southern banks and cities.

For five cents each, the curious could obtain what the advertisement bragged were "perfect FAC-SIMILES." For those who ordered in bulk, Upham offered a discounted price of 100 for $2. Upham also placed classified ads in newspapers offering the $5 and $10 notes. Upham's circular contained several "blurbs" praising his work. One from the *Philadelphia Inquirer* notes that the "engraving is fully equal to that of the originals," while one from the *Philadelphia Evening Bulletin* comments that Upham's copies are sold "at prices even cheaper than they bring in Richmond and Memphis. They are curious and interesting, and will become more so as time advances."

One group in particular found Upham's "facsimiles" very interesting. While Upham cashed in on the rebel curios, other entrepreneurs recognized an opportunity to piggyback on the Philadelphia man's scheme. By simply trimming off the lower edge, Upham's facsimiles could be made counterfeits. For two cents each, one could obtain perfect copies of notes circulating as real money throughout the Confederacy—a tidy profit for the underhanded speculator. Before long, the notes made their way south of the Mason-Dixon Line in quantity, minus Upham's signature of course.

Upham's notes were particularly troublesome in Tennessee—a tweener state in more ways than one. Tennessee twice voted to secede. The first attempt failed, but a second referendum succeeded. Despite the two-thirds majority vote in favor of leaving the Union, the people of the Volunteer State remained deeply divided on the issues of slavery and secession.

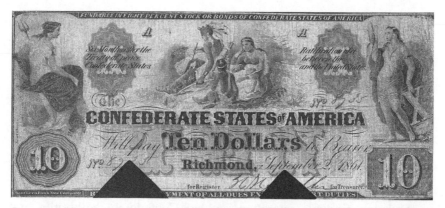

A genuine 1861 Confederate $10 note. The Confederate Treasury canceled notes that were redeemed, often removing a portion of the note (in this case, by punching out triangles of paper where the signatures were located). HERITAGE AUCTIONS, WWW.HA.COM

Most residents of western Tennessee favored the Confederacy, while many residents of the eastern portion supported the Union. Tennesseans fought for both sides, and both Union greenbacks and Confederate currency circulated alongside the issues of the state's local banks. With so many different banknote types floating around, Tennessee was fertile soil for counterfeiters. Profiteers purchased large quantities of Upham's fake money, passed them off as originals, and pocketed the profits.

Upham's facsimile business boomed. At about the same time as forces clashed at the Battle of Yorktown during the Army of the Potomac's massive Peninsular Campaign in the spring of 1862, smugglers waged fiscal war with the Confederacy using what Upham called his "mementoes of the rebellion."

According to some sources, Federal authorities heard whispers that Upham was also making facsimiles of Federal issues. They would turn a blind eye to counterfeiting a rebel government's money, but copying U.S. currency was a no-no. Agents paid a visit to 403 Chestnut and questioned Upham, who quickly asserted that he was doing nothing illegal. After a brief investigation, authorities discovered no wrongdoing on Upham's part. They dropped the matter and Upham went back to work making his facsimiles.

In May 1862, Upham launched another circular. By this time, he had expanded his line even further. He now offered nine different notes and three different types of Confederate postage stamps, which cost three cents each. According to this handbill, "Upwards of 80,000 of the Notes, Shinplasters and Postage Stamps have been sold during the past four weeks, and the cry is still for more." The handbill promises "QUICK SALES

AND LARGE PROFITS," suggesting that perhaps by this time, Sam Upham realized that he had launched one of the most grandiose counterfeiting schemes in history.

On May 30, the day before the Battle of Seven Pines, Upham distributed another handbill, this time offering fourteen different types of notes. The circular boasts of "500,000 SOLD IN THE PAST THREE MONTHS" and warns "BEWARE OF BASE IMITATIONS." The handbill goes on to describe the operation of a New York "shyster" who was selling "shocking bad copies"—an indication that others had joined the paper war against the Confederacy. Upham notes that "Each and every FAC-SIMILE issued by me bears my imprint."

Upham's facsimile operation rankled Confederate authorities and wreaked havoc on the Southern economy. His banknotes, he later bragged, did more to bring down the Confederacy than Federal bullets. "I was the 'best abused man' (by the rebels) in the Union," Upham gloated years after the war had ended. "Senator [Henry] Foote, in a speech before the rebel Congress, at Richmond, in 1862, said I had done more to injure the Confederate cause than General McClellan and his army."[2]

Upham took the operation a step further, which according to some, provided even more help to opportunists who wanted to use Upham's funny money to buy Southern cotton. Until this point, each of Upham's copies contained printed signatures and serial numbers—one way that a facsimile could be distinguished from the genuine article. Confederate treasury officials employed a legion of secretaries who hand-signed each note issued by the Confederate government (except for the fifty-cent notes of 1863 and 1864). Each genuine note contained a handwritten serial number and two signatures—one representing the "registrar" and one representing the "treasurer." Today, the faded ink of genuine signatures appears brown while the printed signatures of an Upham note remain black. In 1862, though, both would have appeared black.

Apparently, Upham realized that his "facsimiles" would more easily pass as genuine if handwritten serial numbers and signatures were fraudulently added instead of printed. So he began to offer his facsimiles without printed serial numbers and signatures. The purchaser could then add a serial number and sign each note, giving it a more authentic look. And although Upham denied it, there is some evidence to suggest that he also offered notes without his imprint at the bottom, sparing his customers the trouble of trimming them.[3]

Even Confederate Treasurer Christopher Menninger gave a disgusted nod to Upham's operation when he told a Confederate congressman that "printed advertisements have been found stating that counterfeit notes, in any quantity, will be forwarded by mail from Chestnut Street in Philadelphia."[4]

Confederate authorities weren't fooled by the handwritten signatures and serial numbers applied to this bogus $10 bill. HERITAGE AUCTIONS, WWW.HA.COM

Years after Lee's surrender to Grant at Appomattox, Samuel Upham still bragged about the damage his facsimiles inflicted on the Confederacy. In an 1874 letter to an authority on Confederate money, Upham claimed to have sold over a million and half copies (of both notes and stamps) during his brief career as a "counterfeiter" between March 12, 1862, and August 1, 1863.

Upham never explained why he quit producing facsimile banknotes in August 1863. Experts believe that it was probably a combination of factors. The Confederate economy began a nosedive following massive battlefield defeats at Gettysburg and Vicksburg, and Confederate money lost much of its buying power. Merchants would no longer take the Confederate scrip, instead insisting on Union cash. Competitors also cut into Upham's profits, which may have contributed to the end of his career as a money maker.

While he was the most widely-known "counterfeiter" of the period, Sam Upham did not invent the facsimile banknote business nor hold a monopoly on it. According to some sources, counterfeiters who wanted to obtain perfect replicas that could pass as currency turned to Upham's New York competitor, Winthrop Hilton.

Hilton, like Upham, advertised his facsimiles in *Harper's Weekly*. "So exactly like the genuine," Hilton boasted in one of his advertisements, "that where one will pass current the other will go equally well."[5] The wording of this ad implies that not only did Hilton know what became of his facsimiles, but he also anticipated that his customers would travel south to "pass current" his copies. For $5, Hilton offered $500 worth of Confederate notes—a penny for each counterfeited dollar. Hilton's presses ran hot and heavy until Federal agents arrested him in December 1863 under suspicion of espionage, alleging they had found a coded message from Hilton to Confederate spies. In a bizarre twist, Hilton was subsequently jailed because Federal agents believed the printer was in league with the rebels by producing authentic Confederate currency and using his facsimile business as a front.

Upham continued to operate his Philadelphia general store and pursued other ventures. In 1878, he published an account of his prewar adventures, *Notes of a Voyage to California Via Cape Horn*. He died in 1885 at the age of sixty-six, leaving an estate worth just under $5,000—a significant fortune at the time.

There is no doubt that Upham's facsimiles circulated alongside genuine Confederate banknotes. In fact, his notes were so good that the illustration of a "genuine" Confederate note in *Harper's Encyclopedia of United States History*, published in 1893, is actually an Upham facsimile.

Although it is impossible to tell exactly how much damage Upham's fakes caused the CSA, they certainly did their part in inflating the Southern economy. By war's end, Confederate banknotes had become virtually worthless; they traded at a rate of $1,200 Confederate for every $1 in Union greenbacks.

As souvenirs of one of the most audacious counterfeiting schemes in the history of money, the Upham facsimiles that survived the war remain a popular curio among collectors. The wily Philadelphia entrepreneur may have gotten the last laugh. Today, his bastard notes are more valuable than legitimate Confederate offspring. Untrimmed notes with Upham's imprint along the margin are almost impossible to find.

CHAPTER 3

Benjamin Butler, Beast of New Orleans 1862

ome Civil War generals overstepped their boundaries. Benjamin Butler—the "Beast" of New Orleans—took several leaps over his. At least, that is how the citizens under his oversized thumb felt.

Butler, the military commander of occupied New Orleans in 1862, was so loathed in the Crescent City that his mug appeared on chamber pots so citizens could relieve their angst while relieving themselves. The portly general's tyrannical reign over New Orleans drew the ire of Confederate president Jefferson Davis, who labeled Butler a felon and sentenced him to death in absentia.

⊕ ⊕ ⊕

One doesn't obtain a nickname like "Beast" for charm and charisma, unless it's a term of endearment from an enraptured lover. That certainly wasn't the case for Union general Benjamin Franklin Butler. There was no love lost between the people of New Orleans and their Federal nemesis.

To be fair to the Beast, the bombastic Butler may have been the right man for the Union as chief of occupied New Orleans in 1862, but among residents, he was loathed and despised.

Most accounts depict Butler as a career politician with little military prowess. When the war began, Butler held the military rank of brigadier general in the Massachusetts state militia, but unlike other general officers who wore the blue or the gray, Butler had not seen any real military action before 1861; his military rank was, for the most part, just a title. The only action he had seen was on the floor of the Massachusetts House of Representatives and later in the Senate.

Despite a lack of experience, when hostilities broke out in 1861, Butler went to war, eventually becoming the Union's major domo in the "Paris of the South." Although Butler was somewhat of a controversy magnet during the War Between the States, it was his uber-strict administration of the city that made him so notorious that Jefferson Davis denounced him as "a felon, deserving of capital punishment." If Butler was captured, Davis declared, he was to be treated as "an outlaw and common enemy of the mankind" and executed on the spot.[1]

Butler's claim to infamy as the military overlord of New Orleans is somewhat ironic, considering that his father, Capt. John Butler, laid his life on the line when defending New Orleans from the British during the War of 1812. That American force, under the command of Andrew Jackson, prevailed. Captain Butler—also a veteran of the American Revolution—survived the Battle of New Orleans and went on to become an American privateer (some say pirate). In 1819, he died of yellow fever on the island of St. Kitts, leaving his widow, Charlotte, to fend for their six children, including one-year-old Benjamin.

Charlotte Seelye Butler moved her brood several times before settling in Lowell, Massachusetts, where she opened a boardinghouse. With a military hero for a father and time spent around a few old-timers fond of swapping war stories, it was little wonder that Benjamin, the youngest of the Butler children, grew up dreaming about military glory.

He wanted to attend West Point to learn the art of war, but was instead sent to Waterville College, a Baptist school. When he graduated in 1838, he began to study law and taught school to make ends meet. As a schoolmaster, Butler acquired a reputation as a strict disciplinarian. A few years later, he passed the bar and became a trial lawyer known for his bulldog-like defense of his clients.

Butler eventually graduated to the big time, opening a firm in Boston, where he became a successful lawyer and a political somebody, first winning a seat to the state legislature in 1853, and then, in 1858, a senate seat. A skilled debater, Butler was also a gifted pundit, and barraged his political enemies with scathing critiques.

Just after the first shots were fired in 1861, Butler went off to war with a regiment from Boston. After his unit's arrival in Washington, Union brass tasked him with reestablishing the rail link between the North and its capital city. That link had been disrupted in April when a secessionist mob brawled with a Massachusetts regiment attempting to transfer trains in Baltimore, an incident that resulted in eighteen deaths. Butler performed his job and went one step further—acting without orders, he seized Baltimore and imposed martial law on the city. The action, which quelled secessionist ardor in Maryland, earned him a promotion to major general; the manner in which he did it got him relieved of command.

Butler was then assigned to Fort Monroe, Virginia, where he made a decision that would shape Union policy throughout the war. He refused to return slaves to their owners, despite the 1850 Fugitive Slave Act, which required it by law. Butler considered runaway slaves "contraband of war," and Union higher-ups soon adopted the policy.

After a series of failures in Virginia, Butler was assigned to Louisiana after Admiral David Farragut seized New Orleans. Butler became the Union man in charge of occupied New Orleans in May 1862. He knew it would be a difficult assignment. In fact, he waited until evening before leading his troops into the city because he thought they might face an angry mob.

The city was a nest of secessionists, many of whom would just as soon spit on a Yankee as look at one. The day Butler walked into town, a man was gunned down for yelling "Hurrah for the old flag." The killers tossed the corpse into the river and disappeared.

If there were any hopes among New Orleans residents that the big Bostonian would be a softy, Butler pushed them aside when he stared down an angry mob that formed when he met with city officials at the St. Charles Hotel.

Amid the increasingly chaotic scene, Capt. Sidney Brooks de Kay managed to fight his way through the rioters, losing most of his uniform on the way. De Kay had come to Butler from General Thomas Williams, who wanted to know what he should do about the mob. Butler, who had had enough of the noise, wasn't going to take any more.

"Give my compliments to General Williams, and tell him to clear the streets with his artillery," ordered Butler. De Kay marched off as the city officials watched in stunned silence.

"Don't, General," they pleaded. "Don't give such an order as that."

"Why this emotion, gentlemen?" Butler asked. "The cannon are not going to shoot our way, and I have borne this noise and confusion long enough."[2]

The city officials begged Butler to hold off until they had a chance to speak to the crowd. The mayor went out on the balcony and addressed the mob, pleading with them to disperse, but the crowd began to shout insults at him.

The angry horde called for Butler, who appeared on the balcony. The way Butler tells it, the crowd immediately quieted at the sight of him, and then fled when the horse-drawn artillery unit of the Sixth Maine tore down the cobblestone street toward the assembled mass. According to Butler, the noise alone was terrifying enough to break up the crowd without a single shot fired.

The incident at the St. Charles Hotel set the tone for Butler's administration of New Orleans. The former teacher with a knack for controlling recalcitrant youth, the former trial lawyer who argued his way from a courtroom into the Massachusetts Senate, rolled up his sleeves and went to work . . . and acquired the nickname "Beast." During his brief, seven-month time in New Orleans, Butler ruled the city with an iron fist. "They will fear the stripes," Butler later quipped, "even if they do not revere the bars of our flag."[3]

Over the next few months, Butler took a switch to the city's residents, reddening their backsides as well as their faces. He shut down newspapers that ran what he considered treasonous text and jailed ministers who refused to say a prayer for President Lincoln.[4]

One proprietor placed a skeleton named "Chickahominy" in his shop window—a morbid reminder of the Federal lives lost in a series of battles fought along the Chickahominy River in Virginia. The skeleton wasn't from a dead Union soldier; it was purchased as an anatomical specimen from the Mexican ambassador. Nonetheless, it insulted Butler, who sent the shopkeeper to Ship Island for "two years at hard labor" for "desecration of the dead."[5] Butler also shipped elderly Judge John W. Andrews to the island for displaying a cross the old man said was made from the bones of a Union soldier.

Big Brother Butler seemed to know all and see all. He kept tabs on people through a network of informers, many of who were servants of the city's elite. These employees acted as Butler's eyes and ears behind the closed doors of the city's mansions. Through them, he heard about seditious behavior. And in return, he offered rewards and even freedom to slaves who snitched on their masters for, among other transgressions, possessing weapons "not held under a written permit from the United States authorities."

The Beast evolved into an almost mythical antagonist who enraged many, including some of his own superiors. Entire books have been written about New Orleans under Butler's thumb, but the girth of his reputation as an ego-bloated ruler came from a few particularly eyebrow-raising incidents.

Butler trampled all over the diplomatic immunity of the city's foreign consuls, creating an international stir, but he really enraged foreign ambassadors when he barged in on the Dutch ambassador and seized a large quantity of silver on May 10, 1862. Through a slave informant, Butler had heard whispers about silver bullion in the ambassador's possession. He suspected that rebels were using the consul to hide the money until they could send it out of the city, or that underhanded bankers were concealing the silver to defraud the bank's customers. So he ordered his men to search for it.

In the cellar of the embassy, they found 160 barrels, each one containing five thousand coins. The cache amounted to $800,000 worth of "Mexican coin bearing the mark of the Citizens Bank of New Orleans" along with

The two faces of Benjamin "Beast" Butler. Left: In this carte de visite, a steely-eyed "Bluebeard of New Orleans" is depicted as a cruel tyrant who does not hesitate to use his sword against the female population of New Orleans—a caricature aimed at Butler's "Woman Order." Right: Charles Stanley Reinhart's rendering of "Gen. Butler Holding the Mob in Check at New Orleans," run in *Harper's Weekly*, portrays Butler as a conquering hero. The dignified appearance of Butler is a sharp contrast to the men of the mob. LIBRARY OF CONGRESS

printing plates for the bank's currency.[6] Butler confiscated the booty, enraging the Dutch ambassador, who immediately cried foul.

The other diplomats, equally angry about this breach of ethics, sent a letter to Butler, dated May 12, 1862, protesting the ill treatment of the Dutch consulate. Word of the scandal reached Washington, and Secretary of War Edwin Stanton demanded answers. The money, Butler explained, belonged to the Citizen's Bank, whose directors had refused to exchange their banknotes for coin upon demand and who were using the consulate as a convenient way to keep the money out of Union hands.

Except for having to explain his actions to Washington politicians whenever he ruffled a few diplomatic feathers, Butler was omnipotent in New Orleans. "Otherwise I was supreme," Butler notes in his autobiography. "Having supreme power, I used it in the manner I have set forth."[7] He may have felt supreme, but Secretary of State William Seward later sent Reverdy Johnson, a Maryland politician, to New Orleans to investigate the matter. Johnson concluded his investigation in late July and ordered the bullion returned to the Dutch.

Butler's already checkered reputation took a seedy turn when he issued "General Order 28," a dictate designed to control the behavior of the city's women. After the order hit the streets, his name became a four-letter word not just in New Orleans but throughout the South. News of the order even traveled across the Atlantic, raising a few voices in the British Parliament.

In Butler's mammoth autobiography, *Butler's Book*, he refers to the controversial dictate as "the woman order." Butler had effectively gagged the men of the city, but the women were another story altogether—they went about fighting the rebellion in their own way. Butler characterizes them as harpies with razor-sharp tongues that they used to cut Yankees with every word.

Federal officers became favorite targets of the New Orleans belles who flocked around them, taunting them with insults. The women openly defied Union authority by toting around the Stars and Bars and whistling "Dixie."

The general himself became a target of harassment when his carriage passed a group of ladies congregating on a terrace. "Just as we were passing the balcony," Butler later recalled, "with something between a shriek and a sneer, the women all whirled around back to a flirt which threw out their skirts in a regular circle like the pirouette of a dancer." Butler, unfazed, had a comeback ready. "I turned around to my aid, saying in full voice: 'Those women evidently know which end of them looks the best.'"[8]

Butler's insult fell on deaf ears and the ladies of the city continued to literally spit on Union officers. In one incident, a woman hacked on an officer—and on the Sabbath, no less.

One of the most flagrant episodes involved Flag Officer Farragut, when one of belles of the city gave him a special baptism from a balcony. Farragut and Col. Henry Deming were walking down a street when "there fell upon them what at first they took to be a sudden and heavy shower." It didn't take them long to realize that the yellow rain came from the balcony above them. One of the city's ladies had doused them with the contents of a chamber pot. Perhaps this incident inspired some clever entrepreneur to later craft chamber pots with Butler's image inside their bowls.[9]

But the ladies of New Orleans had gotten into a pissing contest with the wrong guy. On May 15, 1862, Butler issued General Order No. 28:

> As the officers and the soldiers of the United States have been subject
> to repeated insults from the women (calling themselves ladies) of New
> Orleans, in return for the most scrupulous non-interference and courtesy
> on our part, it is ordered that hereafter when any female shall, by word,
> gesture, or movement, insult or show contempt for any officer or soldier
> of the United States, she shall be regarded and held liable to be treated
> as a woman of the town plying her avocation.[10]

A "woman of the town plying her avocation" was Butler's euphemism for prostitute. The intent of the order was to control the flagrant verbal abuse from the town's women by threatening to treat them like whores. This was more or less a license for soldiers to publicly humiliate women who ridiculed them, to fight fire with fire so to speak. But what exactly did this entail? Butler's chief of staff, George C. Strong, pointed out the problem as soon as he read the order.

"This order may be misunderstood, General," Scott advised. "It would be a great scandal if only one man should act upon it the wrong way."[11] The "wrong way" could be an insult, or worse, a sexual assault or even a rape.

Butler's response suggests that he had considered the possibility of a misunderstanding. "Let us, then, have one case of aggression on our side," Butler said. "I shall know how to deal with that case, so that it will never be repeated." Butler went on to explain that they were "conquerors in a conquered city," yet they were the victims of the abuse. "I do not fear the troops, but if aggression must be, let it not be all against us."[12] Butler, it appeared, had great confidence in his soldiers to keep their hands to themselves. If they didn't, they would have to answer to "Butler the Beast."

The alternative to "the woman order" was to treat the women as he had treated the men: send them off, kicking and screaming, to jail. These women, Butler wrote in a letter about a month later, had no business "in the place where we shut up thieves and assassins and drunken soldiers"

Moreover, the arrests of New Orleans's finest ladies would only fan the flames. Their insults, Butler said, had "come from the balconies whence Juliet made love," and New Orleans folk would cringe at the thought of boys in blue breaking open "private dwellings" and chasing "the fair, feeble, fretful, and ferocious rebels to their bedroom to have seized them."[13] Butler was convinced that Order No. 28 was a necessary step to stop the petticoat rebellion going on inside the city. Sarah Butler, who had accompanied her husband to New Orleans, agreed. "Never has anything been more deserved," she said in a letter to a friend. She even used the same language as her husband: "we, the Yankees, seem like the conquered and they like conquerors."[14]

Sparks flew as soon as Butler ordered the issue. Here was a Union general in Dixie threatening to treat the city's women like whores if they insulted his men. For women of the time, particularly those in the South, their virtue was sacrosanct. Any public suggestion that a woman was a "soiled dove" cut to the quick.

John T. Monroe, the mayor of New Orleans, whipped off a letter to Butler. "To give a license to the officers and soldiers of your command to commit outrages such as are indicated in your order is in my opinion a reproach to the civilization not to say the Christianity of the age in whose name I make this protest."[15]

Butler had Monroe brought to his office, where he scolded the mayor for the language of his letter and threatened to imprison him in Fort Jackson if he couldn't control his people. The general explained that the order wasn't an affront to the virtue of a lady, because a lady wouldn't spit in a man's face. Monroe signed an apology before leaving Butler's office with his tail between his legs. The next day, he rescinded his apology and asked Butler to declare that the order didn't apply to virtuous women. Butler refused.

After that, no one said anything inside New Orleans. At least not out loud. According to Butler, the order "executed itself" and didn't require any enforcement. The fine ladies behaved because they didn't want to be treated like whores. And the whores behaved because they wanted to be treated like ladies.[16]

The slap in the face of New Orleans women caused a sting felt throughout both the North and South. Southerners cried bloody murder and called for Butler's head.

Rebel officers used Butler's order to rally their troops around the Stars and Bars. Confedcrate general P. G. T. Beauregard issued a statement that officers read to their men. "MEN OF THE SOUTH! Shall our mothers, wives, daughters and sisters be thus outraged by the ruffianly soldiers of the North, to whom is given the right to treat, at their pleasure, the ladies of the South as common harlots?"[17]

News of the order even traveled all the way across the Atlantic to Victorian England, where Prime Minister Palmerston described it as an outrage unfit for print in the English language. The *Saturday Review*, a British tabloid, denounced the order. "No Englishman ought to own as kinsmen men who attempt to protect themselves from a handful of women by official and authoritative threats of rape. The bloodiest savages could do nothing crueler—the most loathsome Yahoo of fiction could do nothing filthier."[18]

Butler, writing thirty years after the act that made him infamous, justified the order. "These women, she-adders, more venomous than he-adders, were the insulting enemies of my army and my country, and were so treated." But the "she-adders" knew when to hide—Butler notes of the order that "No arrests were ever made under it or because of it."[19]

General Order No. 28 may have enraged many, but it was the hanging of William Mumford that chafed Jefferson Davis so much the Confederate president pronounced Butler an outlaw and sentenced him to death in absentia.

The Mumford incident began with the desecration of a United States flag on April 28, 1862, a few days before Butler took over the city. When Farragut captured New Orleans, the victorious Yankees raised the flag over the New Orleans branch of the United States mint. Later, a group of young rebels removed the flag, dragged it around the streets, and tore it into pieces. Mumford wore a shred of it in his buttonhole.

When he heard about the flag desecration, Butler vowed to punish those responsible. Not long after arriving, he noticed a man wearing a fragment of the Stars and Stripes. The man, William Mumford, was arrested and charged with treason. The trial took place on May 30, 1862. Mumford pled not guilty. He was not the only one involved and claimed that he wasn't the ringleader. But a police officer testified that he heard Mumford later brag that he was the first one to tear down the flag. Another witness said he saw Mumford coming out of the mint with a flag in his hands. After a brief trial, he was sentenced to death. But no one, not even Mumford, believed that Butler would actually go through with the hanging. The alleged crime, after all, had occurred before the Beast came to town.

Even after Butler issued the execution order on June 5, 1862, people still doubted that the chief of the city had the gall to execute a man for desecrating a flag. They had good reason to question the hanging. Just a day before signing Mumford's death warrant, Butler had commuted the death sentences of six paroled Confederate soldiers who attempted to rejoin the lines.

After issuing Mumford's execution order, Butler received a barrage of hate mail from citizens who tried to scare him into commuting the sentence. It had the opposite effect. When Butler learned that he would be the target of assassination plots if he went through with the execution, he said "I thought I should be in the utmost danger if I did not have him executed; for the question was now to be determined whether I commanded that city or whether the mob commanded it."[20] Mumford's execution wasn't just about a seditious tough anymore; it was now about who was running New Orleans, Butler or "the mob."

Mumford's young wife made an eleventh-hour pitch for mercy. Butler describes the pitiful scene: "She wept bitterly, as did the children, who fell about my knees."[21] Butler explained the reasoning behind his decision and suggested that Mrs. Mumford visit her husband in jail to say farewell. The general also offered to help the soon-to-be widow in any way he could.

Even after a visit from his wife, Mumford still didn't believe he would be hanged, but the day of execution came without a reprieve or commutation. Butler ordered the deed be done, "Imitating the Spanish custom," in the place where the crime was committed: the US Mint.[22] After Mumford said a few words from the scaffold, the floor fell out from under his feet. Although Mumford didn't act alone, he died alone. His confederates were never identified or punished.

"The fate of Mumford caused the greatest excitement throughout the whole Confederacy," Butler later said. "Threats of retaliatory vengeance

The LADIES OF NEW ORLEANS before GENERAL BUTLER'S Proclamation.   After GENERAL BUTLER'S Proclamation.

A *Harper's Weekly* sketch from July 12, 1862, showing one of New Orleans' finest hacking on a Union officer. Butler issued his infamous Order No. 28 two months before this illustration appeared in print. LIBRARY OF CONGRESS

came from the governor of Louisiana, and were circulated by all the cognate rascals south of Mason and Dixon's line, including Jefferson Davis."[23]

Davis viewed the act as a war crime. In a proclamation dated December 23, 1862, Davis described Butler as a "felon," an "outlaw," and a "common enemy of mankind."[24] Any outfit that captured the Beast was ordered to hang him on the spot.

William Mumford would not be the last man to swing on Butler's orders. About a week later, a citizen brought a complaint to Butler. A group of soldiers had entered his house on the pretense of looking for weapons. They had presented a search warrant in the name of J. William Henry, a lieutenant with the Eighteenth Massachusetts Volunteers. The party took $10,000 in cash and all of the jewelry in the house. Butler tracked down one of the thieves—a "paroled" soldier turned burglar—who rolled on the others. For his cooperation, the informant received a sentence of five years; five of the others were hanged.

"From that hour," Butler boasts in his autobiography, "no burglary was ever committed in New Orleans; at least none was complained of."[25]

To many Louisianans, however, the biggest burglar in the Big Easy was the Beast himself. Almost from the day he stepped off the boat, Butler acquired a reputation for using his position to profit and even pilfer from the people of New Orleans. During his time in the city, gossip circulated that Butler stole fine silverware from the houses he occupied. The story snowballed, and he acquired a second nickname, "Spoons." One persistent legend about Butler is that when he left the city, he took with him a coffin full of silver spoons he allegedly pilfered while military governor.

The story of Spoons Butler's love of fine silver spread throughout the area. Louisianan Eliza Ripley told a humorous anecdote of Mammy Charlotte, who "hurriedly secreted the spoons (!) when a Federal cavalry company came prancing down the road toward our gates." When they left, Mammy Charlotte remarked, "It's all right; they didn't say nothin' 'bout spoons."[26]

"Even at that early date and that remote spot from Butler's headquarters," Ripley notes, "the matter of spoons had been so freely and laughingly discussed that the sable crowd of witnesses that surrounded every household must have taken the idea that collecting spoons was the chief end of man."[27]

According to some sources, Butler had even more grandiose schemes for turning a tidy profit from the war. On May 4, 1862, Butler issued the controversial Order No. 22, which guaranteed "safe conduct" of "all cargoes of cotton and sugar."[28] According to Butler, the road to Order 22 was paved with good intentions: The area's planters, fearful that the Yankees would take their crops, had resorted to burning them. To prevent this destruction, Butler extended his hand to the locals by assuring them a "safe conduct" for their products. The order led to accusations that Butler was using his power to line his own pockets by trading with the enemy.

With his brother Andrew Jackson Butler acting as his agent, Butler purchased large quantities of rosin, sugar, and turpentine. He shipped the cargoes north to New York and Boston, where they could be sold at a profit.

In his autobiography, Butler provides an excuse for this insider trading. Several Federal ships had to return to Northern ports without ballast. Since rebel authorities had taken just about everything heavy (including church bells) to make cannon, the city didn't have any adequate ballast for the ships. So, Butler decided to weight down the ships with cargos of sugar he purchased and later planned to sell in the east.

According to Butler, his scheme "gave such confidence" that the city's merchants wanted a slice of the action. So Butler set up a fee schedule: $10 for each hogshead of sugar, with half of the fee going directly to his brother as his "commission."[29]

In a letter to Washington dated May 16, Butler explains his motives and reassures Secretary of War Stanton that he used his own money for this business. He also states that he would "be content" if the government decided to take the cargo and reimburse him. Otherwise, he would pay for the cost of shipping. "I only desire that neither motives nor action shall be misunderstood."[30]

Butler's older brother Andrew was linked to all sorts of graft. The Beast's big brother arrived a few days after he did and immediately became one of the more loathed men in the city. Rumors spread that Andrew used his baby brother to defraud citizens of New Orleans, threatening plantation owners with confiscation of their property unless they divided their crops with him.

There were handsome profits to be made. Under the Confiscation Act, Union occupiers seized just about anything of value from their rebel charges and sold the goods at auction. Since there was little specie in the hands of the citizens, Union speculators purchased valuable merchandise at fixed auctions for a song and sent it north for resale, pocketing thousands in the process.

Some of the Union officers in the city lived like potentates. John William DeForest, a soldier who visited New Orleans in the fall of 1862, remarked about the lavish décor of the home occupied by a lieutenant he stayed with. DeForest related that the lieutenant bragged about looting the wine cellars of the city's finest. The lieutenant boasted that he and a friend downed forty-six bottles of wine in one day alone.[31]

In a letter to Secretary of the Treasury Salmon P. Chase, George Dennison, the collector of the Port of New Orleans, complained that "Ever since the capture of this city, a brisk trade has been carried on with the Rebels, by a few persons, under military permits, frequently with military assistance and as I believe, much to the pecuniary benefit for some of the principal military officers of this Department."

Dennison went on to complain about Andrew Butler. "A brother of General Butler is here, who is called 'Colonel' A. J. Butler, though he occupies no position in the Army. Government officers, citizens, and Rebels generally believe him to be the partner or agent of General Butler. He does heavy business and by various practices has made between one and two million dollars since the capture of the City."[32]

Alarmed, Chase sent a note to Butler, raising Dennison's allegations against his brother. In his response, Butler noted that Andrew was "indeed engaged in commercial adventure in New Orleans, and has been successful." But, he said, his profits had only amounted to eight hundred thousand dollars.[33]

All of this corruption may have added up for Ben Butler. According to New Orleans resident Marian Southwood, Butler used the Citizens Bank as his "pet bank" and the "place of deposit" for "his vast scheme of corruption and extortion."[34]

Although a beast of now-legendary proportions, Butler did some real good in New Orleans. Under his administration, violent crime rates plummeted. Butler also cleaned up New Orleans, literally. It turns out that the "Paris of the South" wasn't very sanitary. During a carriage ride with Sarah, Butler noticed an awful stench coming from one of the canals leading from the city to Lake Pontchartrain. "The whole surface of the canal and the pond was covered with a thick growth of green vegetable scum, variegated with dead cats and dogs or the remains of dead mules on the banking."[35]

Motivated by his belief that the rebels wanted to infect Northern soldiers with yellow fever, Butler had the canals cleaned out and the city's markets scrubbed. He also ordered the citizens to clean out their backyards—including the boxes that held the contents of chambers pots (those not dumped on Union soldiers), sometimes for weeks on end.

It has been said that New Orleans under Butler the Beast was a safer, cleaner city than ever before. The general just couldn't elude scandal, which ultimately caused Federal authorities to sign the death warrant of his administration—and in December 1862, Butler was reassigned.

The women of New Orleans weren't sad to see the Beast leave. In her diary, Julia LeGrand quotes a poem entitled "The Ladies Farewell to Brutal Ferocity Butler." The poem indicts Butler for just about every wrong imaginable, calling him a vampire, a demon, even the Prince of Darkness himself: "In Butler's name the foulest wrongs / and crimes are all comprised."[36] LeGrand watched Butler leave on board the steamer *Spaulding*. "There was not one hurrah, not one sympathizing cry went up for him from the vast crowd that went to see him off—a silent rebuke. I wonder if he felt it!"[37]

As for the New Orleans belles, what they saw as Butler's tyrannical rule left them terrified, indignant, and as angry, if not more so, as when Butler arrived. "Mrs. Norton has a hatchet, a tomahawk, and a vial of some kind of spirits with which she intends to blind all invaders," LeGrand notes in her diary entry of December 20, 1862.[38] In her diary, Marian Southwood describes Butler as a type of "creature" more fit for a penitentiary than the "Paris of the South." His daguerreotype "should have been taken and sent to Barnum's Museum," she notes.[39]

The women of New Orleans weren't alone in their ire for the Beast. A gentleman from Charleston, South Carolina, offered a $10,000 reward for Butler dead or alive. There were others. A would-be hitman placed an advertisement in a Tennessee newspaper: "I understand $50,000 is offered as a reward to whoever will kill the Beast Butler of New Orleans. I accept the offer, and require $25,000 forfeit, to be placed in some good hands. When I accomplish the noble deed, I am to be paid the reward. My name can be found when desired by the proper persons."[40] Butler, however, escaped the wrath of irate Southerners.

From the Big Easy, Butler returned to Virginia, this time at the head of the newly-formed Army of the James. In New Orleans, Benjamin Butler was in his element, but on the battlefield, he wasn't. He suffered a humiliating loss to an inferior force in the 1864 Bermuda Hundred campaign. General

Grant wanted him removed, but Butler's powerful political connections kept him in uniform.

While Butler may have been a failure as a general, he succeeded in scaring the hell out of Southern firebrands. When Union officials caught wind of a rebel plot to burn down New York City during the 1864 election (see page 148), they sent Butler to the Big Apple. When Robert Cobb Kennedy and the other plotters learned the Beast was in New York, they changed their plan and attacked the city later in November.

Butler's next military misadventure took place in Wilmington, North Carolina, where he led the siege of Fort Fisher on December 24, 1864. The assault failed, and Butler ordered his troops off the beach, despite Grant's orders that if the initial attack fell short, the soldiers on the beach should then assault the fortification. Fuming, Grant replaced Butler with Maj. Gen. Alfred Terry.

Lincoln couldn't look the other way after Butler's ignominious failure to take Fort Fisher and relieved him of his command. Butler fought his removal and managed to finagle a congressional hearing. During the hearing, he claimed that taking Fort Fisher was an impossible task, but on January 15—while the congressional committee listened to Butler's arguments—the fort fell to his replacement, Major General Terry. Butler was humiliated and lost his appeal.

After the war, Butler continued to raise Cain. He ran for, and won, a seat in the US Congress, where he fought hard for civil rights. After three terms in the House, he left Capitol Hill and became governor of Massachusetts. He unsuccessfully ran for president in 1884. In 1892, thirty years after he left New Orleans, Butler penned *Butler's Book*, his eleven-hundred-page autobiography. He died a year later at the age of seventy-four, leaving an estate worth seven figures.

Butler's years of civic duty as a legislator and leader have been overshadowed by the six months he presided over New Orleans. Pissed on (figuratively), cursed, and denounced as a war criminal for his execution of a young man who desecrated a flag, Beast Butler never did forget the offer he made to Mrs. Mumford the day before her husband hanged.

Four years after the war ended, in 1869, a desperate Mrs. Mumford sought help from the man who widowed her. Butler was in his first term as a congressman when Mrs. Mumford visited him in his Washington office. True to his word, Butler pulled a few strings, helping the widow to get a job as a clerk.

CHAPTER 4

The Sack of Athens and the Court-Martial of Col. J. B. Turchin

1862

"I shuts mine eyes for two hours," Col. John Basil Turchin supposedly told his troops after they occupied the sleepy northern Alabama town of Athens on the morning of May 2, 1862.[1] What happened when the colonel allegedly turned a blind eye to his soldiers' pillaging became known as the "Sack of Athens."

❂ ❂ ❂

Friends and admirers knew him as the "Russian Thunderbolt." His enemies and detractors preferred to call him "The Mad Cossack." During the Union's foray into northern Alabama during the summer of 1862, he acquired a third nickname: the "Robber Colonel."

John Basil Turchin was a zealous abolitionist who fought valiantly for the Union, but it was his soldiers' off-the-battlefield behavior that gave their officer his colorful monikers.

The Russian émigré was born Ivan Vasilovitch Turcheninov near the Black Sea in Russia on January 30, 1822. By the time he suited up for the Union in 1861, Turchin had amassed an impressive military record. At fourteen, Turcheninov marched off to military school in St. Petersburg, where he spent the next five years studying the art of warfare. Upon graduation, he entered the service as an ensign.

After almost a decade of service to the czar, second lieutenant Ivan was accepted to an elite officers training program. He studied warfare for two years before graduating in 1852 with the rank of captain. A star on the rise, Ivan was given a plush position with the Imperial Guards.

During the Crimean War, Turcheninov put his martial skills to work for the empire by preparing a defense of Finland. His strategy was successful, and Turcheninov received recognition from the imperial high command. By the end of 1855, he had attained the rank of colonel.

At some point he caught the eye of Nedezhda Lvova, the daughter of a Russian aristocrat. The young debutante was a good match for Ivan: She was well educated and could read and write in four languages. The couple wed in a spring ceremony on May 10, 1856. Just days after their wedding, the Turcheninovs decided that they had had enough of king and country. Somewhere along the way, the couple had become disenchanted with the decadent world of aristocratic Russia and its sharp class divisions. Ivan obtained a one-year leave of absence on the pretense that he was ill, and the couple defected to London. A few months later, in August 1856, they boarded a steamer en route to New York.

The democratic west was truly a new world for the couple. They Americanized their names, and within a few years of arriving, John Basil and Nadine Turchin had settled in Illinois, where John went to work as an engineer for the Illinois Central Railroad. When war broke out, the army was looking for a few good men, especially those with education and experience in the arts of war, so the former imperial guardsman became Colonel Turchin of the Nineteenth Illinois Regiment.

The impending conflict with the class-based, aristocratic "Old South" may have struck a familiar chord for the Russian imports. In her diary, Madame Turchin compares the relationship of slaves and their masters to that between Russian serfs and their imperial masters in Mother Russia. "The climate and the countryside remind me of Little Russia or the Ukraine, the sun perhaps a little warmer," she states in an entry dated May 31, 1863. The "Land of the Free," she notes, wasn't free for everyone. It had slaves, whose "landlords" were "the exact copy of the master of white serfs."[2]

By 1862, forty-year-old Turchin was in his middle years. His barrel chest had settled around his waist, his hairline had receded, and his jet-black beard and mustache had become sprinkled with salt. In the few photographs of Turchin that exist, he has the icy glare and somber expression of a man on a serious mission.

"The problem before us is grand," Turchin said about the war. "Universal freedom is at stake."[3]

Madame Turchin, not one to be left behind, followed her husband to war. Although US Army regulations strictly forbade a wife to accompany a soldier, she traveled south with the Nineteenth anyway. Nadine was not just another camp follower. According to numerous sources, she took command of the regiment when her husband fell ill.[4]

Like a good soldier, she never complained, making a thirty-mile trek without so much as a whimper. One source even compared her to Joan of Arc, the "Maid of Orleans" and proclaimed that the men of the regiment wouldn't hesitate to follow Madame Turchin into battle.[5]

From the start, Colonel Turchin was at odds with his superiors over the issue of confiscating rebel property, including slaves. Don Carlos Buell, commander of the Army of the Ohio, didn't want his soldiers to take what didn't belong to them. He feared that taking things from the Southern civilian population would hamper the war effort by making enemies out of noncombatants.

Many of the boys in blue, on the other hand, resented the notion of protecting the private property of people in open rebellion against the United States. Turchin called it the "guarding-potato-patch policy," and later condemned it as "the greatest military absurdity that was ever practiced in the prosecution of the war."

In his book *Chickamauga*, Turchin describes the policy as "gently fighting the rebels in the field, and at the same time preserving their property from the uses of the army." He goes on to explain that US soldiers had to live on their own supplies and "guard the patches of truck and grain, orchards, smokehouses, corn-cribs, and even the water-wells of the rebel citizens from the use of, or spoliation by our soldiers."[6]

An experienced soldier, Turchin knew the limitations of an army on the move. Without "foraging," an army couldn't survive in the field. He also understood the value of knowledge gleaned from slaves, and unlike some of his comrades, Turchin believed in liberating the slaves he encountered along the way.

Apparently, not only did Turchin disagree with the "guarding-potato-patch policy," but he also didn't enforce it, and his men quickly earned a reputation. Stories of pillaging among the Nineteenth Illinois quickly reached the Union high command. Stephen Hurlbut, brigadier general of the Illinois Volunteer Militia, sent a note to Turchin dated July 16, 1861, just three months after the war's onset. "The Nineteenth have now an opportunity of establishing a reputation for orderly and soldier-like behavior," he said. "I have no fears for their reputation for courage and gallantry. I regret that I have reliable information that they violate private rights of property and person. This must be stopped at once," Hurlbut warned.[7]

"The regiment must not be permitted to make friends into enemies and injure the cause of the Nation while in its service by excesses and violence. Peaceable citizens must be protected; offenders against such must be punished."

Hurlbut went on to lay down the ground rules for taking things from civilians. He explained that Turchin, if "compelled by military necessity," could take horses or other private property, but this confiscation should only be done by officers who recorded the names of the legal owners so they could be reimbursed later.[8]

The allegations of pilfering didn't hamper Turchin's advancement, and by March 1862, he was made commander of the Army of the Ohio's Eighth Brigade, which contained four regiments: the Nineteenth and Twenty-Fourth Illinois as well as the Eighteenth Ohio and the Thirty-Seventh Indiana.

The taking of unauthorized materiel by men of the Army of the Ohio's Third Division, of which the Eighth Brigade was part, continued. It became such an epidemic that Maj. Gen. Ormsby Mitchel issued General Order No. 81 on March 15, 1862. "All plundering or pillaging or depredation upon property of any kind is strictly prohibited." Mitchel also said that the officers would be punished alongside the men if they failed to keep them from stealing.[9]

Mitchel apparently found it necessary to issue Order No. 85 a week later, on March 23. In this order, Mitchel warned soldiers of the Third Division that anyone "found engaged in any depredations, or in robbing of private property, or in any infringement of the laws" would be surrendered to civil authorities "in the neighborhood in which the offense is perpetrated" and "dealt with by them according to their laws."[10] Here was a Union major general threatening to send Federal soldiers to Southern civil authorities for punishment.

In May, an arm of the Army of the Ohio under Mitchel's command ventured into northern Alabama. Turchin's brigade, which was part of this force, went about securing the area's railroads and repairing bridges. As a former topographical engineer, Turchin was ideally suited to this task. Central to this area's network of railways was the small town of Athens, which had fallen under Union control. The Eighteenth Ohio was stationed just north of town.

As a railroad hub, Athens was also important to the South, so wily Confederate colonel John S. Scott hatched a plan to retake the town. He slipped some misinformation to a Union informer, and the man rushed to Federal forces with news that fifteen thousand rebel soldiers were massing for an attack on Tuscumbia, fifty miles west of Athens.

The bad information caused Turchin to move his regiment to Decatur. Meanwhile, the Eighteenth Ohio under T. R. Stanley remained in the vicinity of Athens to safeguard the railroad. Instead of attacking Tuscumbia, as Mitchel was led to believe, Scott instead hit the Ohio soldiers at Athens with the help of some of the area's residents.

After a brief skirmish, the Eighteenth Ohio retreated. With their tails tucked between their legs, they marched through Athens on their way out of the area. Jubilant townspeople supposedly tossed insults at the soldiers.

Some eyewitnesses later said that the citizens of Athens did not mistreat the soldiers, but the word spread throughout the Federal forces like wildfire—the townspeople were in it with the rebels.

The loss of Athens was a bitter pill to swallow for the Ohio soldiers. Their ire grew with each step. By the time they reached Huntsville, they were hot. They told their brothers in blue that the townspeople leered and jeered at them as they marched through town. The men of Athens, thrilled at the sight of the Yankees retreating, tossed their hats in the air; the women waved scarves and handkerchiefs. Some of the Ohio boys claimed that the townspeople fired at them from the rooftops.

Although some of the citizens of Athens did help Scott, these claims were likely exaggerated for effect. The Ohio men may also have been misled about the extent of citizen aid to the rebels because a few of Scott's men, including the colonel himself, were out of uniform.

Adding to an already volatile situation, guerrilla warfare was on the rise in the area. One attack in particular vexed the men of Turchin's brigade.

The same morning the Ohio soldiers evacuated Athens, a group of about fifty citizens attacked soldiers guarding the Limestone Creek Bridge a few miles south of town. After the guerrillas overcame the guards, they weakened the bridge by sawing through the support beams. They had just finished when they heard a supply train coming around the bend. They hid in the woods and watched as the trestle collapsed under the weight of the locomotive. The crash killed the train's engineer and pinned two Union soldiers inside a boxcar.

When the boxcar caught fire, a few local slaves attempted to rescue the trapped soldiers, but the guerrillas threatened to shoot them if they tried. The slaves could do nothing but listen to the screams as the two men slowly burned to death.

The men of Turchin's brigade had endured a humiliating defeat at Athens, swallowed insults from the townspeople, and heard about the ghastly murders at the Limestone Creek Bridge. Major General Mitchel sent Turchin to Athens to rout the Confederates. As the Nineteenth Illinois marched, a few of them heard Mitchel say, "don't leave a grease spot."[11]

Turchin's men reached Athens at about eight on the morning of May 2, 1862, but Scott's forces had already moved out. This left the population open to assault by an angry force who felt the townspeople had wronged them.

The men of the Nineteenth may have had a little payback in mind. Mitchel later described what he believed was the pretext for the "terrible excesses" that occurred when the Mad Cossack's men arrived in town: "When my troops were driven from town they were cursed, hooted, and spit upon. Two of their comrades on the day before were burned alive. One of these, caught between the tender and the engine when the train was destroyed at Limestone Creek Bridge, was actually roasted alive, in the presence of barbarians, who swore they would kill the negroes who offered to cut away and rescue the unfortunate man."[12]

What happened during the Sack of Athens—and Turchin's role in particular—has become mired in speculation, innuendo, and finger-pointing. According to some sources, the commander did what he could to control his men, even appointing Colonel Stanley as provost marshal to keep law and order. In this version of events, Turchin rode off to scout the area and was gone when his men raided the town.

Other sources, particularly those from the Southern perspective, contend that while Turchin didn't directly participate, he knew about and even condoned the pillaging. In this version, when the Nineteenth arrived in town, Turchin said he would close his eyes for two hours.[13]

Details of soldiers were sent to search residences for arms, but things quickly degenerated into a free-for-all. The unruly elements of Turchin's brigade went about ransacking the town and terrorizing the citizens. Reports of the extent of the looting vary widely. According to the list of charges specified at Turchin's court-martial, the men did more than just take a few horses. They took items of little or no military value, like women's clothes, a "fine microscope," and "geological specimens."[14] In a wild frenzy, they tore apart books and trampled on Bibles. They menaced citizens with foul language as they rifled through houses as well as stores.

One source contains a humorous, albeit less than accurate, scene of the Mad Cossack during the fray. The author even gave the colonel his idea of a Russian accent. "Vell, Lieudenant, I dink it ish dime to shtop dis tam billaging," Turchin allegedly said to his adjutant.

"Oh, no, Colonel, the boys are not yet half done jerking."

"Ish dot so? Den I schlep for half an hour longer," Turchin replied before going back to sleep.[15]

While violence against citizens was kept to a minimum, in at least one instance a non-combatant was violently assaulted. Charlotte Hine, a widow who lived on a plantation a few miles from town, witnessed a rape. Hine later said that a private named Ayer Bowers demanded that Hine's slave girl put down the child she was carrying. The terrified girl complied, and the soldier raped her while the widow watched, helpless. Turchin had Bowers thrown in the stockade at Huntsville, but after two weeks, the private was released and sent back to his unit.[16]

In the days that followed, Major General Mitchel—the man who allegedly made the remark about not leaving a grease spot—sent a flurry of communications to Colonel Turchin. In a dispatch dated May 3, Mitchel warned Turchin that "anything less than rigid discipline, perfect order, and thorough soldiership will end in disaster."[17] A few days later, he sent another message emphasizing the need for strict discipline.[18]

On May 7, 1862, he sent a message in even stronger language: "Again, I say, be vigilant and repress pillaging. Shave the heads of the offenders, brand them thieves, and drive them out of camp."[19]

On May 16, Mitchel demanded answers for what occurred at Athens. "Colonel: you will report whether any, and, if any, what, excesses and depredations on private property were committed by the troops under your command in Athens"[20]

A few days later, Mitchel sent a letter to Secretary of War Edwin M. Stanton, perhaps in an attempt to cover his own flank. "My own personal attention cannot be given to all the troops under my command," Mitchel said. "The most terrible outrages—robberies, rapes, arsons, and plundering—are being committed by lawless brigands and vagabonds connected with the army, and I desire to punish all those found guilty of perpetrating these crimes with death by hanging."[21]

Mitchel made some attempt to repair the damage done at Athens. He had the officers under Turchin's command search their men and made them swear an oath in writing that they didn't have any loot.[22] He later reported "not a solitary article was found except what was authorized by the regulations."[23] He also went to town and asked citizens to form "a committee to hear all complaints," although his note to Stanton suggests that he had a less than sympathetic ear. "Not that I had any sympathy for the citizens, for I believed they had led the enemy to the Attack upon Athens," he noted.[24]

The citizens committee didn't name names, but they did present a "bill" to the United States Government for $54,689.90—the damage done to the property of forty-five citizens of Athens. In his reply to the committee, Mitchel explained that the government could not reimburse the money because the pillaging was done by individuals not under direct orders of the US Army. Since the committee didn't point the finger at any particular individuals, Mitchel notes, it wouldn't be possible to arrest anyone for the crimes committed at Athens.[25]

This wasn't good enough for Maj. Gen. Don Carlos Buell, who was a staunch advocate of treating the Southern civilians with kid gloves. When he heard about the Sack of Athens, he was furious.

As Buell fumed over the incident, Congress was considering promoting the Mad Cossack to brigadier general. Major General Mitchel himself had put in Turchin's name for promotion in late June for his uncommon valor on the battlefield.

Buell reacted to the news and whipped off a letter to Stanton. "If as I hear the promotion of Colonel Turchin is contemplated," Buell declared in a letter to Washington, "I feel it my duty to inform you that he is entirely unfit for it. I placed him in command of a brigade, and I now find it necessary to relieve him from it in consequence of his utter failure to enforce discipline and render it efficient."[26]

Buell wasn't going to let the Sack of Athens go unpunished. He relieved Turchin of his command and ordered a court-martial. An indignant Turchin resigned immediately. "I was at the head of my brigade everywhere and always on duty," he commented in his farewell notice. "Neither my name nor the name of my brigade was mentioned in the official reports of dispatches. Instead of thanks I receive insults; therefore I respectfully tender my unconditional resignation . . . to be accepted immediately."[27] Buell refused to accept Turchin's withdrawal.

While Turchin awaited trial, Madame Turchin traveled north to Chicago in order to round up political allies. With her entourage in tow, she then headed east to Washington, where she supposedly met with President Lincoln to plead her husband's case.

Back in steamy northern Alabama, Turchin's court-martial got underway on July 7, 1862. It quickly became a headline story and a benchmark for the proper conduct of war. The "Robber Colonel" was charged with three counts: dereliction of duty, conduct unbecoming an officer, and disobeying orders. Brig. Gen. James Garfield, the future president of the United States, acted as the president of the court-martial until he later dropped out due to a case of dysentery.

The sole specification of the first charge—dereliction of duty—alleged that Turchin was negligent as an officer by giving his men carte blanche to plunder Athens. The specification contained twenty different allegations that detailed the gamut of crimes against the citizens of Athens or their property. The allegations ranged from theft of items of little or no strategic value to "indecent outrages" to rape.

One group allegedly tore through the office of B. C. David. They stole about $1,000 and then ripped through David's books. Whooping and hollering, they tore apart Bibles and trampled on them.[28]

Another group allegedly ransacked the home of a lawyer named John Malone. They took clothing, silverware, and just about anything else of value. While they rifled through the house, they "used coarse, vulgar, and profane language to the females of the family." When they were done with Malone's house, they plundered his office and then his plantation on the outskirts of town.[29]

A few soldiers rifled through the home of Milly Ann Clayton. They went through her dresses, took clothes, and threatened to shoot the terrified woman. When they were done pillaging, they "attempted an indecent outrage on the person of her servant girl."[30]

Some of the soldiers took over the home of J. H. Jones. While the family watched, they used the piano as a chopping block, using it "to cut joints with an axe." They stole the silverware and destroyed furniture, and "behaved rudely and coarsely to the ladies of the family."[31]

They were even ruder to one Mrs. Hollingsworth. The soldiers fired their rifles at her house and threatened to torch the place. According to the specification, Mrs. Hollingsworth, who was in the third term of her pregnancy, was so terrified that she miscarried and later died.[32]

Another allegation referred to the rape of Charlotte Hine's fourteen-year-old black servant. "Several Soldiers came to the house of Mrs. Charlotte Hine and committed rape on the person of a colored girl and then entered the house and plundered it of all the sugar, coffee, preserves and the like which they could find," read the report on the incident. "Before leaving they destroyed or carried off all the pictures and ornaments they could lay their hands on."[33]

The record also alleged that "a party of soldiers" burst into B. S. Irwin's house and demanded that Mrs. Irwin make them a meal. As she and her servant cooked, "they made the most indecent and beastly propositions to the latter in the presence of the whole family, and when the girl went away, they followed her in the same manner, notwithstanding her efforts to avoid them."[34]

The second charge leveled against the colonel—conduct unbecoming an officer—contained two specifications. The first alleged that Turchin spent a week in an Athens hotel and didn't pay the landlord. The second alleged that the Mad Cossack failed to prevent his troopers from looting the town.

The third charge—disobeying orders—contained four specifications. The first alleged that Turchin disobeyed Order No. 13 from headquarters: "Peaceful citizens are not to be molested in their persons or property." The second specification alleged that Turchin's men failed to follow the ground rules set up for the seizure of private property for army use when they took items from citizens of Athens without "fair compensation." The third specification alleged that Turchin's men took food and animals "without adequate necessity." The fourth alleged that Turchin violated Army General Order No. 4 when he allowed Madame Turchin to go to Athens with the Eighth Brigade.[35]

Turchin pled innocent of all the charges except one—he admitted to breaking army regulations by allowing Madame Turchin to accompany his regiment into Athens.

The government planned on calling nineteen witnesses, sixteen of them from Athens.[36] Aware of their potential bias, Turchin submitted a written request asking that witnesses against him state under oath whether they were loyal to the Union or the Confederacy. The court rejected this request. The idea of rebel eyewitnesses testifying against a Union colonel shocked some Northerners and angered others, particularly those who favored total war against people in open rebellion against the United States.

The judge advocate, Capt. Peter Swain, went forward with his case. He called residents of Athens, who testified about the destruction wreaked on their town by Turchin's soldiers. Milly Ann Clayton testified that soldiers called her a "God damned bitch."[37] Charlotte Hine described the rape of her slave.[38] W. P. Tanner said several soldiers of the Eighteenth Ohio told him that Turchin agreed to close his eyes for two hours.[39]

A handful of Union soldiers also testified for the prosecution. Joseph Arnold, a soldier from the Eighteenth, said that Turchin sat on the courthouse steps while the looting took place. Another Ohio man, Pvt. Joe Stevens, said that he watched Turchin ride out of town and that the colonel did not attempt to stop the violence right away.[40]

As the witnesses painted a sinister picture for the military commission, Congress approved Turchin's promotion to brigadier general on July 17, creating a surreal scenario in which an officer facing a court-martial and possible dismissal was eligible for promotion.

Turchin's defense began on July 23. A few officers in Turchin's brigade testified on his behalf, downplaying the alleged atrocities and emphasizing the colonel's attempt to keep law and order. Col. Timothy Stanley, the commander of the Eighteenth Ohio, said he didn't see any "depredations" but contradicted himself when he testified that there were men in jail at Athens for committing outrages on citizens.[41]

Col. Carter Gazlay testified that Turchin did everything in his power to safeguard the citizens of Athens. He appointed a provost marshal and later apprehended a few of the culprits responsible, sending them to Huntsville for punishment.

Besides, the order to sack Athens may have come from a higher authority, or at least that is how Turchin's men may have perceived the offhanded remark made by General Mitchel. Three different defense witnesses, including Gazlay, testified that they heard Mitchel tell some of the men in the Nineteenth to "not leave a grease spot" in Athens—a comment they may have taken as a license to pillage the town.[42]

At the end of the trial Turchin addressed the members of the court. During his ninety-minute remarks, he discussed each of the charges, narrated a tale of his military experience, and preached about the proper mode of warfare. He tried to downplay the damage done to Athens. "The three most extensive stores in town, including that of George Mason, who joined the rebel cavalry and fought against us, were not molested, because their owners, or partners of their owners, attended to their business and remained with their property."[43]

Turchin then explained the strategic value of taking slaves from their Southern masters. The former slaves, he said, were the "only friends" the Federal army had in the South, and were invaluable sources of information. To turn them back to their owners, Turchin argued, would only doom them as traitors.[44]

As for his reputation, Turchin said he thought it was a compliment. "I have everywhere in Missouri, in Kentucky, in Tennessee, and in Alabama, been hated by secessionists, and I consider it my best recommendation as a loyal officer"[45]

"The more lenient we are with secessionists," Turchin told the members, "the more insolent they become; and if we do not prosecute this war with vigor, using all the means that we can bring to bear against the enemy, including the emancipation of slaves, the ruin of this country is inevitable."[46]

The colonel's eloquent and impassioned speech wasn't enough to erase what happened at Athens. The court found him guilty of all charges except two: the first specification of the second charge, which alleged that Turchin failed to pay for his room and board at an Athens hotel; and the third specification of the third charge, which alleged that his men took, without need, food and "draught animals" from area's residents. The commission dismissed Turchin from the military.

Despite the guilty finding, Turchin did at least partly win over most of the members. Six of the seven officers recommended leniency "on the ground that the offense was committed under exciting circumstances, and was one of omission rather than commission."[47] While Turchin allegedly closed his eyes and allowed others to terrorize the citizens of Athens, he didn't directly participate.

Buell wouldn't budge on the sentence. The "Robber Colonel's" reputation came back to haunt him. In weighing his decision of whether or not to grant clemency to Turchin, Buell noted that "It is a fact of sufficient notoriety that similar disorders, though not to the same extent, have marked the course of Colonel Turchin's command wherever it has gone."[48]

"The question is not whether private property may be used for the public service, for that is proper whenever the public interest demands it. It should then be done by authority and in an orderly way," Buell explained. "But the wanton and unlawful indulgence of individuals in acts of plunder and outrage is a different matter, tending to the demoralization of the troops and the destruction of their efficiency." When Turchin's men should have been on the alert, Buell noted, they were loading up "with useless plunder."[49] Buell gave Turchin his marching orders, drumming the Mad Cossack out of the army.

❂

Whether or not he closed his eyes—literally or figuratively—John Basil Turchin became the poster boy for Buell critics who wanted to take the gloves off their fighting men, and an epic villain to Southerners, Southern sympathizers, and Northerners who favored what Turchin dismissed as the "guarding-potato-patch policy."

Some characterized the Russian Thunderbolt as a get-it-done type who wasn't afraid to do what was necessary to win the war. "Colonel Turchin has had, from the beginning, the wisest and clearest ideas of any man in the field about the way in which the war should be conducted," a reporter for the *Chicago Daily Tribune* wrote in mid-July.[50]

Others branded the "Mad Cossack" with more than a few scarlet letters. A correspondent for the *New York Times* described Turchin's conduct at Athens as "especially odious, not to say criminal . . . No effort was made to restrain the soldiers till their work was accomplished, if any effort was made at all."[51]

"Sic Transit Turchin"—and thus goes Turchin—the *New York Times* correspondent wrote after the court-martial concluded.[52]

Only Turchin didn't go. On August 5, President Lincoln approved Turchin's promotion, which wiped away the verdict of the military commission. John Basil Turchin, soon-to-be Brigadier General Turchin (he didn't accept the promotion until September 1), returned to Chicago two weeks later. He was given a hero's welcome.

The Mad Cossack addressed the crowd, once again giving a lengthy speech. He told the crowd, "I know also that the same men who were relying on the power of slavery must not be handled with kid gloves, and so I handled them a little roughly." The crowd howled its approval.

He said that he didn't know if it was a "happy or unhappy result" that Buell didn't agree with his methods of handling secessionists. This drew boos for Don Carlos Buell. Someone in the audience yelled, "you shall go back, General."[53] Buell drew more than boos; he also drew the ire of his superiors, who ejected him from his command in late 1862 for allegedly dragging his feet in Kentucky.

As the crowd predicted, Turchin did go back to war. Again, Madame Turchin followed her husband, although this time she stayed a few steps behind him to avoid any further scandal. She kept diaries of her experiences, but only one—covering the period from May 1863 to April 1864—has survived. She wrote about the September 1863 Battle of Chickamauga, which she watched from the outskirts of the battlefield. She also described the Battle of Missionary Ridge—fought outside Chattanooga in November of that year—which she observed from a bluff overlooking the field.

The Mad Cossack remained in the Army until October 1864, when a severe case of heatstroke forced him to leave the service. He returned to

Chicago, where he worked as a civil engineer. He never really left the service entirely. In 1865—before the war had ended—he authored *Military Rambles* followed by *Chickamauga* in 1888.

In 1901, he lost his mind as a result of heatstroke. He was sent to the Southern Hospital for the Insane in Anna, Illinois. The Mad Cossack died a pauper on June 18, 1901, at the age of seventy-nine—a hero in the Land of Lincoln, an outlaw in Athens.

John Basil Turchin spent most of his adult life in one uniform or another, fighting valiantly for czar and country on a hundred different dots on the map. Despite years of service, Turchin's name will be forever linked to the Sack of Athens, whatever he may or may not have seen.

CHAPTER 5

Feuding Generals: The Murder of Bull Nelson and the Walker–Marmaduke Duel 1862–1863

In the heat of battle, sometimes tempers flare and passions take control. During the Civil War, several officers on both sides perished not by enemy grapeshot or bullets, but by their own comrades-in-arms. In two high-profile cases, disagreements between generals ended in violent confrontation.

✥ ✥ ✥

William "Bull" Nelson was a bull in more ways than one. At six feet four, he towered over his fellow officers; tipping the scales at three hundred pounds, he outweighed most of them, too. With a wrestler's broad shoulders and barrel chest, Nelson was a physically imposing character. People who knew Nelson also described him as a Jekyll-and-Hyde type who could change faces from smooth, educated gentleman to coarse, nasty tyrant at the drop of a hat.

Gen. William B. Hazen, who served with Nelson, described Bull's tranquil face as socially refined, well-liked, and often the life of the party. He would titillate dinner guests with exciting stories culled from his worldwide adventures with the US Navy.

Along with Nelson's Jekyll, Hazen noted, came the "harsh and petulant" Hyde, who bullied others and could swear like Sam Hill.[1] Gen. Stanley Matthews—who served under Nelson and later became a justice of the Supreme Court—described a Bull incident in a letter he wrote to a friend.[2]

Nelson and a Dr. Bradford, a surgeon attached to his command, became involved in a heated argument over Bradford's black servant. Nelson accused the servant of some wrongdoing, and when Bradford stood up for his employee, Nelson exploded, assailing the surgeon with a volley of insults.

Later, upset and perhaps a little ashamed, Nelson consulted the future judge and asked him to referee. Reluctant to tangle with the general, Matthews agreed to hear both sides and mediate, if Nelson agreed to accept his judgment, whatever it may be.

After listening to both sides, Matthews sided with Bradford. Incredulous at first, Nelson accepted the "verdict" after a few minutes and immediately apologized to Bradford. Matthews offered a few parting words to Nelson. "You are two different men," Matthews observed. "The outside man is rough, overbearing, inconsiderate, and tyrannical, easily given offence, and not overlooking offence given by others; the inside man is generous, open, frank, fearless, magnanimous."[3]

Matthews went on to point out that most people knew only the "outside" man, whereas just a few friends knew of the "inside" man. He ended with a poignant note: One day, Matthews said, "you will come in contact with some person, in some offensive way, who not appreciating more than he can see from the outside will, in resenting your offensive manner, shoot the outside man, and in doing so kill the inside man."[4]

"You will not be able to acquit him of a sometimes harsh and imperious temper in command," Don Carlos Buell, Nelson's one-time superior in the US Army, said. Buell chalked up Nelson's bombastic behavior to his "strong character."[5] He also speculated that this harshness resulted from the strict discipline of the navy, where Nelson spent his later teenage years and all of his adulthood.

Nelson, born in Kentucky in 1824, began his colorful military record at the age of fifteen when he went to naval school at Annapolis. After graduation, Nelson traveled the world with the navy, accumulating anecdotes and promotions. During the Mexican-American War, he served with Commodore Matthew Perry in the Gulf of Mexico and later took part in the 1847 siege of Veracruz, where he showed a talent for artillery combat.

From the balmy Mexican Gulf Coast, he traveled to the Great Lakes for duty aboard the steamship *Michigan*. After a brief stint up north, it was back to sea duty for Nelson aboard the *Cumberland* in the Mediterranean. After his service in the Med, Lieutenant Nelson took command of the *Tredonia*, docked at Valparaiso, Chile. A few years later in August 1858, Nelson made a transatlantic trek to Africa in command of the *Niagara* on a mission to return the survivors found aboard the *Echo*, a slave ship captured en route to Cuba. The *Niagara* was tasked with delivering the Africans aboard the slaver to Liberia.

By the time the Civil War began, Nelson had accumulated a trove of stories, a long list of credentials, and the nickname "Bull."

Bull began the war as a lieutenant commander in charge of the Union's fleet of boats on the Ohio River. A native of the Bluegrass State, Nelson was familiar with Kentucky, so in April 1861, he was sent home to rally support for the Union.

During the Civil War, Kentucky—like Bull Nelson—had a bit of a split personality. Citizens were deeply divided on the issue of secession. When the war began, some marched off to join the North, while others sided with the South. The state government decided to split the difference and declared neutrality.

Both Union and Confederate forces initially respected Kentucky's neutrality, but they also coveted the railroad lines and strategic areas along the Mississippi River, so they massed forces along Kentucky's borders. Union brass sent Nelson into Kentucky to raise troops for the cause. By late summer, Nelson had managed to whip up enough support from Unionist forces to form Camp Dick Robinson, the first of several recruiting camps in Kentucky. From the camps, the Union equipped soldiers and organized regiments.

Not content to sit idly by and watch the Union assume control of Kentucky, Confederate forces crossed the Tennessee border and occupied Columbus, which at the time was situated on the banks of the Mississippi (much of the city was moved to the bluff overlooking the river after a 1928 flood). To counter this move, the Union sent Ulysses S. Grant into northern Kentucky, where a key railroad line was located.

By the fall of 1861, Kentucky's pro-Union legislature had had enough of neutrality and what they viewed as the rebel encroachment; they ordered out the Confederate forces and declared their allegiance to Washington. The state's secessionists countered by forming a second Kentucky government, which declared its allegiance to Richmond. Throughout the rest of the war, Kentucky remained split by divided loyalties. It became a battleground state marked by vicious guerrilla raids, particularly along the border with Tennessee.

Five weeks after establishing Camp Dick Robinson, Nelson was promoted to brigadier general of volunteers and assigned a division in the Army of the Ohio under the command of Maj. Gen. Don Carlos Buell.

As the war heated up, Nelson found himself in the middle of the kitchen. He played a critical role in the epic clash at Shiloh in April 1862 and helped Maj. Gen. Henry Halleck take Corinth, Mississippi, the following month. He earned back-to-back promotions in July 1862: He was made lieutenant commander in the US Navy on July 17, and a day later, major general in the US Army.

Nelson was a colorful character on the battlefield and the farthest thing from a coward. He supposedly once stood up in the midst of a Confederate lead storm and barked to his men to not be afraid. If the rebs couldn't hit him, he quipped, they couldn't hit the side of a barn.[6]

Major General Nelson was given command of the Army of Kentucky in August. Later that month—on August 30, 1862—his army suffered a major defeat when Confederates under Kirby Smith routed Union forces commanded by Indiana native Mahlon Manson in the Battle of Richmond, Kentucky. More than four thousand of Nelson's men—virtually his entire force—became Confederate POWs. Bull, who arrived on the scene at the end of the battle, sustained a minor gunshot wound. Tail between his legs, Nelson scampered northwest to Louisville.

Enraged, Nelson blamed Manson and fired his immediate superior, fellow Indianan General Lew Wallace. Wallace's removal drew the ire of Indiana governor Oliver Morton, who traveled south to Louisville, apparently to protect Indiana's sons from the wrath of Bull Nelson.

By this point, things had gone south for the North in Kentucky. With Nelson's troops routed at Richmond, the rebels had free reign in the Bluegrass State. Federal forces, including the army of Don Carlos Buell, raced to Kentucky. By late September, Confederate forces under Braxton Bragg were poised to march on Louisville. With Union troops still hurrying to intercept Bragg, the defense of Louisville fell to Bull Nelson. This was the setting for the drama about to unfold at the Galt House, a Louisville hotel that Nelson was using as his headquarters.

In Louisville, Nelson crossed paths with Brig. Gen. Jefferson C. Davis, a Union officer from Indiana with the misfortune of having the same name as the leader of the rebel government. At 5 feet 7 and a featherweight 125 pounds, Davis literally looked up to Nelson, but as a soldier, he stood just as tall.

Davis came from a background every bit as colorful as Nelson's. The son of pioneers who settled in Clark County, Indiana, Davis grew up hearing war stories from his grandfather, an Indian fighter who took part in the Battle of River Raisin during the War of 1812. When he heard word about the Mexican-American War, Davis went south for the action, enlisting in a volunteer company called the Clark Guards.

He fought in several battles during the war, acquiring experience with artillery, and wound up at Fort Sumter in Charleston Harbor in 1861. From the first shots fired, Jefferson C. Davis was in the midst of the action.

After the surrender of the fort, Lieutenant Davis was promoted to captain. During a short stint as a quartermaster, Davis began to long for the action. He was commissioned as a colonel of the Twenty-Second Indiana. Over the next few months, Davis got all of the action he wanted.

In Missouri, his men helped overcome a vastly superior enemy force, capturing a large number of men and confiscating a cache of weapons. He fought at the Battle of Pea Ridge, Arkansas, and elsewhere, somehow finding the time to marry Maretta Athon in Indianapolis during a leave of absence. The wiry Hoosier general was well-liked by this troops, even though he had a reputation as a hothead who could swear with the best of them.

By the fall of 1862, Davis had risen to the rank of brigadier general of volunteers, but illness forced him to leave the field and return to Indiana. But even a fever wouldn't keep the plucky Davis out of the action. When he heard that General Bragg's Confederate forces were in Kentucky, Davis crawled out of bed, traveled south, and volunteered his services to the Army of the Ohio.

Davis wound up under the command of Nelson in Louisville. This was an unfortunate posting for the Hoosier; according to Hazen, Nelson "had it in" for Indiana. For some reason, Nelson harbored a grudge for all things Indiana, including "all the people who came from it," whom he considered "poor trash." To Bull Nelson, the mere mention of Indiana was "like shaking the red rag at the bull."[7]

By the time Jefferson C. Davis entered the picture, Nelson had ousted one general from Indiana (Lew Wallace) and arrested another (Ebenezer Dumont) for leaving his post without orders. One baseless rumor made the rounds that Nelson, enraged during the Battle at Richmond, tried to rally the troops by brandishing his sword. He got carried away and decapitated some of the Indiana soldiers.[8]

Yet Davis may have been a welcomed sight for Nelson. The two had known each other briefly, and Bull may have considered the seasoned combat veteran an asset in his defense of the soon-to-be-besieged city. Nelson assigned Davis the task of organizing a militia amongst the citizens of Louisville—a job that must have seemed like a step down to a division commander with an untarnished record of heroism under fire. Davis may also have felt that Nelson, in asking him to produce an effective fighting force out of untrained civilians, had asked for the impossible. However Davis felt about his mission, the chore wasn't a meaningless one; the rebs were menacing Louisville from the south, and Nelson needed to prepare the city for an all-out defense.

Nelson heard a report that Davis spent his first few days in the city sitting on his behind, so Bull summoned him to the Galt House for a progress report. There are various versions of what happened inside Nelson's office. While the wording differs from one account to the next, the gist remains the same.

When Nelson asked Davis how many men he had mustered, Davis, who had been on the job for just two days, responded "I don't know."

When asked how many companies he had organized, Davis again responded with a flippant "I don't know."

This was an entirely unacceptable answer to Nelson, who went off on the shocked Davis. The giant of a man rose from his chair and pointed a finger at Davis. "I am disappointed in you, General Davis. I selected you for this duty because you are an officer of the Regular Army, but I find I made a mistake."

"General Nelson," Davis retorted. "I am a regular soldier, and I demand the treatment due me as a general officer."

Davis then ducked into the hallway to ask Nelson's medical director, Dr. Bernard Irwin, to witness the rest of the exchange.

"Yes, Doctor, I want you to remember this," Nelson bellowed as he noticed Irwin enter his office.

With Dr. Irwin listening, Davis said "I demand from you the courtesy due to my rank."

"I will treat you as you deserve," Nelson responded in a booming voice. "You have disappointed me," he said, "You have been unfaithful to the trust which I reposed in you, and I shall relieve you at once."

Incensed, Davis fired back, "You have no authority to order me."[9]

Disgusted by this insolence, Nelson ordered Davis out of his office and out of Louisville—he was to report to Gen. Horatio Wright in Cincinnati—and threatened to have him escorted across the Ohio River by the provost guards if he didn't leave town by 9 P.M.

Scalded, Davis acquiesced and left the Galt House. Still feeling the sting from Nelson's rebuke, Davis followed orders and traveled to Cincinnati where he reported to General Wright.

About a week later, Wright reassigned Davis to General Buell, now in Louisville and preparing to go on the offensive against the Confederates. Wright ordered Davis to stay away from Bull Nelson.

Davis first traveled north to Indianapolis, where he found a sympathetic ear in Gov. Oliver Morton. The governor, who knew too well Bull's treatment of Indiana boys, traveled south with Davis. The duo reached Louisville on the evening of September 28. The next morning, they visited the Galt House. Davis was headed straight for the bull's pen.

On the morning of September 29, 1862, the little general waltzed into the lobby with Governor Morton and Thomas Gibson, an old army buddy he had served with in the Mexican-American War. Col. James Barnet Fry, who was also in the Galt House that morning but didn't witness the confrontation between the two generals, later speculated that Davis wanted to goad Nelson into a public apology and if he didn't receive "satisfaction."[10]

As Davis strolled through the lobby accompanied by Governor Morton, General Nelson emerged from one of the rooms and went over to the front desk. The diminutive Davis, with Morton watching, confronted Nelson. Davis demanded an explanation of why Nelson kicked him out of

Louisville. He didn't get one, so he repeated his demand. Nelson became enraged, his face reddening.

"Go away, you damned puppy!" Nelson hollered. By now, all eyes in the lobby were watching the drama unfurl. "I don't want to have anything to do with you!"[11]

Davis tightened his fist, crushing the "visiting card" he held during the exchange. With a quick snap of the wrist, he flicked the wadded up ball of paper in Nelson's face "as boys shoot marbles."[12]

This was just too much for Bull Nelson. He backhanded Davis and then screamed at Morton, "Did you come here, sir, to see me insulted?" Morton shrugged and said he came at Davis' request. Bull had had enough of this insolence. He stomped off toward the staircase.

Unnerved, Davis borrowed a gun from Gibson, who witnessed the entire scene. Pistol in hand, Davis raced after Nelson. When he caught up to him, he pumped a slug into his barrel chest from point-blank range (some sources say from about ten yards away). Clutching his chest, Nelson stumbled up the stairs and then crumpled to the floor.

Alarmed by the sound of gunfire, several bystanders raced to the scene and hovered over Nelson, who lay sprawled out at the staircase landing. Still conscious, he asked for a reverend so he could be baptized, and then added, "I have been basely murdered."

"Tom," Nelson said to his friend, Maj. Gen. Thomas L. Crittenden, "I am murdered."[13]

It took several bystanders to hoist Nelson's girth and carry him to a nearby room. A few minutes after a reverend baptized him, the larger-than-

Jefferson C. Davis shooting Bull Nelson, as depicted in the October 18, 1862, edition of *Harper's Weekly*.

life general died. Fry immediately arrested Davis and took him to another room at the Galt House, where the two men had a conversation that remained behind closed doors for more than two decades.

News of the shooting traveled fast, and the rumors began to fly. The shooter's name led to one tall tale that Confederate president Jefferson Davis had sneaked into Louisville and gunned down the boisterous Bull Nelson.[14]

The crime was a cold-blooded murder, but public sentiment at the time suggests that people saw Nelson's slaying as more like poetic justice. Nelson's reputation as a bully was widely known, and according to some contemporary news reports, Nelson's own troops would have shot him the first chance they had. The *Daily Journal* of Indianapolis stated that Nelson was "heartily hated by every man he ever commanded, and not a few have threatened that if they ever got into battle with him they would not be under him long."[15]

Davis simply beat them to it, and in doing so, fulfilled Stanley Matthews' prediction: The man outside had led to the murder of the man inside.

In the days following the murder, newspapers seized on this theme of Bull Nelson pushing the wrong man over the edge. Davis may have physically murdered Nelson, but reporters assassinated his character. In an ironic twist, the victim became the villain. Reporters pilloried Nelson and depicted him as a bully who brought on his own murder by slapping Davis without provocation. Writing years later, Colonel Fry lamented that "Nelson's habitual violence of character was exaggerated, the idea of retribution supplanted the demands of justice. Public attention became fixed upon Nelson's alleged violent conduct toward men generally, and not upon Davis's specific act of violence in shooting Nelson."[16]

Yet reporters and Union officials alike missed a key part of the story, which Davis confessed to Fry just after his arrest: the fact that he provoked the slap by flicking a wad of paper at Nelson.[17] For reasons known only to himself, Fry remained mum for more than twenty years and only tried to correct these inaccurate accounts when he published an 1885 article. In the papers, Davis was an officer avenging the public insult of an uncalled-for cuffing; in reality, he pinched the Bull's nose.

Not everyone considered the shooting a righteous kill. Many Kentuckians were livid. Jefferson C. Davis had murdered one of their favorite sons, and they wanted an eye for an eye. A lynch mob formed by the Galt House, where Davis was under house arrest, but the provost guard dispersed them before they caused any trouble.

The next day, September 30, a funeral procession made its way down Louisville's Main Street. A riderless horse—Nelson's mount—trailed behind the wagon carrying the casket, followed by Nelson's soldiers.

When the procession reached Christ's Church, six pallbearers lifted the casket from the carriage and carried it inside. Even in death, Bull Nelson was heavy; the men staggered as they carried the coffin. After the ceremony, Nelson made his final march, ending at Cave Hill Cemetery.

Nelson's closest friends and allies wanted justice for Nelson's murderer. They wanted to court-martial and then hang Davis, but it wouldn't happen. It was a bad time for a trial. Buell was gearing up to go after Kirby Smith, and he couldn't spare the personnel that it would take to court-martial Davis. So instead, he recommended that a court-martial convene in Washington.

By late October, however, three of the generals pushing for a trial were gone. Two of them, James Jackson and William Terrill, perished at the battle of Perryville on October 8. The third, Don Carlos Buell, was relieved of command when he failed to chase Braxton Bragg after that same battle. By this time, Davis was a free man. General Wright had ordered his release in mid-October. One of the reasons Wright gave was his belief that Davis acted in self-defense.

There was another factor that may have kept Davis out of a courtroom: he had friends in high places. After the murder, Governor Morton traveled to Washington and met with President Lincoln. Morton later insisted he went to Washington to discuss the exchange of POWs from Indiana, but there is the possibility that he went on Davis's behalf.[18]

There is one other Lincoln-Davis connection. Davis hired James Speed, who would later become Lincoln's attorney general, as his attorney. If Honest Abe influenced the decision to not court-martial Davis, it must have been a difficult decision, as he personally knew Bull Nelson.

While a formal charge of manslaughter lingered against Davis in a civilian court until 1864 (it was ultimately dropped), he escaped any formal punishment for the murder of Bull Nelson. He returned to active duty at the head of a division and served bravely throughout the rest of the war.

If his autobiography is any indication, Davis didn't feel the least bit bad about murdering his superior officer. In a brief memoir he penned after the war, Davis devoted just one clause to the murder, describing it as "a personal difficulty with Gen. Nelson" that "caused my arrest"[19]

After the war, Davis continued his military service. In 1873, he played a key role in putting down an uprising of the Modoc in northern California. He died of pneumonia at Chicago's Palmer House on November 30, 1879, at the age of fifty-one.

Jefferson C. Davis devoted his life to his country's defense, but he is best known as the Union general who got away with murder. He escaped a court-martial, but Davis remains the only Union general who murdered another Union general during the war—a legacy that he can't escape.

Davis avoided the scaffold, but James Barnet Fry made sure that he wouldn't escape infamy. In 1885, twenty-three years after Nelson's murder, Fry authored an article about the shooting.[20] In "Killed by a Brother Soldier," Fry revealed for the first time the details of his closed-door conversation with Davis just minutes after the shooting. A shaken Davis explained that he never intended to shoot Nelson and told Fry about throwing the paper ball at Nelson's face.

Fry concluded that "It seemed to be Davis's purpose to confront Nelson in a public place, demand satisfaction for the wrong done him a few days before, and if he received no apology, to insult Nelson openly, and then leave him to seek satisfaction in any way, personally or officially, that he saw fit."[21]

There could have been a darker motive moving Davis than righting a perceived wrong. The murder of a high-profile character cannot come without a conspiracy theory or two.

Fry raised the possibility that others incited Davis to publicly insult Nelson. The ringleader, Fry suggests in "Killed by a Brother Soldier," was none other than Indiana governor Oliver Morton. "I do not doubt that Morton, and perhaps others, without designing or foreseeing the fatal consequences, encouraged Davis to insult Nelson publicly for wrong done in an official interview. One step led to another in the attempt to place and fix the insult, until the end was Nelson's violent death."[22]

The conspiracy mill really began to turn when Dr. A. M. Ellis, a friend of Nelson, wrote an article about the murder in 1906. Ellis explained that a few hours before the murder, a Kentucky officer named Walter Whitaker told him about a conversation he had overheard the night before at the Galt House. A group of Hoosiers, according to Whitaker, discussed a plot to murder Nelson. The Indiana soldiers had had enough and planned to publicly humiliate Nelson, who would predictably react in a violent way that would then justify shooting him. In this fascinating but dubious conspiracy theory, Davis becomes the weapon for a shadowy cabal. Ellis apparently didn't believe the story; he didn't warn Nelson and later lived to regret it.[23]

The animosity Nelson had for Hoosiers, coupled with the number of Indiana boys that would be under his command in Buell's upcoming offensive, provided a motive, but most historians consider the conspiracy theory baseless. Davis came to the Galt House unarmed—odd if he was planning an assassination.

The real plot occurred when stubbornness, tenacity, and passion—the traits that made Jefferson C. Davis a great general—conspired to make him a murderer.

The Southern episode of "dueling generals" occurred on September 6, 1863, when two prominent officers decided to settle a score the old-fashioned way. Dueling was illegal in Arkansas and discouraged in the rebel army, but that didn't matter.

The sun had just begun to peek over the horizon when the two generals squared off in a grove of trees a short distance from the antebellum mansion of Godfrey LeFevre. The two men stood facing each other, fifteen paces apart, each holding his revolver and awaiting the signal.

They were generals John Sappington Marmaduke and Lucius Marshall "Marsh" Walker—both heavyweight cavaliers in the Confederate Army. This would be the last battle for one of these two old soldiers.

Both men were from prominent Southern families and had amassed impressive records. Marmaduke, the son of the former governor of Missouri, went to both Harvard and Yale before pursuing a martial education at the US Military Academy. He graduated from West Point in 1857 and went west with the Army. When the war began, he left the US Army and signed on as a colonel with the Missouri militia.

The hotheaded Marmaduke resigned after a particularly humbling loss, only to re-up later with the Confederate Army, becoming lieutenant colonel of the First Arkansas. His bravery during the Battle of Shiloh in April 1862 earned him a promotion to brigadier general, but the serious wound he received during the conflict sidelined him for several months. When he recovered, Marmaduke fought in several engagements, including several battles in Arkansas.

"Marsh" Walker was a native of Tennessee. Like Marmaduke, he came from a respected family—he was the nephew of former president James Polk—and he graduated from West Point. He also served on the western frontier before resigning from the military in 1852, when he went into the mercantile business. And, like the man about to shoot at him, Walker served the CSA with distinction. He made brigadier general in 1862, but missed Shiloh due to illness. He wouldn't, though, miss out on the action. He had fought in several battles before being assigned duty in Arkansas.

"Are you ready?" the man in charge of giving the word asked.

"Ready," Walker replied.

"Ready," Marmaduke echoed.

"Fire!"

The seeds of the Marmaduke-Walker duel were planted a few months earlier. During the summer of 1863, the war turned ugly for the Confederacy. The Fourth of July was a particularly devastating date for the secessionists. A day earlier, Lee's army was smashed at Gettysburg, and on the Fourth, Vicksburg fell, leaving the entire Mississippi River under Union control.

The Confederacy also suffered a humiliating defeat upriver from Vicksburg at Helena, Arkansas, on the fourth, which was when a feud arose between the two generals. Confederate forces tried to wrest the city from the Union's grip in an effort to draw Federal troops away from Vicksburg. During the battle, Marmaduke's job was to capture a Union stronghold on "Rightor's Hill" at daybreak. He was to move his men into position under the cover of darkness. They started out for their target at 10 P.M. on the night of July 3.

A few miles from the fort, Marmaduke's cavalry dismounted and made their way through the thick tangles of trees chopped down by the Union defenders. These obstacles slowed their march, and they arrived just before dawn. The shooting began around 4 A.M.

Walker's job was to keep Marmaduke's left flank clear, but he was slow to move his men. His no-show left Marmaduke's boys wide open to attack. By 4:30 A.M., Union soldiers had massed to the left side of Marmaduke's force. Union snipers began picking off the Arkansas rebels one by one.

Marmaduke was stuck in no-man's-land. In his report, he says that his men couldn't advance until the force along his left side was removed. "I twice dispatched to Brigadier-General Walker to advance and assist me in dislodging them. It was not done," he said in his after-action report.[24] Walker did eventually appear on the battlefield later that morning, but by then, it was too late and the rebels withdrew. A petulant Marmaduke "forgot" to tell Walker about the order to retreat, and his troops had to scrap their way back to their horses.

Proud and temperamental, Marmaduke admitted his failure in his report, and then pointed the finger at Walker. He could have taken the fort, he concluded, if Walker had driven the men away from his left side. Marmaduke added that Walker didn't arrive until 7 A.M.; when Walker's horse soldiers first engaged the enemy, they were still more than a mile away.[25]

He wasn't alone in his belief that Walker was to blame. In his report, Lieutenant General T. H. Holmes, the commander of the Confederate forces at Helena, also pointed to Walker as the cause of Marmaduke's failure. It was Walker's duty, Holmes stated, to keep the left flank clear, but he didn't. And, Holmes noted, "No satisfactory reason has been given by General Walker why this service was not rendered."[26]

The relationship between the two generals eroded after the debacle at Helena. It was a tense time for the rebels, with Union forces massing for an attack on the Arkansas capital. The Little Rock Campaign, which consumed the summer of 1863, pitted Union general Frederick Steele against Confederate major general Sterling Price.

In mid-August, Marmaduke and Walker were assigned the task of guarding the army's retreat from Helena to Little Rock. As the senior officer, Walker was in command. Their combined forces could not hold off the much larger Union force, and after a brief tussle at Brownsville, they headed west toward Little Rock.

During their retreat, they concocted a plan. Marmaduke's forces would lure the Union scouts into the forest, where Walker's men would attack. But when Marmaduke entered the woods with the Union advance scouts hot on his heels, he was shocked to find not a single soldier from Walker's group. Once again, Marsh Walker had stood up his brother in gray. Marmaduke was caught in his own trap and had to fight his way out of the woods.[27]

For the next few days, Marmaduke's outnumbered men slugged their way through the dense wood and marshland, all the time dodging bullets from their Union pursuers. While Marmaduke fought his way out of the forest, Walker kept his distance and stayed at his headquarters a few miles away.[28] The skirmishing came to a climax at Reed's Bridge over Bayou Meto. Marmaduke's men destroyed the bridge and then repulsed three Union attempts to cross the river. During the fracas, Walker made a brief, fifteen-minute visit to the battlefield and then left.

Marmaduke sensed that the Union forces were weakening and he asked General Walker to come to the battlefield to advise on a counter-offensive. Walker, for some reason, refused to answer. So Marmaduke sent a written note. Walker refused to answer that. Meanwhile, the Union forces managed to escape.[29] This was the last straw for Marmaduke, who threatened to leave the service if he wasn't transferred. Major General Price didn't want to lose a valuable officer, so he honored the request.

Walker was amused by news of Marmaduke's transfer. Then he heard that Marmaduke accused him of being yellow, and his mood quickly changed. Unwilling to accept this verbal slap in the face, Marsh Walker demanded answers.

The two commanders who had hardly exchanged a word during several battles now sent a volley of notes at each other. Walker fired the first shot in a letter dated September 2, 1863, and brought to Marmaduke by Col. Robert Crockett, the nephew of the legendary "King of the Wild Frontier." "General—I am informed that you have pronounced me a coward, and that I so acted in the fight at Reed's Bridge. You will please inform me whether you have been correctly reported."[30]

Marmaduke sent a lengthy answer, delivered by his friend Capt. John Moore. In the note, he says that while he didn't label Walker a coward, he did say that Walker's "conduct as commander of the cavalry" during the previous month's engagements "was such" that he demanded a transfer. He ended his response by noting that Moore "is authorized to further act in my behalf."[31]

Walker was not satisfied with this evasive answer. The next day, September 3, he sent another note demanding an "explicit explanation." What did Marmaduke mean when he stated that Walker's "conduct as commander . . . was such that I determined no longer to serve under you"?[32]

This time, Marmaduke didn't directly address Walker. Instead, he responded through Captain Moore, who sent a note to Colonel Crockett. "Though Gen. Marmaduke disclaims the use of the specific term 'coward,'" Moore said, Walker did avoid "all positions of danger" during the battles at Brownsville and Bayou Meto.[33]

Colonel Crockett responded immediately. "As a friend of Gen. Walker, and without consultation with him, I demand in his behalf of Gen. Marmaduke the satisfaction due to a gentleman."[34]

As the challenged party, Marmaduke set the rules of engagement. The two would meet at the Old Godfrey LeFevre place at 6 A.M. on September 6. The duelists would stand at a distance of fifteen paces. Their seconds would hand each of them a loaded Colt Navy Revolver, and then each would be asked "Are you ready?" After both men said "ready," the command to fire would be given.[35] If either man broke the rules, he would "be shot on the spot."[36]

This type of duel, with the duelists facing each other and handed a loaded weapon, was often chosen over the back-to-back method where each combatant took a step as a referee counted. The face-to-face arrangement, with the duelists placed the predetermined distance apart, eliminated the possibility of one man turning early and shooting his opponent in the back.

While Colonel Crockett and Captain Moore hammered out the details, General Price caught wind of the impending duel. Unwilling to possibly lose two of his top officers, he ordered both to remain in camp. Marmaduke didn't listen, and Walker never received the order; he had already left for the LeFevre plantation.[37]

The duel went forward as planned, although dueling had been illegal in Arkansas for more than forty years. The ban stemmed from an incident in 1820, when two lawyers settled their differences on an island in the Arkansas River. One of the duelists was shot in the middle of the head and died instantly, but not before shooting his opponent in the chest. The two men were well-known and well-liked in the Arkansas Territory, and legislators promptly outlawed dueling. Little good it did. Duelists just sidestepped the ban by conducting duels in areas just beyond the reach of the law. Marmaduke and Walker, however, didn't even bother to take it outside Arkansas borders.

A few minutes before daybreak, both men arrived at the LeFevre estate, where the fight was to take place in a glade of trees about two hundred yards away from the main house. They waited at the house while Colonel Crockett and Captain Moore measured the agreed-upon distance—fifteen paces, or about twenty yards—and marked the spot where each man would stand.

With the necessary arrangements done, Marmaduke and Walker made their way into the woods. While the seconds loaded the Colt Navy revolvers,

Crockett and Moore flipped a coin to determine who would stand where. Moore won the coin toss, and the two duelists positioned themselves behind their marks. The seconds then handed each man a pistol.

Even at fifteen paces, the nearsighted Marmaduke could barely see his opponent. He squinted but could only make out Walker's silhouette against the curtain of trees. Then Marmaduke noticed three weeds in a line between him and the silhouette, and he used them like the sight of a rifle. The third weed—the one farthest away and about midway between Marmaduke and his target—was at about the height of Walker's abdomen.

The two generals gripped their weapons, anxiously awaiting the signal. On the word "fire," both men raised their arms and fired at the same time, both missing their mark. Marmaduke aimed and fired again before Walker had the chance. This second ball struck Walker in the side, tearing through his kidney before slamming into his spine and leaving him paralyzed from the waist down. His legs went rubbery and he crumpled to the moist grass.

Marmaduke lowered his weapon and ran over to Walker, who was sprawled out on the ground. The attending surgeon examined Walker, but he didn't need to tell the general that the wound was fatal. Walker reportedly turned to Marmaduke and uttered that he was dying.[38]

Colonel Crockett took Walker to Little Rock in Marmaduke's carriage. Marsh Walker held on for another twenty-four hours before dying the next day. On his deathbed, he asked Crockett to tell Marmaduke that he forgave him and wanted his men to do the same.[39]

The story quickly passed through the ranks. Twenty-one-year-old private Thomas Barb, who served under Walker, wrote about the duel in his diary. In an entry dated September 6—the day the duel took place—Barb notes, "There was quite a stir in camp this morning." Barb goes on to describe Walker's "mortal" wound: "It went in the right side just about the belt and was taken out in the back." According to Barb, Marmaduke didn't walk away unscathed but "got a slight wound in his leg."[40]

Marmaduke may have dodged Walker's bullets during the duel, but he was in deep trouble with his superior officer. The duel put Price in a real bind; he had lost one valued officer and now had to punish another for disobeying a direct order.

Incensed over the duel, Price had Marmaduke and both seconds arrested, but it would be a short incarceration. The Yankees were headed to Little Rock, and Price needed all the help he could get to defend the capital. He released Marmaduke. "I did this," Price later explained, "in spite of the apprehension that such leniency toward General Marmaduke might intensify the bitter feelings which had already been aroused in General Walker's division by the result of the duel."[41]

Marmaduke returned to action in defense of Little Rock, but the capital fell to Union forces a few days after the duel, on September 10, 1863. During the fight, one of Walker's former officers, Colonel Archibald Dobbin, didn't obey Marmaduke's order to charge. Dobbin said his men would not serve Walker's killer.[42] Marmaduke arrested Dobbin, but Price later released him to avoid any more aftershocks.[43]

John Sappington Marmaduke never had to answer any formal charge for the death of Marsh Walker. He fought for another year before being captured during the Battle of Mine Creek, Kansas, in late October 1864. He spent the rest of the war in a Union prison camp.

After the war, he went back to Missouri and eventually followed in his father's political footsteps, winning the Arkansas gubernatorial election. His stay in the governor's mansion, however, was a short one. He died in 1887 during his first term in office.

General Marmaduke's face-off with Walker wasn't his first experience with the *code duello*. A few days after Gov. John Sappington Marmaduke passed away, a story revealed that while he was a student at West Point, he fought a duel with a fellow cadet named Presley Craig over some perceived slight. The duelists agreed to face each other with pistols at dawn. As their seconds watched in stunned silence, each man fired, both missing their first shots.

There wouldn't be a second bullet for either one. Perhaps realizing that the curious spectacle could turn deadly and land one of the two in a cemetery and the other in a jail, the seconds stepped in and stopped the fight. "No reference has ever been made publicly to this duel," a reporter wrote in 1888, describing the governor as "a man of great nerve." Governor Marmaduke's dirty little secret, the reporter noted, would have ended his career in uniform.[44]

The governor with "great nerve" was determined, temperamental, and very, very proud, which led to tragic consequences one morning in September 1863.

Like Jefferson C. Davis, Marmaduke killed a fellow officer and got away with it, but unlike Davis, he felt bad about it. He once confided to a friend that he wished the duel had never taken place. "How I prayed for you to be here," he wrote in a letter to a friend. "If you had been present the meeting would never have taken place."[45]

CHAPTER 6

The Faulkner Outrage and Detroit's Draft Riot
1863

Trembling, Lewis Pearce darted out of the burning house. Over the roaring of the flames, he could still hear the voices from the mob: "Kill all the damned niggers."[1] When the rioters noticed Pearce in the yard, they began pelting him with stones. One of the "missiles" struck Pearce in the side of the head, sending him to the ground.

"When I came to myself enough to know anything," Pearce later recalled, "I found the flames so intense that I would soon be burned to death unless I had some shelter, so I drew a wheelbarrow over me that fortunately was just there."[2] The iron barrow saved Pearce from the stones and the flames, but his ordeal had just begun.

Lewis Pearce was a victim of what the *Detroit Free Press* called "the bloodiest day that ever dawned upon Detroit"—an inferno kindled by racial tension and sparked by a crime the *Free Press* dubbed "The Faulkner Outrage."[3]

✥ ✥ ✥

While the "Motor City" wouldn't be born for another fifty years, Detroit in the mid-nineteenth century had become a thriving metropolis. The former fur-trading post of Fort Detroit had evolved into an industrial center. The first blast furnace west of the Allegheny Mountains, the Eureka Iron & Steel Works, a brass foundry, a manufacturer of railroad cars, and other industries attracted people from all over the country, particularly from western New York. Since most Detroiters came from the northeast, they brought with them a strong antislavery sentiment.[4]

During the decade leading up to the Civil War, Detroit became a terminus for the Underground Railroad. Just a stone's throw away from Canada, the city's barns, backrooms, and attics gave fugitive slaves one last hiding place before the last leg of their journey to freedom, the crossing of "Route No. 1"—the Detroit River.

On April 12, 1861, news that the rebels had fired on Fort Sumter reached the telegraph operator in Detroit. Lumberjacks, farmers, and factory workers from all over the state answered the clarion call and marched off to war. Within two weeks, the First Michigan had formed. By the end of the year, twenty-one regiments from the Great Lakes State had suited up to fight for the cause. Michigan boys fought in the "Hornet's Nest" at Shiloh and at the "Bloody Lane" of Antietam. They fought at Fredericksburg. By 1863, Michigan men had participated in virtually every major engagement of the war.

But by March of that year, the war that most people believed would end in a month had dragged on for almost two years. Northern and Southern forces continued to slug it out, trading punches at a hundred points on the map. The decisive Union victories at Gettysburg and Vicksburg were still four months away. People had become war-weary as the news carried names of the fallen, and the worst was yet to come. The US Army needed men for the gristmill, and a draft appeared imminent.

While the boys fought the Civil War on the front lines, a civil conflict began to smolder in Michigan's most populous city. Detroiters were living in a hornet's nest of their own, one buzzing with racial tension. Not all Detroiters rallied around the flag; some of the city's working class felt more passionate about jobs than war. They were not ardent supporters of abolition, Lincoln, or the conflict, which some blamed on African Americans. They were also miffed about the new direction the war was heading, with Lincoln's Emancipation Proclamation having shifted the war's emphasis from preserving the Union to freeing the slaves. Detroit's white workers worried that after the war, blacks from the South would migrate to the city and take their jobs.[5] This didn't sit well with some of Detroit's laborers, but for the most part, their angst didn't escalate beyond grumblings in between shots of whiskey at the corner saloon.

According to some sources, one of the city's two major newspapers, the *Detroit Free Press*, may have fanned the embers by printing news with a flagrantly racist spin. During February, the *Free Press* ran articles condemning what it called the city's "amalgamation dens"—saloons that catered to both black and white Detroiters. One story took the readers into a "den," describing a lurid scene of naked black men and white women lying in bed together. "The sight which met the eyes of the officers, on entering, cannot be excelled in human depravity—three white women and three negroes being all in the same room, and all in the same bed."[6] The ménage included a sixteen-year-old girl who was lying next to a man the *Free Press* reporter described as "a specimen of charcoal." Another story attacked a white woman for becoming "the wife of a black, ugly-looking, disgusting negro."[7] The tone and content of this news coverage may have added to an already volatile situation.[8]

The atmosphere in Detroit became even more flammable in February, when news of the "Faulkner Outrage" broke. The "outrage" was the alleged rape of a white girl by a dark-skinned man named Thomas Faulkner. Faulkner's crime supposedly happened in a back room of a Detroit saloon in mid-February and was so heinous the papers wouldn't print the particulars. The alleged crime became a subject of gossip and rumor, shock and ire.

According to contemporary news reports, a nine-year-old white girl named Mary Brown was on her way to the post office when she came across Ellen Hoover, a black girl she apparently knew. The two went into a tavern owned by Thomas Faulkner, and once inside, they were lured to a back room, where Faulkner allegedly raped Brown and possibly also Hoover.

By late February, the alleged crime was front-page news in the city's two primary newspapers. Although Faulkner's race wasn't clear, both the *Free Press* and its rival, the *Advertiser and Tribune*, jumped to conclusions and labeled him a "negro."[9] The highly biased front-page item in the March 1 edition of the *Free Press* entitled the "Faulkner Outrage" described the preliminary examination of Faulkner, the "negro charged with committing the outrage upon the little Mary Brown."[10]

As for the details, the *Free Press* left most of it to the imagination. The story told by Mary Brown during the examination, the *Free Press* said, was "totally unfit for the imagination," but added that "if the story of this child is entitled to any credit, the crime was one of the most aggravated and fiendish ones ever recorded."[11]

The "examination" of Mary Brown took place behind the closed doors of Justice M. T. Lane's office "For the purpose of saving the child the embarrassment of telling the story in front of so many persons."[12] Brown told a moving story, corroborated by her mother and Dr. Charles H. Barrett, who had also interviewed the alleged victim and said that be found her story credible.

Faulkner's counsel, J. Logan Chipman, decided to wait for the trial to present his case and indicated that his star witness would be Ellen Hoover, Faulkner's other alleged victim who supposedly witnessed the crime. Hoover's version of events apparently differed from Brown's. Initially, she said that she wasn't in the room when Faulkner allegedly raped Mary Brown. This made it a he-said, she-said scenario and much harder to prove in court. The prosecutor believed that Hoover had been intimidated into lying to shield Faulkner. To ensure that Hoover would show up for the trial, the prosecuting attorney asked the court to keep the girl in custody. The court obliged and imposed a bail of $300—a hefty sum that ensured a brief stint in jail for the victim.

While being taken away to the city's jail, the girl broke down, sobbing. "Will he kill me if I tell the truth?" she screamed.[13] This statement appeared to confirm the prosecutor's suspicion that Faulkner had intimidated Hoover into lying. With her fears apparently allayed, Hoover changed her story. She now said that Faulkner had taken both girls into a back room of the saloon and locked the door behind them.

Thomas Faulkner had been tried and convicted in the press as well as in the court of public opinion before even he stepped into a real courtroom. "The evidence of the negro's guilt is overwhelming, and cannot be controverted," the *Free Press* noted in its March 1 front-page story. "The only thing to be regretted is that there is no law sufficiently severe to punish him as the damnable crime he has committed so richly merits. The gibbet or the guillotine alone would subserve the ends of justice in the case of the tenfold worse than murderer, the black fiend, the monster Faulkner."[14]

The newspaper's lament referred to the fact that if found guilty, Faulkner would not go to the guillotine or to the scaffold. Michigan had abolished the death penalty in the 1830s after the hanging of Stephen Simmons, who beat his wife to death in a drunken rage after she refused to drink with him. With the death penalty off the table, some Detroiters had frontier justice on their minds.

Tensions mounted when, on March 5, news of a new draft law hit the Detroit streets. The Federal government had passed the national conscription law two days earlier on March 3 but Detroiters first learned about it on the fifth, the same day the Faulkner trial began.[15]

Some of the city's working class railed at the clause of the new law that allowed a draft exemption for a fee of $300. This raised the issue of "rich man's war, poor man's fight." What the laborers saw as class-based discrimination reminded Detroit's German and Irish immigrants of the Old World, where the aristocracy ruled. Some Detroiters also felt that they were now being forced to fight to free blacks who would then migrate north and take their jobs. Disgust with the new law, coupled with the preexisting racial tensions, created a highly flammable atmosphere.

The trial of the "negro Faulkner" was the kick that knocked over the kerosene lamp. For some Detroiters, the Faulkner trial provided an opportunity to vent their growing frustration with the war, the national conscription law, and racial issues. As the proceedings got underway, an angry crowd began to congregate outside the courthouse.

It wasn't easy to find unbiased citizens for the jury, but after a period of the typical questioning followed by an atypical number of dismissals, a jury was empanelled and testimony began. Mary Brown took the stand first and repeated the story she told to Justice Lane. The *Free Press* described her as having "extraordinary intelligence" and "good moral character." As for her testimony, the *Free Press* noted that "all her actions thus far show that she has been nurtured and educated under an influence which could not, certainly, influence her to make other than an honest and truthful statement connected with this horrific outrage."[16]

Ellen Hoover, the other alleged victim, also took the stand. During her testimony, she said that she originally lied about not seeing the "outrage" because she feared for her life. She testified that she did witness the alleged crime. "Her evidence, however is not needed," the *Free Press* reported in its coverage of the trial, "but, as it is, is good to rivet the guilt more firmly upon the negro."[17] The prosecution rested, and the trial was adjourned for the day.

Meanwhile, the crowd outside the courthouse had become an enraged mob. For officers John Fenn, James Hepburn, and John Esser, the three policemen assigned to escort the prisoner from the court to the city jail, the journey would be a treacherous adventure, with the angry mob following "at their heels" the entire time. The mob pelted Faulkner with bricks, paving stones, empty bottles—anything and everything at hand.

The trial concluded the next day with the defense presenting its case. Chipman's strategy included an attempt to attack the credibility of Ellen Hoover's statements, arguing that the physical layout of the building prevented her from seeing what she claimed to have seen. The jurors traveled to the saloon to look over the scene of the alleged crime.

The real trouble outside the courthouse began just after noon, when the court recessed for lunch. "At a half past twelve, after the adjournment of the court," one imaginative *Free Press* reporter noted, "the clouds which portended the coming storm began to gather."[18] The "clouds" consisted of young men and boys who formed a mob outside the courtroom, berating and lashing out at any black citizen who wandered past. The trial concluded that afternoon. Faulkner was found guilty and sentenced to life in prison. Fearing that the mob would attempt to grab Faulkner and lynch him, the provost marshal ordered his troops to escort the convict from the courtroom to the jail.

When Faulkner appeared outside the courthouse, the mob exploded. They rushed toward the prisoner but were held back by the glistening bayonets the troops fixed to the ends of their rifles. Escorted by the soldiers, Thomas Faulkner made it to the city's jail in one piece with the mob right behind him.

At this point, according to the sensational account published in the *Free Press*, the mob would have disintegrated "had it not been for a wanton and malicious act of certain members of the Provost Guard toward the exasperated citizens. Without orders from any reliable authority," the guard, attempting to quell the rioters, fired several shots into the crowd, with "several of them taking effect, and one man, Charles Langer, being instantly killed, shot through the heart."[19]

Langer wasn't the only casualty in the crowd. A bullet struck Henry Hufnagle in the thigh, causing a minor flesh wound. Another ball supposedly took off a man's finger. The guard then returned to its barracks.

The shots from the provost guard enraged an already angry crowd. "If we are got to be killed up for niggers," someone screamed, "then we will kill every nigger in town!" With the guards gone, there wasn't anything in their way. Unlike other Northern cities, Detroit did not have a permanent, regular police force in 1863. City authorities relied on private security details hired by business owners and the affluent. So when the tornado of rioters tore down Beaubien Street, there weren't any cops to stop them.

While most contemporary news accounts of the riot were greatly exaggerated (newspapers of the time sensationalized the event, describing a mob of thousands that in reality was an estimated fifty), there is general consensus that Friday, March 6, 1863, was one of the most shameful days in Detroit's history.

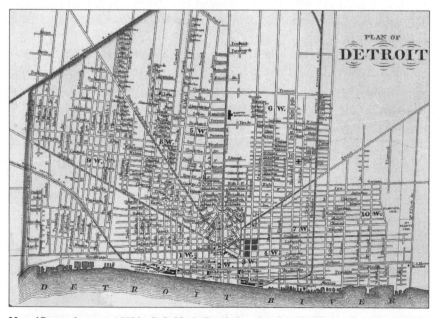

Map of Detroit drawn in 1872 by S. A. Mitchell and altered to show the blocks affected by the 1863 riot. The highlighted areas suffered heavy damage. The jail is just a few blocks east of the damaged districts. From the jail, the rioters made their way down Beaubien Street. At Beaubien and Lafayette, they torched the cooperage and the adjacent house. WIKIPEDIA COMMONS

The mob headed straight from the city jail down Beaubien Street to the district where most of the city's black population lived and worked, hollering "kill all the damn niggers," as they tore through the streets. "This done, they gave the most fiendish yell and started down Beaubien Street," an eyewitness named Thomas Buckner later recounted, "clubs, brick, and missiles of every description flew like hail."[20]

Buckner was standing on the curb when he saw the mob coming down the street. He retreated inside and continued to watch the horrific spectacle. "I could see from the windows men striking with axe, spade, &c. just as you could see men thrashing wheat. A sight the most revolting, to see innocent men, women, and children, all without respect to age or sex, being pounded in the most brutal manner."[21]

The mob descended on a cooperage owned and operated by a black resident named Whitney Reynolds. Several black men—Robert Bennette, Joshua Boyd, Lewis and Solomon Houston, Marcus Dale, and Lewis Pearce—were at work in the shop. Three women and four children were inside the house attached to the shop.[22] Most of these victims survived to tell about their harrowing brush with racial hatred, and their stories were compiled in a publication called *A Thrilling Narrative from the Lips of the Sufferers of the Late Detroit Riot, March 6, 1863: With the Hair Breadth Escapes of Men, Women And Children, And Destruction of Colored Men's Property, Not Less Than $15,000* by an anonymous author and published in Detroit later in 1863.

The mob pelted the shop with stones. They smashed the windows and demanded the men come outside, but the men refused. Someone, probably Joshua Boyd, fired a shotgun into the crowd, the buckshot peppering the rioters. One of the hooligans, a boy named Edward Crosby, was hit in the face with shot, which took out the upper part of his nose, disfiguring him for life. Faced with armed resistance from the shop, the mob attacked the house.

When the men realized what was happening, they raced to the house to protect the women and children. With the men now out of the shop, the mob set it on fire. The wood shavings that covered the floor made the perfect kindling, and within minutes, the structure became a raging inferno. The mob encircled the burning building. From inside the house, a terrified Louisa Bonn heard someone say, "Let us surround the house and burn the niggers up."[23]

"Myself and child, mother, and Mrs. Dale and her three children and brother, kept in the back part of the house while they were throwing stones," Bonn said, "and then someone broke the front door open with an axe."[24]

The fire consuming the cooperage quickly spread to the house, so Louisa Bonn cradled her baby in her arms and went to the front door, praying that the mob would let her pass unharmed. Someone outside yelled, "the women will be protected—no protection for the men."[25] Reluctant to leave their men behind, the women and the children went to the front door, hoping it wasn't an empty promise.

When Louisa Bonn opened the door, a man raced up to her and was about to bash her in the head with a large rock, but someone in the crowd caught his hand. Bonn went back inside the burning house. Trapped, she started to scream.

Some Detroiters who had watched the scene unfold with horror raced to the house, kicked open the door, and helped Louisa Bonn and her baby across the street. Another bystander escorted Louisa's mother and Mrs. Dale out of the burning house. All of the women and children escaped the flames.

Benjamin Franklin Washington Clark, an eighty-year-old man known locally as "the prophet," was also in the house. Terrified, he huddled in a corner, praying for mercy. Accounts vary about what exactly happened to him. According to the *Thrilling Narrative*, he left the house after the women and children and was beaten by the mob. The *Free Press*'s after-action report of March 7 offers a different version: Although the Prophet first refused to leave the burning house for fear of what the crowd might do, good Samaritans managed to coax him into leaving the structure and escorted him safely through the mob.[26] In any event, he survived the ordeal.

The younger men, however, were trapped. Forced to choose between burning alive and being mauled by the angry rioters, men raced out the door one by one. Anyone who tried to leave the house was pelted with stones, bricks, and paving stones. One of them struck Lewis Pearce in the head, knocking him unconscious. "When I came to myself enough to know anything," Pearce later recalled, "I found the flames so intense that I would soon be burned to death," the point at which he took shelter under a wheelbarrow.[27] He huddled under the wheelbarrow until two police officers found him and escorted him away from the yard.

The mob later caught up with Pearce on Antoine Street and drubbed him. "My head was bruised so that for weeks my head and ears run with corruption. My knee cap was broke right in two by a stroke from some weapon. My body was so bruised that for two days I vomited nothing but pure blood," Pearce later said.[28]

When Solomon Houston tried to escape the flames, a man attacked him with a shovel, bashing him twice in the skull. Just as his attacker reared back to hit him a third time, a bystander stepped in and prevented what would have likely become a murder. The bystander chastised the "assassin," who "threw the spade down."[29] Houston limped off, only to suffer another beating before being sheltered by a Mr. Thairs.

Lewis Houston was one of the last ones out of the house. He darted from the burning timbers into the backyard of the property, where he planned to slip through a hole in the fence. Nothing escaped the rioters, who immediately noticed Houston and began pelting him with stones. He made it to the fence, where he recognized a familiar face—a man "who, a few moments before that, worked right at my side." The man "was sitting on the railing of the fence, knocked in the head with an axe. He appeared entirely lifeless, but was being held up by the fence."[30]

The man was Joshua Boyd, a former slave who had settled in Detroit after fleeing the South. Boyd, who had been badly burned in the fire, made it as far as the yard before being struck in the head with an axe. The blade had notched a deep gash in Boyd's head, leaving him comatose.

Pelted with a hailstorm of debris, Houston retreated into the house, but the flames forced him back into the yard. By this time, the body leaning against the fence had fallen down, and when a stone landed squarely on Houston's head, he collapsed on the ground next to Boyd. He lay there for fifteen minutes before he regained consciousness. Two police officers dragged Boyd and Houston out of the yard.

Officer Dennis Sullivan carried Boyd to a nearby saloon with the mob chasing after him. They believed that Boyd had fired the shot that hit Crosby in the face, and they wanted revenge. According to Sullivan, who later testified at the inquest, one of the rioters followed him into the saloon, bought a glass of beer for a dime, then went back outside and complained that it cost him ten cents to catch a glimpse of the man. The rioters then found a clothesline and threatened to lynch the unconscious man on the spot, but they eventually retreated. Boyd was later taken to St. Mary's Hospital.

Houston, meanwhile, slipped into the alley and made it to St. Antoine Street, where the mob found him, beat him, and left him for dead. Eyewitness John Bagley, who later testified at the coroner's inquest, described Houston, lying on the ground, with a swarm of boys "some apparently not over ten years of age," kicking Houston "in the face and head."[31] He managed to stand up and stagger to the city jail, but the jailer kicked him out immediately. Although battered and burned, Lewis Houston survived the ordeal.

Marcus Dale was the last one to escape the flames. A strong man, Dale managed to fight off the rioters who pounced on him as soon as he left the house. He dashed off to safety. His face was seared by third-degree burns, but he also survived.

With the cooper shop and house consumed by flames, the mob moved down the street, looting homes before setting them on fire. According to the *Free Press*, "The houses on Lafayette Street, between Beaubien and St.

Antoine, were literally sacked of their contents, and the furniture piled in the middle of the street and burned."[32] Many of the city's black residents fled across the Detroit River, seeking shelter in Windsor, Ontario.

By late afternoon, local authorities realized they needed help. They sent a telegraph to nearby Ypsilanti, requesting a battalion of soldiers be sent to the city to stop the mob. Five companies from the Twenty-Seventh Michigan hopped onto a train headed toward the inferno.

By 7 P.M., companies A, B, C, F, and G, under the command of Col. Dorus M. Fox and Lt. Col. John H. Richardson, had arrived in Detroit. The four hundred armed men managed to quell the riot by 11 P.M., although by that time, over thirty buildings had been torched, and "the conflagration illuminated the entire city."[33]

While newspapers throughout the north sensationalized the event, the *Detroit Free Press*'s coverage of "The Great Riot" on Sunday, March 8— two days after the event—attempted to dispel some of the tall tales making the rounds after the smoke over Detroit had dissipated.

The "thousands" of rioters were in fact about fifty young hooligans, egged on by others who watched the mayhem.[34] Babies had not been snatched from mothers and smashed on the ground (a story likely inspired by Louisa Bonn's attempts to escape the burning house with a baby in her arms).

As to why the city's fire brigade failed to control any of the fires, the *Free Press* offered an explanation. The firefighters were on the scene "at the time of the first outbreak of the conflagration, accompanied by the efficient and energetic Fire Marshall." As they prepared "to put a stream upon the burning building the Marshall was consulted by a large number of prominent men, who warned him not to endeavor to suppress the fire among the negro houses, but to save the property of the white people adjoining. They assured him that while he would not be molested in the latter course, if he attempted the former, the hose would be destroyed, and the engines thus rendered powerless."[35]

The fire marshal, according to the article, had little choice but to "save what property he could." If he had disobeyed these "prominent citizens" and the firefighting equipment "had been destroyed, the whole city would have been at the mercy of the devouring element."[36]

Detroit survived, but thirty-five structures had been consumed by the flames, totaling more than a million dollars in damage. While dozens of murders had been created by fertile imaginations, in reality, two known deaths occurred: one white man, Charles Langer, and one black man, Joshua Boyd.

During the coroner's inquest into Boyd's death, Officer Dennis Sullivan testified that he carried Joshua Boyd to a nearby saloon, with the mob on his heels, jeering that Boyd was the man who fired the shotgun into the crowd. "The crowd cried 'kill him,' 'hang him,'" as he carried the unconscious man through the streets," Sullivan later recalled.[37] But a lynching would have just been overkill; unlike the others inside the cooperage, Boyd wouldn't recover from his wounds.

He remained in a coma for almost three days before dying of his injuries. Dr. J. C. Gordon, who performed the postmortem, described the injuries Boyd sustained at the hands, feet, and axe of the angry rioters. A correspondent for the *Detroit Advertiser and Tribune* related Gordon's testimony: "Upon examination he found the head badly bruised just below the crown a little to the left. The upper part of his face was beaten all to a jelly; his nose was broken; he was burnt from the right buttox [*sic*] above the hip to the knee; burnt about half an inch into the muscles. The burn of itself would have caused death; either of the injuries would have proved fatal."[38]

No one was charged with either Langer's or Boyd's deaths.

Most of the ruffians escaped punishment, but not all. City authorities rounded up about forty rioters, but because they couldn't find willing witnesses to testify against these suspects, only half of them went to trial. Only six of them were convicted.[39]

The victims inside the cooper shop and adjacent house were scarred—both mentally and physically—for life. So was the city. The "bloodiest day" in Detroit history left its mark on the city and its legacy. Some of the city's black residents fled to Windsor and never came back.

Angst over the draft or not, Michigan men continued to fight for the Union, including the state's first black regiment, which formed shortly after the riot. The Michiganders fought bravely. At the battle of Gettysburg, Joshua Lawrence Chamberlain's Maine troops held their ground at Little Round Top with help from the Sixteenth Michigan Infantry. The Twenty-Fourth Michigan, which was made up of boys from Detroit and Wayne County, also fought at Gettysburg as part of the famed Iron Brigade, sustaining heavy losses.

Ironically, the man whose alleged crime sparked the riot—Thomas Faulkner—wasn't even black; he claimed to be of Spanish-Indian ancestry. He also wasn't guilty. A few years later, the girls admitted that they had lied about his crimes, and Faulkner walked out of prison a free man.

The Detroit Riot was a horrible harbinger of things to come. Just three months later in July 1863 the epic "Draft Riot" shredded the Big Apple. The New York riot was larger, bloodier, and costlier than the Detroit version, but the Detroit riot contained a unique twist: It was a crime sparked by a crime . . . that wasn't really a crime.

CHAPTER 7

The Slaying of
the Beckham Family
1863

The children then were driven to the water's edge, where their father and grandfather had been murdered, and then they were put to death in the most cruel manner. The youngest, Richard aged two and a half years, was thrown into the water alive. Laura jumped in and attempted to rescue him, and whilst in the water, waist deep, begging for mercy, she was knocked on the head by the butt end of a gun, entirely separating her forehead, and then stabbed in the side. Kate Ida, eleven years of age, was then disposed of. She was beaten with guns until her head and shoulders were perfectly soft; her body was bruised all over. Caroline, seven years of age was shot through the head, and so disfigured that she did not look like a human.[1]

According to grieving widow Mary Beckham, this was the tragedy that played out near Tiptonville, Tennessee, on August 4, 1863, when her family was slaughtered by former slaves living on Island No. 10 in the Mississippi River.

It is one of the ghastlier episodes of the Civil War—a crime so brutal, so shocking, even news reporters didn't want to discuss it. Union authorities handled it quickly, harshly, and quietly.

⊕ ⊕ ⊕

Alexander Frank Beckham, a thirty-eight-year-old gentleman farmer, lived with his wife Mary, their seven children, and his elderly father Benjamin on a sizable spread about three miles downriver from New Madrid, Missouri, on the Tennessee side of the "Kentucky Bend."[2] Beckham was somewhat of an entrepreneur and amassed a small fortune in a variety of enterprises, including operating a lumber yard.

His wife Mary spent her entire life at the bend of the river. She was the daughter of Daniel Watson, a prominent planter who owned a large piece of land in the bulb that was the Kentucky portion of the bend.

Major Benjamin Beckham served in the army during the War of 1812. By 1863, he was seventy-five years old. Old age had taken its toll on the former soldier, and he relied on his son and grandchildren to care for him.

The Beckham family lived just a few miles downriver from Island No. 10, the site of a Federal "contraband camp." The camp was part of the Union's answer to the prickly question of what to do with slaves who came into their lines. It was a question that had dogged Union officers since the beginning of the conflict.

Benjamin Butler, who later became infamous as the "Beast of New Orleans," set a precedent when three escaped slaves made their way into his camp in southeast Virginia in 1861. Confederate officers requested that Butler return the property, but the Beast refused to send the slaves back to their masters. Instead, he labeled them as "contraband of war" and put them to work for the US Army. The Confiscation Act of 1861 made Butler's precedent official: Federal forces were legally entitled to confiscate Confederate property in use against Federal forces, and this included slaves.

Not everyone followed Butler's example. Some officers, conflicted or confused, returned slaves that wandered across their lines. So seven months later, Congress passed the Act Prohibiting the Return of Slaves. In July 1862, they passed the Second Confiscation Act—a law that some regard as a precursor to the Emancipation Proclamation, which would be announced in September of that year. This second act gave Union officers the authority to free the slaves of rebels in Union-held territory if those rebels didn't surrender within sixty days.

Over the next few months, thousands rushed to freedom in Union territory. Many of them were disappointed with their newfound "freedom." The former slaves were herded into crowded "contraband camps," where they were given odious tasks that the soldiers didn't want to do themselves, like digging trenches or collecting remains from battlefield graves.

Some of the soldiers assigned to the camps resented the duty and turned on their charges. Physical abuse, including rape, was not unheard of. In a camp at Port Royal, South Carolina, a squad of New York troops gang-raped a nine-year-old girl.

The contraband often lived in squalid conditions. A letter from the Western Sanitary Commission to President Lincoln described the state of the fifty thousand former slaves in the Mississippi Valley between Cairo, Illinois, and New Orleans. "No language can describe the suffering, destitution and neglect which prevail in some of their 'camps.' The sick and dying are left uncared for, in many instances, and the dead unburied."[3]

One of the Union's many contraband camps in the Mississippi Valley was on Island No. 10. The island—so named because it was the tenth island south of the place where the Ohio and Mississippi Rivers diverge—sat at the base of the New Madrid or Kentucky Bend in the Mississippi River. The spot was at the crossroads of three states (Kentucky, Missouri, and Tennessee) and was of tremendous strategic importance to both sides.

An epic clash over the island took place during the spring of 1862. Federal gunboats pushed Confederates out of the area, clearing the river for Union forces all the way south to Memphis. After the battle, the US government created a contraband camp on Island No. 10 where former slaves worked the land.

In January 1863, Lincoln signed the Emancipation Proclamation, but the law did not emancipate all slaves; it did not apply to the slaveholding states of Tennessee and Kentucky, among others. Federal authorities, however, did have the legal right to seize slaves from rebel sympathizers in these areas, which led to an odd scenario in which some slaves were freed and some weren't. Many slaves in non-emancipated states left the plantations, but some loyal servants remained with their masters.

So at the same time former slaves tilled the land at the contraband camp on Island No. 10 in "freedom," slaves worked their masters' plantations at the bend. These masters and mistresses, like Frank and Mary Beckham, lived an uneasy coexistence with both the former slaves and Union troops, who eyed them with suspicion.

The tragedy that took place at Compromise Landing in August 1863 was supposedly set in motion weeks earlier with a dispute over one of Frank Beckham's slave girls. According to this version of events, some of the freed slaves on the island knew a slave girl living with Beckham and working as the nursemaid to his youngest children. Two men, "Corporal" Jim Webb and William Ray, said they went to the Beckham estate to fetch the slave girl and bring her back to the contraband camp at Island No. 10.[4]

In late July, they went to the Beckham home to take the girl, but Frank Beckham shooed them away, brandishing a shotgun. Two weeks later, on August 4, the group returned to the house. This time, they came armed with axes, knives, and a few guns. According to Webb, they also came with an order: "myself and ten other negroes were sent by white men from Island 10 to the Tennessee shore with orders to bring away a colored girl from the house of Frank A. Beckham," Webb later recalled, "and if they resisted to kill every one of the family and burn the house"[5]

Frank Beckham was home with four of his children: fourteen-year-old Laura, ten-year-old Kate, six-year-old Rowena, and three-year-old Richard.

Mary Beckham and three of her other children—Benjamin, Daniel, and Sallie—had traveled to Owensboro, Kentucky. When Beckham told the contraband that his wife had taken the "colored girl" with her to Kentucky, a violent altercation followed.

Emma Beckham, a former Beckham slave, was at home visiting with Benjamin Beckham that morning. She heard loud, angry voices and then a gunshot coming from the Beckham estate, about a hundred yards away. Startled, Emma and the major went to see what was causing the commotion.

At about the same time, twelve-year-old Lelia Dickinson wandered past the Beckham home. Lelia, Frank Beckham's niece, lived with her widowed mother about a mile and a half from Compromise Landing. During her midmorning horseback rides, she often stopped by her Uncle Frank's place.

She heard yelling and trotted over to see what was happening. She saw two black men dragging Frank Beckham out of the house. They wrestled him to the ground and began tying his arms behind his back. When Beckham saw Lelia he yelled at her to go get help. As she galloped off, the men fired at her, their bullets ripping the turf around her horse as she made her getaway. Trembling with fear, she hid in a nearby grove of trees.

Back at the house, Emma Beckham watched in terror as the contraband trussed up Major Beckham. The major begged his captors to let him have a moment with Emma, but they ignored his pleas and continued binding his hands. When they finished, they marched the major and his son toward the river.

Frank made a break for it and raced back to the house, but Jim Webb ran him down and slashed at his shoulder with a large blade. Webb grabbed Beckham by the arm and dragged him back toward the river's edge, where another contraband named William Ray shot Beckham in the jaw at point-blank range. The force of the bullet blew away the lower right portion of his jaw. Ray then slashed Frank Beckham's neck before burying his knife in Beckham's chest.

While Ray dragged Frank Beckham's body into the muddy Mississippi, Jim Webb turned to Benjamin Beckham. Webb swung a small hatchet and leveled the major with one blow to the head. The elderly soldier flopped to the ground. His legs twitched spasmodically as Webb jabbed a long blade into his chest. Ray helped Webb roll the major's body into the river and then they headed back to the house, where the four Beckham children sat trembling on a couch.

Meanwhile, Josh Everett, a neighbor, came across an old friend, Alfred Bashears. Bashears told Everett that he saw a "gang" heading to the Beckham place. He heard gunshots and believed that Frank Beckham had been murdered.

Alarmed, Everett climbed onto his horse and went straight for the Beckham house. By the time he arrived, the men had already murdered Frank Beckham and his father and had herded the four Beckham children—Laura, Kate, Caroline, and Richard—into the river at gunpoint. The oldest, Laura, cradled her baby brother Richard in her arms while her two sisters stood next to her, waist-deep in the muddy water.

"Boys, what in God's name are you killing those four little children for?" Everett gasped, shocked at the sight.[6]

"Shoot him!" one of the men shouted.

Outgunned at least ten to one, Everett bolted. "Josh, don't leave us!" Laura screamed as she watched him ride away.[7]

Everett made a beeline to Island No. 10 to alert the Federal troops stationed there. On the way, he came across a cavalry patrol under the command of Maj. Peter Dobozy. Within minutes, Dobozy and eight troopers were riding to the rescue. But they were too late.

About three miles away from the Beckham house, the Federal soldiers came across the group of contraband—Corporal Jim Webb, Lewis Stevinson, William Ray, Joseph Davis, Wade Good, Abram Cole, George Harris, Aaron Bridgewater, Benjamin Robinson, and Bradley Jones—on their way back to the camp.[8]

"They were crossing the Bend in the direction of Island No. 10," Dobozy later said. "They were all armed with guns and some had pistols, and each one had a load of clothing and other house-hold property on his person."[9]

The Federal soldiers searched the men. During their examination, Dobozy noticed something that made his heart sink: "I found a knife with blood on it."[10] He placed the men under arrest, left them under the watch of a Lieutenant Graham, and raced to Compromise Landing.

When Major Dobozy and his troopers galloped up to the veranda of the Beckham place, Emma was sitting on the porch, her hands buried in her arms, sobbing. Her chest heaved almost convulsively as she swallowed gulps of air. Once Emma caught her breath, she told them the horror story she witnessed a few minutes earlier.

She told them how she watched, helpless, as the contraband dragged Frank and the major down to the river. They disappeared behind the bank but Frank broke free. One of the men slashed at his shoulder with a saber and dragged him back down the bank. She heard a few gunshots coming from behind the bank, and then the men returned for the children. They dragged the kids down to the river, and they too, disappeared behind the bank. Then the contraband ransacked the place and left with armfuls of loot. Dobozy looked around the house and found evidence that appeared to confirm Emma's story. "The house was broken open," Dobozy later said, "the furniture was scattered round in every direction."[11]

Dobozy also found evidence of violent confrontation. "There was blood on the floor in one place," he said, "also blood in the yard before the door."[12]

He noticed a long gouge in the earth leading away from the house, like something had been dragged down to the landing. He followed the tracks for about thirty yards to the bank of the Mississippi River, where they ended in a pool of blood.

"We looked around and found hooks and two skiffs," Lt. Charles Nelson, a soldier in the Fifteenth Wisconsin Volunteer Infantry, later recalled, "and commenced dragging the river."[13]

Josh Everett returned to the scene, and along with local carpenter W. E. Jones and a few other locals, helped the Union men sweep the riverbed. While Dobozy and his men searched the river for bodies, Lt. Graham marched the group of captives to the Mississippi, where they boarded the *Rob Roy* en route to Island No. 10. By this time, three of the men—including Jim Webb—had escaped. Graham's men later collared Webb and brought the entire group of nine aboard the gunship.

On board the *Rob Roy*, the captives were roped together and interrogated about the alleged murder of the Beckham family. According to Lt. Col. William R. Roberts, who was in charge of questioning the prisoners, the men spoke freely about the murders and began pointing the finger at each other.[14]

By the time the vessel docked, all but two of the men had confessed to playing some role in murdering the family. Federal authorities identified the ringleader as Jim Webb, a contraband who held no official rank but often led work details at the camp on Island No. 10, earning him the nickname "Corporal."

After about five hours of sweeping the riverbed in the sweltering heat, the soldiers found the corpse of Maj. Benjamin Beckham. The old man had died a violent death. Someone slashed at his head and neck before running him through with a bladed weapon.

"When we found the body," Nelson said, "the arms were tied with a cord above the elbows and the arms drawn back. There were two cuts on the head and one across the right ear and down the side of the neck, apparently done with an ax or hatchet. About two inches above the left breast was a deep stab. I probed it three or four inches, but did not find the bottom of the wound."[15]

As darkness fell, the search party retired for the night. The next day, they continued the morbid task of searching the river for the missing Beckham family members. Soon after they began their search, they found the body of two-and-a-half-year-old Richard "Dick" Beckham. "The head, face and arms were much bruised," recalled Mrs. Harriet Hatcher, who lived about a mile and a half from New Madrid and who saw the bodies after the Union soldiers fished them from the river.[16]

Over the next few days, they continued to drag the river and managed to find the four missing bodies. Mrs. Hatcher gave a gruesome description of the corpses to the provost marshal. Frank Beckham "had been shot, the ball tearing away the lower right jaw and right eye—his throat was cut and a heavy cut was on the shoulder, severing the joint and cutting the cap of the joint almost off—his arms were tied behind him."

Much of Kate's face and torso were covered with bruises, and her "eyes were started from the sockets, the tongue swollen out of the mouth." Like her sister's, Laura's face and torso were battered. She had been beaten so severely her "left eye burst nearly out and the right eye sunk in." Rowena had been "shot under the left ear. Both eyes were burst out and the hands were raised above the head as in an attitude of great fear or agony."[17]

News of the murders traveled quickly. Although relatively few newspapers carried the story, inaccurate or grossly exaggerated articles popped up in the press. "Murder by Negro Soldiers," the headlines of the *Chicago Post* and *New York Times* screamed. "A FAMILY ASSASSINATED IN COLD BLOOD."[18]

Many articles erroneously reported that the men who "assassinated" the Beckham family were black soldiers. The source of this myth may have been Jim Webb's "Corporal" nickname, although he wasn't a soldier and didn't have a formal rank. To the world outside of the Bend, though, "Corporal" indicated military rank, and reporters were quick to jump to the conclusion that black soldiers murdered the Beckhams.

Reporters vividly recreated the murders as they imagined they occurred. A New Madrid correspondent, perhaps inspired by Mrs. Hatcher's description of the bodies to the provost marshal, described the crimes in nauseating detail.

One negro struck with a saber at Mr. Beckham's head, and missing that, hit his shoulder, nearly severing the arm from his body. Another negro placed the muzzle of his musket at Mr. B's left temple, and, firing, blew away all the front part of his head. Then they stabbed the old major in the side. The old man seized hold of the blade, when they jerked it away, nearly cutting off his fingers. They next thrust a bayonet through his body; one cleft his head with a saber, whilst another shot him through the neck. They then threw his body in the river.

They next turned upon the screaming and frenzied little children, who had stood and witnessed the slaughter of their father and grandfather. By kicks, and cuffs, and punching them with their bayonets, they succeeded in driving the three oldest into the water; then seizing the little baby, dashed it upon the ground and kicked and stamped it to death, and threw its lifeless little body into the river among the girls, who now stood in the water up to their arm-pits. Laura caught the body of her little brother in her arms, and made an attempt to bring it out of the water. When she came in reach of the shore, a negro struck her on the head with a saber, killing her instantly. The other little girls now made an effort to come out of the water. When they had come within reach, the negroes hit them with the butt ends of their muskets, killing them, and they sank beneath the waves."[19]

The correspondent exaggerated his story for dramatic effect. The reporter said that the killers "dashed" Richard "upon the ground and kicked and stamped" him to death. Although Mrs. Hatcher described Richard's body as "much bruised," Lieutenant Nelson, Emma Beckham, and Josh Everett—all of whom examined the body of the two-year-old— said they "did not see any marks of violence on the body."[20]

When the facts didn't suffice, some writers added a little spice to an already hot story. One writer who viewed the bodies after Union soldiers fished them out of the Mississippi said that the oldest daughter—fourteen-year-old Laura—had been "violated."[21] Another correspondent denounced this as a "canard" conjured up by an imaginative writer unsatisfied with the "real horrors" of the crime.[22]

The murder of a prominent local farmer, his elderly father, and his four children by a group of contraband under the protection and watchful eyes of Union troops was a politically inconvenient crime. Opinions around the country remained deeply divided on the issue of slaves and emancipation, and many in the occupied areas distrusted or even despised the occupying soldiers and their contraband camps. For them, the murder of the Beckham family was one of the more hideous incidents in a string of atrocities committed by the Union.

Federal officials decided to end the matter quickly, quietly, and decisively.

Since the accused were under the auspices of the federal government, their trial and punishment fell under Section 30 of the Conscription Act of 1863. The controversial law, which sparked riots throughout Northern cities, contained a rider that gave military courts power to try cases involving "murder, assault, and battery with an intent to kill, manslaughter, mayhem, wounding by shooting or stabbing with an intent to commit murder, robbery, arson, burglary, rape, assault and battery with an intent to commit rape, and larceny."

The military courts were designed to handle law and order in cases where there were no civilian courts available or when the defendants were soldiers, or, in the Beckham case, wards of the Federal government. Unlike a civilian court, the commissions did not empanel a jury. The members acted as judges as well as jury. And they didn't need a unanimous decision to render a verdict, just a simple majority. These military commissions heard entire cases and rendered verdicts sometimes in just a few hours.

Justice wielded her sword two weeks after the murders at the bend. On August 17, 1863, a military commission convened in Columbus, Kentucky, to decide the fates of the alleged Beckham slayers. Over the following week and a half, the commission listened to testimony that recreated various aspects of that bloody Tuesday morning when the Beckham family was murdered.

The defendants, who were tried separately, each faced two charges: murder and robbery. The first charge specified "the murder of Maj. Benjamin Beckham, Mr. Frank A. Beckham and his four children, Laura, Kate, Caroline, and Richard." The second charge alleged the robbery of property valued at $100.

Presiding over the three-man military commission was William T. Shaw, colonel of the Fourteenth Iowa. The Shaw family had a strong presence in the War Between the States. Two months prior to the trial, Shaw's cousin, Robert Gould Shaw, was killed while leading an all-black unit, the Fifty-Fourth Massachusetts Infantry, in an ill-fated attack against Fort Wagner near Charleston, South Carolina.

William Shaw, a native of Maine, was a frontier teacher in Indiana and later Kentucky before enlisting as a private in 1846. He fought in the Mexican-American War, experiencing combat in the Battle of Buena Vista. After the war, he drifted west into Indian Territory, living among the tribes for a while, until he heard that gold had been discovered at Sutter's Mill in California.

He joined the gold rush and headed west. Failing to find the treasure he sought, he came back east to Iowa, where he became a successful real estate speculator. When the Civil War began, he enlisted and was commissioned as a colonel in the Fourteenth Iowa Volunteer Infantry.

Shaw played a key role in law and order during the Civil War. In January 1863, he was assigned the task of investigating the loyalty of prominent St. Louis citizens suspected of having Southern sympathies. A few months later in June 1863 he was in Columbus, Kentucky, serving as the president of a court-martial.

First Lt. David Edmundson of the Fortieth Iowa was appointed as the judge advocate, acting as both the legal advisor to the commission and the prosecuting attorney. During Civil War–era military trials, the judge advocate was also the advocate for the accused and, if the accused didn't obtain defense counsel, the judge advocate provided legal advice. While this dual role would be considered an unbelievable conflict of interest in the modern legal system, during the Civil War, the men who sat on military commissions were expected to be unbiased discoverers of the truth. The trial transcripts suggest that in the case of the Beckham slayers, Edmundson was put in the difficult position of prosecuting the defendants while also providing them with legal assistance.

William Ray and Jim Webb were the only two defendants to plead guilty to the murders, essentially throwing themselves on the mercy of Shaw's commission. Ray pled guilty to the murder charge but not guilty to the robbery charge. It is possible that he denied stealing to avoid the appearance that theft, as some suspected at the time, was the true motive behind the slayings.

The judge advocate did not call witnesses to testify in Ray's case. Instead, Ray gave a statement admitting his guilt in the crime but explained that he was just doing as he was told. "I am a contraband. I formerly lived in Henry Co. Tenn. I was taken from home by a detachment of United States Soldiers and taken to Island 10 where I was placed under the charge of Capt. Thomas and a black man called Corporal Jim was placed over a number of colored men myself among them. I was made to obey the orders of Corporal Jim in every thing: If I did not I was punished for disobedience," Ray said.[23]

Ray then offered an explanation for his part in the murders.

> On the morning of the 4th of August 1863 eleven of us all colored men went over the river to the Tenn. Shore under the charge of Corporal Jim to get a colored girl at the house of Frank A. Beckham. When we got there the girl was not to be found. We were ordered by Copl. Jim to murder the family of Frank A. Beckham. He said he had orders from a white man on the Island to that effect. I helped to murder some of the family of F. A. Beckham. I thought I was bound to do so as I was compelled to obey his orders from the time I had been placed on the Island. I supposed I was obeying lawful orders from men placed over me.[24]

If Ray was looking for mercy, he came to the wrong place. The three-member commission found him guilty of both charges and sentenced him to death by hanging. Like his partner in crime, "Corporal" Jim Webb pled guilty to murder but only to those of Frank and Benjamin Beckham. He denied killing the children and robbing Frank Beckham.

Edmundson called just one witness, W. E. Jones, the thirty-five-year-old carpenter who had assisted in finding the bodies. "State what you know if anything of the murder of Frank A. Beckham and his family in Obion Co. Tenn. on or about the 4th day of August, 1863," the judge advocate asked.

"I did not see the murders but I saw the dead bodies," Jones said, "and from the wounds and bruises on the bodies of all the persons named, I was satisfied they had been murdered."[25]

After hearing from the carpenter, the panel listened to Webb make a statement admitting his guilt. "I was raised in slavery and in ignorance and always taught to be obedient to white men. I was taken from Cairo [Illinois] some time during the last spring against my will and taken to Island 10 and there placed under the charge of white men and made to do their bidding with all the rigor of a state of slavery," Webb said, characterizing "freedom" on Island No. 10 as no better than slavery.[26]

"On the 4th day of August myself and ten other Negroes were sent by white men from Island 10 to the Tennessee shore and with orders to bring away a colored girl from the house of Frank A. Beckham and if they resisted to kill every one of the family and burn the house. When we arrived at the house of Beckham the colored girl was not to be found. I helped to kill Frank A. Beckham and his father Benjamin Beckham, I supposed we were acting under the orders of men who had a right to command us and I believed we were bound to obey them, and that we were fully justified in doing whatever they ordered us to do; if I have violated the laws it was through ignorance and not through malice."[27]

Like Ray, Webb said that he was just doing as he was told "by white men." The commission was not convinced and found him guilty of both robbery and murder. Webb would join Ray on the scaffold; they sentenced him to death by hanging.

While Ray and Webb admitted to murder, the other defendants all claimed they were innocent of both counts. Lewis Stevinson admitted to being at the Beckham house, but denied playing any role in the crime and pled not guilty to both charges.

Lieutenant Edmundson called Major Dobozy, who testified about finding the contraband about three miles from the Beckham place scurrying away with armfuls of loot. He described the sinister blood-streaked knife that, when considering the blood he later saw at the house, became a damning piece of evidence. He also testified to hearing some of the men confess on the *Rob Roy*. "On being interrogated," Dobozy recalled, "they all confessed that they had assisted to kill Frank A. Beckham and his family. Except two who said they only stood by and watched. The prisoner," Dobozy pointed at Stevinson, "was not one of the two."[28] Dobozy testified that he heard the nine men admit that they had murdered the Beckhams, but he didn't hear Lewis Stevinson admit to killing anyone.

"I cannot recollect particularly what the prisoner said about the part he took in the murder," the major admitted, and then added, "They all confessed that they were the party that had murdered Beckham and his family."[29]

Edmundson next called Lt. Charles B. Nelson, who was with Major Dobozy when they searched the Beckham house.

"Do you recognized the prisoner," Edmundson asked, "if so where did your first see him and under what circumstances?"

"I do recognize him," Nelson replied. "I first saw him on examination before Provost-Marshall Montgomery at Island 10. He was undergoing a preliminary examination on a charge of murder of the Beckham family."[30]

The judge advocate then asked Nelson what he knew about the murders. Nelson described the sequence of events: the news of the Beckham murders, the capture of the eleven contraband, the search of the house, and the recovery of the bodies of Major Beckham and two-year-old Richard.

"We started towards Beckham's house; we met eleven negroes of which the prisoner was one," Nelson said. "They all or most of them had bags and other articles of plunder carrying. I asked the prisoner where he had been; he said they had been to Beckhams to get some things belonging to a negro woman of Beckham's who was on the Island."[31]

Later that evening, after dragging the river for the bodies, Nelson said he saw Stevinson and Corporal Jim on Island No. 10, where "they both acknowledged that they were of the party who had killed Beckham and his family."[32]

The judge advocate, apparently, didn't catch an obvious discrepancy in Nelson's testimony. The lieutenant testified that he first saw "the prisoner" at the preliminary hearing on the murder charges, but he also said he spoke to him when the cavalry searched the party of men en route to the Beckham house. The commission also seemed willing to overlook something else: While Lewis Stevinson admitted being "of the party who killed Beckham and his family," he didn't admit to murdering anyone.

In Stevinson's defense Edmundson called a lone witness, a twenty-nine-year-old contraband named Benjamin Robinson, who was also "of the party" at the Beckham estate when the family was butchered. "I was present when they were murdered and saw it all," Robinson testified. "The prisoner stood guard at the gate. Corporal Jim told him to watch the place. He stood at the gate with a gun during the time the family were murdered. He did not take any other part in the murder. He did not lay his hands on any of them that I saw."[33]

After Robinson's brief testimony, the commission members went into deliberations. Following a brief discussion, they announced their decision. Lewis Stevinson was guilty of both robbery and murder. The court sentenced him "to be hanged by the neck till he is dead."

Over the next week, the commission tried the other alleged coconspirators in the massacre of the Beckham family. The prosecution's linchpin against the other defendants was the former slave Emma Beckham.

Thirty-year-old Emma, nervous and still stunned by what she saw, took the stand and testified against several of the defendants. She told essen-

Statement of the Prisoner

I was raised in Slavery and in Ignorance and always taught to be obedient to white men; I was taken from Cairo Some time during the last Spring against my will and taken to Island 10 and there placed under charge of white men and made to do their bidding with all the Rigor of a state of Slavery; on the 4th day of August myself and ten other Negroes were sent by white men from Island 10 to the Tennessee Shore with orders to bring away a Colored girl from the House of Frank A Beckham and if they resisted to Kill every one of the family and burn the House, when we arrived at the House of Beckham the Colored girl was not to be found, I helped to Kill Frank A Beckham and his Father Benjamin Beckham, I supposed we were acting under the orders of Men who had a right to command us and I believed we were bound to obey them, and that we were fully Justified in doing whatever they ordered us to do; If I have violated the Laws it was through ignorance and not through Malice

Handwritten trial document recording the statement of "Corporal" Jim Webb in which he characterizes life on Island No. 10 as a form of slavery. Webb admits murdering the Beckham family but says he was following the orders of white overseers. NATIONAL ARCHIVES

Statement of the prisoner.

I am a Contraband; I formerly lived in Henry Co. Tenn. I was taken from home by a detachment of United States Soldiers. and taken to Island 10. where I was placed under the Charge of Cept. Thomas. and a black man called Corporal Jim was placed over a number of Colored men. myself among them. I was made to obey the orders of Corporal Jim in every thing; if I did not I was punished for disobedience. On the morning of the 4th of August 1863. Eleven of us, all colored men went over the river to the Tenn. Shore under the Charge of Corporal Jim. to get a colored girl at the house of Frank A. Beckhams when we got there the girl was not to be found We were ordered by Copl. Jim to murder the family of Frank A. Beckham. Hee said he had orders from a white man on the Island, to that effect. I helped to murder some of the family of F. A. Beckham.

Statement of William Ray, in which he also admits to murdering the Beckhams, but says that he was just following Corporal Jim's directions. NATIONAL ARCHIVES tially the same story during each of the trials, beginning with the trial of Wade Good on August 21. She identified Good as one of the perpetrators and then began her narrative.

> I was at my own house about a hundred yards from Mr. Beckham's house where I heard Mr. Beckham call me. Major Benjamin Beckham was at my house at the time. We both went to Frank Beckham's house. When I got there he, Frank Beckham, was tied with a rope, his hands tied behind his back. There were a good many in the house, all negroes. I think there were more than ten. The prisoner was one of the men who was there in the house.
>
> They seized Major Benjamin Beckham and tied him. The prisoner assisted to tie him. Some of the negroes took both Beckhams by the arms and led them to the river. They went down under the bank to the water's edge. The river was about a hundred yards from the house. I think the prisoner went to the river with them but am not certain.
>
> They carried Major Beckham down the bank first. Frank Beckham got loose from them on the top of the bank and ran a few steps when one of them by the name of Jim struck him on the shoulder with a large knife. They then took him under the bank.
>
> When they were under the bank I could not see them. After they took them down under the bank I heard the report of either two or three guns, and saw the smoke. Three of the men came back from the river. Some of the company had remained in the house.
>
> They then ordered Laura, Kate, Caroline, and Dick, all the children of Frank A. Beckham, to go to the river. They started to the river; one of the negroes walked before and two behind. The three negroes who took the children to the river were all armed with guns. Some of the negroes were standing on the bank while the others came for the children. When they went out at the gate, I turned round and went into the house. I did not see them nor the two Mr. Beckhams again till they were taken out of the river dead.
>
> Some of the negroes remained at the house all the time. Those who went to the river came back to the house in about fifteen minutes after they took the children away.

After the murders, Emma said, the men ransacked the house. They went into each room and rifled through the furniture, breaking open a desk, where, according to Emma, they found the key to the safe. "After they got as much plunder as they wanted they left," she said. "They told us (my father, sister, and myself) that we had better leave there, that the secesh would think we had done it." The idea that the "secesh"—the local Southern sympathizers—would blame Emma and her family wasn't an altogether far-fetched possibility: Incidents of theft and looting occurred often among former slaves and their former masters in the occupied territories.

"There were no white persons left on the place after the negroes left. When they came back from the river the last time, I asked them what they had done with old master, meaning Maj. Beckham. One of them said they had shot him."[34]

Emma insisted she watched Wade Good tie Major Beckham's hands, although she admitted that she didn't see him shoot her "old master."

Judge Advocate Edmundson next called Lt. Col. William R. Roberts, an officer with the Second Tennessee Heavy Artillery who had interrogated the prisoners aboard the steamer *Rob Roy*. Roberts testified that he personally interviewed Good about a very valuable gold watch supposedly taken from Frank Beckham. According to Roberts, Good "confessed to his having been at the scene of the murder and having witnessed it" He also admitted to taking "plunder," including the gold watch, from the Beckham place. Good said he put the watch in a satchel that was searched by soldiers before he boarded the *Rob Roy* as a prisoner.[35]

Edmundson's questioning came to an end after Roberts's testimony. The court found Wade Good guilty and sentenced him to death.

The next day, the commission moved on to the trial of Joseph Davis. Like Good, Davis pled not guilty to both counts of robbery and murder. Once again, Emma Beckham took the stand and related the tragic sequence of events culminating in the murder of the six Beckhams. Then she fingered Davis as one of the group but admitted that she only "observed him," after the murders, coming out of the house with "a bag of clothes." Davis stopped by Emma and warned her to leave the plantation, Emma said, "because there were a lot of rebels below."[36]

Davis cross-examined the sole witness against him. He attempted to cast a stain on Emma Beckham's testimony by hinting that she was an accomplice in the robbery.

"Did you not get the key of the safe and give it to Jim? Did you not unlock the safe and get out a pocket-book and give it to Jim?"[37]

Emma denied both accusations and Davis took his seat. Without presenting any witnesses in his behalf, he gave a lengthy statement to the court. Corporal Jim, Davis said, approached him on Island No. 10. "He told me to go over the river with him in the morning, that Mr. Gwin had told him to take a lot of us and go over there on a scout."

When they arrived at the Beckham place, Davis continued, "Corporal Jim asked Mr. Beckham where the child was. He answered that his wife had gone away and taken the child with him and not come back yet."

According to Davis, Webb then ordered Wade Good to take Frank Beckham's watch. After they robbed the frightened farmer, Good, Abram

Cole, Joseph Davis, and a young man Davis referred to as "Jo" trussed up Frank and his father, the major. "I had no idea in the world that it was the intention to murder anyone," Davis said.

Then Webb ordered Davis to lead the major down to the river while Good, Cole and Jo took Frank Beckham. "When I heard that I stopped right there," Davis said. "I saw them take them under the bank. Jim killed old Mr. Beckham. William Ray shot Frank Beckham."

Davis admitted stealing from the Beckham home, and he stated that Emma freely helped the thieves by opening the safe and handing papers and a pocketbook to Jim Webb. But he denied playing any role whatsoever in the murders.[38] The court was not convinced and sentenced Joseph Davis to death.

George Harris was next to face the military commission. Like the case against Davis, Judge Advocate Edmundson presented just one witness, Emma Beckham.

"Do you recognize the prisoner as one of the party who committed the murder and robbery?" Edmundson asked.

"I do not," Emma admitted. "I can't recollect his features. He might have been one of them. I could not say whether he was one of them or not."[39]

Because Emma couldn't place Harris at the scene of the crime with any certainty, Edmundson called Lt. Col. William R. Roberts, the officer aboard the *Rob Roy* in charge of the prisoners after Major Dobozy's cavalry collared them en route to Island No. 10. Roberts testified that Harris was one of the men Dobozy brought to him. He then turned over the nine prisoners to the provost marshal.

According to Roberts, the nine men "freely confessed that they had gone to the house of Mr. Beckham and murdered him and his family. It was a common topic of conversation and no one of them denied it." But, Roberts admitted, he did not "recollect anything said by the prisoner in particular."[40]

Edmundson also called Joshua Everett, who told of arriving at the Beckham place when the contraband were in the process of murdering the children. "There was six or seven negro men in a line from the yard gate to the river bank," Everett said. "The children were in the water as deep as their breasts. One of the negroes was knocking them on the head with the muzzle of his gun. I hollered out and said, 'Boys, what in the name of God are you killing them four little children for?"[41]

Everett explained how one of the men yelled out for the others to shoot him, and he fled. He then described, in graphic detail, the bodies he helped recover.

Harris made a brief statement to the court, admitting that he took part in the robbery but denying any role in the murders.[42] None of the witnesses implicated Harris in the slayings, but the graphic depictions by Emma Beckham and Josh Everett were too powerful, and the commission sentenced Harris to hang.

Beckham, Everett, and Lt. Col. Roberts returned the next day and testified against Aaron Bridgewater. Beckham and Everett recounted the events that morning, but neither witness could pin any specific role on Bridgewater. Lt. Col. Roberts testified that Bridgewater was one of the men on board the *Rob Roy*. "They each and every one of them confessed that the party had been to the Beckhams, that among them the said family had been murdered and the house plundered."

Roberts, though, couldn't attribute any particular confession to Bridgewater: "I do not recollect any words spoken by the prisoner in particular; they were all talking together and accusing one another as having participated in the deed."[43]

Bridgewater threw himself on the mercy of the court and gave a brief statement. "I was at Mr. Beckham's when his family were murdered, but, as for touching any body, I did not do it. I was placed as a guard at the back end of the house next the quarters. Corporal Jim placed me there. There was but one bayonet there and that was on my gun and I stood at the back door and did not go near any body. When Jim ordered the children out of the house Benjamin Robinson told Jim that was wrong, not to do it, that the judgment would be on him for that. This is all I have to say."[44]

It wasn't enough for the military commission; Bridgewater was headed for the scaffold with the others.

Abram Cole was the last of the alleged conspirators to face the military commission. Once again, Emma Beckham was the key witness. After recounting the events as she saw them on the morning of August 4, she fielded a few questions from the prisoner.

"Do you recollect of seeing me do anything?"

"No, I don't recollect of seeing you at all," Emma admitted.[45]

Joshua Everett also testified. Everett said he saw Cole under arrest in the guardhouse on Island No. 10. "I walked in and asked him if he knew me, he asked me if I was not the man who rode up to the bank the day they were killing Mr. Beckham's children, he asked me if I did not recollect a man who stood pretty near me with a gun in each hand," Everett testified. "I told him I did not recollect of seeing him, he said he stood there and had the guns that were taken out of the house. I asked him what they would have done with me if they had caught me. He said they would have killed me and put me in the river."

Everett noted that Cole "used the word they and not we both times," which suggested that Cole was not the group at the river.[46] According to

Everett, Cole also admitted to robbing but not murdering the Beckhams—a claim Cole repeated in a brief statement to the court.

Everett's testimony, coupled with the prisoner's statement, placed Abram Cole at the scene of the crime. And the commission had, a few days earlier, heard the statement of Joseph Davis, who said Cole helped to tie up Frank and Benjamin Beckham and then led Frank Beckham down to the river's edge. They decided to send Cole to the gallows.

By August 27, the military commission had wrapped up the trials of the Beckham slayers and sent their findings to Maj. Gen. Stephen Hurlbut, commander of the XVI Corps, for approval.

A legal technicality led to a brief reprieve for some of the defendants. The last line of the commission's verdict stated "All of the members of the court agreeing thereto." But according to the Articles of War, the records "must show that two-thirds of the members of the court concurred in the sentence. To state the court unanimously voted for the sentence though such be the fact, is improper as it does in truth 'discover' and disclose the vote of 'each particular member of the courts.'"

Hurlbut returned the verdicts for correction. Even though this same error in wording appears in every verdict of the Beckham defendants, for some reason, Hurlbut rubber-stamped the commission's condemnations of Ray, Stevinson, and Webb, sending the three defendants to the scaffold while the others awaited the necessary alterations to their paperwork.

Whenever practical, hangings during the Civil War took place on Fridays—the day of the week Christ was crucified. For Ray, Webb, and Stevinson, "Hangman's Friday" came on September 4, 1863.

Just after noon, a company of infantry formed a hollow square and marched the three condemned men to a spot on a bluff about a mile from downtown Columbus. Two regiments of soldiers, the Thirty-First Wisconsin and the Twenty-Third Tennessee Artillery—a black unit—along with a crowd of curious onlookers assembled near the scaffold to witness the execution.

The three men slowly marched up to the platform. Stevinson, nervous, stumbled on the flight of steps. Two black preachers followed the condemned onto the platform. While guards tied the arms and legs of the three men, the preachers began to sing a psalm. Some of the soldiers and citizens gathered around the scaffold joined in the singing, but Ray, Webb, and Stevinson did not.

The three men kneeled while one of the preachers said a prayer. Stevinson, unnerved by his impending death, slumped backward on the platform. After the prayer, Maj. William Reuben Bowley and Capt. I. H. Williams placed white hoods over the heads of the condemned men. Just before one of the officers slid a hood over his head, Webb asked one of the preachers to reach into his pocket and hand him a handkerchief. The man did as requested and placed the white piece of linen in Webb's hand. Captain Williams released the trap and the three men dropped. Corporal Jim squeezed the white handkerchief as he fell.

A news correspondent who witnessed the execution described the last moments of the three men. "Ray died almost immediately, or at least gave no evidence of life after a minute or two. 'Corporal Jim' also lived but about three minutes. Both of these men undoubtedly had their necks broken by the fall, which was about three feet. But Stevinson appeared horribly convulsed for the space of four minutes, when he was also still."[47]

After about twenty minutes, the bodies were cut down and placed in coffins stacked next to the scaffold. Jim Webb was still clutching the white handkerchief when his body was laid in the casket.

A few days after the executions, Shaw's commission fixed the clerical errors in the paperwork of the other defendants and forwarded the new copies to Major General Hurlbut. By this time, military authorities had softened a little and commuted the sentences of George Harris and Aaron Bridgewater to five years in the Nashville penitentiary. Benjamin Robinson, who testified on behalf of Lewis Stevinson, was also granted leniency and given one year in prison.[48] Abram Cole, Joseph Davis, and Wade Good wouldn't be so lucky—their death sentences were approved.

Another Hangman's Friday for the Beckham killers came on October 9, when Cole, Davis, and Good climbed the steps of the same scaffold in Columbus.

Once again, the audience included both black and white soldiers as well as the curious.

"There was prayer, singing," a correspondent described the scene, "then preparation of the fatal noose and its adjustment around the necks of the criminals, placing black caps over their heads, and cutting the cord fastening the drop, when the three colored men . . . were deprived of life, and in a few moments without apparent struggle, hung in mid-air, ready for the coffin, grave and worms."[49]

The murder of the Beckham family largely escaped notice in the press. A short item about the crimes appeared here and there, but reporters didn't devote much ink to the murders of a Southern family along "the Bend" by freed slaves. It was an uncomfortable scenario for many in both the North and South.

But not everyone kept their opinions to themselves. Some seized the opportunity to use the crime as an argument against the freeing of slaves. "We implore Christian men to kill the scheme forever," a writer for the *Dubuque Herald* said.[50]

The *Herald* was quick to add an accomplice to the crimes:

These abolitionists teach these negroes to hate their former masters and mistresses; that they will be serving their God to murder and rob all who deny them their liberty. Nothing but a long course of pupilage in the school of abolitionism could have brought these negroes up to the task of such a cruel, barbarous murder. I will venture the assertion that eleven negroes cannot now be found in the Southern States, who have not left their masters, nor been among the abolitionists, who could be induced, by any process whatever, to commit such a horrid murder. No, sir, slavery has no such record. The ghouls of Dahomey [a kingdom in western Africa], and the abolitionized negro of America, are the only ones equal to such a barbarous, cruel murder.[51]

Other writers attempted to mitigate the public relations damage done by the murders. One tried to absolve Federal authorities entirely and reported, erroneously, that the perpetrators didn't live on Island No. 10 and had no connection to the contraband camp there, positing instead that they had deserted from local plantations.

About a year after the murders, Mary Beckham wrote a letter that she sent to news correspondents. The letter appeared in several newspapers, including the *Charleston Mercury*.[52] Although she was in Owensboro, Kentucky, when the murders were committed, Mrs. Beckham describes them in graphic detail, based apparently on what others told her about the crimes.

On Tuesday morning, about 9 o'clock, August 4, 1863, twelve armed negro soldiers came to the house, there being no one there except my husband, father in law (Benjamin F. BECKHAM), and four of my children, and some of our family negroes. They rushed on my husband and tied him, took off his watch and pin, and rifled his pockets. They then tied my father in law, and dragged them to the river, it being about thirty yards. They killed my husband on top of the bank by shooting him in the head. They then cut off his shoulder blade and rolled his body into the river; his clothes looked as if there had been a great struggle.

They then took the old gentleman, stabbed him three times, once in the heart, and cut one of his ears off. After throwing his body into the river, they proceeded back to the house, where two of them had been guarding my dear little children.

She goes on to describe the murders of her four children and suggests that Island No. 10 was a sort of sanctuary from punishment. "They then started for Island No. 10, thinking or knowing they would be protected if they reached there in safety."[53]

The Beckham matriarch said she had also endured constant harassment from Federal soldiers after the murders. "Various threats were made against my life if I came home; but I came, and I could not tell the number of times the Federals have searched my house both night and day," she said.

"I reported to the authorities at No. 10, but it did no good. I was told that the Lieutenant who arrested the negroes was wearing my husband's watch. I have been robbed five times since the murder of my family; and if this war continues much longer, I do not know how I will live. The negroes that murdered my family are strange negroes, trained by Union soldiers to commit such deeds."[54]

A few unanswered questions remain, a hundred and fifty years after the Bend was stained with the blood of the Beckham family.

What happened to the Beckham fortune? According to gossip around the Bend, the bulk of the loot taken from the Beckham home—more than $5,000 in gold and another $4,000 in banknotes—was never recovered. One news report stated that the man who initially got away, Corporal Jim Webb, must have hid the treasure before Federal cavalry recaptured him.[55]

This explanation makes no sense whatsoever if Major Dobozy's testimony is taken at face value. According to Dobozy, his nine troopers searched the contrabands before they reached the Beckham house. It was during this search that Dobozy found the bloody knife. He then left the contrabands under the watchful eye of Lt. Graham and then went to Beckham's Landing. Webb didn't jackrabbit until after Dobozy left for the house, which indicates that the Federal cavalry had searched him before he ran away.

So where did Beckham's gold go? According to some lost-treasure yarns, the cache is still hidden in some hole in the ground or recess of a hollow tree.

Another piece of property never supposedly recovered was Frank Beckham's gold pocket watch, valued at $300 in 1863. Lt. Col. William R. Roberts testified that he questioned Wade Good about the watch. Good admitted taking the watch and said he put it into a satchel that was later searched by the Federal soldiers. Roberts turned over all of the property found on the contraband to the provost marshal in Columbus, but he apparently never found the watch.[56]

According to Mary Beckham, the watch may have wound up dangling from the pocket of a Union officer. In her statement to the press, she says she "was told that the Lieutenant who arrested the negroes was wearing my husband's watch," raising the disturbing possibility that the soldiers looted the looters.

There is another unanswered question about the murders: Did some-one connected with the military or the oversight of Island No. 10 know about, condone, or even take part in the murder of the Beckham family?

William Ray testified that he was only following Corporal Jim's order, and Jim Webb said that they were doing what "white men from Island 10" told them to do. Joseph Davis went one step further and named a "Mr. Gwin," who sent them out to "scout." In her letter to the newspapers, Mary Beckham said she knew that one of the men who admitted to throwing Richard into the river "did not want to kill any of them, but he was threat-ened by others that, if he did not obey Guynnes' and Captain Thomas' orders, he would meet with the same fate as those children."

The "Captain Thomas" mentioned by Mary Beckham and some of the contraband during the trial was Captain Benjamin Thomas, a Baptist minis-ter from Ohio and an officer with Company D of the Sixty-Second Ohio Infantry. The reverend, who lived at the camp with his wife, played dual roles on Island No. 10: He oversaw the garrison that protected the contra-band while simultaneously providing spiritual guidance. While the presence of "Captain Thomas" lends some credence to the conspiracy theory, the image of a false prophet with a palm full of gold contradicts the minister's reputation as a well-meaning man with a heart of gold.

Joanna Patterson Moore, a missionary from Illinois, arrived on Island No. 10 about a month after the second group of Beckham murderers went to the scaffold. In her autobiography, Moore describes Thomas as a kindly man who opened his home to her. She also details an incident in which two women got into a scrap. Still kicking and scratching at each other, they were dragged in front of Thomas for punishment. "Captain Thomas called me out," Moore recalled, "and in a laughing manner said: 'Miss Moore, I will turn this case over to you. Since you have come here to make people good, try your hand on these women.'"[57] Moore settled the dispute without punishing the former slaves.

Someone else working under the good reverend, however, may not have had such clean hands. There are scattered reports that white soldiers or administrators of Island No. 10 played some role in the massacre, and some accounts even place white soldiers at the scene of the crime. According to one newspaper article, a "dangerous man" named Gwin—a teacher on Island No. 10—was questioned by authorities but released for lack of evidence.[58] Another report mentions a "Grayson" in connection with the murders.[59]

Even if a white soldier played some part in the murders, evidence would have been hard to collect. As a reporter for the *Chicago Daily Trib-une* pointed out, black men could not testify against white men in court.

"The negroes confessed to the main part of the crime . . . of course, had a white man been along with them, *their* testimony could not have convicted *him* of complicity in the damnable act."[60]

While Civil-war era Southern courts did not allow blacks to testify against white perpetrators of crimes and maintained this ban until well after the war, by late 1864, federal military courts regularly heard such testimony. In 1863 at the Bend, if a white person did have a hand the demise of the Beckham family, he got away with murder.

CHAPTER 8

The Lawrence Massacre and the Not-So-Civil War of Quantrill, Anderson, and the James Brothers 1863

As with many of the infamous guerrillas of the Civil War, there are a lot of legends about "Bloody Bill" Anderson. According to one story, Anderson tied a knot in a silk rope for each man he killed. When Union forces finally caught Bloody Bill in 1864, his string contained fifty-three knots.

If the story is true, then Anderson tied more than a few knots after the August 1863 sacking of Lawrence, Kansas, a raid led by the notorious William Quantrill. When Quantrill polled his followers about the raid, Anderson supposedly said "Lawrence or hell, but with one proviso, that we kill every male thing."[1]

⊕ ⊕ ⊕

The "Bushwhackers" that hit Lawrence were a who's who of notorious characters and infamous bandits. Many of them had a personal axe to grind, and they decided that Lawrence would be the grindstone.

At dawn on August 21, 1863, Quantrill and a force of about 450 men reached the doomed town. None of the city's two thousand residents knew what was about to hit them that morning. Quantrill and some of his leaders supposedly carried "death lists" containing the names of men marked for execution.

The "Lawrence Massacre" would become the stuff of criminal legend and the apex of Bill Quantrill's notorious career; for his captain, Bloody Bill Anderson, it was just the beginning of a short-lived blood vendetta; for burgeoning outlaws Frank James and Cole Younger, it was a place to cut their teeth.

The Bushwhackers had years of pent-up angst dating from a civil war that began years before the Civil War started in 1861. Their conflict began in "Bleeding Kansas" of the 1850s, when the US government allowed its new territories to determine the slavery question for themselves. Pro-slavery Bushwhackers warred with antislavery "Jayhawkers," and innocent men, women, and children were caught in the middle.

There were horrific cases of random violence and brutality on both sides. William Phillips, a Kansas lawyer who made the mistake of airing his antislavery views, was kidnapped, tarred and feathered, and then auctioned off. In another spine-tingling instance of random violence, two pro-slavery men were at a Leavenworth tavern downing a few drinks when one bet the other that he would return in under two hours with the scalp of an abolitionist. The half-drunk man stumbled out of the tavern and waylaid the first man he saw. He shot the unsuspecting man before scalping him and running through the streets waving a bloody mane of hair.[2] Another pro-slavery raider supposedly said that he wouldn't die happy unless he murdered an abolitionist, and he wasn't picky about it. "If I can't kill a man," he said, "I'll kill a woman; and if I can't kill a woman, I'll kill a child."[3]

Abolitionists were just as guilty. In 1856, future Harper's Ferry raider John Brown and his hoods hacked five pro-slavery men to pieces with their sabers in an event that came to be known as "The Pottawatomie Massacre." Brown and his minions then mutilated the bodies.

When the Civil War began, the already-violent Kansas-Missouri border erupted, with Unionist and secessionist guerrillas escalating feuds that dated back to before the war. War is ugly anyway, but the face of the conflict along the nation's western fringe was particularly ghastly.

By August 1863, the already violent and bloody place became a no-holds-barred free-for-all. The Confederacy had suffered crippling defeats earlier that summer at Gettysburg and Vicksburg. Rebel forces along the western border began to dissipate as despondent soldiers returned home.

The Confederacy's loss was the Bushwhackers' gain, as the ranks of guerrilla groups swelled. Some of the worst excesses of the war took place along the Kansas-Missouri border during the waning years of the struggle. Groups on both sides committed ghastly outrages. Pro-Union Jayhawkers and Red Legs—so named after their red sheepskin leggings—led ruthless raids against Southern supporters. The Red Legs—who numbered only thirty men—acquired a particularly nasty reputation, made worse by Red Leg impersonators who dressed like the Union guerrillas and committed all sorts of crimes. The genuine Red Legs weren't much better. Their number included notorious figures Charles Jennison and future gunslinger William "Wild Bill" Hickock—heroes of semi-mythical proportion to those on the Union side of the fence, no-good thugs and murderers to those on the Confederate side.

Bands of pro-Southern Bushwhackers sprang up throughout Missouri and terrorized Union supporters. The most infamous of them was the group's head honcho, William Clarke Quantrill. Contemporary sources on the Union side characterize the guerrilla leader of Missouri as nothing more than a glorified thief. He didn't come into the war lacking experience. A native of Ohio, Quantrill began life as a frontier teacher. Somewhere along the way, he realized that crime paid better than teaching.

Quantrill quickly acquired a shady reputation by stealing from farmers along the Kansas–Missouri border, sometimes going by the nom de guerre Charley Hart. Quantrill-as-Hart would rustle livestock or horses and occasionally steal slaves and resell them. After beating a horse-theft rap in Kansas in April 1861, Quantrill fled to Missouri just ahead of a posse carrying an arrest warrant signed by a Lawrence judge. When war erupted a few weeks later, Quantrill sided with the secessionists. By 1863, he found himself at the head of a gang known unaffectionately throughout the North as Bushwhackers.

Quantrill's motives for sacking Lawrence remain a mystery. Some say that he was hunting for a Jayhawker named James Lane who had sacked and burned the Missouri town of Osceola in 1861. Quantrill believed Lane was in Lawrence. "I would have burned him at the stake," Quantrill later said about his Jayhawker mirror image.[4]

Others say that he wanted to destroy Lawrence because he believed it to be the base for Jayhawker raids into Missouri. Or that Lawrence, Kansas, was doomed because it was the center—both literally and symbolically— of antislavery sentiment in the West. Despite the efforts of Missouri guerrillas, Kansas had won the civil war before the Civil War and became a free state. Lawrence represented this victory and all the bloodletting that went along with it.

Or Quantrill could have been motivated by plain greed. He apparently believed that the Jayhawkers were using Lawrence as a storage depot for their loot. "All the plunder (or at least the bulk of it) stolen from Missouri," Quantrill supposedly said to his men, "will be found stored away in Lawrence. We can get more revenge and more money there than anywhere else in the State of Kansas."[5]

Whatever moved him, Quantrill was hellbent on raising Cain in Lawrence, and he didn't have far to look for men to help him. For Missourians, Lawrence represented years of enmity and border conflict spawned by the slavery question. It was also a symbol of the mayhem caused by the Jayhawkers.

One arm that Quantrill didn't have to twist was Bill Anderson's. Bloody Bill Anderson was one of the more ruthless characters of the Civil War. The twenty-something guerrilla (his birth date is uncertain; he was twenty-two or twenty-three when war began) needed little prodding to join Quantrill's raid on Lawrence.

Most accounts depict Anderson as being on a blood vendetta that resulted from two formative incidents. In 1862, his father was gunned down, some say murdered, in Kansas during a dispute over a stolen horse. Bill and his brother Jim in turn murdered their father's killer.

The second event and the one that may have really sent Anderson over the edge was the death of his teenage sister in Kansas City. Union brass, frustrated with their inability to stop the Bushwhackers, decided to go after family members who they believed were aiding and abetting the Confederate guerrillas. They rounded up several women and imprisoned them in a makeshift jail inside an old Kansas City warehouse.

Two of Anderson's sisters, sixteen-year-old Mollie Anderson and fourteen-year-old Josephine Anderson, were arrested and held in Kansas City. A third sister, ten-year-old Janie Anderson, accompanied her older sisters to jail.

The arrest and incarceration of their womenfolk chafed the guerrillas, but then an already bad situation turned tragic. On August 13, 1863, just eight days before Quantrill's strike against Lawrence, the structure serving as the penitentiary collapsed. Of the nine women in the temporary prison, four of them perished in the cave-in, including Josephine Anderson. The other women escaped unharmed, except for Mollie Anderson, who was seriously injured.[6]

Irate Southerners called it murder, and rumors circulated that the building's collapse was a planned "accident"—an atrocity perpetrated by the Union military to punish the Bushwhackers. While historians and researchers have discounted this possibility, at the time pro-Southern guerrillas blamed the Union authorities in Kansas for the deaths of their loved ones. According to some sources, Bloody Bill hit the ceiling when he heard news about his sisters and vowed to murder as many Yankees as he could, recording each one with a knot in a silk scarf he carried with him.

Just eight days after Josephine Anderson's death, Anderson took his silk scarf to Lawrence. Along for the ride was a young Missourian named Frank James. When the war began, eighteen-year-old James signed on with pro-Confederate Missouri State Guard and saw action until measles forced him to leave the battlefield. Captured by Union forces, he swore an oath of allegiance to the Union, but when the governor of Missouri required every man to join the state militia to fight the Bushwhackers, James faced the uncomfortable prospect of fighting alongside his enemies against his friends. So he swore an oath of different kind and became a Bushwhacker.

At Lawrence, Anderson and Frank James rubbed elbows with a lanky, tall drink of water named Thomas Coleman Younger, a disenchanted teenager who joined Quantrill's raiders in 1862. Cole Younger had a lot in common with Bloody Bill; Jayhawkers had wronged his family when they gunned down his father and burned the Younger farmhouse, leaving his mother homeless.

Younger also had family ties to three of the women imprisoned at Kansas City. Two of them, Arminna Selvey and Sue Vandiver, were the daughters of William Crawford, Cole's uncle by marriage. Charity Kerr was his cousin. According to one rumor of the time, Kerr was arrested because she witnessed Union forces murder Cole Younger's father.[7] All three of these women died in the building collapse.[8]

Of the other men Quantrill rounded up for his early-morning raid on the sleepy Kansas town, many of them had similar stories of personal tragedy suffered in the conflict along the Kansas-Missouri border.

The timing for a raid couldn't have been better for the Bushwhackers. During the summer of 1863, Lawrence was ripe for the picking. In the spring, newly elected Mayor George W. Collamore had convinced Union authorities to replace the citizens' guard with a Union contingent. But by August, Union authorities, against Collamore's protests, moved their men elsewhere, leaving Lawrence naked. They believed that any movement against the city would be observed well in advance by Union troops patrolling the Kansas-Missouri border. They didn't think a sneak attack was even possible.

But Quantrill's men managed to stay out of skirmishes by sticking to back roads, streams, and little-used trails. They kidnapped men at gunpoint, used them as guides, and then shot many of them when they were no longer useful, leaving a trail of bodies in their dust. In one eight-mile stretch, they murdered ten guides. Many of these men were Missouri natives who had fled to Kansas.

Along the way, the Bushwhackers stopped at a few homes whose occupants were on Quantrill's death list. One man, a Dr. Shean, managed to tiptoe out the back door while his wife answered the front door. Shean hid out in briar patch while Quantrill's men hunted for him without success.

The Bushwhackers didn't stay completely out of sight. Several people saw Quantrill's force en route to the city, but through a series of misfortunes, no advance warning was sent to Lawrence.

The onslaught began just after sunup on August 21, 1863. Quantrill and a force of about 450 rode into Lawrence after a long night in the saddle. The guerrillas went straight for two camps of Union recruits—mostly young boys—who represented the only Federal Army presence in town. The Bushwhackers mowed down most of the two dozen soldiers in a matter of minutes.

Quantrill and a group of raiders descended on the Eldridge House, one of the town's principal hotels. With four Colt Navy pistols tucked into his belt, the guerrilla chief looked more like a pirate than a soldier. When the hotel guests surrendered without firing a shot, Quantrill realized that the town's citizenry was at his mercy.

"Kill! Kill, and you will make no mistake," he allegedly said to his men. "Lawrence should be thoroughly cleansed, and the only way to cleanse it is to kill! Kill!"[9]

Quantrill reserved that command for only the town's male residents; he ordered his men not to harm a single hair of a single woman or child, but men, including teenagers, were fair game.

Thus began a four-hour orgy of violence. While the town's womenfolk tried to hide their men, the Bushwhackers helped themselves to the town's liquor supply. The inebriated soldiers rifled through homes and stores, taking anything of value, while terrified townspeople watched in horror. When they were finished, they fired businesses and residences alike.

Thirty-three-year-old spinster Sophia Bissell later described the melee in a letter to her cousin dated September 8, 1863. "And oh to hear the yells & hear the firing and to see the people running black & white old and young and the Fiends chasing after them firing as fast as they possibly could. Oh it was perfectly awful!"[10]

When the bandits' agenda became clear, several men tried to escape, but the guerrillas had blocked the town's exits. A few, like the hated Jayhawker James Lane, darted into adjacent cornfields and hid among the stalks. Lane, one of the top names on Quantrill's death list, owned a large plot of land on the outskirts of town. His cornfield became a refuge for many men who escaped the Bushwhackers' Colts. Many others didn't make it that far.

Ghastly, pathetic scenes of murder took place all over town. John and William Laurie, two farm boys who had come to town, were gunned down by guerrillas in front of their mother. "We are fiends from hell," the guerrillas yelled at the terror-stricken woman after murdering her two boys.[11]

Another group plundered the clothing store of Eldridge and Ford. They forced two store clerks to help them find new clothes before shooting both boys and setting the building on fire.

Bushwhackers galloped through town searching for people on their death lists, such as Mayor Collamore. The mayor and another man in the home jumped down a well in the adjacent outbuilding. The guerrillas rifled through the house and then torched it. Carbon monoxide gas filled the well, killing both men. Later, a good Samaritan named Captain Lowe tried to rescue them by shimmying down on a rope. He lost consciousness when he reached the layer of gas. The rope snapped and he fell to his death.

It was a bad morning for the Speer family. The father, John Speer, ran a newspaper called the *Tribune* and was a tax collector. Marked for death, he hightailed it into a cornfield on the outskirts of town before guerrillas reached his doorstep. He survived the Lawrence Massacre unscathed, but the rest of the Speer men didn't.

Nineteen-year-old John Speer Jr. was asleep in the Tribune office when the raid began. He and another newspaperman, M. M. Murdock, took refuge in the basement of an adjacent building. Later, Speer went out into the streets. He was immediately cornered by a guerrilla named Larkin Skaggs.

The Reverend Larkin Skaggs was a one-time Baptist minister who left the pulpit to become a raider during Bleeding Kansas. This wasn't Skaggs's first foray into Lawrence; he was part of the force that had sacked the city in 1856. The Reverend took Speer's wallet, shot the kid, and rode off. Speer lay in a pool of his own blood just a few feet from an inferno that used to be a house. Unable to move, he begged another guerrilla to move him a few feet away, but the guerrilla shot him instead.

Seventeen-year-old Robert Speer was in the printing shop when guerrillas set fire to the structure. He was never seen again, and it is presumed he perished in the flames.

A few Bushwhackers stopped fifteen-year-old William Speer in the street and asked him to identify himself. He lied, telling them he was "Billy Smith." One of the men looked over the death list. There was no "William Smith" on it, so they let him go. Billy Speer then hid out for a while under a porch. He was later found and beaten but survived.

Bandits also descended on the home of Judge Louis Carpenter. He and his young wife lived in a brick house they had just built a few months earlier. The Bushwhackers robbed the Carpenters but left the couple unharmed. A few minutes later, another group rode up to the Carpenter place, but not to steal. They came to murder the judge.

They chased Carpenter through the house, riddling the structure with lead. They eventually hit their target. The wounded judge stumbled into the front yard and collapsed. His wife and her sister clung to the dying man, but they were peeled away by a guerrilla who put the barrel of his Colt Navy revolver to the judge's head and blew his brains out in front of the women. Eyewitness C. Grovenor called the murder of Judge Carpenter "one of the cruel things of that morning of cruelties."[12]

Guerrillas also went looking for the Reverend H. D. Fisher, who hid behind a pile of dirt in his basement and managed to avoid detection. His ten- and twelve-year-old boys were out with twelve-year-old Robin Martin and tried to hoof it to the cornfield, dodging lead with each stride. Bullets ripped the turf at their feet as the Bushwhackers opened fired on the three boys. The Fisher kids survived, but Martin sustained a fatal gunshot wound to the head.[13]

There were some miraculous escapes. The wife of Judge Samuel A. Riggs reached out and grabbed the reins of a guerrilla's horse long enough to allow the judge to scamper away to safety.

Another, more humorous escape took place inside the house of Dr. Charles Reynolds. When a man darted into the house from the street, the women inside, aware that the rebels were not harming the town's females, dolled him up in a dress. They shaved him and applied a generous amount of makeup. When guerrillas smashed through the front door, the women told them to be careful not to disturb "Poor Aunt Betsy." Aunt Betsy's five o'clock shadow was suspicious, but they left her alone.

Even in the midst of terror, romance found a way. According to historian William Connolley, "two marriages resulted from incidents which occurred on that awful 'Black Friday.'"[14] One pair met when both took shelter in, of all places, a pig sty. The other couple met in a tavern. The guerrillas took a man prisoner and carted him off to the watering hole. They shot the bartender, leaving the barmaid to serve them drinks. The crafty barmaid kept the drinks coming, and before long, the Bushwhackers were seeing double.

When they had had their fill, they decided to murder their prisoner and continue their pillaging. They dragged the young man outside, but the barmaid pleaded with them not to shoot him. She said he was her brother, and the Bushwhackers, pleased with the nonstop drinks she had poured, decided to grant her wish and spare his life. The couple later tied the knot.

Sometime around nine—after about four hours of looting and shooting—the guerrillas left town. A sentry posted at the peak of nearby Mount Oread had seen a column of Union soldiers headed toward Lawrence, so Quantrill gave the order to mount up. The Bushwhackers left town with saddlebags filled to the brim with plunder.

Quantrill ordered Capt. William Gregg to round up the stragglers, many of them drunk and scattered throughout town. As the Bushwhackers made their getaway, Gregg did his best to corral the miscreants still in Lawrence. Gregg witnessed some horrific acts of brutality during his last-minute roundup.

He found a few inebriates at a gunsmith's shop. They shot the shop owner and another man before lighting the building on fire. While the store went up in smoke, the rebels bound the hands of the two wounded men and then shoved them into the flames. Bleeding and burning, they tried to jump out of the inferno, but the guerrillas pushed them back in the raging fire. The two unfortunates burned alive.

Gregg managed to gather most of the drunken raiders and they rode out of town to join the others, but there was one who didn't get away. The Reverend Larkin Skaggs—the same Skaggs that shot John Speer Jr., and left him for dead—stayed just a little too long and wound up in the sights of William "Billy" Speer, who had earlier that morning survived a savage beating.

Billy had wobbled back home with dried blood caked around his mouth and nostrils from the beating. His mother gave him a bear hug and then, according to one popular version of the story, handed him an old rifle, telling him to even the score for the Speers murdered that morning. Billy and his buddy Frank Montgomery did just that when they came across Skaggs.

With one shot, Billy unhorsed Skaggs, who hit the ground with a thud. The Reverend was only wounded, but a Delaware Indian named White Turkey finished the job. He stabbed Skaggs in the chest and then scalped him. The Bushwhacker was still carrying the wallet he took from young John Speer Jr.

The former preacher suffered numerous post-mortem indignities. C. M. Chase, who galloped into Lawrence after the rebels had left, found a macabre scene. "The first sight attracting my attention was a negro rushing through the streets on horseback, dragging the dead body of a dead rebel, with a rope around his neck hitched to his saddle. A crowd was following pelting the rebel with stones." Skaggs, the dead rebel, was dragged around until the clothes fell off his body.

"There was an attempt later by the negroes to burn the body," Chase continued, "which was not successful. The bones lay naked all winter in a ravine in the town, and negroes and boys sawed finger rings from some of them. No part of the body was ever given burial."[15]

Reverend Larkin Skaggs was the only rebel caught at Lawrence, but he was not the only one punished. Union forces under Missouri lieutenant Cyrus Leland Jr. later caught a few of them. They hanged one man in his living room and three others from a tall tree. They placed a sign on the swinging corpses: "Don't cut them down!"[16]

Lawrence was a burned-out skeleton. Survivor Sidney Clarke later summed up the damage Quantrill's raiders left in their wake. "More than 200 buildings were burned—96 of them stores and shops, and the rest of them the finest residences in the city. The fires were set as soon as the plundering was done, and by ten o'clock A.M. the old Citadel of Freedom, and the most beautiful city west of the Mississippi was a heap of smoldering ruins."[17] The theft and destruction came to an estimated cost of $1 million to $2 million.

The death toll of Lawrence varies from source to source, but most pin it at about 150. According to Frank James, "Bloody Bill" jerked fourteen knots in his silk scarf after the attack "It was a day of butchery," James later said in his autobiography. "Bill Anderson . . . claimed he killed fourteen and the number was allowed."[18]

There are no known instances of rape or murder of women, but they weren't left entirely unharmed, either. Colt's Navy revolver was a real widowmaker that morning in Lawrence.

The town's Methodist church was used as a temporary morgue, where the bodies of the slain were laid out in rows and left until relatives claimed them for burial. As roaring fires continued to consume the city, women filed into the church in search of their loved ones. A piercing scream or a garbled sob told everyone that another victim had been identified.

"The scene that met me as I went into that church I shall never forget," C. Grovenor later recalled, "and I said then that I hope God would spare me from ever witnessing another like it."[19]

People of Kansas had blood in their eyes, and according to Brig. Gen. Thomas Ewing, were planning an armed incursion into Missouri to fight fire with fire. "The excitement in Kansas is very great," Ewing noted in a letter to Maj. Gen. John Schofield. Ewing went on to say that there existed "a great danger of a raid of citizens for the purpose of destroying the towns along the border."

"My political enemies," Ewing added, "are fanning the flames, and wish me for a burnt-offering to satisfy the just passion of the people."[20] Ewing wouldn't burn at the stake for not protecting Lawrence, but he did issue Order No. 11 on August 25—just four days after the Lawrence Massacre and the same day he wrote the note to Schofield.

The now-infamous Order No. 11 was an attempt by Federal authorities to break the "Bushwhackers" by removing their base of support. Since friends and enemies were so intertwined in the "Bushwhacker" heartland along the Kansas-Missouri border, Federal forces decided to forcibly remove everyone from the three counties considered their base of operations.

The order forced residents of Jackson, Cass, and Bates Counties and part of Vernon County—the four blocks stacked under Kansas City along the Mississippi River—to gather whatever belongings they could carry and leave. The mandate purged about twenty thousand residents from the affected area.[21] Cass and Bates became ghost counties.

With the area vacated, it was payback time for Union guerrillas. Charles Jennison and others pillaged and looted what was left behind and then torched the buildings. They burned so many structures, the area became known as "the Burnt District."

Three months later, Union authorities took their thumb off of the Burnt District with Order No. 20, which allowed residents to return to their homes if they signed an oath of loyalty. Ewing, apparently fearing further reprisals against the Missourians, added a warning: "If any person in the military service of the United States shall knowingly and willfully commit any act of injury to the person or property of any resident holding such safeguard, he shall be arrested."[22]

While the civilians of west Missouri walked their "trail of tears," the men who sacked Lawrence had headed south. Quantrill and his men fled to Texas, where they spent the winter while things cooled off in Missouri. En route to Texas, they hit Fort Blair at Baxter Springs, Kansas, where Bloody Bill may have tied a few more knots in his string. During a brief skirmish, the Bushwhackers killed around a hundred Union soldiers, some of them gunned down after they had surrendered.

During the winter of 1863–64, the Bushwhackers began to disintegrate. Infighting led the gang to break up into splinter groups. Quantrill's influence waned, the attack on Lawrence remaining his signature moment. But Bloody Bill was just getting started.

In March 1864, Anderson headed back to Missouri with Bush Smith, a teenager from Sherman, Texas, that he had courted and married during the winter retreat. By this time, Bloody Bill had tied dozens of knots in his silk scarf and allegedly rode around with scalps dangling from his horse's bridle.

Early on the morning of September 27, 1864, Anderson and his guerrilla force raided a sleepy Missouri town called Centralia. The orgy of bloodletting has become known as the "Centralia Massacre." Anderson's gang included some tough characters, such as Archie Clement, John Koger—who had been wounded twenty-two times—Frank James, and Frank's seventeen-year-old baby brother, Jesse.

Like many of Anderson's men, Jesse had a score to settle with Unionist forces. Often described as a happy-go-lucky type with a constant smile, James watched pro-Union militia string up his stepdad, Dr. Reuben Samuels (Samuels survived the hanging). They also taunted young Jesse. They threw a rope around his head, poked him with bayonets, and slapped him around a little. Riding alongside Bloody Bill, Jesse had an opportunity for a little payback.

Whooping and hollering, the gang rode into Centralia and began plundering the stores and residences. Many of them gulped down the town's stores of liquor. The buzzed Bushwhackers couldn't believe their luck when they heard a whistle signaling an incoming train. This would be the first major train robbery for future outlaw legends Frank and Jesse James.

As the train rolled into the station, Anderson's men showered it with bullets from their six-shooters. The terrified passengers—about one hundred, including twenty-four Union soldiers on furlough—dropped to the floor as the bullets tore through the cars.[23] Anderson, Clement, the James boys, and a few others jumped onto the train and immediately began to rob the passengers. They marched the civilians off the train, lined them up in a row, and picked their pockets.

Next, they led the two dozen soldiers out of the train. The guerrillas marched them to the south side of the railroad tracks and formed them into a line, ordered them to strip down to their underwear, and robbed them. While the Bushwhackers took money and jewelry from the soldiers, Clement asked Anderson what he planned to do with the Union troops. He planned to furlough them, he said, permanently.

Clement suggested they keep one of the soldiers as a hostage and exchange him for an imprisoned guerrilla, and Anderson agreed. Since Anderson had lost a sergeant, he asked if there were any sergeants in the group. Sgt. Thomas Goodman reluctantly stepped forward, and two of Bloody Bill's men took him out of the line and led him away from the scene. The guerrillas then unloaded their revolvers, mowing down the soldiers. One man, a Sergeant Peters, managed to escape the curtain of lead and crawl under the train, but Anderson's men nabbed him on the platform and shot him execution-style at point-blank range.

Later that afternoon, Union forces under Maj. A. V. E. Johnston clashed with Anderson's Bushwhackers. The Union troops outnumbered Anderson's eighty men by almost two to one, but the well-armed, seasoned Missouri men outgunned the Federal forces.

The Bushwhackers' ability to overcome superior forces in the scrape was primarily the result of their guerrilla muscle: the Colt Navy revolver. The powerful six-shooter—the weapon of choice for border ruffians and officers on both sides—meant that they essentially outgunned their Federal nemeses, who typically carried rifles that needed reloading after each shot, by six bullets to one. So while the Union troops reloaded, Anderson's men unloaded their revolvers, perforating the Federal lines.

The battle quickly turned into a rout. Of Johnston's 155 men, 123 of them were killed, including Johnston himself. Frank James later said that it was Jesse who killed the Union major.

Goodman, the lone Union soldier taken hostage during the raid, survived the Centralia Massacre and later penned a memoir about his "Ten Days' Experience with Colonel William T. Anderson." In the short book, aptly titled *A Thrilling Record*, Goodman describes the blood-curdling scene as Anderson's men mutilated the fallen Union soldiers.

"Men's heads were severed from their lifeless bodies, exchanged as to bodies, labeled with rough and obscene epitaphs and inscriptions, stuck upon their carbine points, tied to their saddle bows, or sat grinning at each other from the tops of fence stakes and stumps around the scene"[24]

In a telegraph sent a few days later, Union lieutenant colonel Daniel M. Draper described the massacre of Union troops as "a scene of murder and outrage at which the heart sickens. Most of them were beaten over the head, seventeen of them were scalped, and one man had his privates cut off and placed in his mouth. Every man was shot in the head. One man had his nose cut off."[25]

After toying with the dead Union corpses, Anderson's men returned to town for a second round of looting. When the sun set on Centralia, the death toll had reached around 150.

Union leadership had had enough of Anderson and sent Col. Samuel P. Cox and a detachment of about three hundred soldiers after him. Cox and company finally caught up with Anderson near Albany, Missouri, on October 26, about a month after the Centralia massacre.

The cunning Cox set a trap to bushwhack the Bushwhackers. He positioned his men in a thicket of woods behind a bridge. He ordered a small force to hit Anderson's camp and then hightail it toward the wooden bridge, where sharpshooters would do the rest.

On cue, Union cavalry under Lt. Jacob Baker hit the guerrillas and ran with Anderson and twenty of his men in hot pursuit. Anderson's Bushwhackers reached the bridge "with their bridle reins in their teeth and revolver in each hand," Cox later recalled.[26]

When they realized they had galloped into a trap, many of the guerrillas bolted, but not Bloody Bill. "Others turned and fled," Cox said, "but the grim old chieftain and two of his men went right through the line, shooting and yelling."[27]

It was Anderson's last charge. Bloody Bill was shot twice in the head, one of the balls blowing away a massive chunk of his cranium and leaving a gaping hole. He was dead before he hit the ground. The "grim old chieftain" was only twenty-five-years old (or twenty-six, depending on which birthday one considers the official date).

Bloody Bill's body lay facedown in the tall grass until the bullets stopped flying. While Cox's men chased after the other Bushwhackers, a few soldiers examined the corpse. They didn't know who the fearless guerrilla was when they rolled the bloody mass onto its back. The man's wavy hair was matted with blood and brain matter. True to his fighting spirit, the dead guerrilla wouldn't give up his guns until the Union soldiers pried them from his cold, dead fingers—still clenched in his hands were two Colt Navy revolvers.

A search of the body produced some tell-tale clues about the man's identity: a photograph of Anderson's teenage bride, Bush Anderson, a miniature Confederate flag inscribed to "W. L. Anderson," and a written order to "Captain Anderson." Cox and his men now realized that they had taken down Bloody Bill. The troops also found grim reminders of the hate that drove him: the infamous silk scarf with fifty-three knots and a human scalp hanging from his saddle.

Anderson's corpse was taken to Richmond, Missouri. Everybody wanted to see Bloody Bill Anderson in the flesh and rushed to the courthouse to catch a glimpse. Soldiers propped Anderson's body against a wall and placed a revolver in his hand, so a local dentist and sometime photographer, Robert Kice, could snap a few shots of the legendary raider. In Kice's ambrotypes, Bill is missing a digit; a souvenir-seeker took Bloody Bill's ring by hacking off his left index finger.

After taking advantage of a postmortem photo op in Richmond with the notorious guerrilla, Union militia had its revenge on Anderson's corpse. They cut off his head and mounted it on a pole for all to see. They then dragged his headless body through the streets before burying the remains in a local cemetery in an unmarked grave. Later that night, a few soldiers tiptoed into the cemetery for one last parting shot—they urinated on the spot where Bloody Bill's body lay six feet under.

After Anderson's demise, Jesse James went to Texas with Archie Clement, while Frank James joined up with Quantrill, who had moved his operation. Officially in disfavor with the Confederate government and unofficially with several of his former chums, Quantrill went east in 1865. In north-central Kentucky, he linked up with other rebel guerrillas and continued to cause as much mayhem as he could muster.

Quantrill's reputation preceded him. All sorts of nefarious activity, some done by other bullies, was pinned on the infamous Quantrill and his men. In *Noted Guerrillas*, nineteenth-century historian John Edwards told the story of one such event.

Two bandits accosted a Mrs. Clark, who was traveling along a lonely road, and "monstrously abused" her.[28] Everyone assumed that Quantrill's men did it, even though Quantrill himself despised crimes against women and banned his men from committing them. The incident particularly bothered Frank James, who took it upon himself to hunt down the real culprits for a little frontier justice.

James and fellow Missourian William Hulse tracked one of the two men to a remote cabin, where James "blew his brains out across the table."[29] A small posse formed to hunt down the second perpetrator, who was shot dead in a brief firefight. Federal soldiers took both corpses to a nearby town, where Mrs. Clark identified them as her assailants.

This frontier justice, according to Edwards, satisfied Union major general John M. Palmer, who was in charge of the Military District of Kentucky at the time. "The Guerrillas had washed out the stain cast upon them in blood," Edwards wrote.[30]

Quantrill planned to travel farther east to make even greater mayhem in Washington, DC; he even contemplated a plot to assassinate Lincoln, but another nefarious character did the deed in April.

Bill Quantrill's life of crime ended on a Kentucky farm about a month after Lee surrendered to Grant at Appomattox Court House. Union guerrilla-hunter extraordinaire Capt. Edwin Terrell and a posse of men tracked Quantrill to James Wakefield's farm on May 10, 1865. On that drizzly morning, Terrell and his group ambushed Quantrill and about twenty other men who were asleep in the barn.

As he was trying to hop on a horse, Quantrill was hit in the back by a slug that tore through his torso and severed his spinal cord, leaving him paralyzed. A second ball took off his right index finger.

The fallen Bushwhacker said that his name was Captain Clarke, a pseudonym he used on occasion. Terrell believed him and galloped off after the fleeing guerrillas. When he realized Quantrill's ruse, Terrell returned to the Wakefield farm, put Quantrill in a carriage, and took him to Louisville, where the Bushwhacker legend lingered for almost a month. Bill Quantrill—the ruthless raider who tried to wipe Lawrence, Kansas, off the map—died on July 6, 1865. He was just twenty-seven-years old.

After the war, Frank and Jesse James teamed up with Cole Younger to form the James-Younger gang. They became outlaw legends in their own right. Both Frank and Cole lived into their elderly years, and both wrote about their experiences in the saddle. Cole later called the mayhem in Lawrence "a day of butchery."[31]

Frank never forgot about "the grim old chieftain" who was lying in an unmarked grave. In 1908, he gave Bloody Bill Anderson a proper funeral and then, finally, in 1967, the infamous guerrilla got a gravestone.

Or did he? According to legend, Anderson didn't die from Union "lead poisoning." As the story goes, the man gunned down after Centralia was some other, unfortunate guerrilla mistaken for Anderson. The real Bloody Bill survived and lived to the ripe old age of eighty-seven as a farmer named William Columbus Anderson. In an interview published a few years before he died, this Anderson claimed to be the infamous guerrilla. Short of some shocking DNA revelation, however, the Anderson-has-survived legend will remain just that—a legend.

Unlike that of his former crony in the saddle, Quantrill's body made it to burial in one piece. Like Anderson, though, he was placed in an unmarked site to prevent any desecration of his remains. The sexton did a good job of picking a site that would stay unmolested, because when Quantrill's mother later came looking for her son's burial place in 1887, the grave had been undisturbed.

Quantrill took one last postmortem ride after his mother, Caroline Clarke Quantrill, accompanied by a newspaper editor from Ohio named William Walter Scott, exhumed the infamous Bushwhacker's body. Scott placed the bones in a box and took them back to Quantrill's native Ohio for reburial. The cemetery officials there didn't want the notoriety that they believed would come along with a headstone bearing the name "William Quantrill," so the box of Bill's bones went into the ground in an unmarked grave once again in 1889.

Scott, however, had done a little sleight of hand and double-crossed Quantrill's mother. While transporting the bones, he kept five arm and leg bones, the skull, and some hair. He kept the purloined bones in his office and later tried to sell Bill's skull to the Kansas State Historical Society, but they failed to reach an agreement. The Society later bought a few of the bones from Scott's widow and put them in a display about the Lawrence Massacre along with a lock of Bill's hair and the wallet of John Speer Jr., which was found on the body of his killer, Larkin Skaggs.

Meanwhile, the cranium collected dust for a while before changing hands again, this time winding up in a college fraternity. The fraternity eventually folded, and the skull passed on to Ohio's Canal Dover Historical Society. (It was easy to identify—Quantrill had a cracked molar in the lower right side of his jawbone). The skull remained on display in Ohio until 1992.

Eventually, like Bloody Bill, Quantrill received a proper burial. Two of them, actually. A disagreement about the terms of burial erupted between the Missouri Sons of Confederate Veterans, who obtained the five bones purchased by the Kansas Historical Society, and the Canal Dover Historical Society, which possessed Bill's skull. The Sons buried Bill's five bones, along with a lock of hair the Kansas Historical Society also acquired, in Higginsville, Missouri. A week later, his skull went into the earth inside a child-sized coffin in Dover, Ohio, ending Bill Quantrill's final ride.

The guerrilla chieftains Bloody Bill Anderson and Bill Quantrill were gone but not forgotten. The surviving Bushwhackers had regular get-togethers, beginning with an informal gathering in 1888. Even Frank James and Cole Younger made appearances. The guerrillas swapped stories of the good old days until 1929, when the last reunion took place with just five in attendance. Quantrill and Anderson, as losers fighting for a lost cause, shoulder most of the blame for what went down along the Kansas-Missouri border, while the equally dastardly deeds of Union Red Legs and Jayhawkers haven't been given as much ink over the past century and a half. The Bushwhackers may have felt justified in their cause, but that one scorching August in Lawrence was just plain murder.

CHAPTER 9

The Murder of Gen. Earl Van Dorn
1863

At five feet five, Confederate general Earl Van Dorn may not have been tall in the saddle, but it didn't matter to several belles of the South. Something about the cavalier—his love of poetry and the arts, his long, flowing mustache, or the uniform and all the stories that went with it—proved irresistible to one particular lady. It would be a fatal attraction. While the men in blue and gray fought on the battlefields, Earl Van Dorn died in a civil war of a different sort.

Although many of his lady friends were taller than he was, Earl Van Dorn's shortness didn't stunt his social growth. He became a fixture at wartime soirees in Spring Hill, Tennessee, which would prove to be the last stop in his epic journey as a military man. The small, sleepy town about thirty miles south of Nashville wasn't the center of the war, but it wasn't far from the action, either, as Van Dorn quickly learned after his posting there in March 1863.

For the lonely women and widows of Spring Hill, Van Dorn must have seemed larger than life. One writer from Virginia glowingly described him as "rather undersized—of a spare frame, erect and graceful in his movements; his mustache is long but light; otherwise he is closely shaven, which is one cause of his youthful appearance." And then there was that uniform, which was "a gray tunic with buff collar and cuffs, heavy gold braiding on the sleeve, and three stars on each side of the collar, the one in the center the largest."[1]

The diminutive cavalier dazzled friends with stories culled from more than two decades in uniform. And he had the scars to prove it; his body was a canvas illustrating the numerous engagements he experienced as a young soldier.

Van Dorn put on his first uniform when his distant relative, former president Andrew Jackson, pulled a few strings so Van Dorn could go to West Point. He was not a stellar student, graduating fifty-second out of fifty-six in the class of 1842.

A year after graduation, Van Dorn married Caroline Godbold, the sixteen-year-old daughter of an Alabama planter. Their marriage would have its ups and downs; Van Dorn spent most of his time away from home with the military, which seemed to be the real love of his life. "I never could be happy out of the Army," he later said. "I have no other home—could make none that would be congenial to my feelings."[2]

Van Dorn's first battlefield experience came during the Mexican-American War. The young cavalier seemed to like the taste of battle, and his later comments suggest that he found the thrill of combat intoxicating. "Don't you poor helpless female population wish you were men so that you might snatch a sword and join in the game for glory?" Van Dorn asked in a letter to his sister Octavia in 1846. He goes on to say that combat is much riskier than a gambler who wages a million dollars on a card. "But here life is to lose—glory to win. Who can know what the bosom feels, how the heart swells with burning emotions, hopes, proud longings for distinction."[3]

He also had a flair for the dramatic. In one particular fight, he dodged enemy lead to raise a US flag that had fallen. He later described the incident in another letter. "I dodged several bomb-shells which threatened to fall on my head," he boasted. He side-stepped "a howitzer ball" while all the time "musket balls flew around me at one time like a thousand humming-birds—so I had the sound of all kinds of music." Van Dorn couldn't dodge them all, and he wound up with the first of many war wounds, although he described it as "a scratch on the ankle in dodging a shell."[4]

During skirmishes with the Comanche in Texas and the Indian Territory following the Mexican-American War, Van Dorn—by now a captain in the Second Cavalry—was wounded four more times. In one fight, Van Dorn's wrist and chest were perforated by arrows. There wasn't a doctor in sight, so Van Dorn gritted his teeth and pushed the arrows through the wounds.

Van Dorn found more than combat out west. While stationed in Texas, Van Dorn began an affair with a young woman named Martha Goodbread, an Alabama native who had moved to the Lone Star State with her family in 1854. While Van Dorn penned lengthy love letters to his wife Caroline, he was busy with Martha—so busy in fact, that by 1861, he had fathered three children by her. The outbreak of war essentially ended the relationship.[5]

By the time the Civil War began, Van Dorn had a distinguished record in the saddle. During the secession crisis, he followed his native Mississippi against the United States and became a brigadier general in the state militia. In March 1861, he was mustered into the Confederate Army as a colonel of infantry and was sent back to Texas. In April, Van Dorn led a successful raid against Union shipping in Galveston, becoming the first rebel to capture a Federal ship.

His early success led to a rapid promotion to major general, but infantry wasn't really his forte. Van Dorn suffered an embarrassing loss to Union forces at the Battle of Pea Ridge (Elkhorn Tavern) in Arkansas in March 1862, even though it was a rare occasion in which Confederate forces outnumbered Union troops. The battle was a comedy of errors for the Confederacy, and Van Dorn ultimately retreated after sustaining heavy losses.

Later that same year, Union forces whipped Van Dorn's men at the Second Battle of Corinth in Mississippi. Instead of first looking over the situation, Van Dorn led a hasty charge against a well-entrenched Federal force. Once again, the general retreated after his command suffered heavy casualties. Van Dorn's critics characterized him as a glory-hunter who made spur-of-the-moment decisions that cost his men dearly, and the Second Battle of Corinth gave them plenty of evidence.

By the end of 1862, Van Dorn was back in the saddle at the head of a cavalry division. What doomed him as an infantry general—his impetuous streak—served him well as a horse soldier. He won a series of skirmishes in late 1862.

In February 1863, Van Dorn moved into Tennessee and set up his headquarters in Spring Hill. His job as cavalry commander was to scout for and protect Gen. Braxton Bragg's Army of Tennessee. He continued to enjoy a string of wins on the battlefield.

In April 1863, Van Dorn had a blowout with Nathan Bedford Forrest that nearly ended in a duel. The fight took place in Van Dorn's Spring Hill office. Van Dorn had heard whispers that Forrest had said some unflattering things about him to Gen. Joseph E. Johnston. Van Dorn later described the ugly confrontation: "One thing led to another, until at length I threw off all restraint, and directly expressing my belief in his treachery and falsehood, suggested then and there was a good time and place to settle our differences"[6]

The two men started toward each other and had begun to draw their swords when Forrest said, "General Van Dorn, you know I'm not afraid of you—but I will not fight you—and leave you to reconcile with yourself the gross wrong you have done me." Forrest suggested that a duel would set a bad example for their men.[7] Forrest's words cut deep. Van Dorn apologized and the two parted company on good terms.

Van Dorn would not live to see Forrest again. It wasn't a colleague's saber or an enemy bullet that did him in, but rather his own indiscretion and a fatal attraction to the young trophy wife of a local doctor.

In Spring Hill, Van Dorn acquired a reputation as a ladies' man and a flirt. Although he may have been neither one of those things, both acquaintances and the press alike considered him somewhat of a womanizer. A reporter for the *Mobile Advertiser and Register* described him as "the terror of ugly husbands and serious papas."[8] The reporter also added an embarrassing snippet of conversation he apparently overheard. The little general was conversing with a twenty-four-year-old widow who remarked, "General, you are older than I am, but let me give you a little advice—let women alone until the war is over."

"My God, madam!" Van Dorn retorted. "I cannot do that, for it is all that I am fighting for. I hate all men, and were it not for the women, I should not fight at all; besides, if I accepted your generous advice, I would not now be speaking to you."[9]

While the newspaper reporter may have engaged in a little character assassination by taking this comment out of context, some of Van Dorn's acquaintances also insinuated that Van Dorn found plenty of action off the battlefield. In a letter to his wife, Lt. William L. Nugent noted "you can see at times some fine looking ladies driving about in his splendid four-horse Ambulance. I do not relish such an officer"[10]

One of those "fine-looking ladies" was Jesse McKissack Peters, a real stunner with chocolate brown hair and hazel eyes. She was also married. The twenty-five-year-old beauty was the third wife of Dr. James Boddie Peters.

Dr. Peters came to Tennessee in the 1830s and worked for a while as a country sawbones. He became a prominent personage in the area, at one time winning a seat in the state legislature. He also invested in real estate and by the time war began, owned several pieces of land in Tennessee and Arkansas.

While he was fortunate with finances, he was unlucky in love. His first wife died a few months after giving birth. His second wife died at the age of thirty-seven in 1855. Three years later, the forty-six-year-old Southern aristocrat married debutante Jesse Helen McKissack, twenty-six-years his younger. They were an odd couple; she liked parties, and he liked quiet evenings at home in his study. That is, when he was home. Dr. Peters spent much of his time on the road.

Jesse wasn't going to just sit home while her husband pored over medical texts. She took full advantage of the Spring Hill social scene. She went to soirees and tea parties, balls and card gatherings. At some point, Mrs. Peters caught the eye of Van Dorn, or vice versa. Jesse's sheets may not have been completely white when she met the dashing Confederate cavalier. Dr. Peters later remarked that he had left Jesse once before because she had had an extramarital tryst.[11]

If Mrs. Peters and the general did hit it off, they were well-matched. Both had spouses they rarely saw, both were vivacious personalities who liked action, and both apparently enjoyed each other's company. With little regard for how things appeared, they strolled through the streets of Spring Hill and took rides together in Van Dorn's carriage. At the very least, they were both guilty of reckless disregard for the rules of nineteenth-century high society. In that prim and proper world, husbands and wives didn't take walks and rides with other people's husbands and wives. Whether these rides were just rides and conversation, or rides and "rides," the rumors of an affair began to make the rounds.

There is no doubt that Van Dorn had some type of relationship with Jesse Peters, although it could have been platonic. At least some of his officers believed this. In a letter published in the *Mobile Advertiser and Register*, several of Van Dorn's men insisted that there was "no improper intimacy" between the general and Mrs. Peters.[12]

Whether they were confidantes, lovers, or just friends, Van Dorn's relationship with Mrs. Peters was a dangerous liaison. Even one of his aides pointed out the risks. "General, as your friend, may I take the liberty of warning you that your friend, Mrs. Peters, can cause you a lot of trouble."[13]

Van Dorn took the hint but denied any wrongdoing. "I have no intention of getting involved with her," he retorted. "However, I find her to be pleasant company." Then he went on to catalog Mrs. Peters's various attributes, including a head for business, a sharp wit, and an infectious charm.

Inevitably, the rumor mill worked overtime. People whispered about what the dashing general and Dr. Peters's trophy wife did behind closed doors. Dr. Peters later said that when he returned to Spring Hill on April 12, he heard the rumors about an alleged affair. Capt. G. A. Hanson, a local boy attached to Van Dorn's command, later said that Dr. Peters came back to Spring Hill because of the rumors. According to Peters's later account, he wasn't about to sit still and play the role of cuckold while Van Dorn and his wife played Romeo and Juliet.

The final act of this triangle took place either late in the evening of May 6 or early in the morning of May 7, depending on who's telling the story. One version of the murder is told by an unnamed officer on Van Dorn's staff, whose story appeared in *A Soldier's Honor*, a 1902 compilation of documents by Van Dorn's baby sister, Emily Van Dorn Miller.[14]

According to this officer, on the morning of May 7, 1863, Dr. Peters waltzed across the lawn toward the Nathaniel Cheairs house, where Van Dorn's office was located. He nodded and uttered a good morning to two officers standing outside chatting. The men—a Colonel Brownlow and a

Colonel Dillon—immediately recognized the visitor as Dr. Peters and thought nothing about it, since the physician often visited the house. He knew the Cheairs family and on occasion he would call on Van Dorn to obtain a pass to cross the lines.

A few minutes later (the officer estimates not more than five to ten), Dr. Peters came out of the house, got onto his horse, and rode east, apparently headed out of town. Just as Peters rode off, Cheairs' daughter came running across the lawn. In a panic, she gasped "Come here! Come here! Dr. Peters has shot Van Dorn!"[15]

The officer then raced to Van Dorn's office and found a ghastly sight: Van Dorn sitting at his writing desk with his left arm in his lap and his right arm on the table, as if he had just been writing something. His head was "against the window pane," and "blood was flowing from the back of his head against the glass, and he was convulsively shuddering."[16] Bullets to the head sometimes cause slight convulsions, and the victim's body will shake or quiver.

According to this anonymous source, Van Dorn had been shot in the back of the head, the bullet tearing through his brain and settling in his left frontal lobe, causing his left eye to swell and blacken. "There was a very small round hole in the back of his head evidently made from a parlor pistol which makes no noise louder than the snapping of a cap, and hence it was not heard in explosion though so near," wrote the officer.[17] Even the Cheairs girl who found the body didn't hear the gunshot, even though she was in the room across the hall.

Capt. G. A. Hanson, however, did later claim to have heard a gunshot. He was going past Van Dorn's headquarters when he heard the "very loud report of a pistol." Like his anonymous colleague, he also went into Van Dorn's office and found his boss slumped over in his chair, shot "in the back of the head with a Derringer pistol of the largest calibre."[18]

The crime scene baffled the anonymous officer, who later noted that Van Dorn always wrote out passes while facing his visitors. He simply would not have allowed someone to stand behind him. The glass window hadn't been broken, so Van Dorn's murderer wouldn't have shot him from outside, either. These facts led the unnamed officer to reconstruct the crime later, but at the time he had to track down the general's killer.

The pursuers were slightly delayed because there were no available horses—an embarrassing fact since Van Dorn's outfit was cavalry. The officer explains this quirk as bad timing; he claims that several riders were out delivering messages at the time.

Within minutes, however, Van Dorn's men managed to find horses and search parties went out in all directions. One search party included Captain Hanson, who later said he found parts of fences removed along Peters' escape path. From this, he deduced that Peters had planned his escape route ahead of time. Van Dorn's murder, it appeared, wasn't an argument that turned violent. It was an assassination.

Van Dorn's men failed to nab Peters, who successfully crossed the lines into Union territory and made it to Nashville, where he showed up at the Union Office of Army Police and spilled his guts about the murder.

"I arrived at my home on the 12th of April and was alarmed at the distressing rumors which prevailed in the neighborhood in relation to the attentions paid by General Van Dorn to my wife," Peters claimed. "I was soon convinced of his intentional guilt, although a doubt still lingered in on my mind as to the guilt of my wife."[19]

According to Peters, he personally witnessed several "incidents" that "confirmed the guilt of General Van Dorn," including one time when he intercepted a note from Van Dorn to his wife. After reading the note, Peters threatened to kill the messenger, literally. "I distinctly told him I would blow his brains out if he ever entered the premises again," Peters said, "and to tell his whiskey-headed master, General Van Dorn, that I would blow his brains out, or any of his staff that stepped their foot inside of the lawn"[20]

Van Dorn, Peters said, didn't heed his warning. When he returned from Nashville on April 22, he heard rumors of Van Dorn spending every night in his wife's company, so he set up a ruse to catch them in flagrante delicto. He told Jesse that he was headed to Shelbyville, but instead hid out at his estate and waited.

"The second night after my supposed and pretended absence, I came upon the creature, about half-past two o'clock at night, where I expected to find him," the doctor said.[21] Peters planned to kill Van Dorn on the spot, but the terrified general offered to write a letter "to exonerate my wife from dishonor and to inculpate himself completely"[22]

On the morning of May 7, Peters said, he called on Van Dorn for the letter. The general balked but eventually consented. After a brief time with pen and paper, however, Van Dorn had written only a partial confession, so an argument erupted. Peters again threatened to shoot him if he didn't write the letter. Van Dorn scoffed, "You damned cowardly dog, take that door, or I will kick you out of it."[23]

"I immediately drew my pistol," Peters said, "aiming to shoot him in the forehead, when, by a convulsive movement of his head, he received the shot in the left side of his head just above the ear, killing him instantly. I picked up the scroll he had written, for evidence."[24] And then Peters made his getaway, eventually turning himself in.

Peters's account didn't seem to fit with the facts. No one heard an argument. As the unnamed officer cited in *A Soldier's Honor* would later point out, if there had been a row, Van Dorn wouldn't have turned his back. Perhaps the most damning piece of evidence was that Van Dorn was shot in the back of the head, not above the left ear, as Peters claimed. The doctor said he shot Van Dorn while facing him, but the evidence indicated that instead, he tip-toed behind the general and shot him from point-blank range.

Nonetheless, Peters would avoid any official punishment. He requested a pardon for the crime, claiming that he was defending the honor of his home. Neither Union nor Confederate officials charged him. In fact, the Confederate governor of Tennessee, Isham G. Harris, pardoned him for the murder. Dr. George Peters never spent a single day behind bars for the killing.

He did, though, fear an unofficial punishment. He apparently worried about a reprisal from one of Van Dorn's friends. While in Nashville, Peters checked into the boardinghouse of Ben Weller. The house was full, and Peters spent the night with another boarder. In an anonymous letter dated 1901, that man told a strange tale about his sleepless night with the infamous murderer.

Dr. Peters told his roommate about the killing and his subsequent dash for Nashville. "His conversation was rational," wrote the boarder, "but he labored under great mental excitement, and expressed a fear that some friend of General Van Dorn in Nashville would assassinate him if he stayed in that city."[25]

After reassuring Peters that no one would attempt to gun him down inside a Union-controlled city, the man fell asleep. A half hour later, he was roused by the sound of a gunshot. He turned on the gas lamps and found Peters, now in a near panic, against the wall holding a pistol and "shaking like that of one with palsy" Peters said that he saw an assassin at the window and shot at him.

"He then talked in a wild crazy way. I tried to reassure him nobody had shot at him; that it was an hallucination; but I could not," the man wrote. "I then regarded him as temporarily insane, and sat up with him the remainder of the night, as he would not give up his pistol."[26]

While Dr. Peters feared for his life, Van Dorn was given a hero's burial. Because Van Dorn's hometown in Mississippi had fallen to the Federals, he was buried in a plot belonging to his in-laws in Mount Vernon, Alabama. A few glorified Van Dorn. The *Mobile Register and Advertiser* described Van Dorn as "every inch a soldier" and quoted an eyewitness who saw the funeral procession and the "grand casket in which the dead hero lay" and "thought with sorrow of the handsome face still in death and the heart-broken wife thus cruelly widowed."[27]

Others vilified the general. One Tennessee newspaper reporter, writing in the *Fayetteville* [Tennessee] *Observer* on June 4, 1863, described the cavalier as "unfit to live." Another described him "as a rake, a most wicked libertine—and more especially of late. If he had led a virtuous life, he would not have died the death of a dog—'unwept, unhonored, and unsung.'"[28]

Even in death, the glory Van Dorn craved would elude him. Farther north in Virginia, the beloved Stonewall Jackson had died of pneumonia on May 10, just a few days after Van Dorn's demise, capturing headlines across the nation. News of Jackson's death made Van Dorn's murder back-page fodder. The timing led to the inevitable comparison between the two generals—one a devoutly religious man, the other an alleged philanderer.

"Think of the universal respect paid to the lamented Jackson," wrote one reporter. "The whole country is filled with mourning and tears at his death, while no man expresses even a regret at the fate of Van Dorn. Here is a striking illustration of the difference between sin and righteousness— between the devotion of a man's life to the most infamous and debasing of all human vices and the most commendable and elevating Christian virtues. The country has sustained no loss in the death of Van Dorn. It is a happy riddance. He was unfit to live, let alone having charge of such important trusts as he had."[29]

The coverage was so anti-Van Dorn that his own staff officers wrote a letter attempting to clear his name. In the note, which was published by the *Mobile Advertiser and Register*, the officers declared that Van Dorn and Mrs. Peters were innocent of any affair. They also blame some newspapers for publishing "false rumors" that were "injurious to the living and to the dead"[30]

Dr. Peters may have escaped prosecution in Tennessee, but he was still a wanted man in the Confederacy. During a visit to a relative in Mississippi in the fall of 1863, he was apprehended by a Texan named Lt. Dan Alley. Peters thought that the soldiers would avenge Van Dorn's murder with a lynching, but he made it to court in one piece. He went before a judge, but after a brief hearing, was released.

Dr. Peters later returned to Jesse, but she booted him off her plantation. She denied the affair and denounced her husband as a murderer, refusing to live with him. Shortly after this separation, they divorced. A few years later, though, they reconciled, living as husband and wife until George died in 1889.

According to Van Dorn's sister Emily, Peters spent the rest of his life in "mortal terror" of a bullet from one of Van Dorn's friends, and at least one attempt at revenge was made. "At one time a pistol ball passed through the pillow on which he was sleeping," Emily wrote.[31]

Jesse lived another thirty-two years, dying in 1921. Although to her final day she steadfastly denied any illicit relationship with Van Dorn, she couldn't undo the gossip caused by those carriage rides.

The Van Dorn murder isn't a whodunit—all the sources agree that Dr. Peters pulled the trigger. The real mystery involves what transpired in those minutes during which the doctor and the general were behind closed doors together. Since the murder occurred without an eyewitness, and since the murder of a luminary always gives birth to a conspiracy theory or two, there has been a great deal of speculation about those few minutes and Dr. Peters's motive for the crime.

In his statement, Dr. Peters suggested that the killing occurred during a heated argument after Van Dorn refused to sign the document Peters requested. Dr. Peters said he shot Van Dorn in the side of the head, but more than one person said that Van Dorn was shot in the back of the head, casting doubt on Peters's story.

According to the account related in *A Soldier's Honor*, as Van Dorn began writing the pass, Dr. Peters asked if he could pour himself a glass of water from the pitcher on the table behind the general's desk. Instead, he slipped behind Van Dorn and shot him in the back of the head. He grabbed the pass that Van Dorn had just inked and went straight for his getaway horse.

As for motive, Van Dorn's friends didn't buy the story that Dr. Peters was defending the sanctity of his home. They believed there was a more sinister motive behind it all. They believed that Dr. Peters colluded with Federal authorities in an assassination plot to off one of the Confederacy's top men in the area.

Advocates of this theory note that Peters owned land in Arkansas that Union forces had confiscated. In exchange for having his land returned, Dr. Peters agreed to do the dirty work. "It is stated," Emily Van Dorn Miller writes in *A Soldier's Honor*, "that the assassin went at once to Nashville to claim his reward, and it is a fact that his plantation on the banks of the Mississippi, which had been confiscated, was soon recovered, and he remained upon it until his death"[32]

The officers who defended Van Dorn's reputation in the newspapers also alluded to this theory, saying "for our own part, we are led to believe that there were other and darker motives"[33] As for evidence of these darker motives, they note that Dr. Peters had made an enigmatic comment prior to the murder, "that he had lost his land and negroes in Arkansas, but he thought he would shortly do something which would get them back."[34] It was also suspicious, they said, that Dr. Peters had sworn allegiance to the Union just two weeks prior to the murder.

A variant on this theory has Jesse acting as a witting accomplice. In this version, the oh-so-beautiful yet treacherous wife of an older man set the rumor mill churning through her public appearances with the little general. This gave her husband the "sanctity of home" motive. Proponents of this theory note that Jesse later remarried her husband after a cooling-off period to avoid any suspicion.

Another fanciful theory has Dr. Peters catching Van Dorn with his pants down. In this scenario, Peters murders the general on the spot, flees the vicinity, and concocts a cover story to beat the rap. To avoid further scandal, Van Dorn's men move the body to his office and then cry bloody murder.

There is another minor mystery concerning the Van Dorn murder: the location of the crime scene. Writers can't agree where the shooting took place. Some accounts place the incident inside the Spring Hill mansion of Nathaniel Cheairs. Others say it took place in a smaller home in the town.

Van Dorn biographer Arthur Carter presents a third possibility, based on statements made fifty years after the murder by the general's aide, Manning Kimmel. Kimmel's version of the shooting is similar to the story told by the anonymous officer in *A Soldier's Honor*, with two key differences: time and place. According to Kimmel, the crime took place on the evening of May 6 (not the morning of May 7) in a cabin on the Peters plantation about six miles from town (not at the Cheairs home in Spring Hill). Van Dorn had been using the structure as a temporary headquarters.

According to Carter, there is an explanation for these major discrepancies. Kimmel left out a key part of the story: Eager to avoid controversy and protect Van Dorn's legacy, his officers took his body to the Cheairs residence in Spring Hill. It's a fascinating theory, but as Carter acknowledges, "it cannot be substantiated at this day and time."[35]

Van Dorn's legacy included five children by two women and possibly a sixth by a third; there have been whispers that his progeny may have included Medora Wharton Peters. Jesse's daughter was born eight and a half months after Van Dorn's murder.[36] The timing would be about right if the pair had had an affair during the spring of 1863.

In 1899, Earl Van Dorn's body was exhumed and transported to his native Mississippi for reburial. When the casket arrived, it was opened. Even as a corpse, Earl Van Dorn was quite an impressive sight. Emily Van Dorn Miller described her brother's body. The general was still in uniform after three decades spent six feet under: "after an internment of thirty and more years the grave disclosed his soft, light hair, and all the emblems of his rank—the belt, buckle, buttons, and epaulettes of his military clothing."[37]

CHAPTER 10

No Quarter: Bedford Forrest and the Fort Pillow Massacre
1864

On a drizzly April afternoon, one of the worst atrocities of the war—a mass murder allegedly perpetrated by rebel soldiers—took place at a lazy bend in the Mississippi River.

"I saw one of them shoot a black fellow in the head with three buck shot and musket ball," a survivor of Fort Pillow later recalled. "The man held up his head, and then the fellow took his pistol and fired that at his head. The black man still moved, and then the fellow took his saber and stuck it in the hole in the negro's head and jammed it way down, and said 'Now, God damn you, die!'"[1]

The incident became known as "The Fort Pillow Massacre," and the "fellow" was supposedly under the command of Confederate horse soldier Nathan Bedford Forrest.

But was this murder most foul, or was it political propaganda? Or both?

A native of Tennessee, Nathan Bedford Forrest didn't have a formal education, but he had a certain saddle sense that earned him the nickname "The Wizard in the Saddle." He suffered from boils on his backside, which made it miserable to mount a horse, but that didn't harm his reputation. The "massacre" at Fort Pillow did.

Whether Forrest knew about, condoned, or even ordered the slaughter of surrendering soldiers remains a bone of contention among Civil War buffs and historians, but the damage has been done. The Fort Pillow Massacre has become one of the defining moments in the colorful and controversial career of Gen. Nathan Bedford Forrest.

Forrest was born in a log cabin near Chapel Hill, Tennessee, on July 13, 1821, the first of William Forrest's dozen children. As the eldest child of a frontier blacksmith, Forrest grew up knowing privation and sacrifice. He occasionally went to school, but more often than not, he was needed at home to help the family make ends meet. At the time, Tennessee was the frontier, and life was a tug-of-war between the elements and human endurance. Five of Forrest's siblings, including his twin sister, didn't survive to adulthood, suffering premature deaths from typhoid fever.

The stories about Forrest's youth illustrate the derring-do that would later make him a legend on horseback. One story has the young Forrest killing a rattlesnake that threatened a group of children picking berries.[2] Another incident taught the future general about boldness—a lesson he would apply during the war. One of Forrest's former soldiers, John Allan Wyeth, later wrote a biography about Forrest in which he describes the incident in detail. Forrest, like many other pioneer boys, mastered horse riding at a young age. While he was out riding, a neighbor's two dogs chased after his horse. The mount threw its young rider to the ground. Sure that the two canines would shred him when he landed, Forrest was shocked when the dogs, afraid of the horse, ran away.

According to Wyeth, Forrest later said the incident taught him a valuable lesson: "He had learned there the value of a bold attack, even when he knew he was inferior in strength to the enemy."[3]

William Forrest died in 1837, leaving his fifteen-year-old son in charge of his mother and siblings. Forrest made a go at farming and raising cattle, accumulating a significant herd. It was the beginning of a rags-to-riches tale.

In 1842, he went to work with his uncle Jonathan in Hernando, Mississippi, as a cattle broker. Their partnership ended abruptly in 1845, when a violent scuffle—the climax of a feud—occurred between the Forrests and the four Matlock brothers. Jonathan Forrest was killed in the fray, but not even a lead slug could stop Nathan, who gunned down two of the Matlocks and wounded the other two with a Bowie knife.

Undeterred by the loss of his uncle and business partner, Forrest continued in the cattle business. His fortune snowballed after he invested his profits in cotton plantations and opened a slave-brokerage firm. An acquaintance later described Forrest as "kind, humane, and extremely considerate of his slaves"[4]

He also had a sort of reckless bravery. When Forrest lived in Memphis, a sensational murder took place. An inflamed lynch mob formed and stormed the Memphis jail. Forrest, armed only with his knife, wedged himself between the prisoner and mob. At six feet two and a husky 210 pounds, he was a physically imposing figure, made even more intimidating by the Bowie knife he usually carried. Brandishing the blade, he threatened to kill any man who rushed the prisoner. No one apparently questioned his intent, and the mob dispersed.[5]

By the late 1850s, the eldest son of a frontier blacksmith had become a major player in the antebellum South. He owned a large population of slaves, dabbled in local politics, and had amassed a fortune. When the war began, thirty-nine-year-old Nathan Bedford Forrest was a self-made millionaire and one of the richest men in the South.

In June 1861, the millionaire cotton planter enlisted as a private in Tennessee. This raised more than a few eyebrows, since wealthy planters were exempt from military service. Forrest's bravado caught the eye of Tennessee governor Isham Harris, and he was promoted to colonel and given his own regiment, "Forrest's Tennessee Cavalry Battalion," which he equipped largely from his own funds.

Forrest's horse sense and uncanny knack for cavalry tactics made him one of the war's most successful leaders, a soldier who defied odds and defeated opponents of vastly superior numbers. Southern generals turned to him; Northern generals turned away from him, if possible.

By 1864, Forrest had become a brigadier general and a living legend. He and his troops, both black and white horse soldiers, had fought and prevailed in various engagements, but a falling out with Gen. Braxton Bragg led Forrest to request reassignment; he was sent to northern Mississippi.

By the spring of 1864, Tennessee had become a battleground in more ways than one. The Volunteer State had hosted battles such as Stones River and the siege of Chattanooga, and guerrillas like Champ Ferguson and Dave Beatty harassed and terrorized people along the border with Kentucky.

Tennesseans were also deeply divided on this issue of secession. A majority of residents in East Tennessee remained pro-Union; while the majority in West Tennessee favored secession. Pockets of Union supporters existed all over the state. Occupying Union soldiers also foraged resources from the area, which to the locals seemed more like theft. "While at Jackson and other points in West Tennessee," Forrest later said, "I learned, from I believed to be reliable sources, that the Tennessee troops under Major Bradford, at Fort Pillow, had pillaged the whole country."[6]

Confederate soldiers also heard stories like that of the murder and mutilation of a rebel soldier allegedly perpetrated by Union forces under the command of Col. Fielding Hurst. The unfortunate rebel grunt was "left to die after cutting off his tongue, punching out his eyes, splitting his mouth on each side to his ears, and inflicting other mutilations."[7]

Into this mix of loyalties, uncertainty, and animosity trotted Nathan Bedford Forrest and his horse soldiers. In the spring of 1864, Forrest led a series of raids—hit-and-run operations designed to harass the enemy—into Union-controlled West Tennessee. Many of his soldiers despised the white

Tennesseans who enlisted with the Union, known as "homegrown Yankees" or "Tennessee Tories," and felt an equal disgust for the blacks who wore blue. This was the situation when Forrest's men attacked the tiny garrison at Fort Pillow on April 12, 1864.

Fort Pillow was a fortification about forty miles upriver from Memphis. Originally constructed by Confederate brigadier general Gideon Johnson Pillow, the fort fell into Union hands when the rebels abandoned it as Federal forces took control of the area in 1862. Sited on a bluff overlooking the Mississippi, the fort provided an ideal spot to protect Union-occupied Memphis from gunboats moving north on the river.

An assault on the fort would literally be an uphill battle. Attackers would first need to bypass two lines of defense: The fort itself, which consisted of eight-foot-tall walls, and a moatlike trench twelve feet long and six feet deep. Spring showers turned the ditch into a swamp of muddy water.

A besieging army would also have to overcome a force of well-armed men. On the morning of April 12, a garrison of 557 soldiers—295 white and 262 black—manned the parapets under the command of Maj. L. F. Booth.[8] The garrison included the Thirteenth Tennessee Battalion—the "Homemade Yankees" so despised among the Tennessee Confederates.

Adding to the security of the fort, a Federal gunboat named *New Era* hovered in the river, ready to repel any assault with its cannon. Federal authorities believed that Fort Pillow could survive a siege for two days—long enough for reinforcements to arrive. But they didn't count on Forrest.

At about 5:30 in the morning of April 12, after a lengthy ride through a light rain, about fifteen hundred Confederate soldiers under the command of Brig. Gen. James Chalmers arrived at Fort Pillow. An intense firefight followed.

By 9 A.M., the rebels had beaten the Union soldiers back inside the fort. They took cover behind trees, and sharpshooters took up positions on high ground around the fort. The Federal forces, outgunned and outmanned three to one, were fish in a barrel. At some point, both Major Booth and his adjutant were killed, leaving the defense of the fort to a young, inexperienced officer named Maj. William Bradford.

An hour later, Forrest himself reached Fort Pillow after a hard ride from Mississippi. Not one to shy away from a fight, Forrest rode up close to the action to survey the scene. A volley of Federal fire struck Forrest's horse, throwing him to the ground. Undaunted, he climbed onto another horse, which was also shot out from under him. For a second time, he mounted a new horse and looked over the scene.

For the next few hours, rebel soldiers crept closer to the inner fort, picking off defenders from the adjacent bluffs. The *New Era* shelled the Confederate lines, but by 1 P.M. it had used almost all of its ammunition and moved into the river to cool its guns.

By 3:30 P.M., Forrest concluded that the Union soldiers could no longer hold the fort, and under a flag of truce, he sent a note asking Major Booth to surrender. He praised the gallantry of the defenders and said they would be treated as prisoners-of-war, then added an ultimatum: "My men have received a fresh supply of ammunition, and from their present position can easily assault and capture the fort. Should my demand be refused, I cannot be responsible for the fate of your command."[9]

The exact wording of Forrest's threat differs according to the source. Forrest later said in an 1868 interview that during this exchange with the fort's authorities "I stated that the animosity existing between the Tennessee troops in my command and the Tennessee troops at the fort was such that I could not be responsible for the fate of the garrison."[10]

Meanwhile, during the cease-fire, soldiers inside Fort Pillow noticed men moving closer to the stockade, which later led to allegations that Forrest abused the flag of truce to gain field position. The other side of the allegation is that the Confederates had already obtained strategic positions in the ravines close to the fort before the flag of truce was called, and that the movement noticed by the fort's garrison was instead a group of Confederates pulling back from a position they already held.[11]

Since Booth had been killed in action six hours earlier, command decisions had fallen to Major Bradford. He sent a note to Forrest, which he signed in Booth's name, asking for an hour to mull over his options.

Forrest decided to give him twenty minutes instead and sent a note to "Booth." He had seen smoke coming from around the bend on the river and, he later said, believed that "Booth" was attempting to buy time in order for reinforcements to arrive.[12]

While the two commanders exchanged notes, the garrison and the rebel soldiers, now just a stone's throw apart, began tossing epithets and insults at each other. According to several Confederate officers, Fort Pillow's soldiers were buoyed by liquid courage; Bradford had given them free use of the fort's liquor stores.[13]

After a few minutes, Forrest received word from Fort Pillow. "I will not surrender," Bradford (or rather Booth, since this note was also in his name) said. He had already made plans for a worst-case scenario. Bradford and Capt. James Marshall of the *New Era*, through signals, had worked out an escape plan. If the garrison failed to hold the fort, they would flee down the bluff at the fort's back side to the river's edge where the gunboat would support their retreat.[14]

The assault on the breastworks began immediately. Within minutes, Forrest's men had crawled through the mud-filled ditch and had begun scaling the walls of the inner fort. From the tops of the walls, they fired at the defenders from point-blank range.

As the rebel troops clambered over the earth wall and into Fort Pillow, the decimated garrison fled down the slope toward the Mississippi River, where they may have expected covering fire from the *New Era*. But the gunboat remained floating in mid-river and didn't engage.

Captain Marshall later defended his decision to stay away from the action. The steamboat didn't have enough ammunition left to repulse the rebels, he said, and he feared that the rebs would fire on his boat with Fort Pillow's cannons, so he kept his distance.[15]

Surrounded by Confederate soldiers, the garrison had nowhere to run, except into the river. What happened next, on back side of the bluff, became the subject of hearsay and allegation later known as the "Fort Pillow Massacre."

According to many eyewitness accounts, the decimated, exhausted, and terrified survivors of Fort Pillow's garrison threw down their weapons and surrendered, at which point the "secesh" soldiers began to slaughter the men. Although both black and white soldiers died in the "massacre," contemporary retellings indict the rebels for targeting the garrison's black soldiers. "Kill all the niggers," some of the rebels screamed, according to one eyewitness.[16]

"I was going up the hill," Daniel Tyler, a black soldier who survived the incident, later recalled. "A man came down and met me; he had his gun in his hand, and whirled it around and knocked me down, and then he took the end of his carbine and jabbed it in my eye, and shot me."[17]

"The slaughter was awful. Words cannot describe the scene," Sgt. Achilles Smith wrote in a letter home. Smith was a soldier from Tennessee who fought for the Confederacy. "The poor, deluded negroes would run up to our men, fall upon their knees and with uplifted hands scream for mercy but they were ordered to their feet and then shot down."[18]

In a note to Gen. Leonidas Polk, Forrest described the battle as a total victory. He said that the exact number of Union dead may never be known, because some of the men ran into the river and were shot or drowned, or both. "The river was dyed with the blood of the slaughtered for 200 yards," Forrest said.[19]

According to some survivors, the murdering continued throughout the night and into the next morning, but by nightfall, Forrest's troops had left the scene. They returned at daybreak the next morning and set fire to the barracks on Forrest's orders.

Just after eight on the morning of April 13, a flag of truce was called, and Union soldiers from gunboats on the Mississippi came ashore to tend to the wounded and bury the dead. They found a revolting scene: a line of hands and feet jutting out of the soil. The Confederate soldiers, it appeared, had tossed the bodies of the dead into one of the trenches and covered them with a thin layer of dirt.

The sickly sweet stench of burning flesh filled the air as the crew began to disinter the bodies for reburial. The source of the smell was the nearby tents, which the rebels had set on fire, apparently with men—either dead or alive (accounts vary)—inside. Eli Bangs, the *New Era*'s master's mate who came ashore the day after the battle, later described one of the charred bodies. "He lay on his back, with his arms stretched out. Part of his arms were burned off, and his legs were burned nearly to a crisp," Bangs related.[20]

Bangs and his mates slid a few board planks under the corpse to move it. When they lifted it from the floor of the tent, Bangs noticed "that nails had been driven through his clothes and his cartridge box, so as to fasten him to the floor."[21]

Another burned man, later identified as Private Ackerstrom of the Thirteenth Tennessee, was supposedly nailed down, crucifix-style, with nails through his hands and feet.

After the dust from the battle settled, the rumor mill began to churn out shocking allegations. Rebel troops back-shot soldiers who jumped into the river; they raised wounded soldiers to their feet before shooting them down again; they hacked men to death with their sabers; they burned men alive, nailing men to barrels before igniting them. When the killing was done, they threw the bodies into a mass grave and tossed a thin layer of dirt over them. In some cases, they didn't wait for a soldier to die; macabre stories of twitching hands and feet jutting out of hasty burial pits began to make the rounds.

Stories also circulated about rebel officers bragging about, and then toasting, the slaughter with their Union counterparts onboard Federal gunboats after the battle. And, rumor had it, Major Bradford, who disappeared after the battle, was murdered in cold blood by his rebel captors.

Bradford, in fact, was captured at Fort Pillow. He later escaped but was caught before he got very far. When being transported to Forrest's headquarters, he was shot. Some on the Union side said that the hated "homegrown" major was taken into the woods and executed. But according to Forrest, in a note he wrote to Confederate general C. C. Washburn in June 1864, he received a report that Bradford was shot while trying another escape.[22]

Newspapers screamed that bloody murder had occurred at the tiny fort on the Mississippi. The *New York Times* headline of April 16, 1864, proclaimed "Horrible Massacre by the Rebels. Fort Pillow Captured After a Desperate Fight. Four Hundred of the Garrison Brutally Murdered. Wounded and Unarmed Men Bayoneted and Their Bodies Burned. White and Black Indiscriminately Butchered. Devilish Atrocities of the Insatiate Fiends."[23]

Word of the alleged massacre reached Congress, and the Joint Committee on the Conduct of the War authorized an official investigation on April 21, 1864—just nine days after the battle. The two-man team of Representative Daniel Gooch and Senator Benjamin Wade traveled throughout Union territory to interview eyewitnesses and survivors, who were all from the North.

Gooch and Wade spoke with key players; they also solicited information from soldiers who heard about the "massacre" secondhand, such as doctors who treated survivors and soldiers who heard rumors.

At Mound City, Illinois, the investigators interviewed a surgeon named Horace Wardner who wasn't at Fort Pillow but was treating several black survivors. Wardner, a battlefield doctor, described the survivors as "the worst butchered men I have ever seen." He also noted that the men claimed they had received their wounds after they surrendered.[24]

Wardner told a hair-raising anecdote about a little boy, a contraband, who was in Fort Pillow's infirmary with a fever. "The rebels entered the hospital, and with a saber hacked his head, no doubt with the intention of splitting it open," Dr. Wardner explained. "The boy put up his hand to protect his head, and they cut off one or two of his fingers."[25] The boy survived the alleged attack but died under Wardner's care the day before Gooch and Wade interviewed him. Warder conducted a postmortem and found that the boy had been stuck in the head with such force that a piece of his skull was driven into his brain.

The congressional detectives questioned several black troops who, unlike the surgeon, had lived through the fight at Fort Pillow. Daniel Tyler, a private from Company B of the Sixth U.S. Heavy Artillery, claimed that the rebels shot him after he had surrendered. Then, he said, they buried him alive. "I lay there till about sundown," Tyler told Gooch, "when they threw us in a hollow, and commenced throwing dirt on us."[26]

The terrified private played possum, but the rebels realized that he was still alive. "I hard them say they ought not to bury a man who was alive," Tyler recalled. The rebels then pulled him out of the trench.[27]

George Shaw, another black private from Company B, said that a rebel soldier approached him and yelled, "Damn you, what are you doing here?"

"Please don't shoot me," Shaw pleaded.

"Damn you," the soldier replied, "you are fighting against your master." And then he shot Shaw in the face.

Although most noncombatants were evacuated before the battle started, a few were caught in the middle of the melee. Shaw claimed to have witnessed the murder of three teenaged "contraband boys" who were gunned down while in the river.[28] Dr. Black claimed to have treated a soldier's wife named Mary Jane Robinson who had been shot in both of her knees.[29]

Gooch and Wade also interviewed white soldiers who survived Fort Pillow. John Penwell, a volunteer from Detroit, said he was shot after he surrendered. "I threw my musket down. A fellow who was ahead asked 'if I surrendered.' I said 'Yes.' He said, 'Die, then, you damned Yankee son of a bitch,' and shot me, and I fell." According to Penwell, a few Confederates later stripped him of his clothes, his boots, and about $50 in Union greenbacks.[30]

Others eyewitnesses said they saw men nailed to barrels and burned alive; others said they saw other atrocities. Their stories varied in the details, but one thing remained consistent: Just about all of the men who spoke about the massacre claimed to have received their wounds after they surrendered.

Just shy of two weeks after they began, Gooch and Wade submitted their report, which has over time become as controversial as the alleged massacre. The pair didn't interview one single person from the South, they ignored obvious contradictions in eyewitness testimony, and they spoke to many people who heard about but didn't see the massacre in person. The result, according to some historians, is an exaggeration of what really happened. Others claim the report, although a vehicle of political propaganda, is substantively accurate on one point. There are just too many voices from both sides, they argue, to deny that some of the soldiers were murdered in cold blood.

Gooch and Wade concluded that "the atrocities committed at Fort Pillow were not the results of passions excited by the heat of conflict, but were the results of" a deliberate policy. The report vilified Forrest, and described the "Fort Pillow Massacre" as "a scene of cruelty and murder without a parallel in civilized warfare, which needed but the tomahawk and scalping-knife to exceed the worst atrocities ever committed by savages."[31]

Gooch and Wade described their trip to the scene of the crimes. "We could still see the faces, hands, and feet of men, white and black, protruding out of the ground, whose graves had not been reached by those engaged in re-interring the victims of the massacre," they said, and added that even though it had rained in the two-week interval between the battle and their visit, "the ground at the foot of the bluff where the most of the murders had been committed, was still discolored by the blood of our brave but unfortunate men"[32]

Their stirring report made interesting reading, and forty thousand copies were ordered for use by the members of the House. The report provided powerful ammunition for the upcoming November election. An official account of rebel crimes might strengthen the resolve of a war-weary public.

Since that drizzly day in April 1864, the "massacre" at Fort Pillow has been examined and reexamined from both Southern and Northern perspectives. The voices from the time, while partisan and often exaggerated for effect, tend to agree that something foul happened at Fort Pillow.

Confederate brigadier general Tyree Bell pointed the finger at the drunken garrison and Major Bradford and called the reports of a massacre a "tissue of lies from end to end."[33] Another man under Forrest at Fort Pillow, Col. Clarke Russell Barteau, described the garrison as "in a frenzy of excitement and drunken delirium. Some even, who had thrown down their arms, took them up again and continued firing."[34]

One alternate theory of the event, supported in part by a few soldiers Gooch and Wade interviewed and described in detail by Wyeth, has an entirely different feel to it than the massacre depicted in the congressional report. It goes something like this.

The Union soldiers fled from the fort down the bluff, where they intended to hold their position until the *New Era* arrived (after the fight, Confederate soldiers found a cache of more than 250 rifles apparently left for the continuation of the battle).

When the Union soldiers realized the *New Era* couldn't support their retreat, they panicked. Some soldiers, inebriated from Fort Pillow's liquor stores, continued to shoot at the rebels; others dropped their weapons and surrendered; and some continued their futile flight into the river. In the confusion that followed, soldiers from both sides continued to shoot at each other, and some men who tried to surrender died in the crossfire.

Even Forrest biographer Wyeth admits that some men were shot trying to surrender. "A number who had thrown their guns away, holding up their hands, ran up towards the Confederates on the bluff and were spared, while others who did this were shot down."[35]

Even though one Union soldier told of Forrest riding over his body with a horse and another claimed to have seen Forrest amidst the slaughter, there is no concrete evidence that Forrest ordered or condoned the carnage, or that Forrest's ultimatum to Major Booth was anything other than an intimidation tactic designed to scare the remaining soldiers into surrendering. In fact, the soldiers who Gooch and Wade interviewed only heard talk of Forrest ordering "no quarter" secondhand.

"I heard several of them (Confederate soldiers) say it was General Forrest's orders to them to shoot us and give us no quarter at all," Commissary Sergeant Daniel Stamps recalled.[36]

"The general cry from the time they charged the fort until an hour afterwards," recalled James Stamps, another soldier from the Thirteenth

Tennessee, "was, 'Kill 'em, kill 'em; God damn 'em; that's Forrest's orders, not to leave one alive."[37]

Other soldiers said things that contradicted the image of a bloodthirsty Forrest bent on murder of the fort's black soldiers. Pvt. Major Williams, a black artillerist, said that he heard a rebel officer yell "Kill all the niggers," and another officer respond, "No; Forrest says take them and carry them with him to wait upon him and cook for him, and put them in jail and send them to their masters."[38]

Confederate eyewitnesses go a step further, claiming Forrest demanded that the shooting stop. One Confederate officer, Lt. J. L. Knox, later said that Forrest rode up to the scene and ordered the firing to cease. Dr. W. J. Robinson said that after Forrest's order, the shooting stopped.[39]

But there is a possibility that neither Forrest nor any of his officers were in control of the situation during the massacre. Lt. William Clary told Gooch that he spoke with Col. James Chalmers, one of the rebel officers in the engagement, after the fight. "He concluded that he could not control his men very well, and thought it was justifiable in regard to negroes; that they did not recognize negroes as soldiers, and he could not control his men."[40]

After the engagement, Confederate soldiers directed Union survivors to bury the dead, so if anyone was buried alive, Wyeth notes, it was done by their own men.[41] And if anyone was buried alive, he suggests, it was because they were dead drunk or playing possum.[42]

As for the allegations that men, such as Private Ackerstrom, were burned alive, Wyeth calls them "so absurd as to scarcely call for notice"[43] He cites statements from John Ray, Ackerstrom's comrade in the Thirteenth Tennessee. Ray said he saw Ackerstrom fall from a bullet. Wyeth also notes that since fierce fighting occurred around one section of barracks that was torched by the garrison, it is likely that some of the dead bodies were seared.[44]

One Confederate officer, Capt. Walter Goodman, later suggested that when the rebels set fire to the fort's remaining structures the day after the battle, some of the dead may have been burned as a result, and "this probably gave rise to the horrible stories about burning wounded prisoners which were afterward invented and circulated."[45]

Wyeth presents another explanation for the alleged atrocities of the massacre: They took place after dark. He suggests that by nightfall of April 12, the Confederates had abandoned Fort Pillow, leaving the wounded in the care of a surgeon. If any atrocities occurred between nightfall on the twelfth and early morning on the thirteenth—when Union soldiers came ashore to bury their dead and tend to their wounded—they were done by "guerrillas, robbers, or murderers" not associated with Forrest's army.[46]

Clary's comments and Wyeth's version of events suggest that the massacre may not have resulted from the policy of a bloodthirsty general, as Gooch and Wade's report concluded. It didn't matter. The congressional report, abetted by Northern news reporters, pinned the massacre on Nathan Bedford Forrest, and the Confederate cavalier became a demonic villain of epic proportions.

The controversial cavalry general avoided Federal bullets during the war and a war-crimes trial after it, but he never lived down the alleged atrocity. The "Fort Pillow Massacre" dogged Forrest for the rest of his life. In an 1868 interview, he offered his explanation of the events.

> There were with me many citizens who had been wronged, and, I think, without waiting for the surrender of the men who had wronged them and their families, they shot them down. When I found out they were doing this (understand this was during the twenty minutes of the engagement and not after the capture) I ordered it stopped; and was compelled to shoot one of my own men who did not obey me promptly.

Forrest concluded by stating, emphatically, "No man was killed after the capture by my order; and any killing that was done was without my knowledge."[47]

After the war, Nathan Bedford Forrest may have jumped back into the saddle as the head hood of the Klu Klux Klan. Confederate veterans formed the group in Tennessee sometime in 1866 or 1867. According to some sources, they turned to their ex-cavalry hero, Forrest, to lead them in their new "war." Although he denied even being involved with the Klan in 1868, many believe that the "Wizard of the Saddle" became the first Grand Wizard of the KKK.

Today, a century and a half later, Forrest and the battle at Fort Pillow remain divisive topics. The primary sources on Fort Pillow come from two opposite, strongly biased perspectives. Gooch and Wade presented a Northern Republican spin on the Fort Pillow incident, strategically timed for the 1864 elections. Early Forrest biographers, writing during the Lost Cause era, took a decidedly Southern viewpoint. Modern historians generally agree that "massacre" is the correct word for what happened below the bluffs of Fort Pillow and often point to the statistics: There was an unusually high casualty rate during the battle, and while Fort Pillow's garrison included roughly equal numbers of black and white troops, the rebels took three times as many white prisoners as black prisoners. What exactly these numbers indicate, and what really happened at Fort Pillow, remain the topics of an ongoing debate.

CHAPTER 11

Manhattan Burning: The Rebel Arson Plot 1864

In late November, 1864, a group of Confederate spies gathered at a small cottage near New York's Central Park. Their objective was to burn down New York City in retaliation for Gen. Philip Sheridan's scorched-earth campaign in Virginia's Shenandoah Valley. The plot was simple: overwhelm the local fire departments by setting ablaze as many buildings as possible. But their grand scheme was foiled by the smallest detail.

At about 6 P.M. on Friday, November 25, 1864, a shadowy group of Confederate agents met to discuss their plans to incinerate New York City's business district. Each agent slipped ten bottles of "Greek Fire" into the pockets of his overcoat and they headed off to their respective targets. Greek Fire was a nineteenth-century Molotov cocktail made from a highly flammable mixture of phosphorous and hydrogen sulfide.

The plot was simple. Each man had previously checked into rooms at various hotels in the heart of the city. They would start fires in their respective rooms by dousing the furniture with Greek Fire. The fires would spread, turning the hotels, adjacent buildings, and much of Manhattan to ash.

The "incendiaries," as contemporary news accounts later called the perpetrators, agreed to begin setting fires at exactly 8 P.M. According to one of the fire-starters, Confederate agent John Headley, the timing was vital. The former rebel spy, who devotes two chapters of his memoir to "the attempt to burn [the] business section of New York," explains that the conspirators chose 8 P.M. "so that the guests of hotels might all escape, as we did not want to destroy any lives."[1]

The attempt to incinerate Manhattan was the brainchild of Confederate colonel Robert Martin. The expedition was funded by Confederate senator Clement C. Clay and rebel spymaster Jacob Thompson, whose name is often in the byline of Confederate-engineered conspiracies aimed at the Union during the Civil War. They tabbed Martin to lead the eight-man force.

According to Headley, the plan was originally conceived as a giant diversionary tactic so the "Sons of Liberty," an underground network of Southern sympathizers, could take over New York and Chicago, establishing a "Northern Confederacy" in the Windy City. Authorities would be so busy trying to control the inferno they would not be capable of withstanding an attack from within. The coup would take place on election night—November 8, 1864.

In late October, a cadre of rebel agents visited New York City on a scouting mission to choose targets. The group included Martin, Headley, and Robert Cobb Kennedy, the man whose name would become forever linked with the plot. The "climax" of the trip, Headley notes, "was reached when a monster torchlight procession was formed to march the full length of Broadway, which was reviewed by General George B. McClellan."[2] About a month later, Headley and the others would attempt to engineer a "torchlight procession" of another kind.

But then the Confederate spies received news that Benjamin Butler—who by 1864 had earned the nickname "Beast" for his iron-fisted control of occupied New Orleans—had been stationed in New York with a detachment of thirty-five hundred men. New York newspapers carried front-page stories proclaiming Butler's arrival to safeguard the city against a possible rebel-led strike during the election. To make a bad situation worse for the Confederate plotters, Federal authorities had sniffed out and arrested some of Chicago's Sons of Liberty.

This news changed everything. Confederate agents thought twice about tangling with the Beast and his troops and shelved the plot for a later date. The plan itself had also changed, from a diversionary tactic to an act of revenge. Robert Cobb Kennedy later said the plan to burn New York in late November was payback for the "atrocities of Sheridan in the Shenandoah Valley." No one was supposed to get hurt, although Kennedy later admitted the possibility of collateral damage.[3]

According to Headley, the general idea was to "set the city on fire and give the people a scare if nothing else, and let the Government at Washington understand that burning homes in the South might find a counterpart in the North."[4]

They were going to fight fire with fire and send a smoke signal to Washington, but not everyone cared for the idea of a strike against a civilian target. Even some Confederate agents flinched at the idea. Nevertheless, the plan moved forward and a date selected. The Big Apple would go up in smoke on November 25, 1864.

With the date set, Headley fetched the "rotten eggs" that the group would use to destroy the city. These consisted of twelve dozen four-ounce bottles of foul-smelling Greek Fire. The chemist who mixed the potion placed the bottles in a large valise, which the unflappable Confederate agent took aboard a crowded New York City streetcar.

In one of the more humorous anecdotes in his memoirs, Headley describes the foul odor emanating from his carry-on. "I soon began to smell a peculiar odor—a little like rotten eggs—and I noticed the passengers were conscious of the same presence." As he departed, he overheard one of the car's passengers remark, "There must be something dead in that valise."[5]

At about six on the evening of November 25, the six spies met to divvy up their chemical weapons. Meanwhile, Manhattan was buzzing. It was Friday night, and it was "Evacuation Day," a holiday held near and dear to New Yorkers at the time. It was on November 25, 1783, that British forces had abandoned the city during the American Revolution.

There was further cause for celebration in the city: The North was winning the war. Ten days earlier, Sherman had begun his March to the Sea, leaving behind him a smoldering skeleton that was once Atlanta. The end seemed near.

While the city's residents engaged in Friday-night revelry, the arsonists went to work. Headley reached his first hotel, the Astor House, at about 8 P.M. as planned. "After lighting the gas jet I hung the bedclothes loosely on the headboard and piled the chairs, drawers of the bureau and washstand on the bed," Headley wrote.

He wadded up newspaper and poured turpentine over the pyre, then dumped a bottle of Greek Fire on it. "It blazed up instantly," Headley later recalled, "and the whole bed seemed to be in flames." Similar scenes were taking place in hotels up and down Broadway.[6]

From the Astor, Headley quickly made his way to the City Hotel and repeated the routine. From the City Hotel he went to the Everett House. Then he headed to the United States Hotel. On the way, he could see the flickering orange glow inside his room at the Astor House, but so far, no alarm had sounded. The plan appeared to be working perfectly. By the time anyone realized what was happening, it would be too late to control all the fires.

At about 9 P.M., fire bells erupted all over the business district. Headley managed to get to his room in the United States Hotel and set it on fire. While leaving his last assigned hotel, Headley noted, the clerk looked at him "a little curiously." This ominous glance would later come back to haunt the Southern spy.[7]

Detail of an 1855 engraving of New York City's business district. This area was the target of the 1864 rebel arson plot. One of the city's foremost tourist attractions, Barnum's American Museum, wasn't part of the plan but became a target of opportunity for Robert Cobb Kennedy. "I know that I am to be hung for setting fire to Barnum's Museum, but the fact is that that affair was simply a reckless joke," Kennedy said. "There was no fiendishness about it. The Museum was set on fire by merest accident, after I had been drinking, and just for the fun of the scare."
LIBRARY OF CONGRESS

After lighting a fire in the United States Hotel, Headley took a look around to watch the bedlam he and his cohorts had just created. "As I came back to Broadway," Headley recalled, "it seemed that a hundred bells were ringing, great crowds were gathering on the street, and there was general consternation."[8]

As he surveyed the scene, Headley noticed pandemonium at P. T. Barnum's Museum. Frantic New Yorkers were pouring out of the building. "People were coming out and down ladders from the second- and third-floor windows and the manager was crying out for help to get his animals out," Headley later said of the scene. "It looked like people were getting hurt running over each other in the stampede, and still I could not help some astonishment for I did not suppose there was a fire in the Museum."[9]

Headley was shocked because Barnum's Museum was not part of the plan. One of Headley's cohorts, Robert Cobb Kennedy, had gone off script and dashed a bottle of Greek Fire on a staircase in the museum.

While panicked people poured out of Barnum's, four rooms at the St. Nicholas were ablaze. Twenty minutes, later, fires were spotted in rooms at the La Farge House, followed by a conflagration at the Winter Garden Theatre adjacent to the hotel.

At ten, a fire was discovered at the Metropolitan Hotel. By this point, the particulars of the plot had become evident: Hotels up and down Broadway had been targeted and set on fire. The word spread faster than the flames and warnings went out to all the city's hotels. Pails filled with water were placed strategically throughout the lodging houses.

Constables on the lookout for anything suspicious collared a woman coming out of the Metropolitan and arrested her for questioning. The woman, a native of Baltimore, had been seen emerging from several of the hotels just before the fires erupted. Detectives later discovered that she was just an innocent bystander in the wrong place at the wrong time.

Delighted with the bedlam he helped create, Headley went down to the wharf. "I picked dark spots to stand in," he said, "and jerked a bottle in six different places. They were ablaze before I left." He was hoping that a half dozen bottles of Greek Fire would burn up the row of ships and barges tied closely together.[10]

After lighting up the boats, Headley ran into fellow incendiary Robert Cobb Kennedy on the street. Excitedly, the two coconspirators described their arson, including Kennedy's unplanned attack on Barnum's American Museum.

According to Headley, Kennedy said his decision to torch Barnum's was a last-minute improvisation. After he unleashed the Greek Fire in his hotel rooms, he said, he ducked into Barnum's. He was inside the museum when the fire bells sounded, so he joined a growing exodus to the street. While trotting down the stairway, Headley later recalled, Kennedy said "it occurred that it would be fun to start a scare."[11]

In his pocket, Kennedy had the four-ounce bomb to do it. He told Headley that he smashed one of the bottles on a step "like he would crack an egg." When the fluid mixed with the air, a blaze started.[12]

After swapping stories, the two arsonists walked to the heart of the action on Broadway, where a crowd had gathered. Headley describes the scene as "the wildest excitement imaginable. There was all sorts of talk about hanging the rebels to lamp posts or burning them at the stake."[13] As Headley soon found out, it was much ado about nothing.

The great plot to incinerate Manhattan had failed. Headley and the other plotters were shocked when they discovered that "the fires had been put out in all the places as easily as any ordinary fire."[14]

Several of the hotel rooms had been destroyed, but the flames failed to spread as planned. The actual destruction turned out to be minimal. The estimated damage to the four rooms at the St. Nicholas amounted to about

$3,000. The conspirators were left to ponder how their plan had turned into such a fiasco.

"It seemed to us," Headley concluded, "that there was something wrong with our Greek fire," or that the chemist had betrayed them "because of a disagreement about the plot."[15]

In his memoir, Headley admits that none of the arsonists knew much about the flammable substance, "except that the moment it was exposed to the air it would blaze and burn everything it touched."[16] So if the brew failed to "blaze," it must have been flawed.

But at the Metropolitan Hotel, detectives found a clue that suggested the Greek Fire wasn't the culprit that caused the plot's downfall. Inside one of the rooms, they found a "box of inflammatory material." They carefully removed the box and took it to police headquarters, "and after being exposed to air for a short time, [it] burst into flames."[17]

The concoction worked, if it was used properly. The rebels didn't use it correctly—a fact that New York Fire Marshal Alfred Baker uncovered during his investigation. During the commotion, Baker visited several of the hotels targeted. Inside the Fifth Avenue Hotel, he discovered a room that hadn't lit up. It was an opportunity to study the arsonists' methods.

The man responsible for the Fifth Avenue, Col. Robert M. Martin, had created a pyre in the center of the room by stacking the furniture and then dousing it with turpentine, which would act as an accelerant. It appeared that Martin had left the room in a hurry, because he left behind a smoking gun: three still-corked bottles of Greek Fire.

Baker took two of the bottles and analyzed their contents. He found that the bottles contained "phosphorous dissolved in sulphuret of carbon." Then Baker replicated the formula. "I had some of the mixture prepared," Baker explained. "By saturating muslin or paper with it I found that a blaze was produced in from four to eight minutes."

Baker believed that the mixture had been designed to allow the "incendiaries" the time needed to escape the inferno. "They calculated on its acting as a sort of fuse, which would give them the requisite time to make their way out of the building without danger of detection."[18]

"The chemist had done his work sagaciously," Baker concluded, "but in carrying out the plan a blunder was committed which defeated the anticipated results. In each case the doors and the windows of the room were left closed."[19] According to the fire marshal, this was a critical error. Without oxygen to breathe, the fires smoked but didn't ignite.

The great plot to incinerate New York failed because the fires took place behind closed doors (and windows). Ironically, the arsonists kept the doors shut to keep the fires from being discovered, and in doing so, smothered their own bonfires and foiled their grand scheme.

This *Harper's Weekly* illustration appeared in the December 17, 1864 edition. While the child says her goodnight prayers, the sneering rebel arsonist has piled up furniture and bedding that he hopes to ignite with a bottle of the flammable chemical agent, "Greek Fire."

In addition to this miscalculation, their failure to set the fires simultaneously gave the firefighters time to extinguish the flames and police time to warn hotel managers of the potential danger. "[T]hanks to the Police, Fire Department, and the bungling manner in which the plan was executed by the conspirators," a *New York Times* reporter gloated in his day-after coverage of the plot, "it proved a complete and miserable failure."[20]

There was one other factor: Federal authorities had learned about the possibility of such a scheme from a paid informer. So when the rebel agents began setting fires, the authorities—alerted to the possibility of a possible plot to burn Manhattan—were quick to respond.

The morning after their failure, Headley, Kennedy, and the others needed to find a way of avoiding a short rope and a tall lamppost. Headley and fellow arsonist Robert Martin took a room at a nearby hotel at about two in the morning on November 26.

While the Confederate spies slept, their work was still being uncovered throughout the city's hotels. Just to be on the safe side, the manager of the Astor Hotel made a sweep of the hotels' rooms. When he opened the door to room 204, plumes of smoke poured out as the Greek Fire doused on the mattress ignited.

At about ten o'clock, the headlines of the morning papers shouted out news about the previous night's attempt to torch New York. The conspirators' horror grew as they read the news, which listed the aliases they had used when checking into their respective targets.

Investigators also had a face to go with one of the names. An observant clerk at the Metropolitan Hotel—the same one who cast a curious glance at Headley as he rushed out of the hotel—gave a detailed description of the suspicious stranger.

The city's officers hunted for the mysterious plotters. "If they are detected," Maj. Gen. John Dix said, "they will be immediately brought before a Court-martial or military commission, and, if convicted, they will be executed without the delay of a single day."[21] Dix's ominous statement wasn't an empty threat. As spies, Headley, Kennedy, and the crew of arsonists could wind up with nooses around their necks.

The group managed to make their way north via train to Albany and then across the "Suspension Bridge" into Canada to Toronto, where they met up with shadowy Confederate spymaster Jacob Thompson. Federal bloodhounds followed their trail to the border.

Like his confederates, Robert Cobb Kennedy had made his way across the border into Canada. Two weeks later, he took part in another plot engineered by Thompson, this one designed to free a group of captive Confederate generals by hijacking the train transporting them. The plan was simple: strong-arm the guards and divert the train to Canada. But through a series of mishaps, they missed the train.

After the abortive rescue operation, Kennedy was back in Canada, but he didn't stay long. "I was restless . . . and wanted to rejoin my command," he later said when explaining his decision to reenter the US. "I started with my friend via Detroit." Carrying a loaded revolver and passport in the name of "Richard Cobb," Kennedy hopped onto a train en route to Detroit for the first leg in his journey south. Leaving Canada was a critical mistake.[22]

Kennedy didn't feel the heat at his heels. Detectives had tracked his movements and were waiting for him at the train depot in Detroit. They nabbed him when the train pulled into the station. A search of "Richard Cobb's" clothing revealed the tell-tale signs of a spy: Inside the lining of his coat, they found Confederate currency and a "paymaster's certificate."

So instead of heading south, Robert Cobb Kennedy's journey took a detour east, back to New York, where he faced the dual charges of "acting as a spy" and violating the rules of war by attempting to burn down New York.

Kennedy was a feisty prisoner. On the train trip back to the Big Apple, he held up his shackled hands and announced to the shocked passengers that they were "iron ornaments" that he was proud to wear for his cause. He also tried to jump out of the train.

Friends and acquaintances characterize Robert Cobb Kennedy as a stubborn man with a bulldog's tenacity. One of his fellow officers described him as "a perfect dare-devil, and no situation, however perilous, seemed to daunt his courage."[23] It was a quality that had served him well during the war.

Robert Cobb Kennedy was a twenty-five-year-old planter when the war broke out in 1861. Kennedy had some experience in the military, having spent two years at West Point before he washed out and went back home.

When a regiment formed in New Orleans, he joined the ranks and went to war. In October 1863, the now-Captain Kennedy was dispatched to Chattanooga, Tennessee, where he served under Maj. Gen. Joseph Wheeler. He was captured and sent to the Union POW camp on Johnson's Island in Lake Erie.

It wasn't the first time Kennedy saw the inside of a Union prison—he later boasted that he had "been in half a dozen prisons"—but Johnson's Island would be different. The frigid Lake Erie rock was an escape artist's nightmare.[24]

When Union brass had realized that the war would last longer than a few months, they had begun searching for areas to confine large numbers of captured enemy soldiers pending exchange. They found the ideal spot on a small, remote island about two-and-a-half miles from Sandusky, Ohio.

The port city of Sandusky had a well-established rail line that the army could use to transport prisoners and supplies to the area. The island's entire population consisted of just one family, the L. B. Johnson family, and there was a forty-acre clearing fit for a camp holding as many as three thousand prisoners as well as a garrison to police them. Sandusky Bay provided both fresh water for use at the camp and a natural barrier keeping enemy soldiers from the civilian population.

Work began on a stockade in 1861, and the first prisoners came through the gate in April 1862. The prison consisted of twelve prisoner barracks inside of a sixteen-foot-high perimeter. A combination of guards and geography made Johnson's Island virtually escape-proof.

The island's limestone bedrock made tunneling impossible. The only way out was over the fence, but that wasn't the only barrier to freedom. Escapees who managed to climb over the sixteen-foot-high stockade wall would need to make their way across the bay to Cedar Point (the current site of the amusement park of the same name). In the winter, they could walk across the ice, but the frigid temperatures and frequent snowstorms ensured that they wouldn't get far. In fact, during the four-year life of Johnson Island POW camp, only a handful of prisoners managed to escape. One of them was Robert Cobb Kennedy.

Using pieces of scrap lumber, Kennedy built a crude ladder. Then on October 4, 1864—a dark, moonless night—Kennedy and an accomplice named Turk Smith carried the ladder to the wall. While Smith held the ladder, Kennedy climbed up and over the stockade wall. He tiptoed to a skiff and shoved off the rock for good. After almost a year on Johnson's Island, he was free.

Unlike most escapees who made it off the island, he didn't head south or north to Canada via Detroit. He traveled east, skirting the north shore of Lake Erie through Ohio and into New York. At Buffalo, he crossed the border into Canada, where he made his way to Toronto—the headquarters of Confederate spymaster Jacob Thompson. Perhaps realizing the value of a man who made it off of the Union's rock, Thompson recruited Kennedy as one of the incendiaries.

⊕ ⊕ ⊕

As the other arsonists watched from the safety of Canada, Kennedy faced a military tribunal on the dual charges of acting as a spy and "violating the laws of war." Since he was the only one caught, Kennedy became the poster boy of the plot to burn New York. The case became a sensation as people snatched up newspapers carrying headlines about the trial. The "Southern Terrorist" was the talk of the town.

The press demonized Kennedy. One *New York Times* reporter described him as "a man of apparently 30 years of age, with an exceedingly unprepossessing countenance. His head is well-shaped, but his brow is lowering, his eyes deep sunken and his look unsteady. Evidently a keen-witted, desperate man, he combines the cunning and the enthusiasm of a fanatic."[25]

Kennedy was taken to Fort Lafayette in New York Harbor where he went in front of a military commission led by Gen. Fitz-Henry Warren. Kennedy's former West Point classmate, Brig. Gen. Edwin Stoughton, represented him at the proceedings. The trial began on January 17, 1865, and ended in early March, but the commission didn't announce its findings until March 20.

Kennedy whiled away the hours by keeping a journal from "Room No. 1" at Fort Lafayette. Most of these pages were destroyed at his request, but a few of them have survived and throw some light onto an otherwise shadowy character.

In his March 2, 1865, entry titled "IN HELL," Kennedy contemplates his fate. "If I am executed," he says, "it will be nothing less than judicial, brutal, cowardly murder."[26] In his March 5 entry, he complains about his accommodations at Fort Lafayette. "The damned vermin are so numerous that I am . . . afraid to sneeze, for fear the damned lice would regard it a gong for dinner, and eat me up."

Then, at the end of the note, Kennedy breaks into verse:

Oh, never, never, never will a true Confederate soldier
Forsake his friends or fear his foes;
For while our Lord's Cross proudly floats defiance,
I don't care a damn how the wind blows.[27]

On March 20, the commission delivered its verdict; Robert Cobb
Kennedy should hang for his role in the attempt to burn New York. All that
remained to do was to erect the scaffold and set the date. The Rebel incendiary stood mum for most of his incarceration and trial, but after sentencing, he
began to speak as if there would be no tomorrow. And for Kennedy, there
would be no March 26—his execution had been set for Saturday, March 25.

Kennedy did try one last prison break. Using a red-hot poker, he
attempted to sear the lock off his cell. A guard who sniffed burning wood
caught him in the act. There would be no escape this time.

The five days between the verdict and execution weighed heavily on
Kennedy, who experienced a range of emotions. He hoped that President
Lincoln would commute his sentence, but then railed against the authorities for treating him as a scapegoat. He screamed at the guards but listened
attentively to the parson who came to visit him.

"It's a hard thing to be swung off in such weather as this and to go you
don't know where," Kennedy remarked on the eve of his execution. "Now
my father was a good straightforward man and my mother was a Methodist,
and I always said my prayers and all that, but what does it amount to; I'm
to die tomorrow and don't know where I shall go, or what will be done
with me."[28]

"I suppose I ought to be a Christian," Kennedy said when offered religious services, "but damn it all, I can't. No I can't, and I shall die uncertain
as to my fate."[29]

But there was one point on which Kennedy was certain. "I'm not a bad
man," he said. "I haven't injured anyone except in war, and I think my character will stand investigation."[30]

And then, he confessed his role in the conspiracy to Col. Martin Burke
and *New York Times* editor Joseph Howard. "I know that I am to be hung
for setting fire to Barnum's Museum, but the fact is that that affair was simply a reckless joke," he said. "There was no fiendishness about it. The
Museum was set on fire by merest accident, after I had been drinking, and
just for the fun of the scare."[31]

Kennedy's gallows confession agrees with Headley's account of that
night, when Kennedy admitted to setting fire to Barnum's for the thrill of
it. The attempted burning of the famous museum was an arsonist's ad lib,

but the whole plot was to be a demonstration and that was it, Kennedy said. No one was to get hurt.

"I wish to say that the killing of women and children was the last thing we thought of," Kennedy said. "We wanted to let the people of the North understand and feel that there are two sides to this war, and that they can't be rolling in wealth and comfort while we at the South are bearing all the hardships and privations."[32]

The goal was to destroy buildings, not lives, "although that would of course have followed in the train," Kennedy admitted. He insisted that the press publish his statement verbatim so that the public would not consider him a "fiend."

He spent the rest of the night writing letters—including a tribute to the detectives who worked his case—and sipping the small amount of whiskey his jailors gave him. The condemned also snipped a few locks of hair and packaged them for his relatives

The next morning, Kennedy made his way to the gallows, where a small contingent of reporters awaited the spectacle. The man who tried to burn down Barnum's was going to be launched into eternity, literally. Unlike the typical hanging where the floor comes out from under the condemned, the scaffold used in Kennedy's execution employed a counterweight mechanism that jerked the condemned man upward, breaking his neck.[33]

It took ten minutes for an army captain to read the verdict, during which Kennedy sneered, "It's a damned lie."[34]

After a short prayer, Kennedy asked for a few last words: "Colonel I wish to make a statement. Gentlemen, this is a judicial murder. Colonel. I am ready. This a judicial, cowardly murder. There's no occasion for the United States to treat me this way. I say, Colonel, can't you give me a drink before I go up?"[35]

The noose was placed around his neck and the black hood pulled down over his face. And then, to the surprise of the audience, Robert Cobb Kennedy began to sing a few lines of verse:

Trust to luck, trust to luck,
Stare Fate in the face,
For your heart will be easy
If it's in the right place.[36]

Just after his last word, the counterweight was released and Kennedy's body was yanked off the floorboards, the sharp movement snapping his neck. Robert Cobb Kennedy died instantly.

The great Confederate plot to incinerate New York fizzled out, failing to wreak the havoc intended. In the end, the only casualty was Robert

Cobb Kennedy—the last Confederate soldier executed by the United States government during the Civil War.

But the news coverage of Kennedy's execution wouldn't be the final word about the "Rebel incendiary." Kennedy's story has an interesting epilogue. On April 14, less than a month after Kennedy's execution, John Wilkes Booth murdered President Lincoln at Ford's Theater in Washington. Booth didn't survive to talk about his plot, but his fellow conspirators did. Within days, investigators had rounded up a group that they believed was responsible for a conspiracy to murder Federal heads of state.

The nation was gripped with conspiracy hysteria as the accused stood before a military tribunal. In an attempt to link Lincoln's assassination with the Confederate Secret Service and CSA president Jefferson Davis, witnesses testified about various plots to wreak havoc on the Union, including the failed attempt to burn New York to the ground.

Kennedy's confession was read during the trial as evidence of a greater conspiracy allegedly engineered by Confederate higher-ups in Richmond, and his name became part of the Lincoln conspiracy record.

Robert Cobb Kennedy was just one of eight arsonists, but he was the only one punished for the attempt to torch New York.

Colonel Robert Martin, who most sources credit as the progenitor of the burning plot, was arrested after the war and taken to Fort Lafayette for a trial. Apparently, Martin was going to follow in Kennedy's footsteps to the scaffold. But the trial never took place. Martin was released in 1866 for lack of evidence. He later moved to New York where he ran a tobacco warehouse. Martin died in 1901 at the age of sixty-one from a lung ailment caused by an old war wound.

Headley, the only one of the eight "incendiaries" who wrote about the event, returned to Kentucky after the war. He served one term as Kentucky's Secretary of State before moving to Los Angeles, where he died in 1930. He was ninety years old.

In *Confederate Operations in Canada and New York*, Headley justifies the arson plot by linking it with the burning of Atlanta. In all caps for emphasis, Headley states "It is fair to all concerned to record the fact here that TEN DAYS BEFORE THIS ATTEMPT OF CONFEDERATES TO BURN NEW YORK CITY, GENERAL SHERMAN HAD BURNED THE CITY OF ATLANTA, GEORGIA, AND THE NORTHERN PAPERS AND PEOPLE OF THE WAR PARTY WERE IN GREAT GLEE OVER THE MISERIES OF THE SOUTHERN PEOPLE."[37]

They wanted the people of New York to feel the heat too, but they failed.

CHAPTER 12

Sue Mundy,
Terror of Kentucky
1864

One of the most ruthless characters of the entire Civil War was a female guerrilla named Sue Mundy who robbed, burned, and murdered her way across central Kentucky during a five-month period between October 1864 and March 1865. Thanks to the newspapers, everyone knew her name, but no one knew her true identity.

While the *Louisville Daily Journal* referred to her as a woman, some believed that she was a man who dressed as a woman, while others believed that she was a woman who sometimes masqueraded in a Confederate uniform.

In fact, she was a character invented by George Denison Prentice, a Louisville newspaper editor who based Sue Mundy on a twenty-year-old rebel named Marcellus Jerome Clarke. It is one of the weirdest, most confusing episodes of the entire war. The plotline, which includes a secret trial and a news blackout, is so twisted that questions about the real "Sue Mundy" lingered for years after the war.

The drama that unfolded in Kentucky during the waning six months of the war contained a motley cast of characters: Prentice; Union general Stephen Burbridge, who was so tyrannical he was nicknamed the "Butcher"; a group of rebel troublemakers who wore blood-red clothes; a felonious guerrilla hunter; and a young marauder known as "Sue Mundy."

These actors performed in front of a backdrop of political and military intrigue. Kentucky in late 1864 was a tangled mess of conflicting loyalties, guerrilla warfare, ruthless Union overlords, and murder.

Throughout the war, a deep dissention split Kentuckians on the issues of secession and slavery. This rift grew deeper when, in early 1864, the

Union Army began to deploy black troops—a move that chafed many Kentuckians on both sides.[1]

Into this melee of mixed emotions came thirty-two-year-old Brig. Gen. Stephen G. Burbridge, who took command of the Military District of Kentucky in February 1864. A year later, he would leave as one of the most despised men in the Bluegrass State.

A native Kentuckian, Burbridge graduated from Georgetown College and later the Kentucky Military Institute. He fought bravely at Shiloh and was promoted to the rank of brigadier general. He participated in fights at Vicksburg and elsewhere; by 1864, he had amassed a short but distinguished resume of military experience. He did not, however, have experience governing civilians in a war zone.

In his new command, the young general had his hands full. In the spring of 1864, the Union moved the bulk of its forces out of Kentucky to the front lines, which left the state vulnerable to attack. Recognizing the weakness, Confederate raiders targeted Kentucky. The state's growing number of Southern sympathizers made an ideal support network for these armed incursions. And the state was rich in a resource vital to both sides: horses.

In June, Confederate raider John Hunt Morgan entered Kentucky. Morgan and his men took eight hundred horses from the Union forces at Lexington before Federal troops under Burbridge rousted him at Cynthiana on June 12. The victory earned Burbridge another promotion, this time to Major General of Volunteers, on July 4.

After Morgan's defeat, elements of his cavalry unit scattered throughout central Kentucky. Many Kentuckians who had fought with Morgan struck out on their own, believing it absurd to fight in Virginia when they could fight for the cause at home. Some of them formed small units to conduct viable military operations, like disrupting communications or foraging for strategic materiel such as horses. Others, convinced the war was already over, took a different course.

Kentucky, like Missouri, had been plagued by roving bands of lawless brigands since the onset of hostilities in 1861, but the climate in 1864 made a bad situation worse. The absence of a strong Union military presence and the disintegration of regular Confederate forces lured even more marauders to Kentucky. According to historian L. L. Valentine, Morgan's defeat opened the floodgates for guerrilla groups in Kentucky. "After Morgan's rout," Valentine wrote in his landmark article about Sue Mundy, "both irregular warfare and lawlessness burst into full bloom."[2]

By the summer of 1864, outlaws terrorized citizens and soldiers alike. While some of them fought under the guise of supporting a cause, others were nothing more than opportunistic gangs of degenerates, including

"Guerrilla Depredations," screams the picture caption from this *Harper's Weekly* illustration, published on Christmas Eve 1864. During the Civil War, Kentucky became a favorite hunting ground for horse thieves and irregular soldiers alike. LIBRARY OF CONGRESS

deserters from both sides. To make matters more confusing, they would often masquerade as regulars as a way to pin their crimes on soldiers. Union authorities, though, simply blamed all of the violence on rebels.[3]

Burbridge didn't have a large military force to police his jurisdiction and relied on citizen units called "Home Guards." By summer he was losing the battle with the guerrillas; there was chaos in Kentucky.

He was also losing the battle of public perception. The Kentucky newspapers—the *Louisville Daily Journal* in particular—ran daily articles about guerrilla raids. Some alleged that the *Journal*'s editor, George Prentice, used a little literary license and embellished stories of guerrilla outrages; others accused him of fabricating some "news" altogether.

Prentice had an agenda beyond merely reporting the facts. He didn't like the way Burbridge and the Union leaders had handled their affairs in Kentucky. As he saw it, they opened the door for invasion when they depleted their troops, and now they couldn't control the guerrillas menacing the state's hamlets and highways.

Thanks in part to Prentice's reporting, the public grew increasingly disenchanted with the young major domo and the Union regime in Kentucky. By July 1864, things had gotten out of hand. On July 2, Congress passed the "guerrilla bill," a law that gave military courts broad, sweeping authority to bring to trial and punish "guerrilla marauders" for various crimes, including rape, theft, and arson. Three days later, on July 5, President Lincoln declared martial law in Kentucky and suspended habeas corpus.

For Union officials in the Bluegrass State, the phrase "guerrilla marauder" became an all-inclusive term and included anyone who took things for the wrong side. This included John Hunt Morgan and his boys. Many of them were in Kentucky behind enemy lines and engaged in legitimate acts of war, but that didn't matter to Federal authorities. Detached Confederate units were now lumped together with roving bands of outlaws fighting for no other cause than their own stash of loot.

Burbridge was under intense pressure to capture and bring these "guerrilla-marauders" to justice, so he formulated a vicious policy of retaliation. On July 16, 1864, he issued Order No. 59 to quell "the rapid increase of lawless bands of armed men engaged in interrupting railroad and telegraphic communications, plundering and murdering peaceful Union citizens," and other offenses.[4]

He put Kentuckians on notice: "Rebel sympathizers living within five miles of any scene of outrage committed by armed men . . . will be arrested and sent beyond the limit of the United States"[5] The order gave Union authorities carte blanche to arrest just about anyone, but it was the last sentence of Burbridge's dictate that contained the teeth. "Whenever an unarmed Union citizen is murdered four guerrillas will be selected from the prisoners in the hands of the military authorities and publicly shot to death in the most convenient place near the scene of the outrage."[6]

Judicial executions began almost immediately. Whenever guerrillas killed someone, rebel prisoners drew lots. The losers were dragged, kicking and screaming, out of their jail cells and shoved in front of a firing squad.

The pawns in Burbridge's deadly game of chess weren't always guerrillas. This was indiscriminate, equal-opportunity slaughter. Even a seventy-year-old minister died in one retaliatory execution. "In county after county," Valentine notes, "Confederate prisoners, innocent of that or any other crime, were shot like hogs at a hog-killing."[7] This policy earned Burbridge the nickname "Butcher."

Through the bloody summer and fall of 1864, guerrilla bands and "Butcher" Burbridge's Home Guards exchanged bullets, with rebel prisoners caught in the crossfire. Burbridge's iron fist also came down hard on civil liberties in an attempt to curb dissention in the state. He suppressed the press and arrested reporters and editors who wrote what he considered to be treasonous remarks. The Butcher also tried to control the 1864 election, going so far as imprisoning some of Lincoln's political foes in Kentucky.

Kentuckians, even staunch supporters of Lincoln and the Union, blanched at their Union overlord. They were forced to endure random violence from guerrilla bands, what many saw as state-sanctioned murder under Order No. 59, and brutal suppression of their civil liberties. With the presidential election on the horizon, Stephen Burbridge, in his zealous desire to control Kentucky, turned many Kentuckians into Southern sympathizers and converted many hard-line Republicans, like *Louisville Daily Journal* editor George Prentice, into Democrats.

A native of Connecticut, Prentice settled in Kentucky three decades before the Civil War. The gifted writer became the guiding force in transforming the *Louisville Daily Journal* into the city's premier newspaper. The plucky news editor had a reputation for fighting feuds with his pen, often outdueling his political foes with scathing satire and ingenious puns.

Prentice was also a workaholic, sometimes spending as many as eighteen hours a day scribbling notes and articles.[8] The long hours eventually came back to haunt him. He developed a condition called *Chorea Scriptorum*, or scrivener's cramp, an ailment that caused uncontrollable tremors in his writing hand. Even this debilitating physical ailment couldn't stop Prentice. He taught himself to write with his left hand, but before long, his left arm failed. Undaunted, he continued to compose articles by dictating to a team of scribes.[9]

When the war began, Prentice was sixty-one years old. The conflict literally tore apart his family. While Prentice was a Lincoln supporter and a loyal Union man, both of his sons fought for the Confederacy. His younger son Courtland died at the Battle of Augusta, Kentucky, on September 29, 1862, just weeks after enlisting with the Confederacy.

Prentice had also watched Kentucky morph into a quagmire of mixed loyalties. The pullout of Federal forces left Kentucky wide open to attacks by both Confederate raiders such as Morgan and ruthless bandits with itchy trigger fingers. Burbridge's attempt to control the situation in the state created blood-drenched civil war within the Civil War, and in the process he had stepped all over the right of free speech that Prentice held near and dear to his heart.

Prentice knew he couldn't overtly criticize the Butcher without risk of going to jail, so he took a different approach. He discovered the ideal way to mock Union authorities when he heard about a guerrilla raid in Mercer County.

On October 7, 1864, five raiders dressed in Union garb held up a stagecoach and then rode into nearby Harrodsburg. Two of the marauders were former soldiers under John Hunt Morgan, who had been killed about a month earlier: Capt. Samuel "One-Arm" Berry and a mysterious, long-haired youth named Marcellus Jerome Clarke, who went by his middle name.

Clarke, a twenty-year-old native Kentuckian, was mustered into the Confederate forces as a seventeen-year-old recruit in 1861. He was the sixth son of Mary Hail and Hector Clarke, a farmer and high-ranking member of the Kentucky militia. When Jerome's mother died in 1849, Hector Clarke moved his family to Logan County, but Jerome stayed behind and lived with his fifty-two-year-old aunt Nancy Clarke Bradshaw.

After the war began, the younger Clarke joined the First Kentucky and fought valiantly for the South. He later said that he was captured after the February 1862 Battle of Fort Donelson and sent to a Louisville prison. He returned to duty after being exchanged a few months later, this time fighting under John Hunt Morgan.

When Morgan was killed during a skirmish in Tennessee in September 1864, Clarke drifted back across the border into his native Kentucky, where he remained a "detached" soldier carrying on the war there with a small group of others.[10] In early October, he and "One-arm" Berry took part in the raid at Harrodsburg.

They were after a cache of firearms held in the local bank's vault. During their getaway, they skirmished with a group of armed citizens and Home Guards. The fight resulted in just one casualty. A man named Robinson, caught in the crossfire, was hit more than a dozen times and fell from his horse. He was dead when he hit the ground, his body peppered by lead from the guerrillas' Colt Navy revolvers as well as buckshot from a citizen's shotgun.

Inspired by the gunfight at Harrodsburg, Prentice decided to create a paper bandit for the readers of the *Louisville Daily Journal*. To add insult to the beleaguered Federal authorities, he decided to make the guerrilla a female. The long-haired rebel captain, Marcellus Jerome Clarke, was the perfect model for Prentice's fictional desperado, whom he dubbed "Sue Mundy."[11]

No one is sure exactly why Prentice decided to create Sue Mundy in the pages of the *Louisville Daily Journal*, but the fictitious guerrilla was most likely the editor's way of embarrassing what he saw as corrupt and ineffective Union leadership. Since Burbridge couldn't catch the figment of Prentice's imagination, he would look like he was chasing his own tail.[12]

On October 11, four days after the Harrodsburg robbery, "Sue Munday" galloped into the news, making her debut in Prentice's *Louisville Daily Journal* under the bold headline "GUERRILLA DESPERADOS IN MERCER—A FEMALE GUERRILLA."[13]

The article described the shootout at Harrodsburg and then introduced the "she-devil" that Prentice would turn into a legend. "One of the peculiarities of this band of cutthroats is the officer second in command, recognized by the men as Lieut. Flowers. The young officer in question is a woman, and her right name is Sue Munday."[14]

Prentice's description of the female highwayman comes right out of a swashbuckler. "She dresses in male attire, generally sporting a full Confederate uniform. Upon her head she wears a jaunty plumed hat, beneath which escapes a wealth of dark-brown hair, falling around and down her shoulders in luxuriant curls. She is possessed of a comely form, is a bold rider and a dashing leader."[15]

Mundy, Prentice continued, "is a practiced robber, and many ladies, who have been so unfortunate as to meet her on the highway, can testify with what sang froid she presents a pistol and commands 'stand and deliver.' Her name is becoming widely known, and, to the ladies, it is always associated with horror. On Friday evening she robbed a young lady of Harrodsburg of her watch and chain."[16]

So began Sue Mundy's career as a criminal. Typically, Prentice would report a raid, sometimes by Clarke's group but sometimes by other guerrillas, add a little spice to the story, and report it as a "depredation" of Sue Mundy's gang.

A few days after her introduction, Kentucky's criminal debutante made another appearance in the *Journal* after One Arm Berry and Jerome Clarke visited Jeffersontown, where they captured a Union mail carrier named Hugh Wilson. The guerrillas led the terrified soldier out of town and shot him half a dozen times. One of the bandits then buried his knife in the dying man's chest.

Although who pulled the trigger hadn't been established, Prentice was quick to finger Sue Mundy for the cold-blooded killing. "All the circumstantial evidence," Prentice noted, "goes to prove that the murder was committed by one hand, that of Sue Mundy, the outlaw woman, the wild and daring leader of the band."[17]

"Sue Mundy, the tigress," Prentice concluded, "seems to be wholly abandoned; lost to every kind, womanly feeling, and exulting in scenes of blood, leads her desperate followers on to the perpetuation of the most damnable outrages. Her many atrocities will be remembered, and we trust, will be the means of bringing her to the gallows."

While Mundy wreaked havoc among civilians, real Confederate forces headed toward Nashville. There was a growing concern that they would cross the Tennessee River into Kentucky and meet up with the various guerrilla groups there.

With this looming threat, Burbridge raised "the black flag," declaring that guerrillas would not be taken as prisoners of war. Union authorities adopted a shoot-on-sight policy. On October 26, Burbridge issued Order No. 8, which declared that "Hereafter no guerrillas will be received as prisoners, and any officer who may capture such and extend to them the courtesies due prisoners-of-war will be held accountable for disobedience of orders."[18] Union soldiers had a license to kill.

Burbridge's order did not deter violence; it enhanced it. The guerrillas had nothing to lose. In the eyes of the law, it made little difference if they looted or if they looted and then murdered. Of course, Sue Mundy didn't hesitate to murder even before Burbridge's take-no-prisoners order. By early November, stories of her crimes had spread all over the state.

About a week after Burbridge threw down the gauntlet, Sue Mundy made an appearance in the official report of Union major Samuel Martin of the Thirty-Seventh Kentucky Infantry. Martin's forces had caught a group of guerrillas red-handed in Bloomfield. The five guerrillas had traded lead with the soldiers. Three of them were killed but two managed to hobble away, wounded. "The notorious Sue Mundy and Berry are said to be the ones who were wounded and made their escape," Martin reported. "Sue's pipe fell a trophy to my men, and various other articles." [19]

But Mundy was Prentice's baby, and he didn't want the military to feel like they were closing in on his "she-devil."[20] So a few days later, he ran an article implying that the Sue Mundy mentioned in Martin's report was an imposter who put on a skirt and pretended to be *the* Sue Mundy. While there is no evidence that Clarke ever masqueraded as a woman, this theme would endure in the various stories about his paper alter ego.

"It appears that some ambitious youth aspires to the reputation as made in a few brief months by Sue Mundy, the notorious outlaw woman and the leader of a desperate cut-throat gang," Prentice wrote in the November 9, 1864, edition of the *Journal*.[21]

Prentice identifies this "ambitious youth" as "Mr. Clark," the leader of the gang that hit Bloomfield and who "would associate his name with the terror by assuming the title of Sue Mundy." Prentice then issued an ominous warning: "We would advise Mr. Clark to abandon this field or, if he will persist in traveling the road to the gallows, let him sail under his own name and stand on his own reputation."[22]

In early December, Sue Mundy was back in the saddle and back in the *Louisville Daily Journal*. On December 3, a well-armed gang of guerrillas led by Jim Davis raided Springfield, Kentucky. The gang included Clarke and his cronies, One-Arm Berry and Henry Magruder, who got into a firefight with the locals.

Prentice featured the skirmish in the December 8 edition of the *Daily Journal*, but he put Sue Mundy in the front saddle instead of Jim Davis. At the end of a lengthy article detailing "A Chapter of Robberies and Murders," Prentice fires a shot at Kentuckians.

"Surely, if a proper effort was made, some means could be devised for the capture of Sue Mundy and her horse-thieving, murdering gang. If the citizens would exhibit a spirit of bravery worthy of Kentuckians, the handful of marauders might be picked up and turned over the military authorities as prisoners without anybody getting very badly hurt."[23]

After the Springfield raid, Sue Mundy disappeared into the backwoods, conspicuously staying out of the *Louisville Daily Journal* for about a month while Prentice ventured to Richmond, Virginia, to visit his son, Col. Clarence Prentice.[24]

Clarence had apparently inherited a little of his father's feistiness and landed in prison after murdering a fellow Confederate. With special permission from both Presidents Lincoln and Davis, Prentice traveled to the rebel capital to attend his son's trial. When the trial ended with an acquittal, both father and son went back to work. Clarence returned to active duty. Meanwhile, the editor returned to his writing desk in Louisville, and Sue Mundy returned to the front pages of the *Daily Journal*.

In mid-January, Prentice did an about-face and attempted to unmask Sue Mundy in a curious story buried on page three of the *Journal*. According to Clarke biographers Thomas Shelby Watson and Perry A. Brantley, the story was the editor's attempt to admit his deception, since people generally believed that Sue Mundy was a man.[25] Once again, Sue Mundy is depicted as a man who masqueraded as a women, but this time the "true" identity of the bandit is revealed. The story names "Jerome Clarke" as Sue Mundy and relates a humorous anecdote in which Clarke, in full drag, introduces himself to John Hunt Morgan as a woman named Sue Mundy. Fooled by Clarke's disguise, Morgan remarks, "All right boys, we will have use for Sue Mundy."[26]

Clarke supposedly later denounced this as a tall tale, but Sue Mundy had become attached at Jerome Clarke's hip. Because Prentice had dressed his infamous rebel guerrilla in a woman's clothes, and because people believed that "Sue" was a man named Jerome, cross-dressing became a feature of "Sue Mundy" myths both during and after the war.

Despite the tentative identification, Prentice went back to describing Sue Mundy as a ruthless female guerrilla, and Sue was a busy girl. In late January, a group of guerrillas attacked a convoy of cattle en route to Camp Nelson. The gang, which included Bill Marion, One-Arm Berry, and Henry Magruder, slaughtered a contingent of black soldiers. While it is uncertain if Jerome Clarke took part in the raid, Prentice placed Sue Mundy at the scene of the alleged crime. "It is presumed that the Negroes surrendered and were shot down in cold blood," Prentice noted in his article about the massacre.[27]

In the next day's edition, Prentice chided the military for not catching Sue. "How very strange that she isn't caught," Prentice noted. The menace "goes where she pleases, and does what she pleases, and none of our military leaders seem to have the ability, if they have the disposition, to lay their hands upon her. We can't imagine what the matter is; surely they are not afraid of her. To permit this she-devil to pursue her horrid work successfully much longer will be . . . a military scandal and shame."

Prentice deepened the mystique surrounding Sue. "Some say Sue Mundy is a man, and some say a woman. We don't suppose the sexes will quarrel for the distinction of owning her. If she were captured and it should become important to ascertain to which sex she belongs, should the committee consist of women or men?

"We have this moment received a communication, assuring us that it has been settled that Sue is a compromise between a man and a woman—a hermaphrodite. Sue, whether of the masculine, feminine, or neuter gender—whether he, she, or it—is certainly a grammatical puzzle." Prentice goes on to wonder which pronoun he should use to "parse Sue Mundy."[28]

Desperate to stop the marauders, Union authorities hired mercenaries to do their dirty work. Some of these men, such as Edwin Terrell, were criminals in their own right. The twenty-year-old Terrell had a checkered past. When the war began, he enlisted with the First Kentucky and fought for the Confederacy. In August 1862, he joined John Hunt Morgan's cavalry but deserted the following September. According to legend, he murdered a fellow officer but the case didn't go to a court-martial. Later that fall, he switched sides and joined the Thirty-Seventh Kentucky and fought for the United States. He did a brief, five-month stint in prison before leaving the service altogether.

By 1865, Terrell had left both militaries and was living as a civilian when Union colonel Thomas Farleigh hired him to rid Kentucky of the guerrilla menace in early January. Terrell immediately went to work. When he wasn't hunting, he was plundering.

On January 28, Terrell and his gang of Home Guards rode into Bloomfield, where they came across a suspected guerrilla named Ike Dudley. They shot Dudley and began ravishing the town, some say pretending to be Sue Mundy. Their pillaging came to an end when a group of rebels surprised them. More than a dozen of Terrell's Home Guards were killed in the ensuing firefight.

At first, Prentice pinned Terrell's actions on Sue, but he apparently changed his mind and pointed the finger at Terrell in the next day's edition.[29] "Capt. Terrill and his Home Guards behaved outrageously, robbing stores, relieving citizens of watches and money," an incensed George Prentice wrote. "He plundered after the fashion of the guerrilla."[30]

By February, Prentice's monster began to appear all over Kentucky. Marauders and bandits had committed all sorts of atrocities and chalked them up to Sue Mundy. More pressure was heaped onto overwhelmed Union authorities when William Clarke Quantrill rode into Kentucky in late January. An outlaw out west, the bushwhacking cavalier came east when things became too hot for him in Missouri. At some point, Jerome Clarke's group met up with Quantrill's gang.

It didn't take long for the two outlaw legends—Quantrill and Mundy—to become intertwined, and their association further cemented the connection between Clarke and Mundy. While Quantrill was in Kentucky, he went by the name of Captain James Clark.[31] This made two "Clarks" for one Mundy.

On February 1, a nervous Union officer noted that Quantrill was likely headed for Owen County, and "also Sue Mundy." The next day, Prentice also linked the two legendary bandits. In an article in the February 2nd edition of the *Journal*, Prentice reported that Quantrill and Mundy had murdered four Federal soldiers.

The day the *Journal* hit the streets, there were Mundy sightings in two different places about sixty miles apart. At approximately 2 A.M. on February 2, a well-armed force of about thirty riders attacked a group of soldiers near New Castle. Capt. E. W. Easley identified the group as "Sue Munday's command."[32]

Later that same day, Lt. Thomas Howes wired that "Rebels under Clarke or Sue Munday burned depot at Midway tonight."[33] The distance between the two points on the map made it highly unlikely that the same Sue Mundy appeared at both places.[34] Prentice reported on the Midway raid but didn't mention Mundy. Instead, he placed Mundy at New Castle, where he said the female bandit oversaw the murder of four unarmed soldiers.[35] In fact, the group that hit New Castle was led by Bill Marion, another rebel guerrilla.

While Union soldiers beat the bushes looking for Quantrill, Mundy, and others, Union higher-ups gave Burbridge his walking papers in mid-February. Prentice was elated. "Thank God and President Lincoln," he declared.[36]

Maj. Gen. John M. Palmer took the reins from Burbridge and reassigned him to Tennessee. The new Union chief was just as serious about stopping the guerrillas as his inglorious predecessor. "Kentucky was cursed at the time I assumed command of the department by the presence of 'Sue Mundy' (Jerome Clark), Marion, Magruder and Quantrell, who finally came into the state, and others," Palmer recalled in his autobiography.[37]

Unlike the Butcher, however, Palmer didn't punish guerrillas by gunning down their friends; he "waged war upon the guerrillas personally."[38] He relied on a network of spies to track guerrillas and employed mercenaries to hunt them down. On March 4, just a few weeks after he took over,

Palmer hit paydirt. An informer brought news that three guerrillas—Henry Metcalf, Henry Magruder, and Jerome Clarke—were holed up in a barn after a shootout.

The day before, the men, along with another rebel named Sam Jones, were ambushed by eight Home Guards. Jones was killed, and Magruder took a bullet in the chest. A chunk of hot lead tore through his right lung, leaving him tottering on the brink of death. Metcalf and Clarke took their critically injured friend to a barn near the town of Brandenburg where a sympathetic doctor tended to him.

When Palmer received the tip about the three men, he immediately brought in a trusted ally, a retired major named Cyrus J. Wilson, to lead the expedition against the guerrillas. To keep word from leaking out, they plotted their strategy behind closed doors.

While Palmer made plans to bring in the rebels, dead or alive, the *Louisville Daily Journal* ran an interesting piece about Sue Mundy. According to the article, Mundy herself sent a note to the *Journal* asking for her "communication" to be published in return for whatever payment the *Journal* would like.

Prentice hit a rhetorical all-time high with his pun-filled "response" to the request.

> We don't desire it [payment] in lead, for we have mettle enough in us already. We don't want it in steel, for we have quite as much point now as we need. We prefer not to take it in hemp, for we are a temperance man and have decided objections to getting high. We won't accept it in kisses, for we would rather be kissed by the Devil's daughter with her brimstone breath than by a tomboy. We'll not submit to have it in hugs, for those who have seen Sue in her guerrilla costume say that she is a little bare. So we'll not sue Sue for favors of any sort.

The fresh editor continued to jibe with Sue. "We should be almost as willing to see the nipples of your bosom as the nipples of your firearms . . . Many think that it makes no difference on what day of the week a man dies, but we confess that we shouldn't like to die of a Mundy."

Prentice ended his playful article on an ominous note.

> You have been an awful girl, Sue, we must say. You have killed so many persons, of all colors, that no doubt white, yellow, and black ghosts haunt you continually, the black ones coming at night because black doesn't show at night. Our Journal may bring you and your fellows to justice and thus be to you and them not only a newspaper but a noose-paper. The authorities civil and military command us to cut down you and your gang wherever we

can find you, but, if we wake up some morning and see you all hanging about here, we'll be hanged ourselves if we'll cut down one of you.[39]

This was more than a statement; it was a prophecy. As Prentice waxed eloquent about Sue's nipples and chastised her for being "an awful girl," Jerome Clarke remained by the side of his critically injured friend, unaware that Union authorities knew his whereabouts and were about to close in for the kill.

While Palmer eagerly waited in Louisville, his men made a beeline for the barn and the three unsuspecting guerrillas. At dawn on Sunday, March 12, 1865, Wilson and a company of Wisconsin soldiers under the command of Capt. Lewis O. Marshall surrounded the barn. One of the men knocked but no one answered. After a few seconds of silence, two Wisconsin boys threw a boulder at the barn door.

This brought a reaction from the rebels, who perforated the wooden door with a dozen shots. The volley of bullets injured four soldiers, who returned fire while they stumbled away from the barn. Wilson called a flag of truce and Clarke agreed. Without hesitation, Wilson went into the barn. Clarke puffed on a cigar while Wilson tried to talk him into laying down his four revolvers. According to Wilson, Clarke said that if he surrendered, he believed the Union soldiers would shoot him on the spot.

The major assured Clarke that he would survive until they reached Louisville but admitted that Clarke would likely wind up on a scaffold there. Still, Wilson managed to persuade the reticent rebel that a few days of life was better than none at all. Magruder, who believed he wouldn't live long enough to stand trial, agreed that surrender was Clarke's best option. After a little more prodding, Clarke said he would surrender if the Union soldiers treated them as prisoners of war, not common criminals. Wilson agreed to treat them as prisoners of war until they reached Nashville, and the three guerrillas laid down their arms.

Wilson took no chances. He watched as his prisoners were trussed up. "Mundy," he said, "this is rather hard treatment for a prisoner of war, but we are determined that you are not to get loose."[40]

The group returned to Louisville on board the riverboat *Morning Star*, arriving the next morning, Monday, March 13. Word reached town before the ship did, and a large crowd gathered around the wharf to see the infamous Sue Mundy in the flesh. If there was any doubt about the true identity of Sue Mundy, it was dispelled when the *Morning Star* docked; the public and military alike now identified Jerome Clarke as Prentice's female guerrilla.

Magruder was in bad shape and was taken to a nearby hospital. Clarke and Metcalf went in different direction. Boxed in on all sides by soldiers, they were marched to prison. Prentice described the Federal prisoner as an effeminate boy. "Sue Mundy is a rosy-cheeked boy, with dark eyes and scowling brow," Prentice wrote in the March 15 edition of the *Journal*. "He is of medium height, beardless, with small hands and feet. He has a soft feminine voice but bore himself as a man of culture and gentlemanly refinement."[41]

According to Valentine, Prentice had an ulterior motive in describing the prisoner as a "rosy-cheeked boy." It was an attempt to cover his journalistic backside for reporting Mundy as a female when everyone now believed her to be a him.[42]

In describing Clarke as a refined, cultured gentleman, Valentine notes, Prentice may also have planted a subtle hint that this Sue Mundy was not his Sue Mundy. Throughout Mundy's five-month tear through Kentucky, Prentice characterized her as a coarse, unrefined ruffian. As a "man of culture and gentlemanly refinement," Clarke was so unlike the character depicted in earlier *Journal* stories, they couldn't possibly be the same person.[43]

Such minor discrepancies didn't bother General Palmer, who realized that bagging the biggest bandit in Kentucky besides Bill Quantrill would go a long way toward restoring public confidence in the Union authorities. The court-martial paperwork was drawn up while the prisoners were still en route to the city.

Palmer apparently had an itchy writing hand; he signed the commission's findings on March 13, a day before they even convened. This paper trial even included Clarke's sentence: death by hanging.[44]

Even though Clarke's fate had been decided the day before the trial, the military commission went through the motions anyway. Testimony began behind closed doors and off-limits to the public. The secrecy of the trial furthered the mystery surrounding Clarke and Sue Mundy. Some even believe that a trial never took place and that the court-martial document was completely fabricated, as was the prosecution's case against "Jerome Clark, alias Sue Mundy."

Jerome Clarke faced one charge: "Jerome Clark alias Sue Mundy, being a guerrilla." The indictment came with two specifications: acting as a guerrilla, defined as warring with the United States while not belonging to any "organized military force," and wounding four of the Wisconsin men when they surrounded the barn.[45]

The prosecution presented six witnesses, including the two officers who made the arrests: Maj. Cyrus Wilson and Capt. Lewis Marshall. Wilson testified about the capture of Clarke in the tobacco barn. He recollected their conversation just before Clarke handed over his pistols. Judge Advocate William Coyl asked Wilson whom he meant by "Sue Mundy." Wilson said he meant Clarke, who was known as Mundy. The elderly major also said that Clarke admitted some of the stories about him were true, but some weren't. According to Wilson, Clarke denounced as a tall tale the story that he fooled Morgan by dressing as a woman.

Marshall also fingered Clarke as Mundy and testified that Clarke said was the man known as Sue Mundy. According to Marshall, Clarke even offered an explanation as to how he acquired the pseudonym: A girl named Sue Mundy stole a horse and pinned the theft on him.[46] But Prentice's girl-guerrilla "Sue Mundy" first appeared in his October 11 article, which cast a long shadow of doubt over the captain's testimony.

Clarke's defense quizzed Wilson on this identification. "Did not the accused say Prentice gave him the name?"

"I don't think he did," Marshall responded.

"Did he not say there were three men who went by the name?" Mundy's defense asked.[47]

Marshall admitted that Clarke may have said something along those lines to another officer, but he hadn't really paid attention at the time. According to Valentine, these two questions together suggested that the military "knew—or at least strongly suspected—how and why Editor Prentice had been dramatizing Sue Mundy."[48]

The judge advocate called four witnesses who testified about Clarke's alleged crimes. One soldier described the bloodbath at New Castle when Sue Mundy and Bill Quantrill attacked a group of Union soldiers. Sue Mundy appeared in both military dispatches and in the *Louisville Journal* as one of the bad guys at New Castle, but the soldier couldn't positively say that the man on trial—Clarke—was even in the fight.

Wisconsin private Hiram Meadows testified that Clarke and a contingent of guerrillas captured him and a few other soldiers, including his brother. The guerrillas forced the captives to march, but Meadows's brother, who couldn't keep up, was shot by Clarke.

Pvt. Alfred Hill identified Clarke as one of the men who held up a train. According to Hill, one of the train's passengers pointed at Clarke and said he was Sue Mundy. The private didn't specify the date of the train robbery, but it was likely a train robbed by Henry Magruder in early September, when Clarke was in Tennessee with Morgan.

Clarke asked the commission for a delay in the proceedings so he could muster up witnesses to testify that he wasn't a guerrilla but a detached Confederate soldier. The commission denied this request on the grounds that even if Clarke was a detached Confederate regular, the crimes he allegedly committed would warrant criminal charges anyway. The members went into deliberations without hearing from a single defense witness. Their verdict came as no shock (especially since Palmer had signed it before the trial began). They found Clarke guilty of both specifications and sentenced him to hang. Federal officials were apparently in a hurry to tie up the Sue Mundy affair. They scheduled the execution for the next day. Clarke would take the long walk to the scaffold on Wednesday, March 15, 1865. A minister broke the news to the condemned man earlier that afternoon.

Clarke asked the minister to baptize him in his cell. The minister also wrote, as Clarke dictated, four letters to the condemned man's friends and family. One of these was addressed to his girlfriend, Mary Porter Thomas.[49] "I have to inform you of the sad fate which awaits your true friend. I am to suffer death this afternoon at four o'clock," Clarke said in the note. "I send you from my chains a message of true love; and as I stand on the brink of the grave, I tell you, I do truly and fondly and forever love you."[50] Clark enclosed a lock of hair with the note as a memento.

Around 3 P.M., the procession made its way down Broadway to the scaffold. The drums of a regimental band played the death march as Clarke rode in a carriage flanked by soldiers.

Other executions of guerrillas had taken place behind fences or in closed courtyards, out of public view, but officials decreed the execution of the infamous Sue Mundy must be public. Palmer had to kill the legend as well as the convict, so the hanging would take place in the city's center where everyone could see it.[51] A crowd of several thousand gathered around the scaffold to watch Sue Mundy's last moments.

Clarke muttered a few prayers as the charges were read. When asked for his last words, he said, "I am a regular Confederate soldier, and have served in the Confederate army for four years. I fought under General Buckner at Fort Donelson, and belonged to General Morgan's command when he entered Kentucky. I have assisted and taken many prisoners and have always treated them kindly. I was wounded at Cynthiana and cut off from my command. I have been in Kentucky ever since; I could prove that I am a regular Confederate soldier, and I hope in, and die for, the Confederate cause."[52]

The provost marshal then placed a white hood over Clarke's head and then stepped back. At the count of three, the floor came out from under Clarke's feet. He dropped just three feet and died an agonizingly slow death by strangulation. "He struggled convulsively for two or three minutes, after which all was still," a correspondent for the *New York Times* wrote, "and in his death the majesty of the law was vindicated."[53]

A few morbid curiosity-seekers approached Clarke's corpse and plucked buttons from his jacket as mementoes of the infamous Sue Mundy. After about twenty minutes, Clarke's body was cut down and placed in the pine box lying by the scaffold. As he requested, his remains were taken to his elderly aunt in Franklin, Kentucky, and buried alongside his mother and father.

Taking down Sue Mundy was a coup for Palmer. News traveled all over the United States that the new military man in Kentucky had caught the infamous bandit. In its coverage of the execution, the *New York Times* described "Jerome Clarke alias Sue Mundy" as "the most famous outlaw among the whole guilty fraternity in these parts" and whose name was "a terror to every honest household throughout the country."[54]

Mundy was Palmer's first major score, but the "she-devil" wouldn't be his last. Politics makes for strange bedfellows, and Palmer went to bed with some real harlots. To rid Kentucky of its guerrilla "curse," Palmer hired men like Edwin Terrell. With Terrell on the prowl, Kentuckians had to sleep with one eye open and the other on a gun. "Terrell was an exceedingly dangerous man," Palmer later said about the young guerrilla hunter. "I never let him enter my quarters without keeping a revolver at hand."[55]

In April, he put Terrell on the payroll as the chief of his secret service at a rate of $50 a month. Terrell earned every penny. In mid-April, he delivered Bill Marion, literally, when he supposedly dropped Marion's bloody corpse on the steps of Palmer's office.

A month later on May 10, Terrell's group ended the career of notorious bandit William Clarke Quantrill, who was asleep in a central Kentucky barn when Terrell and company burst in, guns blazing. One piece of hot lead struck Quantrill in the spine, paralyzing him. He died a few weeks later in a Louisville hospital.

Shortly after bringing in Quantrill, Terrell was discharged from service, but he wasn't finished killing. A few months later, he murdered a blacksmith. In August, he murdered again, the victim this time a traveler who was reportedly carrying a quantity of gold.

Terrell beat the rap in court but was then arrested for the blacksmith's murder. A bunch of his former cronies busted him out of jail, but he took a bullet in the back during a shootout with a posse and was captured. Paralyzed, he lived for two years until he died during a surgery to remove the slug from his spine in 1868. He was twenty-three years old.

Trials and hangings of alleged guerrillas continued throughout the rest of the war and beyond. Six months after Clarke was hanged, Henry Magruder still hadn't given up the ghost. He wound up in front of a military commission facing seventeen counts of murder, including six killings he allegedly committed with Jerome Clarke. He pled guilty to several of the crimes and received a death sentence. Before his execution, he dictated a memoir to his jailor, Maj. Cyrus J. Wilson—the same retired officer who led the expedition that resulted in Clarke's capture.

The title of Magruder's book, *Three Years in the Saddle: the Life and Confession of Henry C. Magruder, the original "Sue Munday," the Scourge of Kentucky*, raised a few eyebrows at the time, particularly among those who believed that Jerome Clarke was framed by Union authorities desperate to bring the "she-devil" to justice. Modern historians, however, believe that Wilson, eager to boost book sales, decided to capitalize on the Mundy myth by inserting the book's subtitle.[56] Magruder was hanged on October 29, 1865.

The third man arrested with Clarke and Magruder, Henry Metcalf, was tried and convicted, but his sentence was commuted.

Sam "One-Arm" Berry was tried and sentenced to hang in January 1866, but his sentence was later commuted to prison, where he died of tuberculosis in 1872.

Maj. Gen. John Palmer resigned from the military shortly after the war and started a law partnership. He was elected governor of Illinois in 1868.

The "Butcher," Maj. Gen. Stephen Burbridge, settled in New York after the war. "He lived in exile and died in exile, a fate which he won by the bitterness of his rule," E. Polk Johnson wrote in his *History of Kentucky and the Kentuckians*.[57] He died in 1894 in Brooklyn.

George Prentice continued to helm the *Daily Journal* after the war, writing articles through scribes. He died in 1870 of influenza. The paragon of journalism is perhaps best known today for his Sue Mundy stories.

Union authorities in Kentucky managed to nab and kill the legendary Sue Mundy, but they failed to kill her legend. She lived on in countless stories that appeared in the years following Clarke's execution. But Sue just couldn't shake her reputation as a cross-dresser; most of the Sue Mundy tales contain some element of gender-bending, possibly because Prentice's "she-devil" was female, and the person the public came to associate with Sue was a male.

A news item published a little more than four years after Sue Mundy hanged in Louisville tells the curious story of a Detroit woman named Sue Kiteradge. According to the article, Ms. Kiteradge came from a wealthy Kentucky family and often spent time with the neighbor boy—the son of a wealthy planter named Mundy.

One day, vicious Yankees plundered their plantations, murdering their parents and leaving seventeen-year-old Sue and "young Mundy" without means to survive. The traumatized boy could only manage to utter the name of his sweetheart, "Sue," as he was being carried away, "probably the effects of a disordered brain." The soldiers found the name "Mundy" stitched on his "linen," and "Sue Mundy" was born.

Vowing vengeance, Sue Mundy became the most feared guerrilla in Kentucky alongside his sweetheart Sue, who disguised herself as a man named "Kit." Kit later went to work for the Confederate army and wound up as one of the most feared guards at Andersonville prison. According to the fanciful story, when Sue Mundy was hanged, "the bleeding and broken heart of Sue Kiteradge was buried with it."[58]

Another humorous story appeared in a Richmond newspaper in 1898. The tale is about a woman who claimed to know Sue Mundy personally. According to the story, which is told by the unnamed woman's daughter, the woman's sister returned home from boarding school with "one of the most effeminate men she ever saw."

This man was none other than Sue Mundy, who came to spy on the Yankees in drag. This Sue Mundy "came prepared with an extensive wardrobe and carried off his part of a fashionable and fascinating young lady." All went well until Mundy and the narrator's mother went to a party attended by Union officers. As a sort of petticoat rebellion, the mother wore over her dress an apron fashioned after the Confederate flag.

"About the middle of the evening, mother and Miss Sue went into the smaller room for a drink of water. A man bearing the bars of a sergeant on his arm was just raising the dipper to his lips when mother said mischievously: 'A health to Jeff Davis.'"

Offended, the sergeant said, "Yes, miss, here's a health to your apron," and tossed the ladle of water on her front porch. Mundy, seeing this insult to his flag, leveled the sergeant with one punch.[59] Exposed as a man and a rebel spy, Mundy fled with the Federal soldiers on his heels.

As for the "real" Sue Mundy, some writers have described Marcellus Jerome Clarke as a ruthless guerrilla, while others have depicted him as a sort of martyred saint. Like most of the Civil War's controversial characters, the reality is probably somewhere in between these extremes.

While questions about the real Sue linger today, "her" story makes one thing crystal clear: While there many sinners in Kentucky during the Civil war, there were very few saints.

CHAPTER 13

The Trial of the Lincoln Assassination Conspirators 1865

A procession of eight prisoners, their hands and feet pinioned with chains and their heads covered with thick canvas masks, clanked their way into the makeshift courtroom on the third floor of the arsenal in Washington, DC. Government prosecutors believed the group had plotted the country's most infamous murder, committed less than a month earlier at Washington's Ford's Theater.

At about 10:15 P.M. on April 14, 1865, actor John Wilkes Booth jumped onstage to play the role for which he would be forever remembered: the perpetrator of perhaps the most notorious crime in US history. But what about Booth's supporting cast? Were they all guilty as charged, or were some of them only guilty by association?

☻ ☻ ☻

As an actor, John Wilkes Booth had a flair for the dramatic. After he shot Abraham Lincoln in the back of the head with a Derringer pistol and briefly tussled with Lincoln's companion, Maj. Henry Rathbone, he leaped from the president's box onto the stage below, fracturing his leg in the process. "Sic Semper Tyrannis," he hollered before he hobbled backstage, hopped onto his horse, and rode off into the night.

This is the traditional rendition of Lincoln's murder, albeit perhaps flawed. Oddly enough, the person left to correct the small errors in this popular version is none other than the assassin himself. He kept a diary in which he claimed to have yelled "Sic Semper Tyrannis" (the motto of Virginia) just before (not after) he shot the president. Some historians also believe that Booth broke his leg while mounting his horse, not during his theatrical jump from Lincoln's box.

One way or the other, Booth climbed onto his horse and disappeared into the black night. The thespian-turned-assassin rode out of the city and into ignominy as the first man to assassinate an American president.

At about the same time Booth shot Lincoln, Lewis Powell (alias Lewis Paine or Lewis Payne)[1] attacked Secretary of State William Seward, who was home recovering from injuries suffered in a carriage accident. Payne, accompanied by David Herold, arrived at Seward's place at about ten o'clock.

Under the guise of delivering medicine to the secretary, Payne pushed his way past William Bell, the servant who answered the door. Armed with a Whitney revolver and a knife, Payne headed up the stairs towards Seward's bedroom. The secretary's son Frederick attempted to stop Payne, who bashed him over the head with the butt of his revolver, fracturing his skull.

The secretary's bodyguard, George Robinson, also tried to stop Payne. The conspirator knifed Robinson and then stabbed the secretary several times in the face and neck before Robinson and two other men pulled him off. Like Booth, Payne escaped and darted off into the night. Seward survived the attack, but Payne's rampage left him permanently disfigured by a large indentation running from his bottom lip to his neck.

While Booth sneaked up behind Lincoln with Derringer and Payne pushed his way into Seward's house with a Bowie knife, George Atzerodt was supposed to be dispatching Vice President Andrew Johnson. To get close to the VP, Atzerodt checked into the Kirkwood House, the Washington, DC, hotel in which Johnson was staying, on April 14. Later that evening, Atzerodt plied himself with liquid courage at the hotel saloon. But the only assault he made that night was on the bar's whiskey bottle. He apparently chickened out on his role in the conspiracy.

Federal authorities immediately dispatched a team of investigators to sniff out Booth and his coconspirators. From the start, detectives suspected John Surratt, a known associate of Booth's. They traced Booth to a boardinghouse run by Mary Surratt, but they came up empty-handed; Booth was long gone.

After the assassination, Booth and coconspirator David Herold (who met up with Booth after the botched attempt on Seward) made a midnight ride southeast, eventually arriving at the farm of Dr. Samuel Mudd in Charles County, Maryland, at about 4 A.M. on the morning of April 15. Mudd patched up Booth's leg and quartered the two men for the remainder of the day.

Lincoln died a few hours later at 7:22 A.M. on April 15. The city that just days before had celebrated the end of the Civil War now mourned the first US president to be assassinated. While shocked citizens grieved, detectives turned over every stone in the nation's capital, hoping to find the conspirators hiding beneath. They arrested dozens of people, including anyone and everyone connected in any way with John Wilkes Booth.

Detectives pounded the pavement searching for Booth, John Surratt, and other alleged conspirators, including George Atzerodt, identified as a prime suspect after a search of his hotel room revealed a few possible links to Booth's plot. Just a few hours after the shooting, investigators had raced to the Kirkwood House to protect the vice president. While there, they received word from an employee about a suspicious fellow who had checked into the hotel on the morning of the assassination. Believing this man somehow connected to a murder conspiracy, detectives searched George Atzerodt's room, where they found some incriminating evidence: a pistol under the pillow and a Bowie knife tucked under the sheets. They also found a direct link to Booth: his bankbook. Detectives combed the city for Atzerodt, but he wouldn't turn up for almost a week.

Despite some promising leads, government sleuths still hadn't collared Booth and his alleged cohorts more than forty-eight hours after the shooting. Then, on April 17, they managed to nab five people that they came to believe played key roles in the plot.

Two alleged conspirators, Samuel Arnold and Michael O'Laughlen, were arrested that morning. When detectives had learned of Arnold's longstanding friendship with Booth, they decided to bring him in for questioning. The discovery of an incriminating note didn't help his case; during a search of Booth's room at the National Hotel, investigators found a letter to Booth from "Sam." In the letter, Arnold says "None, no, not one were more in favor of the enterprise than myself." The letter also mentioned a "Mike."

Detectives tracked Arnold to Virginia and arrested him for his role in "the enterprise," which they believed meant the murder of Abraham Lincoln. During questioning, Arnold broke down and confessed to plotting, along with Booth, Payne, Atzerodt, John Surratt, and Michael O'Laughlen, an abduction of the president in March. Although Arnold denied participating in the murder conspiracy, he was cuffed and taken into custody.

Michael O'Laughlen, Booth's childhood chum, who detectives believed may have been the conspirator tasked with murdering General Grant, surrendered to authorities in Baltimore when he learned they were looking for him. He wanted to spare his family the embarrassment of a public arrest.

Later that night, detectives hit paydirt during their second visit to Mary Surratt's boardinghouse. Now convinced that Mary's son John had a hand in the plot, authorities ordered the arrest of everyone in the house. While law enforcement officers questioned boarders, a man arrived and told authorities that he had come to dig a ditch for the landlady, but Mary Surratt said she didn't hire the man. Suspicious, detectives arrested the alleged ditchdigger, who turned out to be Lewis Payne.

A search of Mary Surratt's home also produced several provocative pieces of evidence suggesting a connection with John Wilkes Booth, including a picture of Booth concealed behind another picture.

Earlier that evening, authorities arrested Edman Spangler,[2] an employee of Ford's Theater and an acquaintance of Booth's. The stagehand had been hauled in for questioning just hours after the assassination, released, and then rearrested when investigators came to believe that he helped Booth flee the scene of the crime. Another conspiracy domino fell three days later on April 20 when investigators nabbed George Atzerodt in Maryland.

Less than a week after Lincoln's assassination, investigators had managed to collar six chief suspects they believed had entered into a conspiracy to kill President Abraham Lincoln, Vice President Andrew Johnson, Secretary of State William Seward, and Gen. Ulysses S. Grant.

But they had not yet found the assassin. Booth and his alleged confederates David Herold and John Surratt were still on the lam by April 20, so President Johnson offered a huge reward: a king's ransom of $100,000 to anyone who brought in the three men. Wanted posters with the portraits of Booth flanked by John Surratt and David Herold began to appear everywhere. The long arm of the law, represented by a large hand, points to the "$100,000 REWARD!" and then the ad notes that "THE MURDERER of our late, beloved President, Abraham Lincoln, IS STILL AT LARGE."

Meanwhile, Alexander Lovett had followed Booth's bootsteps to the farm of Dr. Samuel Mudd. On April 18, Lovett questioned the doctor about his association with Booth. Mudd, an outspoken critic of Lincoln, told Lovett about the men who arrived at his farm at about four o'clock on the morning of April 15. One of them was hobbled with a leg injury. Mudd admitted to splinting the stranger's fractured leg, but insisted he didn't know the man. Dr. Mudd seemed nervous, and the further investigators probed, the more they believed that Mudd did know the identity of the injured man when he came to the Mudd farm and was now lying about it.

Three days later, Lovett returned to the Mudd estate. Dr. Mudd again insisted that he hadn't recognized the man whose leg he fixed. During this second visit, Mudd's wife Sarah gave Lovett the boot her husband cut off of Booth's leg. Lovett found the name "J Wilkes" inscribed inside the boot.[3] Mudd denied seeing the name, but the boot's inscription suggested that he likely knew the stranger's identity. His suspicion piqued, Lovett took Mudd to Bryantown for further questioning.

During interrogation, Mudd admitted that he had met Booth before the morning April 15, but insisted it was on just one prior occasion—a lie that would ensnare him later at trial. Mudd now appeared more of an accomplice after the fact than a country doctor duped into helping an assassin. He was arrested and joined the others in chains.

Booth and Herold managed to remain on the lam for a week after Johnson put a price on their head, but their luck ran out on April 26, 1865. Federal investigators led by Everton Conger tracked the duo to the Virginia farm of Richard Garrett. At first Garrett told Conger that Booth had hightailed it into the woods, but Conger didn't buy it. Not one to mince words, Conger threatened Garrett with a bit of frontier justice: If Garrett didn't tell Conger where Booth was hiding, Conger would string him up until he did. The son of the terrified man immediately pointed at the barn.

Conger's men surrounded the barn, trapping the two fugitives. Herold surrendered, but Booth refused, vowing to fight instead. Once again, the actor illustrated his flair for the dramatic when he yelled, "Well, my brave boys, prepare a stretcher for me."[4]

Federal troops torched the barn to smoke out the assassin. As the flames ate away at the structure, Booth grabbed his rifle and started toward the barn door. He apparently wasn't going to go down without a fight. Sgt. Boston Corbett, a survivor of Andersonville who would go on to testify at the trial of Henry Wirz, shot Booth.

As he lay dying, Booth—paralyzed by Corbett's shot—asked to have his hands lifted up so he could see them. He looked at his hands. "Useless, useless," he uttered, dying a few minutes later. Booth's body and Herold went back to the capital; they both would end up inside the Old Arsenal Penitentiary.

Booth's body took a strange, twisted journey after it left Garrett's farm sewn up in a horse blanket. According to Lafayette C. Baker, who recounted the incident in his memoir *History of the United States Secret Service*, Booth's corpse became the target of relic hunters looking for macabre souvenirs of the century's most infamous crime.

"I was greatly surprised and indignant," Baker said, "to find persons of high position, and some of secession proclivities, around the dead body, the coarse shroud parted at the seam, and a lady at that moment cutting off a lock of the black, curled, and beautiful hair."[5] Except for the one curl of hair, Booth's body made it back to the capital unscathed, at least by souvenir hunters.

The corpse was taken to the *Montauk*, a Federal monitor docked at the Washington Navy Yard. After an autopsy, it was taken out to sea and dropped, or so the authorities wanted people to think. The newspapers believed the ruse, reporting Booth's burial at sea.

Richmond's infamous "Castle Thunder." The alleged cruelties that took place in this former tobacco warehouse led the Confederate Congress to conduct an investigation. LIBRARY OF CONGRESS

Castle Thunder's most famous inmate, Dr. Mary E. Walker. The battlefield doctor was one tough customer. "I am a lady, gentlemen, and I dare any man to insult me," she told fellow inmates. LIBRARY OF CONGRESS

Jefferson C. Davis (left) confronted William "Bull" Nelson (right) at Louisville's Galt House. Davis was half Nelson's size, but he refused to let the imposing general's insult go unanswered.
LIBRARY OF CONGRESS

John Sappington Marmaduke defended his honor on a private battlefield. Unlike Jefferson C. Davis, Marmaduke spent the rest of his life feeling guilty about his duel with fellow CSA general "Marsh" Walker.
LIBRARY OF CONGRESS

Conditions for contraband could be harsh, as suggested by this sketch from *Frank Leslie's Illustrated*. Often, former slaves were exploited as laborers and sometimes even became the victims of violent crime. LIBRARY OF CONGRESS

Contraband and black soldiers alike were given the least desirable chores. In this picture, a group of black soldiers exhume bodies from the battlefield of Cold Harbor, Virginia, in 1865. LIBRARY OF CONGRESS

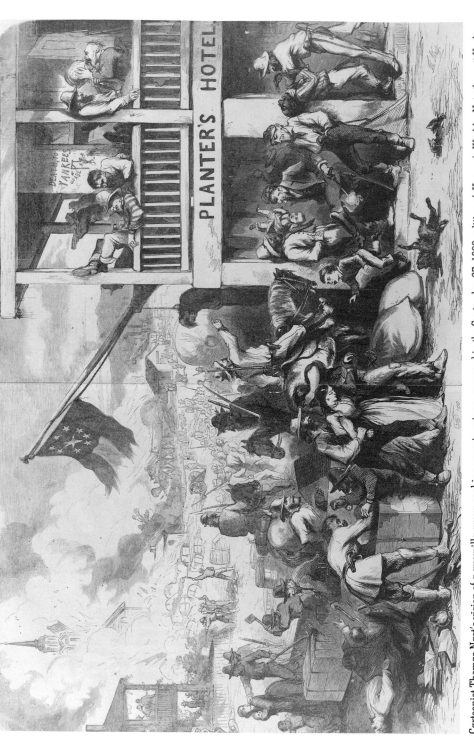

Cartoonist Thomas Nast's vision of a guerrilla group sacking a western town appeared in the September 27, 1862, edition of *Harper's Weekly*. Note the anti-Yankee graffiti on the second story of the "Planter's Hotel," the desperado holding the baby upside down, the Northern sympathizer strung up from the flagpole, and the two ruffians manhandling the woman. Quantrill's Bushwhackers, unlike these desperadoes, rarely harmed women. LIBRARY OF CONGRESS

Above left: This sketch of the Lawrence Massacre appeared in the September 5, 1863, edition of *Harper's Weekly*. Above right: Infamous Jayhawker Jim Lane. Lane was in Lawrence when Quantrill's men sacked the town, and according to some sources, he was the primary target on Quantrill's death list. In one interview, Quantrill said that if he caught Lane, he would skin him. Lane survived the raid by hiding in a cornfield. LIBRARY OF CONGRESS

This sketch of the "Fort Pillow Massacre" appeared in the April 30, 1864, edition of *Harper's Weekly*. "The annals of savage warfare nowhere record a more inhuman, fiendish butchery than this," the *Harper's* writer proclaimed. Inset: The "Wizard of the Saddle," Nathan Bedford Forrest. LIBRARY OF CONGRESS

Stephen "the Butcher" Burbridge tried to discourage guerrillas by executing prisoners in retaliation for their raids. When he was reassigned in February 1865, he left Kentucky as one of the most despised men in the state. LIBRARY OF CONGRESS

"I chose to pursue a different course, and made war upon the guerrillas personally," Palmer later said when comparing his methods to those of Burbridge. Palmer's mercenaries captured "Sue Mundy" and later William Quantrill. LIBRARY OF CONGRESS

Gen. Lew Wallace, who played a key role in the two biggest courtroom dramas of the era: the trials of the Lincoln assassination conspirators and Henry Wirz. LIBRARY OF CONGRESS

The War Department's wanted poster offering a reward for the assassins "Of our late beloved President, Abraham Lincoln." LIBRARY OF CONGRESS

Four of the men who presided over the conspiracy trial. From left: Gen. Joseph Holt, Gen. Robert Foster, Col. H. L. Burnett, and Col. C. R. Clendemin. LIBRARY OF CONGRESS

Facing page: After their arrests, Mary Surratt and Dr. Mudd were taken to the Old Capitol Prison. The other six conspirators were taken aboard Federal monitors, where they were photographed. Note the nineteenth-century handcuffs with a crossbar, which restricted movement. After Payne tried to commit suicide by ramming his head against the ship's bulkhead, his jailers also put a padded box over his head. LIBRARY OF CONGRESS

Payne: death by hanging

Atzerodt: death by hanging

Arnold: life in prison

O'Laughlen: life in prison

Spangler: six years in prison

Herold: death by hanging

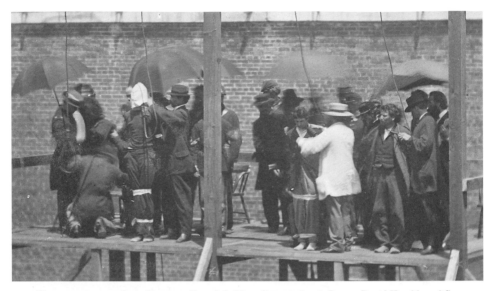

The executioners adjust the ropes. From left, Mary Surratt, Lewis Payne, David Herold, and George Atzerodt. Atzerodt's anxiety is evident in his facial expression as he watches the hangman place a noose over Herold's neck. LIBRARY OF CONGRESS

The four condemned conspirators hanging in the yard of the Old Arsenal Penitentiary. From left: Mary Surratt, Lewis Payne, David Herold, and George Atzerodt. Payne strangled slowly, lifting his legs a few times in his death throes. LIBRARY OF CONGRESS

The government spared all expense in the burials of the conspirators. They were interred in rifle boxes in the yard of the Old Arsenal Penitentiary. LIBRARY OF CONGRESS

Below: Dr. Mudd's failed escape attempt from Fort Jefferson as depicted in the October 21, 1865 edition of *Harper's Weekly*. Right: John Surratt in 1867, at about the time of his arrest. While Surratt faced charges, Mudd was at Fort Jefferson battling the yellow fever epidemic that killed Michael O'Laughlen. LIBRARY OF CONGRESS

Champ Ferguson, a Guerilla on trial, with guard of 9th. Infty Mich

Champ Ferguson stands tall in this photograph taken after his capture. One of his guards was a Michigan man, and the photograph (one of the very few of Ferguson that exist) made its way back to the Great Lakes State and is now part the University of Michigan's collections. LOUIS E. SPRINGSTEEN COLLECTION, BENTLEY HISTORICAL LIBRARY, THE UNIVERSITY OF MICHIGAN

The hanging of Champ Ferguson as sketched for the November 11, 1865, edition of *Harper's Weekly*. The skirt around the drop and the lines of soldiers surrounding the gallows on three sides led to conspiracy theories that Champ, in collusion with Federal authorities, survived the execution.

Temperance Neely's champion in court, the honorable Nathaniel Boyden. LIBRARY OF CONGRESS

The picket fence that served as Andersonville's "dead line." Did Wirz entice his men to shoot POWs inside the line? The military commission pondered this question during the trial.
LIBRARY OF CONGRESS

This sketch of Henry Wirz's trial appeared in the October 21, 1865 edition of *Harper's Weekly*. Wirz became so ill in the waning days of the trial that he watched the proceedings from a couch.

In this detail from a larger image, Henry Wirz bows his head as he listens to the charges read on the scaffold. LIBRARY OF CONGRESS

The floor drops from beneath the feet of convicted war criminal Henry Wirz. The execution took place in the closed courtyard of the Old Capitol Prison. Desperate to watch the hanging, a few men climbed trees to catch a glimpse. LIBRARY OF CONGRESS

During the Civil War, both civilian and military perpetrators were tried by military commissions. Justice was swift and harsh: Trials sometimes lasted only a few hours and capital punishment was common for more severe crimes. In this early stereoview, a Private Johnson is hanged following a conviction for rape. LIBRARY OF CONGRESS

In fact, Booth's body was taken to Washington's Old Arsenal Penitentiary, a former prison that had been transformed into an ammunition depot, and secretly buried according to Secretary of War Edwin Stanton's orders. Swathed in a blanket, Booth's body was deposited under a stone slab in a ground-floor cell where it remained for two years—a postmortem prison stint intended to protect Booth's corpse from desecration. Stanton had the only key to the cell.

In 1867, the body was exhumed, placed in a pine box, and moved to a prison warehouse where it lay for another two years. Booth's remains were exhumed for a second time in 1869. After an inquest, the remains were released to the Booth family, who buried them in an unmarked grave in the family plot at Baltimore's Green Mount Cemetery.

Booth's death deprived authorities the satisfaction of trying and executing the man who staged and committed the crime of the century. But the crime wouldn't go without a trial. As investigators probed, they discovered a sinister conspiracy and a mysterious cabal assembled to execute it. The murder of Lincoln was just the closing act in a play that allegedly involved a shady lineup of nine (excluding Booth) suspects.

By late April, investigators had netted eight of the nine. Only one suspected conspirator—Mary Surratt's son John—remained on the loose. He had simply vanished and would not reemerge for more than a year after the trapdoor was sprung on his confederates.

Everywhere they went, the alleged conspirators all wore canvas hoods, as ordered by Secretary Stanton, in order to keep them completely isolated. Although a hood was stitched for Dr. Mudd, he escaped being forced to wear the oppressive canvas contraption. A headpiece was also made for Mary Surratt, but authorities worried that such treatment of a woman might not sit well with the public, so she too avoided the sinister-looking hood. Mary Surratt and Dr. Mudd went to the Old Capitol Prison, while the rest had been taken to ships anchored offshore. On April 27, Lewis Payne attempted to kill himself by ramming his head into the wall of his cell, so his canvas hood was replaced with a padded hood known as a "muffler."

As the trial approached, the prisoners were relocated to the Old Arsenal Penitentiary (the same place that served as Booth's temporary grave), where they were confined to individual cells with the highest security possible. Nails were pulled out of the cell walls and the prisoners were deprived of eating utensils to keep them from harming themselves or others, and guards kept a constant vigil over the prisoners twenty-four hours a day.

President Johnson ordered the formation of a military commission to try the eight alleged conspirators. Maj. Gen. David Hunter, a friend of Lincoln's, presided over a panel of officers, which included Maj. Gen. Lew Wallace. The future governor of New Mexico and author of the novel *Ben Hur* would, a few months later, preside over another such trial when Andersonville's commandant faced charges of murder and conspiracy to commit murder.

The decision to try the conspirators by a military commission was a point of contention from the outset of the trial. The defense argued that the eight defendants should be tried in a civilian, not a military court. "My conclusion," Attorney General James Speed said in later defending the decision to use a military tribunal, "is, that if the persons who are charged with the assassination of the President committed the deed as public enemies, as I believe they did . . . they not only can, but ought to be tried before a military tribunal. If the persons charged have offended against the laws of war, it would be as palpably wrong of the military to hand them over to the civil courts, as it would be wrong in a civil court to convict a man of murder who had, in time of war, killed another in battle."[6]

Critics of the trial argued that the standards of the military commission stacked the deck against the conspirators. Instead of a unanimous decision needed for a guilty verdict, the commission only needed a majority. For a sentence of death, the commission needed a two-thirds majority. If convicted, the defendants could not appeal their verdicts to a higher appellate court. They could only appeal to the nation's highest authority—President Andrew Johnson.

And the speed with which the trial proceeded hindered the defense. Testimony began just three days after the defendants were asked if they wanted counsel. In order to be ready, their defense attorneys had to scramble to piece together their cases. "Public enemies" one through eight went before Hunter's military commission less than a month after the assassination. The arraignment took place on May 10 in a large room specially prepared for the purpose on the third floor of the Old Arsenal Penitentiary.

The prisoners, each wearing shackles (except for Mary Surratt, who was not required to wear restraints on her hands or feet during the trial), shuffled their way into the makeshift courtroom to face the military commission. The fetters around Atzerodt's and Payne's ankles were attached to iron balls, which guards carried when the men traveled from their cells to the courtroom. The prisoners also wore manacles; Dr. Mudd wore police-style handcuffs, or "bracelets," while the other male prisoners wore cuffs separated by ten-inch bars that kept their hands apart.

The defendants lined up in the dock—a raised platform on one side of the courtroom—with uniformed soldiers between them. Ben Perley Poore, a Washington correspondent who covered the trial, studied the infamous eight as they listened to the charges. Poore, with a journalist's eye for detail, described the alleged conspirators as they sat in the dock from right to left. At the time, people generally believed that a person's character could be determined by their physical appearance, which is evident in Poore's descriptions of the defendants.

Samuel Arnold: "curly brown hair and restless eyes."

Dr. Mudd: "rather tall, and quite thin, with sharp features, high bald forehead, astute blue eyes, compressed pale lips, and sandy hair, whiskers, and mustache."

Edman Spangler: "a large, unintelligent-looking face, evidently swollen by an intemperate use of ardent spirits."

Michael O'Laughlen: "uneasy black eyes, bushy black hair, a heavy black mustache and imperial, and a most anxious expression of countenance, shaded by a sad, remorseful look."

George Atzerodt: "short, thick-set, round-shouldered, brawny-armed man with a stupid expression, high cheek-bones, a sallow expression, small grayish-blue eyes, tangled, light-brown hair, and straggling sandy whiskers and mustache" with a "stoical indifference to what was going on in the court," unless it directly concerned him.

Lewis Payne (Powell): "motionless and imperturbed," with an "athletic, gladiatorial frame" and "unflinching dark gray eyes, low forehead, massive jaws, compressed full lips, small nose with large nostrils, and stolid, remorseless expression."

David Herold: "a slender frame" and "a narrow forehead . . . small dark hazel eyes" and "thick black hair."

Mary Surratt: "a belle in her youth, who has borne her five and forty years or more bravely. When she raised her veil in court that some witness might identify her, she exposed rather pleasing features, with dark gray eyes and brown hair."[7]

These were the eight individuals charged with "maliciously, unlawfully, and traitorously . . . combining, confederating, and conspiring together to kill and murder" Abraham Lincoln and conspiring to murder Vice President Andrew Johnson, Secretary of State William Seward, and Gen. Ulysses S. Grant.

The charges specified the roles each defendant allegedly played in the conspiracy supposedly authored by Booth and his Confederate backers: Spangler aided Booth by helping him flee the theater; Herold aided Payne in the botched attempt on Seward's life; O'Laughlen intended to murder Grant; Atzerodt intended to murder Johnson; Arnold, Surratt, and Mudd played supporting roles in this vast, shadowy conspiracy to topple the heads of the US government. To prove its case, the government turned to Judge Advocate Joseph Holt, who was assisted by Judge Advocates Henry L. Burnett and John A. Bingham.

The defense included a few legal luminaries. Thomas Ewing, chief justice of the Kansas Supreme Court before the war, represented

Arnold, Mudd, and Spangler. Former Maryland Attorney General Reverdy Johnson represented Mary Surratt, but he was a controversial character in his own right. Johnson didn't endorse the use of loyalty oaths during the 1864 election, which led to the question as to whether or not he had the right to defend a person suspected of high treason. The commission ultimately decided he could represent Surratt, but the controversy destroyed his credibility, so Mary Surratt's case was handled primarily by two young attorneys named Frederick Aiken and John W. Clampitt.

Testimony began on May 12, two days after the arraignment. Over the next six weeks, more than three hundred witnesses appeared before the commission. Holt wanted to connect Lincoln's murder to a grand rebel conspiracy, so he called several witnesses to talk about the rebel espionage department. The witnesses claimed to see conspiracies behind every corner and offered testimony about various plots concocted by agents working for the Confederate government.

They testified about a plot to poison New York's water supply; about a scheme to infect northern cities with yellow fever; about the plan to burn New York, executed in part by Robert Cobb Kennedy; about plans to destroy Union steamboats; about an attempt to blow up part of Richmond's Libby Prison while it was filled with Union prisoners; and the plot against the Union commander-in-chief. One witness even told about an advertisement supposedly posted in the *Selma* [Alabama] *Dispatch* by a man who offered to murder Lincoln for $1 million.

This testimony indicted the Confederate government for just about every crime imaginable, from vandalism to terrorism to the murder of President Lincoln.

Although Judge Advocate Bingham attempted to prove that the defendants plotted to murder Lincoln from the start, testimony established that Booth, along with the team of conspirators he recruited, originally intended to kidnap Lincoln, take him to Richmond, and later ransom him for imprisoned Confederates. Booth hatched a plan to nab the president while he and first lady were en route to see a play on March 17, but the president altered his schedule. A few weeks later, Richmond fell to Grant's Federal troops, and at some point after that Booth changed the plan from a kidnapping to a murder.

According to Louis Weichmann—a friend of the Surratt family who testified at the trial—Booth made a veiled reference to an assassination plot after hearing about Lee's surrender to Grant at Appomattox Court House on April 12. Booth remarked that he wanted to present the play *Venice Preserved*, a story about murder conspiracy, although Weichmann claimed that at the time he didn't understand Booth's allusion.

The government's case was strongest against Lewis Payne, who was caught red-handed following his attempt to murder Secretary Seward. Payne, a native of Alabama, spent much of his youth in Georgia, where his father worked a farm and ran a Baptist ministry. A shy teen, Payne delighted in helping wounded animals, earning him the nickname "Doc." At seventeen, Doc Payne enlisted with and fought for the Second Florida. He fought at Gettysburg, where he was wounded and captured by Union forces. He was eventually transferred to a Baltimore hospital, where he fell head-over-heels for a nurse.

Payne managed to escape and joined Mosby's Rangers, a famed Confederate cavalry unit under the command of John Singleton Mosby. Payne fought valiantly but in January 1865 he signed an oath of allegiance to the Union (as "Lewis Paine") and returned to Baltimore. He took a room in that city at the Branson boardinghouse, which was frequented by members of the Confederate Secret Service—the organization that allegedly masterminded various plots against Union cities, including the failed attempt to incinerate New York. According to some sources, Payne went to work for the group.

During his time in Baltimore, Payne met John Surratt, who knew John Wilkes Booth. Surratt introduced the two future conspirators, and Payne agreed to join Booth's plot to kidnap the president. Later, when Booth decided to instead assassinate the heads of state, he assigned Payne the role of assassinating Secretary Seward.

The attempt on Seward wasn't Payne's first criminal assault of a non-combatant. While at the Branson boardinghouse, he trounced a black servant for doing what Payne felt was a substandard cleaning job. He pushed the startled woman to the floor and violently kicked her. He wound up spending two days in jail but never faced charges for the assault.

William Bell, Sgt. George Robinson, and Seward's son, Maj. Augustus Seward, all testified about Payne's attempt to murder the secretary. Each man began his testimony by pointing at Payne as the one who bashed Frederick Seward, slashed Robinson, and then stabbed the secretary. When Bell pointed at him, Payne laughed out loud—an emotion that startled some in the courtroom, given the circumstances.

During his testimony, Maj. Augustus Seward recounted the attack. After hearing a commotion, he said, he ran to his father's room. "During this time," Seward said, Payne "repeated, in an intense but not strong voice, the words 'I'm mad, I'm mad.'"[8]

Augustus briefly tussled with Payne, who bashed the major with a bottle. The would-be-assassin then darted down the stairs and through the front door. The major ran to his room, grabbed his revolver, and went to the door, but by then Payne had jumped onto his getaway horse and galloped off into the night.

Col. H. H. Wells, who took custody of Payne after his arrest on April 17 and examined his clothes aboard a Federal monitor, described what appeared to be spots of blood on Payne's coat and shirtsleeve. A box containing the clothes Payne wore during his arrest was entered into evidence. Wells pointed out the blood spatter on the white shirt. "I called Payne's attention to this at the time," Wells testified, "and said 'What do you think now?' He leaned back against the side of the boat and said nothing."[9]

Wells also took a pair of boots from Payne. Inside the boot cuff was a black ink blotch that may have been used to cover something. During a bit of nineteenth-century forensic work, Spencer Clark examined the mark and saw some faint writing beneath it. Using oxalic acid, Clark managed to remove the upper coat of ink to find a name. "The name appeared to me to be," Clark testified, "J. W. Booth."

When the judge advocate asked about the clarity of the inscription, Clark admitted that "The J and W were distinct; the rest of the writing was obscure." He went on to say that the inscription "left very little doubt upon my mind that the name was Booth."[10]

In his cross, Payne's attorney William E. Doster questioned Clark about this evidence.

"You had, then, an impression that it was your duty to discover some name; had you not?"

"Yes, sir; if it was there," Clark responded.

"And someone in connection with this case?"

"I expected to find the name of Payne," Clark admitted.

"And, not finding that, you naturally expected to find the name of somebody else connected with this case?"

"I then followed out the letters until I thought I plainly discovered 'th' at the end; and then the name of Booth came to my mind. That was before I had clearly determined upon the B."[11]

Clark also admitted that acid had obliterated the inscription. So the only evidence left to prove his findings was his word.

The boot wasn't the only thing connecting Payne to Booth. Weichmann, who was originally arrested in connection with the conspiracy, testified that he saw Payne at Surratt's boardinghouse on several occasions, where he would disappear behind closed doors with Booth and John Surratt for hours at a time.

Doster faced an uphill battle in his attempt to keep his client from the gallows. He decided on an insanity plea. "I intend to set up the plea of insanity," Doster informed the court. "I claim that the whole conduct of the alleged murderer, from beginning to end, is the work of an insane man."

Doster laid down his argument in front of the commission. Only an insane man would drop the intended murder weapon—the Bowie knife—

on the doorstep of the victim. Only an insane man would slowly ride away and then not flee the city, instead riding "around like a maniac" and then returning to "the very house which, if he had any sense, he knew must be exactly the house where he would be arrested."

And then, Doster noted, there was his behavior at the trial: "Instead of showing the slightest feeling, he has displayed an indifference throughout this trial. You yourselves noticed that at the time of that solemn scene, when the negro [Bell] identified him, he stood here and laughed at the moment when his life was trembling in the balance."[12]

To prove his case, Doster called a woman who witnessed Payne savagely beating the servant at the Branson boardinghouse in Baltimore, and two doctors, Dr. Charles H. Nichols—the supervisor of the "Government Hospital for the Insane"—and Dr. James Hall, who examined Payne for forty-five minutes on the morning he testified.

"I should say that, from the whole examination" Dr. Hall testified, "there was reasonable ground for suspicion of insanity." But, Dr. Hall noted, he would need more time to be sure. "I can not give a positive opinion that he is laboring under either moral or mental insanity."[13]

Doster also called eyewitnesses who testified that Payne said he was weary of life and just wanted them to hurry up and hang him so he didn't have to return to the courtroom. That Payne was physically uncomfortable was confirmed by another one of Payne's jailors, who testified on June 3 that Payne suffered from a serious case of constipation and hadn't had a bowel movement since April 29.

To rebut Doster's defense, the judge advocate called a series of doctors, including Surgeon General J. K. Barnes. Even Dr. Hall returned and gave testimony rebutting his earlier statements. During his second trip to the stand, Hall did a one-eighty, reversing his earlier opinion about Payne's mental fitness. "I think I am now prepared to say," Dr. Hall testified, "that there is no evidence of mental insanity. Payne's mind is weak and uncultivated, but I can not discover any sufficient evidence of mental insanity."[14]

Doster's insanity defense had unraveled before his eyes, so he changed his approach. Doster based his closing argument on the supposition that Payne suffered from a form of fanatical mania caused by a combination of factors that included growing up around slavery and the war. This mania had made Payne delusional, believing that he was doing the right thing. This mental state, Doster argued, made Payne a tool used by Booth. He was a willing accomplice, just not a responsible one.

The government also had a strong case against David Herold, who had fled Washington with Booth and was caught hiding out with the president's assassin. At the trial, the most damning words against David Herold came from Herold himself. The twenty-two-year-old bragged about the conspiracy to murder Lincoln during his time on the lam with Booth. "We are the assassinators of the President," Herold proclaimed to a former rebel soldier as he and Booth crossed the Rappahannock River from Maryland into Virginia. Herold meant the "royal we." After making the statement, he pointed to Booth and said "Yonder is the assassinator."[15]

What David Herold did do on the night of April 14 was wait outside the Seward residence with Payne's getaway vehicle; while Payne scrummed with Seward's sons and bodyguards, Herold held the reins to the would-be assassin's horse. At some point during the struggle, he lost his nerve and galloped away. Then he fled the city and met up with Booth, hiding out until Conger tracked them to Garrett's barn.

Herold's role in the affair, it appeared, was assisting in Booth's escape from the city—a role he apparently prepared for earlier on the afternoon of April 14. John Fletcher testified that David Herold rented a horse from his stables on the day of Lincoln's assassination. It wasn't Herold's first visit to Fletcher's business; both he and George Atzerodt had visited the stables in early April. On April 14, Herold rented a horse from Fletcher until 9 P.M. at the latest. When Herold didn't return the horse, Fletcher went looking for it around 10 P.M. From a distance, Fletcher caught sight of Herold and another man matching the description of George Atzerodt, but he didn't manage to catch them.

Like Doster's defense of Payne, Herold's lawyer Frederick Stone argued that his client was nothing more than a tool used by John Wilkes Booth. Unlike Doster, though, Stone didn't try to prove that his client was crazy, only dimwitted. Through a series of witnesses, Stone tried to depict his client as a simpleton, a ventriloquist's dummy, with Booth's hand in the glove.

Character witnesses for David Herold testified about a boy in a twenty-two-year-old's skin. Francis S. Walsh, who ran a drugstore where Herold worked for awhile, described the defendant as "more like a boy than a man." Herold was "easily persuaded and led, more than is usually the case with young men of his age; I considered him boyish in every respect."[16] Another acquaintance, Dr. Samuel A. H. McKim, characterized Herold as slow. "In mind," Dr. McKim testified, "I consider him about eleven years in age."[17]

Stone argued that even Booth exonerated Herold. "I declare, before my Maker, that this man is innocent," Booth said when he was captured. If Herold was guilty of anything, Stone said, it was "his aiding in the escape of Booth, and no more. It by no means follows, because he aided Booth to escape, that he aided him to kill the President"[18]

George Atzerodt, according to his defense, also played no role in the conspiracy—he didn't have the guts to be an assassin. The twenty-nine-year-old Atzerodt had immigrated to the states from Germany at age eight. During the war, Atzerodt came into contact with Confederate spies, including John Surratt. Atzerodt followed Surratt to Washington and stayed for a while in Mary Surratt's boardinghouse. John Surratt introduced him to Booth, who later recruited Atzerodt to play a role in the kidnapping scheme.

When the kidnapping plot turned to one of murder, Booth tapped Atzerodt as Vice President Johnson's assassin, according to the prosecution. Witnesses placed Atzerodt in the same hotel Johnson was staying in, the Kirkwood House, on April 14. Investigators testified about the things found in Atzerodt's room there, including the revolver under the pillow and the knife under the mattress. A witness testified that Atzerodt's room was advantageously positioned for a strike against the vice president.

Col. W. R. Nevins, who had visited the Kirkwood on April 12, testified that the man now sitting between Michael O'Laughlen and Lewis Payne in the prisoners' dock approached him and asked the whereabouts of the vice president.

John Fletcher said that on the afternoon of April 14, Atzerodt came to his stable with Herold and a mare. He asked Fletcher to keep the saddle and bridle on the mare until 10 P.M. He left and then returned later that night, around 10 P.M., and asked Fletcher to have a drink with him. The two men went to the Union Hotel. "I had a glass of beer and he drank some whiskey," Fletcher recalled. "Returning to the stable, he said 'If this thing happens to-night, you will hear of a present,' or 'Get a present.'"[19] The cryptic remark, the prosecution argued, suggested premeditation.

Due in part to Fletcher's testimony, prosecutors linked three of the suspects to Booth—a bit of horseplay that would turn out to be lethal for the alleged conspirators. Atzerodt had rented a stable from Fletcher for the horse identified as the one Payne used to flee from Seward's house (and which was later found abandoned). This was the same horse Booth had purchased from a neighbor of Dr. Mudd.

The prosecution also called James McPhail, a provost marshal for the State of Maryland. On May 1, Atzerodt summoned McPhail to his cell and made a partial confession. As the prisoner spilled his guts, an assistant hurriedly scribbled the admission onto a piece of paper. In his statement, Atzerodt said that on April 14 he tossed his knife into the street; he also claimed that the gun and knife found in his room belonged to David Herold. Atzerodt said more, but the court ruled portions of his confession inadmissible. The actual text of the statement was lost for more than a century; the document often referred to as the "Lost Confession" turned up in 1977 among the papers of Atzerodt's attorney, William Doster.

In his rambling confession, Atzerodt admitted meeting with the others to plan the kidnapping of Lincoln. "Arnold, O'Laughlen, Surratt, Harold, Booth, and myself met once at a saloon or restaurant," Atzerodt said. He also said that he was "certain Dr. Mudd knew all about" the kidnapping scheme.

Atzerodt went on to insist that he didn't participate in the murder plot, which he said Booth only told him about a few hours before it happened. He didn't believe Booth would actually kill Lincoln.

"Herold came to the Kirkwood House, same evening for me to go to see Booth. I went with Herold & saw Booth. He then said he was going to kill the President and Wood, the Secy. of State. I did not believe him. This occurred in the evening about 7 ½ o'clock. It was dark. I took a room at Kirkwood's. Both Herold & I went to the room left Herold's coat, knife, & pistol in room and never again returned to it."[20]

In his defense of George Atzerodt, William Doster argued that Atzerodt lacked the constitution to commit murder. Doster called a series of witnesses who testified that Atzerodt was too yellow to have plotted an assassination.

Although he had planned to nab the president as part of the initial plot, Doster argued, Atzerodt didn't do anything on April 14 other than down a few cocktails. "This man is principal in an attempt to abduct the President of the United States. He has assaulted no one; he has sheltered no one that did assault," Doster explained. "He has killed no one, nor has he sheltered anyone that did kill. You can, therefore, only find him guilty of a crime for which he is not on trial."[21]

Mary Surratt sheltered some of the alleged conspirators in her boardinghouse, but did she know what they were plotting?

The forty-two-year-old Surratt grew up in Maryland and at age seventeen married John Surratt. Together, they had three children; their eldest child, John Jr., grew up to become a Confederate spy and alleged Lincoln conspirator.

The Surratts lived on a large parcel of land that eventually evolved into "Surrattsville," a village with its own post office and saloon. John Sr. died in 1862, so in 1864, Mary leased Surrattsville's saloon to John Lloyd and moved to Washington, where she operated a boardinghouse.

John Jr.'s cronies included most of the alleged conspirators, who used Surratt's boardinghouse as a place to meet and discuss their plots. But did the mistress of the house know what they were talking about? And did she help them with their scheme?

Prosecutors believed that she did. Among the dozens of witnesses called to testify against Mary Surratt, former boarder Louis Weichmann and saloon operator John Lloyd proved to be the most incriminating. Weichmann said that he saw Mary Surratt with John Surratt and some of the other alleged conspirators on several occasions. Surratt even went behind closed doors with John Wilkes Booth. They were talking about something, and the prosecution alleged the topic was murder.

Lloyd said that a little more than a month before Lincoln's assassination, John Surratt, George Atzerodt, and David Herold came to Surrattsville with a cache of guns and ammunition. They secreted the stash under the floorboards of a room above the tavern. According to Lloyd, on the evening of the assassination, Mary Surratt said that the "shooting irons" would be needed soon—a remark that, according to the prosecution, suggested she knew about the murder plot.

Surratt's lawyer, Frederick Aiken, noted that the prosecution's entire case rested on three "circumstances": Lloyd's testimony about the "shooting irons," Surratt's statement that she didn't know Lewis Payne when he came to her boardinghouse after the assassination, and her association with John Wilkes Booth. "These three circumstances constitute the part played by the accused, Mary E. Surratt, in this great conspiracy," Aiken said. "They are all that two months of patient and unwearying investigation, and the most thorough search for evidence that was probably ever made, has been able to develop against her."[22]

Lloyd's testimony must, according to Aiken, be mitigated by his heavy drinking. "But on the 14th of April," Aiken said, "and at a time when, as testified by his sister-in-law, he was more than ordinarily affected by intoxicating drink."[23] Even though Lloyd had apparently dried his own bar supply on April 14, he stuck to his story. But, Aiken implied, how reliable could it be?

As for Surratt's claim that she didn't know Payne, Aiken suggested that his middle-aged client suffered from poor eyesight. Besides, Payne was disguised as a ditchdigger when he returned to the boardinghouse on the evening of April 17.

That left Surratt's association with John Wilkes Booth as the remaining piece of evidence. Her lawyer argued that it made sense that a mother would at some point come in contact with her son's acquaintance—a "common acquaintance," as Aiken characterized it, not an "intimacy."

Another defendant who was guilty of associating with Booth was the country doctor whose name has become synonymous with dirt. Like Mary Surratt, Dr. Mudd was a native of Maryland. The young Samuel Mudd grew up on his father's sizable tobacco plantation about a day's ride from the nation's capital. His father, Henry Lowe Mudd, owned about ninety slaves who worked the plantation.

Mudd graduated from medical school at the University of Maryland in 1856. He practiced medicine, but when his father gave him a parcel of land as a wedding gift, Mudd became a gentleman farmer in addition to his practice. While he tended to the sick, his five slaves worked his small tobacco plantation.

When the war began, the institution of slavery began to atrophy in Maryland until it died altogether when the state abolished it in 1864. At this point, Mudd considered selling his plantation. One prospective buyer was John Wilkes Booth.

Booth wasn't really looking for land, though. At this point, historians believe, Booth was formulating a plan to kidnap Lincoln and was in Mudd's area scouting an escape route. The question was whether or not Mudd aided Booth in his plot.

During the trial, Dr. Samuel Mudd became, according to his lawyer Thomas Ewing, the victim of an assassination attempt of sorts: a character assassination, which Ewing described as an attempt to "blacken his character." Witnesses testified about his allegedly harsh treatment of his slaves, which Ewing called "utterly false," and disparaging remarks Mudd supposedly made about President Lincoln.[24]

But as damaging as these allegations may have been, it was Dr. Mudd's association with Booth and the other conspirators that doomed him at the trial. In an attempt to prove that Mudd played a role in the conspiracy, the prosecution focused on his prior relationships with the alleged conspirators, which indicated that he lied to investigators when he at first told them that he didn't know the man whose leg he splinted and when he later said he had met Booth on only one prior occasion.

A few of Mudd's former slaves testified to Mudd's involvement with John Surratt and other men believed to be involved in Confederate espionage. An acquaintance named Daniel Thomas even alleged that Mudd, just a few weeks before the assassination, made statements insinuating that the president would be killed. Although the validity of Thomas's testimony became a source of controversy during the trial, it cut deeply into Mudd's defense.

Col. H. H. Wells, who interviewed Mudd several times after the assassination, also testified for the prosecution. Wells recounted Mudd's story about the enigmatic man who appeared in the early hours of April 15 with a broken leg. Mudd fixed the man's leg, but he told Wells that he did not know the stranger. "I exhibited to him a photograph of Booth, but he said he could not recognize him from that photograph," Wells testified.[25] Wells claimed that later, on recollection, Mudd remembered the stricken man as John Wilkes Booth, whom he first met the previous November. Mudd admitted to him, Wells testified, "that he could now recognize the person he treated as the same person he was introduced to—Booth." And, the colonel added, Mudd insisted he had met Booth just once before that night.

According to Wells, Dr. Mudd also gave Booth and Herold directions. The doctor "said that Herold . . . asked him the direct route to Dr. Wilmer's, saying he was acquainted with the doctor. Dr. Mudd described the main traveled road, and was then asked if there was not a nearer way. He replied that there was a road across the swamp, and described it."[26] Dr. Mudd then showed Wells the route.

Wells described Dr. Mudd's demeanor during his various interviews. "Dr. Mudd's manner was so very extraordinary, that I scarcely know how to describe it," Wells said. "He did not seem unwilling to answer a direct question; he seemed embarrassed, and at the third interview alarmed, and I found that, unless I asked direct questions, important facts were omitted."[27]

Several witnesses testified about Mudd's previous association with Booth. According to testimony, the two had met in November 1864 when Mudd assisted Booth in buying a horse from a neighbor and was interested in purchasing Mudd's property. Judge Advocate Holt called a number of witnesses who testified that this wasn't the only time the two men came into contact with one another. Evans, a minister, told a story that raised a few eyebrows among the commission. Evans testified that he saw Mudd—whom he knew only as a "slight acquaintance"—in Washington, DC, around the beginning of March 1865.

Yet Evans was bewildered. The minister couldn't remember the names of all the people he visited that day. "I am so confused at present that I cannot recollect," Evans said. "I have been so confused since the death of President Lincoln that I really at times am bordering on insanity almost."[28] But he was lucid on one point: Evans said he watched Dr. Mudd go into Mary Surratt's house. The minister's dubious testimony didn't fool Thomas Ewing, who denounced him as a "false witness." In his closing argument, Ewing said that the only credible statement Evans made was that he had "been on the verge of insanity."

But other, more reliable witnesses also provided links between Dr. Mudd and Booth. Marcus Norton, a lawyer staying at the National Hotel, said that a man matching Mudd's description came into his room. The man apologized for the error, saying that he was looking for Booth and had arrived at the wrong room. Louis Weichmann also said that he saw Dr. Mudd with Booth outside of the National Hotel in late December 1864. Mudd recognized John Surratt, who was with Weichmann, and called out his name. According to Weichmann, the trio of Booth, Mudd, and Surratt went off together to discuss something in private.

This testimony was very damaging to Dr. Mudd. It indicated that he knew John Wilkes Booth before the assassin showed up at his home with a broken leg and made it hard to believe that he didn't recognize him that morning. The evidence suggested that Dr. Mudd had lied to the investigators. But was there any guilt beyond his association with Booth?

Not according to Thomas Ewing, who argued that Dr. Mudd was guilty of association only and played no role in the conspiracy. "As for Dr. Mudd," Ewing said, "there is not one particle of evidence tending to show that he was ever leagued with traitors in their treason."[29] Nor, according to Ewing, was Mudd guilty of being an accessory before or after the murder by aiding or abetting Booth and Herold in fleeing the authorities. Yes, Ewing argued, Dr. Mudd fixed Booth's leg, but Mudd's claim that he didn't know the identity of his patient was credible.

Ewing pointed out that there was no evidence that Booth said anything to Mudd, and that Booth was an actor "accustomed by years of professional practice to disguise his person, his features, and his tones, so that if Mudd had been an intimate associate, instead of a mere casual acquaintance, it would have been easy for Booth to maintain a disguise"[30]

If Mudd didn't recognize Booth and Herold, even though he fixed the assassin's leg, and even though he pointed out the way through the swamp, he was not, Ewing argued, an accessory. If Dr. Mudd was guilty of anything, it was of simply knowing the now-infamous assassin, John Wilkes Booth. And that wasn't a crime.

The prosecution's case against thirty-year-old Samuel Arnold hinged on a note. Investigators found what they believed amounted to a conspiratorial "smoking gun" in Booth's Washington hotel room: a letter dated March 27 from "Sam" to Booth alluding to an "enterprise."

A native of Washington, DC, Sam Arnold went to school in Baltimore, where he crossed paths with Booth. The school chums remained close, and when Booth masterminded his plot to kidnap Lincoln, Arnold agreed to help. The two conspirators met on March 15 and planned to spring their trap on March 17. When Lincoln foiled the plan by changing his itinerary, Arnold went back home to Baltimore.

The linchpin of the prosecution's case against Arnold was the letter. Dated March 27, ten days after the kidnapping was to take place, it suggested that the "enterprise" referred to another plot. That other plot, the judge advocate argued, was the plan to murder Lincoln.

Walter Cox, representing Samuel Arnold, argued that the letter referred to the aborted kidnapping scheme and not Booth's murder plot. Cox attempted to show through witnesses that Arnold had left the capital in late March; while he had planned to kidnap the president, he played no role in the planning or execution of Booth's murder conspiracy.

Arnold, Cox pointed out, wasn't even in the city when Booth executed his plot; he was clerking at Fortress Monroe in southern Virginia from April 2 through April 17, when he was arrested. "It was, therefore," Cox noted, "impossible for him to participate in the murder or assaults in Washington. Nor is there the slightest evidence, or even pretense, that he had any part to perform, in the execution of the deadly plot."[31]

Like Samuel Arnold, twenty-four-year-old Michael O'Laughlen was tied to Booth's murder conspiracy by a very thin thread. A native of Baltimore, he grew up in the same neighborhood as Booth and the two became lifelong friends. O'Laughlen did a brief stint in the Confederate army before returning home in June 1862.

Prosecutors presented evidence in the form of telegrams from Booth that appeared to incriminate O'Laughlen as part of Booth's scheme. In a telegram dated March 27, Booth says "Get word to Sam. Come on, without or without him, Wednesday morning. We sell that day for sure. Don't fail."

O'Laughlen's role in the murder conspiracy, prosecutors surmised, was to assassinate Ulysses S. Grant. According to the prosecution's theory, O'Laughlen believed that Grant was staying at the home of Secretary of War Stanton. To prove their case, they called witnesses who fingered O'Laughlen as the man who showed up at Stanton's house during a party held in Grant's honor the night before the assassination.

But O'Laughlen, according to his lawyer Walter Cox, had an alibi. Cox called a series of witnesses who claimed that O'Laughlen was nowhere near Stanton's residence on either April 13 or the night of Lincoln's murder. Instead, like George Atzerodt, he whiled away the night of the 14th at a saloon with friends, who provided an alibi for the crucial time when Booth shot Lincoln and Payne attacked Seward. The prosecution's eyewitnesses, Cox claimed, were mistaken when they said they saw O'Laughlen at Stanton's.

"The specific charge against him is, that he did, on the nights of the 13th and 14th of April, lie in wait for General Grant, with intent then and there to murder him," Cox argued. "The whole evidence on the subject shows a mistake of identity that would be ridiculous but for the serious consequences it involves to the accused."[32]

Thirty-nine-year-old Edman Spangler worked as a stagehand at Ford's Theater, where he became acquainted with John Wilkes Booth. A heavy drinker, Spangler typically spent the night at the theater. John T. Ford, the theater's proprietor, described Spangler's association with Booth when he testified for the defense: "Spangler seemed to have a great admiration for J. Wilkes Booth," Ford said. "Booth was a particularly fascinating man, and controlled the lower class of people, such as Spangler belonged to, more, I suppose, than ordinary men would." Ford went on the say that "Spangler was not in the employ of Booth, that I know, and only since the assassination have I heard that he was in the habit of waiting upon him."[33]

It was this alleged "habit of waiting upon" Booth that placed him next to the other seven defendants. Two witnesses in particular offered testimony that appeared to implicate Spangler as an accessory.

Joseph Burroughs, known as "Peanuts," worked at Ford's Theater with Spangler. Peanuts testified that Booth came to the theater between five and six on the evening of April 14 and put his horse in the stable behind the theater. Booth then "Hallooed out for Spangler; when he came, Booth asked him for a halter."

Booth returned later that night between nine and ten. According to Burroughs, Spangler asked him to hold Booth's horse. "When Spangler told me to hold the horse, I told him I could not; I had to go in to attend to my door," Burroughs testified. "He told me to hold it, and if there was anything wrong to lay the blame on him; so I held the horse." Burroughs also testified that when he and Spangler were preparing the president's box, Spangler snarled "Damn the President and General Grant."[34]

A few seconds after the shot that felled Lincoln, Booth fled through the back door into the alley, bashed Peanuts in the head with the end of his knife, and rode off.

The prosecution's key witness against Spangler was Jacob Ritterspaugh, a carpenter at Ford's Theater. Ritterspaugh said that on the night of the assassination, he was backstage when he heard a shot and then saw a man moving toward the back door. He tried to intercept the man but jumped back when the man swiped at him with a knife. After a brief chase down the alley, Ritterspaugh returned to the theater and said that he recognized the man as Booth.

Ritterspaugh's statement suggested that Spangler at least attempted to cover Booth's tracks away from the theater: "I came back to the stage where I had left Edward Spangler, and he hit me on the face with the back of his hand, and he said, 'Don't say which way he went.' I asked him what he meant by slapping me in the mouth, and he said, 'For God's sake, shut up.'"[35]

As damaging as these statements were, they didn't amount to evidence that Spangler knew about a plot to murder the president, according to Spangler's defense attorney, Thomas Ewing. The lawyer called James Lamb, a "scene painter" at Ford's, to rebut Ritterspaugh's testimony. Lamb testified that Ritterspaugh was still smarting the next day from Spangler's slap and carped about it to Lamb. According to Lamb, Ritterspaugh told a slightly different version of what Spangler said after cuffing him: "Then he represented Spangler as saying, when he slapped him, 'Hush up; hush up; You know nothing about it. What do you know about it? Keep quiet.'" Ritterspaugh never told him, Lamb added, that Spangler said "Don't say which way he went." Two other witnesses testified that Ritterspaugh told them about the incident but omitted the incriminating "Don't say which way he went" statement.

The devil was in the details. Ritterspaugh's recollection made Spangler look like an accomplice after the fact; Lamb's made him look more like an irritated stagehand in disbelief that his friend Booth just shot the President. If Lamb and the others correctly remembered their conversations with Ritterspaugh, Ewing argued, "there can be no question but that his statement of the conversation, made on the witness stand, is incorrect."[36]

After seven weeks of testimony, the trial came to an end. On June 29, the Commission went behind closed doors to contemplate the evidence and decide the fates of the eight alleged conspirators. It took just two days for the officers to sift through the testimony of more than 350 witnesses; on June 30, they returned their verdicts to President Johnson. The commission found all eight guilty of various charges. George Atzerodt, David Herold, Lewis Payne, and Mary Surratt received death sentences for their roles in the conspiracy. Mary Surratt was to become the first woman executed by the United States government. Samuel Arnold, Dr. Samuel Mudd, and Michael O'Laughlen received life sentences, while Edman Spangler received a six-year term for helping Booth to escape.

President Johnson approved the commission's verdicts on July 5, and the execution was set for July 7, 1865. The morning after Johnson signed the papers, Maj. Gen. John Hartranft, the officer who oversaw the conspirators' imprisonment at the Old Arsenal during the trial, went from cell to cell with sealed envelopes containing the death warrants. Hartranft stood by and watched as each of the four condemned tore open the envelopes and read their sentences.

The now-convicted conspirators were shocked by the commission's quick deliberation and judgment. George Atzerodt, the man whose attorney tried to depict as a coward, began to tremble.

Within hours of reading their death warrants, the four condemned could hear from their cells the ominous sound of hammers as workmen began building a wooden scaffold outside in the courtyard of the Old Arsenal.

Surratt's attorney made a last-ditch attempt to keep his client from the noose by submitting a writ of habeas corpus. Surratt's daughter Anna went to visit President Johnson to personally plead for her mother's life, but Johnson did not see her. He would not budge on Anna's mother's sentence, calling Surratt the one who "kept the nest that hatched the egg."[37] Johnson ordered the writ suspended and the immediate execution of Surratt's sentence.

With such little time between sentencing and execution, Hartranft scrambled to find relatives and spiritual counsel for the condemned. He managed to round up a few relatives who, dressed in black, visited their loved ones.

On the eve of the executions, the affair was debated on the floors of the city's taverns. The *New York Herald*'s coverage of the hangings captures the general feelings of the time. "Everything has been done decently and in order, and the majesty of the law and of the nation has been vindicated," the *Herald* proclaimed. But feelings were less unanimous regarding the hanging of a woman in the United States. "The sympathy in favor of Mrs. Surratt gained ground by discussion, and hundreds who admitted her guilt inveighed bitterly against the mode of punishment," wrote a *Herald* reporter.[38]

The execution took place on July 7 in the Old Arsenal Yard—a large courtyard enclosed by high walls. Amid the scorching heat of the summer's hottest day, the condemned, with their hands in manacles and their ankles shackled, shuffled their way to the scaffold. First came Mary Surratt, followed by Atzerodt, Payne, and Herold. Surratt was so distraught that she needed help walking. Atzerodt continued to tremble, while Payne walked like a man without a worry in the world.

The condemned sat on the scaffold as preparations were made. The arms of each were tied with strips of white muslin. Then their legs were also bound with muslin. From the raised platform, the four condemned could see the newly dug holes in the Arsenal yard that would serve as their temporary graves and a stack of four rifle boxes that would be their coffins.

The hangman and Lewis Payne exchanged a few words. The executioner said that he hoped Payne would die quickly. "You know best," Payne replied. Atzerodt was terrified, but Payne just stared at the clouds in the distance as white hoods were placed over the condemned's heads. "Gentlemen, beware!" George Atzerodt exclaimed. "Goodbye gentlemen!" A few seconds later, Atzerodt said his final farewell. "May we all meet in another world."[39] Mary Surratt also managed a few final words. "Don't let me fall," she said.

At about 1:30 P.M., the floor came out from under the four convicted Lincoln conspirators. The fall snapped Mary Surratt's neck, and her body remained motionless like a "bag of old clothes" in the words of the *New York Herald*.[40]

Atzerodt and Herold twitched as they dangled below the scaffold. Payne, who during the trial told a guard he wanted to die and when first imprisoned try to do the deed himself by ramming his head into a wall, took the longest to die. The crowd witnessed a macabre sight as Payne strangled to death. He pulled his legs up, as if sitting in a chair, then stretched them out, then pulled them up again. Payne violently twisted and shook for more than six minutes before he died.

After the last spasm, a small crowd gathered around the dangling bodies before they were cut down. The government spared all expense when it came to burying the four convicted conspirators: The bodies were interred, with white muslin hoods still over their heads and glass capsules containing their names (for future identification), in ammunition boxes. The bodies were later exhumed and moved to the same warehouse that temporarily held the remains of John Wilkes Booth and from there, to various locations.

The conspirators may have been six feet under, but they didn't disappear altogether. A few morbid souvenir seekers had obtained locks of Mary Surratt's hair and the Boston hemp rope used for the hangings and sold them as mementoes of the nineteenth-century's most sensational crime, trial, and execution.

The four conspirators who escaped the scaffold—Arnold, Mudd, O'Laughlen, and Spangler—were sent to one of the more remote places under US control: Fort Jefferson, a massive brick edifice on a tiny sand spit in the Dry Tortugas southwest of Florida. The hexagonal fortress had been converted to a prison for Union deserters and held about six hundred prisoners when the convicted Lincoln conspirators arrived there.

A life sentence for O'Laughlen amounted to just two years in captivity. In 1867, a yellow fever epidemic swept through Fort Jefferson, taking O'Laughlen and the fort's physician with it. With the unexpected vacancy, Mudd once again had a chance to practice medicine and took over as the prison's doctor.

Dr. Mudd missed the death penalty by one vote, but the commission did not give him a light sentence. For his role in the conspiracy, he received life in prison. He seemed content in captivity and initially didn't try to escape, but that changed on September 25, 1865 when the steamer *Thomas A. Scott* stopped by Fort Jefferson.

Mudd saw an opportunity and colluded with a sailor. Dressed in civilian clothes, he simply walked aboard and hid beneath some floorboards below deck. When a count of the prison's inmates came up short, guards searched the ship and found Mudd, hiding.

The incident later made it in print, albeit converted into a humorous yet inaccurate anecdote in the October 21, 1865 edition of *Harper's Weekly*. In the *Harper's* version of Mudd's escape, the doctor crawls into the cannon of a ship. He was a little too tall, however. A Lieutenant Tappan spied Mudd's shoes sticking out of the barrel, and the prisoner was returned to Fort Jefferson. A passenger aboard the steamship sketched the humorous scene and sent it to the nation's top-selling news rag.

Mudd eventually left the island prison as a free man. In 1869, President Johnson, swayed by Mudd's attorney Thomas Ewing and moved by Mudd's part as a doctor in the yellow fever epidemic, pardoned him. While his prison sentence was brief, Mudd received a life sentence of a sort; his name lived in infamy as the source of the common expression "His name is Mudd," which is synonymous with shame.

Mudd stayed out of the spotlight for a while, and then returned to the public eye when he unsuccessfully ran as a Democrat for the Maryland House of Delegates. He died of pneumonia in 1883 at the age of forty-nine.

Arnold and Spangler escaped the yellow fever epidemic and, in March 1869, the rest of their sentences as well. Three weeks after he pardoned Mudd, President Johnson extended his leniency to Arnold and Spangler. Spangler returned to Ford's Theater, where he worked until 1873. His health failing, he relocated to Maryland, moving in with Dr. Mudd's family. The two had become friends at Fort Jefferson. He died in 1875.

After his release, Samuel Arnold authored his memoirs, in which he admitted his role in Booth's plot to kidnap Lincoln. He died of tuberculosis in 1906 and was buried in the same cemetery as fellow conspirators Booth and O'Laughlen.

And what about the one who got away? In April 1865, alleged conspirator and former Confederate spy John Surratt fled north across the border into Canada. While the others stood trial at the Old Arsenal Penitentiary, Surratt laid low. In September, two months after his mother swung from the scaffold, he left North America for Europe. The long arm of the law finally caught up with Surratt in 1866. He was arrested in Egypt and brought back to the United States, where he stood trial as the tenth conspirator.

More than 150 witnesses testified at Surratt's trial, which took place during the summer of 1867. Unlike his alleged coconspirators, Surratt faced a civilian jury, which could not unanimously decide on his guilt or innocence. Following the hung jury, the charges were dropped and Surratt walked out of prison a free man in 1868. Surratt became a highly sought-after lecturer. Like Arnold, Surratt admitted that he plotted the president's kidnapping, but he adamantly denied playing any role in the assassination.

Surratt eventually settled down in Maryland and went to work for a transportation company. In 1916, he died of pneumonia just a week after his seventy-second birthday—the last of the alleged Lincoln conspirators to die.

As for the dastardly mastermind behind the Lincoln assassination, there were those who refused to let John Wilkes Booth die. The ultra-secret manner in which he was buried, and then exhumed, stored, and later re-buried encouraged speculation from the conspiracy machine, which churned out the story that Booth did not die in Garrett's barn. Each time Booth was buried, his remains were identified by several people (he had a tumor removed from his neck, which left a telltale mark); nonetheless, the rumor that Booth survived, and that Boston Corbett had shot someone else, continued to swirl.

A judge denied a 1995 request to exhume Booth's remains, leaving undisturbed, at least for now, the remains of the man who engineered the sensational crime.

The trial remains controversial nearly 150 years after the fact. Law schools debate the military commission's jurisdiction to try the case. Professional and amateur historians are divided on several key questions about the defendants and the roles played by Dr. Samuel Mudd and Mary Surratt in the drama authored by John Wilkes Booth. Were they guilty of wrongdoing or just by association? Or did their actions lie somewhere in the gray area between those two extremes?

According to some researchers, Booth's diary indicates that he changed his plan from one of kidnapping to murder at the last minute. This tidbit, the argument goes, exonerates Mary Surratt in a murder conspiracy. If she had prior knowledge of anything, it would have been Booth's kidnapping scheme. Some even call Surratt's execution a "judicial murder."

Under the conspiracy laws of the time, however, people who had knowledge of Booth's kidnapping plot would also have been guilty of a murder conspiracy, even if they didn't know that Booth had changed his plan. According to the 1865 law, if they knew about any plot against Lincoln, they had a legal obligation to take the information to authorities, an action which historian Edward Steers notes, might have saved Lincoln's life.[41] And many historians agree that both Surratt and Mudd knew about and probably played some part in Booth's kidnapping scheme.

There have been several efforts to clear Mudd's name through legal channels, but all of them have fallen just short of an official exoneration, and according to some sources, these attempts have actually further muddied the waters of the doctor's involvement. The image of a country doctor who innocently helped a man in need, according to many historians, just doesn't jive with the evidence that the two men knew each other and had met on several occasions prior to the assassination. Most agree that Mudd acted as an accomplice at least to some degree in helping Booth flee.

And then comes the eternal question: Who was the hand ultimately behind the assassination? Booth was the shooter, but was he the mastermind or merely the weapon of a shadowy cabal engineered by someone else? There is substantial evidence suggesting that Jefferson Davis knew about and possibly even condoned Booth's kidnapping plot, but what about the murder? Entire books have been devoted to conspiracies that indict, among others, Davis and even then-Vice President Andrew Johnson for planning the murder.

One theory posits that Lincoln's assassination was Confederate payback for an alleged Federal plot to murder Jefferson Davis. Despite exhaustive efforts at the trial and beyond to indict Jeff Davis and other CSA leaders as the minds behind the murder plot, there is not one shred of documentary evidence proving Davis directed the drama that unfolded at Ford's Theater. If such a link did exist, it went into the fire years ago or remains locked away in someone's attic.

CHAPTER 14

Fifty-Three Counts of Murder:
Champ Ferguson's Private War
1865

His name was Champ, and according to eyewitness testimony at his trial, he was a kind of criminal Davy Crockett, a "King of the Wild Frontier" that was the Kentucky / Tennessee border. He made a name for himself on the Cumberland Plateau, where conflicting sympathies led to constant feuding between Confederate and Union guerrillas, with innocent noncombatants often caught in the crossfire.

When official hostilities ended in April 1865, the Federal victors treated the defeated rebels with kid gloves. Most of the soldiers who fought for the Confederacy laid down their arms, swore a loyalty oath, and then went home. Not Champ Ferguson, a captain and cavalry scout who worked along the border between Kentucky and Tennessee. After finally collaring Ferguson, Federal authorities charged him with more than fifty counts of murder.

One of the fifty charges was for the killing of John Crabtree, who Ferguson shredded with his Bowie knife one night in October 1863.

On the evening of October 1, 1863, infamous guerrilla leader Champ Ferguson and a dozen of his cronies showed up at the cabin of Patsy Huff. Ferguson knew the family personally and once even spent a night at the house.

This wasn't a social visit. The guerrillas were looking for specific men they believed were Union sympathizers. They found William Delk, John Williams, and John Crabtree inside the home. Huff's sixteen-year-old son John witnessed the pathetic scene inside the cabin and lived to tell about it at the trial.

While some of the men trussed up Delk, Williams, and Crabtree, others looted the place. Ferguson told his men, John Huff later said, to take whatever they wanted, so they rifled through the home.

Young John Crabtree's mother begged Ferguson to spare her son. It was too late, Ferguson told her. He was going to kill the kid. As Crabtree's hysterical mother watched, Ferguson and his men led Crabtree, Delk, and Williams into the night.

A half an hour later, John Huff went to a neighbor's house and discovered the bodies of the three men in a horse stall. Huff later described the scene he found—supposedly Champ Ferguson's doing.

"Williams was shot about the centre of the forehead, and a piece of his skull was blown off," Huff said. "Delk was shot once through his breast, and a bayonet run through his breast—it looked like it might have been a bayonet."[1]

Ferguson had apparently made good on his threat of knifing Crabtree. "Crabtree I don't think was shot at all—he was just cut; he was cut all over the breast," Huff said, "and in the forepart of the shoulder, between the neck and collarbone; also in the back, under the shoulder blade." After he sliced the man to death, Ferguson committed an odd postmortem mutilation: He rammed a cornstalk into one of the stab wounds.[2]

Patsy Huff's daughter Lucinda Hatfield was also home that night and also saw Crabtree's body. "I counted twenty-eight holes cut in Crabtree's coat when we washed it after he was cut up so; I saw two cornstalks driven in his left shoulder."[3]

Such graphic testimony went on for weeks in a sensational trial that consumed most of July and August 1865 and commanded headlines in Nashville, Tennessee.

The summer of 1865 was the season of atonement for Southern sins, real and imagined. The trial of the Lincoln conspirators set the tone in May, and in midsummer, two men were tried as war criminals for their acts during the Civil War. One of them, former Andersonville prison commandant Henry Wirz, faced the music in Washington. At the same time, in Nashville, Champ Ferguson met judgment for his alleged crimes.

Ferguson had been arrested May 26, the same day that four of the Lincoln conspirators went to the gallows for their roles in the assassination plot. The testimony at Ferguson's ensuing trial, recounted in every detail by the Northern press, depicted Ferguson as a ruthless, almost sadistic murderer who used the war as an excuse to settle scores with his enemies and satisfy his seemingly insatiable bloodlust.

By his own admission, Ferguson murdered in cold blood, but over time, he had become a larger-than-life fiend and was blamed for some crimes that others committed and for some that may not have occurred at all. Eyewitness testimony tainted by personal bias, highly exaggerated trial coverage, and the political climate of the time all colluded in creating the legend of Champ Ferguson.

The man himself was born on November 29, 1821, near Albany, Kentucky. Unlike William Quantrill and his gang, who were already seasoned criminals by the war's outset, Ferguson was a middle-aged farmer when the war began. Named after his grandfather Champion, Ferguson was the first-born in a family that eventually grew to include ten children. His father was a pioneer who settled in the rugged area along the Kentucky–Tennessee border and eked out a living as a farmer.

Champ followed in his dad's footsteps. He worked long hours tilling the fields and spent his spare time hunting in the mountains, learning every nook and cranny of the highlands. He also became a crack shot and later bragged that he always hit what he aimed for, with one exception: his archrival, Federal raider Tinker Dave Beatty. This exception would later come back to haunt him when Beatty, a ruthless guerrilla himself, testified against Ferguson.

Few contemporary images have survived of Ferguson. One photograph shows Ferguson standing next to, and half a head taller than, one of his guards. Union major John A. Brents described Ferguson as six feet tall and about one hundred and eighty pounds "without any surplus flesh."[4]

According to Brents, Ferguson was a large man with "long arms and large hands, broad round shoulders, skin rather dark, black hair a little curled, a broad face, large mouth, and a tremendous voice, which can be heard at a long distance when in a rage." As well as possessing a powerful build, Ferguson had a curious gait. He "gives his legs a loose sling in walking, with his toes turned out," Brents said.[5]

Basil W. Duke, John Hunt Morgan's right-hand man, crossed paths with Ferguson and later described him in his post-war memoir *Reminiscences*. According to Duke, Ferguson possessed "great bodily strength" and "savage energy." Duke made a curious observation about the mountaineer: "He had one peculiarity of feature which I remember have seen in only two or three other men, and each of these was, like himself, a man of despotic will and fearless, ferocious temper. The pupil and iris of the eye were nearly the same colour."[6]

When the war began, Ferguson sided with the Confederacy. This set him, both literally and figuratively, against his brothers. Of his nine siblings, Champ was the only one who supported secession. This also put him at odds with many of his friends and neighbors in east Tennessee, where Unionist sentiment ran high.

During the war, the border area of Kentucky and Tennessee was rife with paramilitary units that bullied soldiers and civilians alike. Groups of men took sides, attained a nominal rank, and waged war with and against their former friends and neighbors. War in the Cumberland Mountains was constant, bloody, and very, very personal.

As befitted a larger-than-life character, Champ Ferguson's motives for warring against his neighbors became the topic of several legends. One story had Union soldiers gunning down his infant son after the boy waved the Stars and Bars at them from his porch. In reality, Ferguson's only son died before the war.

In another story, Union soldiers allegedly forced Ferguson's wife and his teenage daughter to strip in public and march through their neighborhood in their birthday suits. Ferguson himself later called his tale ludicrous.

According to Champ, he went to war not out of a strong belief or righteous indignation, but because it was a way for him to beat a murder rap. He stabbed a local constable to death during a feud in 1858. By the time the war began in 1861, his case still hadn't made it to court, and Ferguson apparently believed that he would win clemency if he fought for the Confederacy.

Ferguson's lawyer, Willis Scott Bledsoe, had outfitted a guerrilla unit to fight for the Southern cause. Eager to enlist Ferguson's help, Bledsoe may have played on Champ's fear of prosecution by leading him to believe that the murder indictment would be waived should the area become part of the Confederacy.[7] Ferguson, eager to dodge a prison sentence, joined Bledsoe's force in November 1861.

In truth, Champ didn't need too much coaxing. A few months before Ferguson took up arms with Bledsoe, Unionist Home Guards arrested him as a disloyal citizen and marched him to Camp Dick Robinson in central Kentucky, where he was going to be forced to enlist with the Union. Champ slipped away, and in November, joined up with Bledsoe.

By the end of the year, Ferguson led his own paramilitary group. "While Ferguson undertook many expeditions on his own private account and acknowledged no obedience to Confederate order generally," former Confederate cavalier Basil Duke later recalled, "he nevertheless served frequently with the Confederate cavalry commands, particularly Morgan's, and not only did good service, but for the time being strictly obeyed commands and abstained from evil practices."[8]

Over the next four years, Champ Ferguson hunted Union supporters throughout the Cumberland region. And they hunted him. He carried on several long-standing feuds with opposing guerrillas Tinker Dave Beatty and Elmer Huddleston.

Ferguson caught up with Huddleston on New Year's Eve 1863. Ferguson attacked Huddleston and one of his companions with his Bowie knife, killing both of them. "I shall never forget how that terrible weapon looked when Ferguson showed it to me the next day and related the story I have just repeated," Duke later recalled in his memoirs. "I had been severely wounded in the head a few days previously, was still faint and sick from the wound, and the sight of that knife, still covered with clotted blood, thoroughly nauseated me."[9]

Champ Ferguson's reputation preceded him, and the mention of his name sent shivers down the spines of the area's Union sympathizers. Murders that others committed, or crimes that weren't really crimes at all, were assumed to be his handiwork.

Ferguson contributed to his own legend by boasting about the number of men he killed. Basil Duke first met Ferguson in July 1862, little more than a year into the war. At that time, Ferguson's band had joined forces with Duke's superior, John Hunt Morgan. Duke, no doubt knowing the mountaineer's reputation, warned him not to kill Union soldiers they captured during their raids. Curiosity overcoming him, Duke then asked, "Champe [*sic*], how many men have you killed?"

"I ain't killed nigh as many men as they say I have; folks has lied about me powerful," Ferguson replied. "I ain't killed but thirty-two men since this war commenced." The war would rage for another three years.[10]

Word of Ferguson's brutality reached the Union high command, which sent a force to comb the Cumberlands in search of the infamous guerrilla. Ferguson, who knew every crevice of the mountainous region, proved an elusive and dangerous target.

On December 15, 1862, Maj. Gen. William Rosecrans sent Col. Frank Wolford and the First Kentucky Cavalry after Ferguson. Maj. Gen. George Thomas, who issued the order, apparently recognized the risk of tangling with Ferguson's bunch; he warned Wolford to "be careful not to get caught himself."[11] Wolford didn't get caught, but he didn't capture Ferguson, either.

Six months later, the Federal Army sent another group after Ferguson. Capt. Wendell Wiltsie of the Twentieth Michigan Infantry was dispatched into the Cumberland Mountains in early May 1863 and ordered to "proceed, with a force of 100 men, to where a band of guerrillas, under the notorious [Champ] Ferguson, was supposed to be lurking in the mountains" and stop him.[12] Wiltsie skirmished with the rebels, but came out of the Cumberlands without Champ Ferguson.

Ferguson continued to harass his enemies throughout the rest of 1863. In early 1864, Federal forces raided Ferguson's farm and found a cache of goods, including horses that Ferguson's band had stolen. Once again, though, they didn't find Ferguson.[13] Union colonel T. J. Harrison expressed his frustration with the Cumberland guerrillas in his report. "We had 2 men captured by straggling, but they were stripped of horses, arms, and valuable clothing, and turned loose," Harrison wrote. "Before we left the valley these bandits would fly to the mountains on the approach of even a squad of our men."[14]

While Union troops hunted for him, Champ Ferguson continued his wars, both personal and public. He and Unionist guerrillas battled constantly. Ferguson lost his farmhouse when a group of Union partisans torched it. On the other side, Tinker Dave Beatty lost his son in a skirmish

In the fall of 1864, Ferguson and his group were attached to Maj. Gen. John C. Breckinridge's forces in the southwest toe of Virginia. There Ferguson notched one of his most infamous murders when he marched into a hospital and gunned down Union officer Eliza Smith, who was recovering from a wound he received earlier that month in the Battle of Saltville.

The fight at Saltville was a skirmish between Federal cavalry and a small Confederate force that included Ferguson. Several eyewitnesses later claimed that after the shooting stopped, they saw Ferguson walking among the wounded, shooting both black and white soldiers alike—accusations that would ultimately contribute to Ferguson's postwar fate.

More than one hundred wounded Union POWs were taken from Saltville to the hospital at Emory and Henry College in the town of Emory. To prevent a possible escape attempt, the Confederates placed the wounded men on the third and fourth floors with guards posted at each stairwell.

Ferguson and about a dozen followers visited the hospital on a blustery Saturday afternoon in early November. They manhandled a guard and headed straight for Lieutenant Smith, allegedly shooting two wounded black soldiers along the way. Numerous contemporary accounts suggest that Smith had earlier abused Ferguson's wife, making her strip and then march down the road in the buff. Champ later said that this was false. Smith was always decent to his family, Ferguson later said, and was in fact a relative of his first wife. But Smith was a Kentuckian who took up arms with the Union and had killed several of Ferguson's men, so Champ decided to take revenge.[15]

When Ferguson came into the room, Smith sat up in bed. Champ walked over to him, raised his revolver, and shot the officer in the head from point-blank range. The bullet tore through Smith's skull, splattering the wall behind him with blood and flecks of brain matter.

Union authorities were furious upon hearing of the murder. Gen. Stephen Burbridge, who had taken over the Department of Kentucky a year earlier, expressed his disgust in a note to Brig. Gen. Basil Duke of the Confederate States Army. "The murder of Lieutenant Smith at Emory and Henry Hospitals by Champ Ferguson was one of the most diabolical acts committed during the war," Burbridge said in the February 24, 1865, communication, "and I am surprised at its being passed over without notice by the Confederate authorities."

Burbridge ended his letter on a solemn note: "Should he or any of the band that accompanied him on this occasion fall into the hands of US forces they will not be treated as prisoners."[16] The note left little room for interpretation. Burbridge, a somewhat ruthless character is his own right, considered Ferguson a criminal, meaning he would be sent straight to a trial and not a POW camp if Union forces managed to catch him.

Confederate authorities were also unhappy with Ferguson for the murder of Smith. Breckinridge ordered Champ jailed for the crime, but after just two months behind bars in Virginia, Ferguson was released in early April. He remained an elusive target throughout the remaining days of the war. Three months after Burbridge condemned Ferguson for the murder of Lieutenant Smith, the guerrilla leader was still at large and roaming the Cumberland Plateau.

On May 1, 1865, a week after Joseph E. Johnston's surrender in North Carolina ended the war's major hostilities, a general order went out from the Department of the Cumberland. The directive called for "every band of armed men" in the area to surrender at once. Groups that ignored the order would "be regarded as outlaws, and be preceeded against, pursued, and, when captured, treated as outlaws."[17]

By May 16, Ferguson and his band still hadn't come forward. Union authorities in Nashville branded Ferguson a criminal. "Champ Ferguson and his gang of cut-throats, having refused to surrender are denounced as outlaws, and the military forces of this district will deal with and treat them accordingly," read a Federal order.[18] With the Confederate guerrilla now officially on the other side of the law, the US Army made plans to capture him. They drew up plans for an expedition to the Cumberland Gap to search for the elusive bushwhacker.

The hunt would not be necessary. On May 23, Ferguson laid down his Bowie knife and surrendered. He later claimed that the Federal authorities, who had hunted him since 1863 with no success, promised him parole and then went back on their word when they arrested him a few days later. Union sources, not surprisingly, tell it a different way; they claim they finally caught Ferguson.

One way or another, Ferguson's confederates went home while their leader faced two charges: acting as a guerrilla, and murder. The second charge contained twenty-three separate counts comprising fifty-three alleged murders. Nineteen of the victims were named; the others were nonspecific. One count alleged that Ferguson murdered nineteen unnamed men in Tennessee; another suggested that he killed a dozen unnamed men following the skirmish at Saltville.

Ferguson's alleged murders of Federal prisoners of war, known as the "Saltville Massacre," is still a controversial subject among Civil War historians. The evidence that Ferguson murdered wounded soldiers on the battlefield is sketchy at best, but the Federal prosecution of the time felt the accusations were legitimate enough to be included in the formal charges.

The military commission convened in Nashville and testimony began on July 11. Ferguson pled not guilty. His defense attorneys argued that the killings were done in self-defense in a no-holds-barred, kill-or-be-killed atmosphere where the only survivors were the ones who shot first.

Ferguson's counsel objected to a trial in front of a military commission. Like the lawyers for the Lincoln conspirators a few months earlier, Ferguson argued that if a trial was to take place, it should be in a civilian, not a military court. The tribunal waved aside his objection and the trial began on July 11, 1865.

The prosecution didn't have to look far for witnesses. Friends and relatives of Ferguson's alleged victims came out of the woodwork and volunteered to testify. Some critics suggest that many of these witnesses exaggerated. Eyewitness after eyewitness testified about Ferguson's alleged misdeeds, and news reporters printed the juicy parts. The August 15 *New York Times* headline read "THE TRIAL OF CHAMP FERGUSON; Details of Atrocious Barbarities."[19]

Esther Ann Frogg, who had known Ferguson since their childhood, testified about how Ferguson made her a widow when he murdered her husband William on November 1, 1861. According to the widow Frogg, her husband was sick in bed when Champ Ferguson came knocking on their door. He apparently suspected that Frogg had been to Camp Dick Robinson, the Federal recruiting station in Kentucky set up to enlist Union troops from the area.

"Ferguson walked in the house to the bed, and said, 'How are you, Mr. Frogg?'" Esther Frogg testified. "My husband told him he was very sick, that he had the measles, and had taken a relapse. Ferguson said, 'I reckon you caught the measles at Camp Dick Robinson.' Mr. Frogg told him he never was there. Ferguson then shot him with a pistol, and I started out of the house, and just as I got out I heard another shot." According to Esther Frogg, her five-month-old son was in a cradle next to the bed when Ferguson shot her husband.[20]

Elizabeth and Robert Wood testified about the murder of their father Reuben on December 4, 1861. According to Elizabeth, Ferguson gunned down her unarmed, elderly father after meeting him in the road by their house. Like many of the alleged victims, Reuben Wood had known Ferguson for years.

Ferguson asked if the elder Wood had visited Camp Dick Robinson. After Wood admitted that he had been to the camp, Ferguson shouted a stream of expletives that Ms. Wood did not want to repeat under oath. She called it "vile and bitter language," and added that Ferguson said "nobody but a damned Lincolnite would be caught at any such place." After berating the frightened man, Ferguson pulled his pistol and said "Don't you beg, and don't you dodge."[21]

"By this time," Elizabeth continued, "mother was standing in the doorway with me, and she begged Ferguson not to shoot father. I also begged for the sake of God not to shoot him. Father said, 'Why Champ, I nursed you when you were a baby. Has there ever been any misunderstanding between us?'"

"No," said Ferguson, "Reuben, you have always treated me like a gentleman, but you have been to Camp Robinson, and I intend to kill you."[22]

Ferguson shot Reuben Wood in the stomach. In abject pain, the old man hobbled into his house. Ferguson chased Wood into the home, and from the yard, Elizabeth Wood heard a second shot and the sound of a violent scuffle. She and her mother ran to a neighbor's house.

When they returned a few minutes later, they found Reuben sitting by the fire. He had managed to fend off Ferguson with a hatchet, but he was dying of the bullet wound in his abdomen. In agony, Reuben Wood described his epic fight with Champ Ferguson.

Inside the house, the two mountaineers had gone at it. During the fight, Wood hit Ferguson in the side of the head with the axe. Ferguson stumbled out of the house with Reuben Wood on his heels, brandishing the axe overhead.

Rains Philpot, Ferguson's companion, threatened to shoot Wood if he touched Ferguson again, and he and Ferguson rode away. Wood returned to the house and waited, the axe in one hand and a pitchfork in the other, for Ferguson to return, but he never did. Wood later died from the gut shot.

An eyewitness with the colorful name of Orange Sells testified about the murder of Eliza Smith. Sells, a soldier with the Twelfth Ohio Cavalry who was also wounded and captured at Saltville, was in the room when Smith was murdered.

Ferguson went straight to Smith's bed and asked, "Smith, is that you?"

"Champ!" Smith said. "For God's sake, don't shoot me here in this manner."

Ferguson ignored the plea. He raised his pistol and shot Smith in the head. As he watched Smith's bedsheets turn from white to pink and red, he remarked, "He is damned dead."[23]

Even Ferguson's longtime enemy, Unionist guerrilla Tinker Dave Beatty, got in the action and took the stand. For Ferguson and other South-

ern sympathizers, Beatty's day in court was like salt in the wound; the elderly mountain man, they believed, was as savage as the defendant.

In his defense, Champ managed to present just a small cadre of character witnesses, such as his former commander, Confederate general Joseph
Wheeler. These witnesses depicted an altogether different Champ Ferguson than the ruthless murderer described by prosecution witnesses, but
they couldn't deflect the barrage of testimony the tribunal heard during the
prosecution's case.

The trial concluded on September 26, 1865. Two weeks later, the six-
man commission delivered its verdict. While the members found Ferguson
not guilty on some of the unspecified charges, they found him guilty of both
counts: acting as a guerrilla and murder. They sentenced him to hang and
set the date of execution for Friday, October 20.

October 20 came without a kind word from Washington. Rumor had it
that President Andrew Johnson would commute Champ's sentence. But
Johnson had no interest in seeing the mountain man live. Johnson, the
Federal wartime governor of Tennessee, had seen his state plagued by Ferguson's guerrilla activities. Champ had even put a price of $2,000 on John-
son's head.

Just before he made his way to the scaffold, Champ said his goodbyes
to his wife Martha and daughter Ann. The distraught Martha wailed "Have
I not suffered enough? Is my agony never to cease? Oh God! Is there nothing that will save my husband?" She clung to him for a few seconds, "Die
bravely, Champ, die bravely."[24]

The condemned man hugged Ann, holding her in one final embrace.
The forlorn girl managed to choke out one last goodbye as the guards
escorted her and her mother to a nearby house.

Ferguson, dressed in a new black suit, made the "long walk" across the
yard of the Tennessee State Penitentiary in front of a crowd of onlookers. He
passed his own cherrywood coffin on the way to the scaffold. He nodded to
a few of the spectators as he slowly made his way to the execution spot.

Ferguson stood on the scaffold, patiently listening as Col. W. R. Shafter
read the list of charges. According to some accounts, Ferguson nodded to
ten of the charges. After one particular charge, he supposedly added, "I
could tell it better than that."

"I presume you could," Shafter replied.[25]

After reading the charges, Shafter asked the condemned man if he had
any last request. "Well," Ferguson began, "I don't want to be cut up by anybody; and when you've done with me I want you to put my body in that
coffin and give it to my wife. She'll take me home to White County [Ten-
nessee], on the Calf Killer [River]. There I wish to be buried—not on soil as
this. There is a little graveyard near my house (she knows it), and I want to

lie there. If I had my own way, I'd be there now, and not here. I wish you would wipe my face before I go."[26]

Colonel Shafter swiped Champ's face with a handkerchief, pulled the hood over his head, and stood aside. Ferguson managed to utter one last statement just before the drop: "Lord have mercy on me, I pray you!"[27] Ann Ferguson, watching from the window of a nearby house, fainted when her father dropped.

The crowd watched a slow death by strangulation. Champ's body trembled and he clenched his fists. Splotches of crimson—blood from his nose—seeped to the outside of his hood. After about five minutes, the tremors stopped. Thirty minutes after the drop, his body was cut down and placed in a carriage.

Champ Ferguson—a terror to Union sympathizers in the area—was dead just a few days before his forty-fourth birthday.

Or was he? There is a fascinating footnote to the Ferguson folklore. According to legend, Ferguson didn't die on October 20, 1865. In the years after his death, several stories circulated that Champ cheated the hangman. Union authorities had constructed a skirt around the lower half of the scaffold and then encircled the scaffold with soldiers so that when Ferguson dropped, the lower half of his body fell out of view. This led to an intriguing, albeit far-fetched, conspiracy theory.

In this account, Federal authorities, realizing the absurdity of executing Ferguson while other guerrillas like Tinker Dave Beatty went free, hatched a plan to fake Champ's death. This way, they could give a guy a break while still appearing tough on lawbreakers. The rope was made extra long and when the executioner released the trap, Ferguson fell harmlessly to the ground. They placed his living body in a coffin and loaded it into the nearby carriage. Champ later went west with his family to begin a new life where no one would gun for him—a sort of nineteenth-century witness protection relocation. The legend does not account for the fact that Martha went on to remarry an affluent farmer.

There is not one shred of evidence to support this tall tale except for the fact that Ferguson's tombstone contains a curious misspelling: "Capt. C. Furguson."

There is also the issue of the many eyewitnesses to Ferguson's execution. Undeterred, conspiracy theorists sidestepped this problem by offering an alternate version of events. In this telling, Union officials decided to fake Champ's death and pulled it off by substituting another convict for the notorious mountain man.Conspiracy theories aside, Champ Ferguson would make one appearance from beyond the grave—in the nation's newspapers.

As was customary at the time, Ferguson did not testify in his own defense, but he did talk about his alleged crimes in a partial confession. To avoid influencing the members of the court, Champ waited until after the verdict to come clean. He gave detailed statements to reporters on the condition that they wouldn't be published until after his execution.

The *Louisville Daily Journal* published "Champ Ferguson's Full Confession" on October 24, 1865. The *New York Times* ran a parallel article, "Confession of the Culprit," on October 29.

"The testimony in this case," Ferguson said, "was, with very few exceptions, false."[28] In a lengthy statement, Champ Ferguson denied the charges. He admitted to several killings, but attempted to justify each as something other than cold-blooded murder.

Ferguson admitted killing Reuben Wood, but argued that it was out of self-preservation—a sort of preemptory self-defense. According to Ferguson, Wood was a pro-Union guerrilla who was hunting him. "I knew that he intended to kill me if he ever got the chance," Ferguson said. "If I had not shot Reuben Wood I would not likely have been here, for he would have shot me. I never expressed a regret for committing the act, and never will. He was in open war against me."[29]

Ferguson also said that Wood's children embellished during the trial. "The touching story about his piteous appeals to me—that he had nursed me when a babe, and tossed me on his knee—are false, and were gotten up expressly to create sympathy; and set me forth as a heartless wretch."[30]

Ferguson admitted shooting William Frogg as he lay sick in bed. Again, Ferguson said, he was acting in self-defense. According to Ferguson, Frogg was gunning for him and waiting for the right opportunity, so he decided "to settle the matter by going direct to Frogg's house and killing him." He described the shooting: "He was lying in bed, and, on seeing me, pulled the cover over his face. I then shot him twice."[31]

He also admitted shooting sixteen-year-old Fount Zachary, because he had "orders to shoot down any person who might be seen with guns. As we neared a creek, the lad emerged from a thicket with a gun on his shoulder. I shot him on sight in obedience to orders."[32]

The confessions didn't stop there: "I killed John Crabtree," he said. "I went to Piles' house in the night and stabbed him, and did another good job when I killed him. He was a murderous villain, and had went to men's houses and shot them to get their money."[33]

Ferguson denied any role in the alleged massacre at Saltville. "I am charged with killing twelve soldiers at Saltsville [*sic*]," he said. "I am innocent of the charge. I know they were killed by Hughes' and Bledsoe's command, and they were fairly killed in battle. There were thirty instead of twelve that fell on that day, and it was in a regular fight."[34]

He admitted to shooting Lieutenant Smith at the Emory and Henry Hospital. "I had motive for committing the act," Ferguson said. "He captured a number of my men at different times, and always killed at least one of them." Ferguson went on to say that "He is the only man I killed at or near Saltsville, and I am not sorry for killing him."[35]

The trial's outcome, Ferguson argued, was a foregone conclusion. "I told my lawyers, and you will recollect of my telling you, that that court was bound to convict me. I was not fooled on that. I think the Judge-Advocate run things entirely too far. My counsel did well, but it was useless, for every point of law in my favor was overruled, and they intimidated."

According to critics of the trial, Ferguson pretty much hit the nail on the head. Someone had to pay for the carnage in the Cumberland region, and that person was Champ Ferguson. While Union authorities strung up Ferguson, they turned a blind eye to murders committed by guerrillas like Tinker Dave Beatty. In short, Tinker Dave was on the winning side, and Champ wasn't.

The morning of the execution, Ferguson gave one last statement to the world during an interview with reporters. Like the confession, it wasn't printed until after the scaffold floor fell out from under him.

"I was a Southern man at the start," Ferguson said defiantly. "I am yet and will die a rebel. I believe I was right in all I did. I don't think I done anything wrong at any time. I committed my deeds in a cool and deliberate manner. I killed a good many men, of course, I don't deny that; but never killed a man whom I did not know was seeking my life."[36]

CHAPTER 15

Murder or Misadventure?
Temperance Neely
Kills Her Former Slave
1865

The ink on the surrender was barely dry when a North Carolina aristocrat shot her former slave, and the same issues that sundered the country emerged in the courtroom where a military tribunal decided Temperance Neely's fate.

While the trial was all about race, it was anything but black and white. Was this murder or manslaughter? Malice aforethought or misadventure? Would Temperance Neely go to the gallows, or pay a fine?

✦ ✦ ✦

Before the Civil War, residents of Davie County, North Carolina, opposed secession, but when the war began, more than one thousand Davie County men sided with their home state and enlisted with the Confederacy.

Just a few months after the war-weary veterans returned home, a different kind of civil war took place on the old Neely plantation, where sixty-year-old widow Providence Neely lived with her two daughters, Temperance and Meek, and a few former slaves who had nowhere else to go. One of those former slaves, twenty-four-year-old Galina, was raised on the Neely estate. Her children, including ten-year-old Ellen, were born there.[1]

The old widow, accustomed to the servile attention of her former slaves, became irate when Ellen didn't do as ordered and copped an attitude with her former mistress. As the slaves-turned-workers came in from the fields on the afternoon of July 1, Ellen did not come to the mansion as requested. Providence, who had a long list of chores for the girl, chastised Ellen for not obeying her and threatened to keep her from supper if she didn't immediately go the cookhouse and fetch a pail of water.

Ellen retorted that she would have dinner, and there was nothing that the old woman could do to stop her. She pivoted on the balls of her feet and stomped off to the cookhouse. An enraged Providence said she would redden Ellen's backside when she returned. "No, you won't whip me," Ellen yipped.[2]

The matron had had enough of Ellen's lip. She went into the yard, broke a branch off of a peach tree, and waited for the sassy girl to return. When Ellen trotted into the mansion, she took one look at the switch and turned for the door, but the widow Neely grabbed her arm. She began beating the child with the tree branch, and Ellen screeched.

Ellen's mother, Galina, was a few yards away strolling with an infant in her arms when she heard the commotion. She set down the baby and headed straight for the mansion. When she saw Miss Providence whacking away at her daughter, her pace quickened.

Galina raced into the mansion and grabbed Ellen. They came out with Providence on their heels. Twenty-nine-year-old Temperance Neely followed them into the "piazza" with her sister's antiquated four-barrel revolver in hand.

There are two different versions of what happened next: one told by former slave Sallie Neal, who claimed to have seen the entire incident from the front door of her cabin on the other side of the cookhouse, and another, entirely different tale told by Providence Neely. Regardless of the version, it is agreed that two shots were fired; one of the bullets wound up in Galina's chest.

Sallie's husband, Henderson, was sitting by the cabin's back door when he heard gunfire. Then he heard Galina call for him. She staggered into his cabin. "Miss Temperance has shot me," she mumbled before she collapsed.[3] She died fifteen minutes later. Who pulled the trigger was never in question. Temperance Neely admitted to firing the shot that killed her former slave. But was it murder "with felonious intent," manslaughter, or a "misadventure"?

If Temperance Neely had shot Galina a few months earlier, the case would never had made it to trial because the only witnesses against her—former slaves—would not have been allowed to testify in court. But this was the "New South," and there were new rules.

As Confederate forces laid down their weapons and returned home during the spring and summer of 1865, the Federal military faced the difficult task of picking up the pieces of the shattered Union. One of their biggest challenges in rebuilding the South was reestablishing law and order in former rebel territories.

In the weeks after rebel forces surrendered in North Carolina, gangs of cutthroats, including former soldiers from both sides, harassed and terrorized citizens. Racial tensions reached an all-time high, as slaves and their former masters and mistresses lived an uneasy coexistence that sometimes turned violent.

During this turbulent time of reconstruction, swift justice was meted out through the use of military commissions. These military courts did not have a jury; they typically consisted of between five and thirteen soldiers who acted as both judges and jury.

Unlike a civilian court, a military commission did not need a unanimous vote to reach a verdict; a simple majority ruled. A two-thirds consensus was needed to send a defendant to the scaffold. And their decision was almost sacrosanct. Short of an appeal to the president, there was no higher court to review the case.

From the start, military commissions became the subject of controversy not just in North Carolina, but throughout the South. The primary bone of contention involved the testimony of former slaves. In many antebellum Southern courts, blacks could not testify against whites; in some cases, perpetrators got away with murder because the only witnesses against them couldn't testify.

When the war ended, state laws had not yet caught up to the times, and many civilian courts retained the same trial guidelines. The military commissions, on the other hand, did allow the testimony of former slaves. Perpetrators who would have gone unpunished in the past now went to court. Nonetheless, justice wasn't exactly colorblind in the Tar Heel State.

While military commissions handled more serious criminal cases, provost marshal courts took care of some minor crimes, like petit theft, particularly those perpetrated by former slaves. Contemporary news stories suggest that the punishments meted out to "freedmen" were a bit harsh. The *Raleigh Daily Standard* ran an article describing the fate of "Abram (colored)": for stealing bacon, he was "suspended by the thumbs to a lamp post" for all to see. The story said "A card affixed to his back, marked 'Abram stole meat,' informed all passers-by of the reason for his punishment."[4]

Gen. Thomas H. Ruger, who became chief of the Department of North Carolina in June, worked alongside the Freedman's Bureau—an arm of the military dedicated to protecting the interests of former slaves—in leveling the legal playing field and creating a colorblind justice.

In Ruger, who eyed the Southern aristocracy with suspicion, the Freedman's Bureau had a strong advocate. He ran North Carolina as a de facto governor, censoring media who criticized the military's policies in the state. He and the Bureau made waves in North Carolina, but it was the testimony of black witnesses that really caused a ruckus. By late July, military commissions not only heard testimony from former slaves, they also began to accept it as equal in value to that of white witnesses.

Temperance Neely's trial began in Salisbury on July 28. Five soldiers from Indiana would hear testimony, much of it from former slaves owned by Providence Neely, and render a verdict. Lt. Col. Reuben Kise of the 120th Indiana Volunteer Infantry presided over the trial, and fellow Hoosier Lt. J. G. Wood, the court's judge advocate, played the role of prosecuting attorney.

The single charge of murder carried one specification: "In this; that the said Temperance Neely, did on or about the first day of July, A.D. 1865, in the County of Davie, State of North Carolina, willfully, maliciously, and with a felonious intent, shoot 'Galina'—a freewoman formerly a slave, the property of Providence Neely, wounding her, said 'Galina,' so severely that from the effects thereof, she, the said 'Galina,' did die, on or about the 1st day of July, A.D. 1865."[5]

Since the prosecution's only witnesses were former slaves who would testify against their ex-mistress's daughter, it was clear from the beginning that race would be a major factor during the trial.

Neely hired Nathaniel Boyden and J. M. Clement to defend her. Boyden, a War of 1812 veteran just days from his sixty-ninth birthday when the trial began, brought decades of legal experience. He had also served terms in both the North Carolina House of Commons and Senate before heading to Washington for one term as a US Congressman from 1847 to 1849.

Boyden wasted no time in questioning the jurisdiction of the military commission. Neely, he argued, should face a "speedy trial by a jury of the county in the civil courts of law."[6] Boyden knew that the case against Neely would not and could not go to trial in a North Carolina civil court—the state had not yet amended its pre-war law banning Negro testimony in trials, and the government's only witnesses were Providence Neely's former slaves.

Not surprisingly, the court rejected Boyden's challenge. Temperance Neely may have been a civilian and the alleged crime may have taken place during peacetime, but her trial would take place in a military court. She pled not guilty.

The prosecution opened its case on Monday morning, July 31, 1865. Testimony began around 9 A.M. It was a balmy, still morning outside the courtroom when Wood called the prosecution's first witness, Sallie Neal.

Wood had barely enough time to swear in the former slave when Boyden objected. He reminded the commission that the laws of North Carolina, predating the state's secession on May 20, 1861, were still in effect. According to these laws, Boyden pointed out, the "free negro" Sallie would be "not competent" to testify against a white woman.[7]

The commission overruled Boyden's objection and Wood began his line of questioning. Sallie said she was at home—a cabin she shared with her husband Henderson on the Neely plantation—when the shooting occurred. "State if you saw Temperance Neely have a pistol and if she fired it on the day you mention—and if so at whom did she fire it," Wood asked.[8]

"She did have a pistol and she fired it at Galina," Sallie said, and followed with the synopsis of the events leading to the murder. "The hands were in the fields harvesting," Sallie explained. When they finished around four o'clock, Ellen went to the main house where Providence began chastising her for not coming earlier, since "she had plenty of work for her to do." After a brief exchange of words, Ellen went off to the cookhouse to fetch the pail of water, grumbling something as she stomped out of the mansion, and Providence went into the yard, broke a branch off a peach tree, and waited for the indignant girl to return. When Ellen saw Providence with the switch, she started toward the door, but Providence caught her arm and began striking her with the tree branch.

When she heard the commotion, Galina marched toward the house. According to Sallie, Temperance warned Galina not to go in. "The prisoner [Temperance] told her not to come in there—if she did she would shoot her."

Threat or no threat, Galina went in to rescue her daughter from the clutches of her former mistress. According to Sallie, Galina got her child and came out "and the prisoner fired at her as she was going out with Ellen. Galina said something in reply to the prisoner which I did not understand and thereupon the prisoner jumped down, ran around her, and shot her in the breast."[9]

If Sallie was telling the truth, then Temperance Neely fired two shots at Galina. She missed with the first, then ran in front of her and fired again, this time hitting her at point-blank range. It was cold-blooded murder—unless Neely could prove she felt threatened.

"Did Galina strike or attempt to strike Temperance Neely or her mother?" Wood asked.[10]

"No, sir, she just pushed Miss Providence down and got her child," Sallie answered.

Boyden then cross-examined Sallie, asking a series of questions designed to depict Temperance as a gentle soul who kept Galina and her children safe by allowing them to stay in her mother's employ instead of evicting them.

"Had not Galina been directed by Mrs. Providence Neely to remove herself and children from the plantation before 1st July 1865?"

"Yes sir," Sallie said, "she had been but Miss Temperance Neely would not let her go after she had started."

"What did Miss Temperance Neely say and do to stop Galina from removing?"

"She told her she should not go for she would take her children out in the woods to perish to death."[11]

"Was not Galina crying at the time she was fixing to leave and did not Miss Temperance Neely take her youngest child in her lap and tell Galina to go on to her work—she could stay?" Boyden asked.

"I don't know anything about Galina's crying, but Miss Temperance did take the child in her lap and tell Galina she could stay," Sallie admitted.[12]

He fired off another volley of questions about Galina. How many children did she have? Did she have a husband?

Galina had five children and no husband, Sallie explained.

Boyden had subtly managed to make the victim appear to be an indigent and the perpetrator seem a selfless humanitarian who saved the victim before she shot her to death. Since Galina and her family depended entirely on the plantation for survival, and Temperance interceded on their behalf to keep them "home," she looked a lot less like the cold-blooded killer Sallie described.

Boyden continued to hammer away at Sallie. "Was not Temperance Neely very kind and much attached to Galina and her children, and did she not treat her and her children with more kindness than she did any other colored people on the plantation?"

"Yes, sir," Sallie replied. "She was and I think treated Galina and her children more kindly than the other colored people on the plantation."

"Did not the other colored people on the plantation feel and express some jealousy towards Galina on account of her receiving better treatment from Miss Temperance Neely than they did?"

Sallie nodded. "Yes, sir."[13]

With this question, Boyden had provided the commission an ulterior motive for Sallie's testimony. If she was jealous of the attention Temperance Neely gave to Galina, it would explain her animosity toward the defendant.

Sallie testified that the shooting took place in the "piazza" outside of the mansion, near a large log positioned between the manor house and the cookhouse. She also said she was just a few steps outside of her front door when she witnessed the shooting. This positioning would later play a major role in Boyden's case, but now, he had to undo the damage of Sallie's earlier testimony.

During Wood's questioning, Sallie said that Temperance fired two shots "at Galina," but during Boyden's cross-examination, she revised her earlier statement.

that night. She replied to Miss Providence, that she would have supper, and she could not hinder her either. Then Mis Providence, told her that she would whip her when she came back, for talking to her so. – the girl said back to Miss Providence. "nor you wont whip me" when she came back Miss Providence went to whipping her. then Galina the mother of the girl being whipped laid down her child and went into the big house. and pushed Miss Providence down. The prisoner told her not to come in there – if she did she would shoot her. Galina said she would – she was going to have her child – then Galina got her child and came on out and the prisoner fired at her as she was going out with her child. Galina said something in reply to the prisoner which I did not understand and thereupon the prisoner jumped down ran around her and shot her in the breast.

Question by the same

You state that Temperance Neely told Galina not to come in the house – if she did she would shoot her – was this before or after the time Mrs Neely. was whipping the Child.

Answer – It was at the time.

Question by the same.

Did Galina strike or attempt to strike Temperance Neely or her Mother.

Page from the record of Temperance Neely's murder trial. Sallie's statement that "the prisoner jumped down, ran around her, and shot her in the breast" led to a debate about her credibility.

"Was not the pistol fired into the air the first time as if to frighten Galina?" Boyden asked with a coy smile and the tone of a schoolteacher addressing a student who lied about her homework.

"Yes sir, the first time it was."

Then Boyden asked if Galina threatened to hit Providence.

"Did not Galina raise her hands in the act of striking Mrs. Providence Neely after Galina got out of the piazza?"

"No, sir. She just turned around on the log."

Boyden pressed her. "What was the position of Galina's hands when she turned around on the log and faced Mrs. Providence Neely?"

"She held them up and turned around. She said something I didn't know what it was."

Then Boyden fired off one final question. "Were you not examined on oath before Brig. Gen. [John] Schofield about this matter and did you not then give a very different account of the transaction?"[14]

The court advised Sallie that she didn't have to answer, and she didn't. Boyden didn't need an answer. The old attorney's last question was a direct hit. Sallie looked confused on the stand, or worse.

Wood quickly popped out of his seat. He had to do a little damage control.

"You stated that the pistol was first fired in the air. Was it not towards Galina?"

"It was above her head," Sallie answered.

"You stated that Galina turned around on the log and raised her hands. How far was she then from Mrs. Providence Neely?"

"About five steps."

"Did she have her fists drawn at that time?"

"No sir."[15]

The distance between Galina and Providence was significant. If she stood five paces away from the fallen woman, did she present a viable threat that would justify the shooting in defense of the elderly Neely?

Next, Wood called Henderson, Sallie's husband and another former slave who lived in a small hut on the Neely plantation. Once again, Boyden objected to the former slave's "competence" to testify against his former mistress. Once again, the commission overruled the objection and Henderson was sworn.

Henderson said he heard two shots. A few seconds later, he heard Galina calling for him. "I was sitting right at the back door of my house. I got up immediately as soon as I heard her call for me. I asked her what she wanted with me. She said she wanted me to go after Abe Barber right quick. I asked her what she wanted, she said 'Miss Temperance has shot me,' them was the last words she said to me."[16]

Under cross-examination, Henderson described what happened after Galina collapsed. Temperance burst through the door, frantic, screaming for a horse so Galina could be taken to a doctor. Then she "caught a horse and went over to Arthur Neely's," Henderson said.

Boyden quizzed Henderson about Sallie's position when the shots were fired. Henderson said his wife was heading in the direction of the mansion when the first shot was fired, and was about twenty steps from their cabin when the second shot was fired.

Wood next called Cassandra, and Boyden reiterated his objection to the testimony of the former slave. Again, the commission overruled the objection. Sallie and then her husband had already testified over the objections of the defense. It was a moot point.

Cassandra said that she was at work in the fields, "helping to haul wheat," on July 1, 1865. She was at her mother's house, about four hundred yards away from the mansion, when the incident occurred.

Her version of the argument between the Neely matron and Ellen was similar to Sallie's, but Cassandra described an angrier, more violent Providence. "Mrs. Neely kicked the girl and told her to go and bring her a bucket of water," Cassandra testified. "Mrs. Neely also told her she would whip her when she came back at the risk of her life."[17]

Cassandra explained that she didn't see the actual shooting, but she did see Galina afterward, wounded on the left side of her chest.

"When you came up and saw the wound on Galina, was it dark?" Boyden asked during his cross.

"Getting dusk."[18]

With a single question, Boyden created a reasonable doubt about Cassandra's testimony. She witnessed the altercation, but not the shooting, from a distance of four hundred yards in limited light.

After Cassandra's testimony, the prosecution concluded its case and the commission adjourned until 8 A.M. the following morning.

Nathaniel Boyden had shot holes in the prosecution's case. With a well-executed barrage of questions, he had the prosecution's only eyewitness to the crime contradicting herself. At one time, Sallie said the defendant fired two shots at Galina. Later she admitted that Temperance deliberately fired the first shot in the air. Sallie also said the others were jealous of Temperance's favoritism toward Galina and her kids, which hinted at an ulterior motive for her testimony.

Henderson helped little more than his wife. He didn't see anything except Sallie moving toward the mansion—a statement that would later help the defense. And the third witness, Cassandra, didn't see the actual shooting, only the initial altercation, which she witnessed from a quarter a mile away in the falling darkness.

Although Boyden managed to exploit flaws in the prosecution's case, he still had two major obstacles to overcome: the fact that Temperance Neely killed an unarmed woman, and Sallie's statement that Temperance "jumped down, ran around her, and shot her in the breast," which made the shooting appear to be premeditated.

Boyden began his defense on August 1, 1865, when he called his first witness to the stand: the other eyewitness, Providence Neely. It came as no surprise when Providence told an altogether different version of events than Sallie had. She depicted Ellen as more violent than she appeared in Sallie's rendition, and described Temperance as a peacemaker rather than a murderess.

Seeing the branch, Temperance pleaded with her mother not to harm the child. "Then the prisoner said to me, 'Ma, don't whip her. I will call her here and shame her,'" Providence recalled. "When she came in the prisoner called to her saying, 'Come here, Ellen, I want to talk to you.'"

Ellen went for the door, but Providence grabbed her by the hand before she could escape. "She took hold of my hand," Providence said, "and attempted to bite me. I pressed my hands up against her mouth, then I took hold of both of her hands and led her into the dining room and picked up my switch as I went along to whip her. By me having the switch in my hand she got one of her hands away and attempted to scratch me in the face but did not get it done. Then I commenced whipping her with the switch."

Providence continued her tale. "She ran out to the far corner of the piazza—I having hold of her hands and still trying to whip her, and the next thing I knew, I was lying sprawling on the floor, Galina having thrown me over on the floor."

As the Neely matriarch pulled herself up, Galina and Ellen moved into the piazza. Providence was following them when she saw a flash and heard the report of a pistol behind her. The ball whizzed over her left shoulder "a good piece" above her head.

Undeterred by Temperance's warning shot, Galina and Ellen continued on a wooden plank that served as the path between the mansion and the cookhouse. "I followed them and struck at Ellen with the switch," Providence testified, "whereupon Galina let go Ellen and wheeled suddenly around on the log and raised both her hands up. At that instant, the pistol fired the second time." When this second shot occurred, she said, Galina "was in arms length of me, was a taller woman than me, and was standing on the log and I on the ground."

"State as near as you can the expression of Galina's countenance and her exact attitude at the instant she wheeled and faced you," Boyden asked.

"She looked as if she intended to push me down. She held her hands up as if she intended to push me again."

After the fatal shot, Providence said, Galina "slapped her hands upon her breast and the prisoner said to Galina, 'Why Gill! Did I shoot you?' Galina then ran through the cookhouse down to Henderson's house." According to Providence, the shooting took place about midway between the mansion and the cookhouse.

Providence also testified about the firearm they kept on the mantle. "We were helpless women," she said, "and we kept a pistol there to defend ourselves."

A few minutes after the shooting, Providence went to Henderson's cabin where Galina lay on the floor, dying. Frantic, Temperance was yelling for a horse. "She was crying, fretting, and declaring, 'What shall I do? I never expected to have my hands put into human blood,'" Providence recalled. "[She] also said Galina was her favorite negro."

Providence admitted that she asked Galina and her children to leave the plantation in May, but her daughter interceded on their behalf. "'Ma, you are so easily fretted. What are you going to turn these four children away for?'" Temperance said as she held Galina's four-month-old in her lap. The old woman softened and let the former slaves stay.[19]

Providence Neely's story placed the murder weapon in her daughter's hand, but her testimony didn't harm Temperance's defense. It depicted her daughter as a benevolent soul who would never murder her "favorite negro" in cold blood.

Unlike Sallie's version, in which Temperance runs in front of Galina to shoot her, Providence's version opened the door for two other possibilities: Temperance shot the former slave to protect her mother, or she fired another shot intended to frighten Galina, and the bullet accidentally hit her.

During his cross, Wood challenged Providence on some of the details of her story. "You stated that when Galina wheeled around on the log immediately after the first fire she raised her hands, was she so close to you that she could have struck you with her hands from where she was standing? Did she have her fists drawn?"

"She was close enough to have struck me. She did not draw her fists. The motion was as if to push me down. It all occurred in one instant."

"When she pushed you down on the piazza, did she strike or attempt to strike you afterwards?"

"No, sir. She picked up her child and started off. My arm was bruised by falling against the wheel when she pushed me down."[20]

Lt. Col. Kise asked the witness if Galina was a "strong, healthy woman," and Providence said she was "at least a head higher than I am. I suppose she weighed 150 lbs. She was very stout and very strong."

"While you were attempting to chastise the child Ellen and before the first shot was fired," Kise asked, "did you hear the prisoner tell

Galina not to come into the house of if she did she (the prisoner) would shoot her?"

"No sir. I don't think there was a word spoken by us on either side until the prisoner said, 'Why Gill! Did I shoot you?' and this was after the second shot. If there was any spoken before that I did not hear it."[21]

When Wood concluded his cross of Providence Neely, her brother-in-law, Arthur, took the stand. Arthur Neely lived about a half a mile away and heard the shots fired.

About thirty minutes after the gunshots, he said, Temperance showed up at his door, sobbing and in a state of panic. "I met her at the door," Arthur said. "She gripped me by the hand telling what she had done—that she had shot Galina, that she had no intention in the world of killing her, that she shot to scare her, that Galina pitched at her mother again then she shot her." According to Arthur, Temperance spent the entire night crying.

Arthur had lived next door to his brother's estate for thirty years and knew his family well. Despite appearances, he said, the widow Neely was always good to her slaves. She was generous with food and clothes and didn't employ an overseer to keep them in line.

Boyden's last question for the witness was the most important one. Since the prosecution's entire case depended on Sallie's version of the shooting, he continued his attempts to discredit her testimony.

"Do you know the general character of the witness, Sally, for truth?" Boyden asked.

"I think I know her general character for truth—it is not good," Arthur replied.[22] This last question was strategically placed to set up Boyden's next witness.

The defense called a professional surveyor, John D. Johnson, to the stand. Johnson wasn't exactly an impartial witness; he grew up on the plantation next door to the Neelys and had known Temperance since they were kids.

Johnson presented defense exhibit A—a plat he had drawn of the Neely estate. The plat map, Boyden believed, was the final piece of evidence impeaching Sallie's testimony. With a skillfully worded series of questions, he quizzed Johnson about the position of the buildings, particularly Henderson's front door, from where Sallie said she watched Temperance race around Galina and shoot her in the chest.

Sallie said she was a few steps from her front door when the shooting occurred, and her husband Henderson verified this during his testimony. According to Johnson, the cookhouse "was in a direct line between" the spot where the shooting took place and the spot where Sallie said she was standing when she saw the whole thing.[23]

Although the witness stopped short of saying it, the gist of his testimony became crystal clear to everyone in the courtroom: Sallie lied through her teeth about seeing the homicide. According to Johnson, all she could have seen from her front door was the back of the kitchen building.

Johnson's testimony, apparently backed up by his plat map, was damning to Sallie's story—if the map was accurate. In his cross, Wood quizzed the surveyor about every detail in his map and his methods. Johnson explained that he measured each distance "by stepping it," but admitted that he didn't know the exact scale he used when making the plat.

"What is the scale by which you laid off this plat—how many yards to the inch?"

"I don't remember the scale," Johnson said, "forty (40) or eighty (80) I expect."

During his cross, Boyden got right to the point. Was Providence Neely an honest woman? Johnson said he knew Providence as an honest woman.

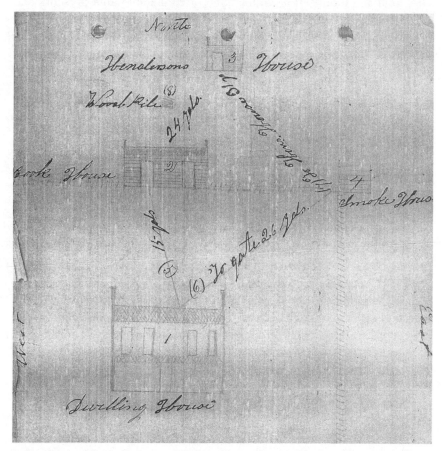

Defense exhibit A in the Neely case. If Sallie had stood between Henderson's house (no. 3) and the cookhouse (no. 2), Boyden argued, she couldn't have seen the spot of the shooting (no. 5).
NATIONAL ARCHIVES

"Did you take position two yards from the back piazza on the hewn log and could you see the front door of Henderson's house from that point?"

"I did and could not see the door."[24]

Sallie said she was standing by her front door, and Providence said the shooting took place halfway between the mansion and the cookhouse. One of them was lying.

Next, Boyden called Temperance's sister, Meek. The woman had been at her in-laws' on July 1 and said that the gun used to shoot Galina belonged to her. She had acquired it a few years earlier, and the pistol was kept on a mantel in her mother's room at the mansion.

"State if you know the feelings which existed between the prisoner and the deceased Galina," Boyden asked.

"They were on very friendly terms. My sister, the prisoner, was always very kind and indulgent to Galina. She often made Galina presents, and Galina was regarded as a favorite of hers."[25]

Boyden next summoned George W. Campbell, who had lived next to the Neely plantation for more than twenty years. Campbell wasn't another character witness. Boyden brought him to the stand for one reason: He had once made a remark about Meek Neely's handgun.

Boyden held the gun in front of the elderly planter. "Did you ever see the pistol now shown you, and did you make any remarks to the prisoner as to its efficiency to kill? If so, state what you said to her."

Campbell leaned forward and eyed the gun. "Yes, I think I have seen it. I think I have told the prisoner that it was no account to kill, that no body [sic] could be killed with it, that it was only fit to kill horse flies or something of that sort. This was between six months and a year ago."

According to Campbell, the murder weapon was incapable of murder. Clearly, this wasn't the case, but Boyden was hoping the members would see the planter's assessment of the murder weapon to indicate a lack of malicious forethought on the part of his client. If Temperance believed the weapon couldn't hurt anything but "horse flies," then clearly she didn't intend to use it to murder Galina.

Defense counsel continued its attempt to assassinate Sallie's character. "Do you know the general character of the colored witness Sally for truth? If so, state what it is," Boyden asked.

"I know her general character for truth—it is very bad. This is her reputation among her own color," Campbell said.[26]

Boyden called twenty-four-year-old C. W. Pearson, a friend of Temperance Neely, who also testified about the non-lethality of Meek Neely's pistol.

"I have seen one like it," Pearson said when shown the pistol. "I can't say it is the same one. I told the prisoner that I had very little idea that the pistol would kill a man, this was about the last of April 1865."[27]

The defense called one final witness, forty-three-year-old Alexander S. Nail, another longtime familiar of the Neely family. Once again, timing was everything; Nail would be the last witness to testify, and Boyden wanted a statement that would resonate when the commission went into deliberation.

He asked Nail just one question. What was Sallie's "general character for truth?"

"I know her general character," Nail responded. "It is very bad for truth."[28]

With that, Boyden rested his case, and the commission adjourned for the afternoon. The court reconvened the next day, August 2, 1865. Both Judge Advocate Wood and Neely's attorneys presented lengthy written arguments to the members. With these documents and Johnson's plat map in hand, the five Indiana soldiers went into deliberation.

The stakes were high. In passing sentence, military commissions followed the laws of the state where the crime was committed. In North Carolina, murderers went to the scaffold. If the commission decided that Neely committed the lesser crime of manslaughter, she could be fined, receive a scarlet letter "M" branded on her left thumb, and be sent to jail for a year at the most.

The case had been anything but black and white. In court, however, it was just that. The prosecution had called only former slaves to testify, and the defense called just white witnesses. Perhaps aware of the sensitive nature of the case, defense attorney J. M. Clement noted in his written closing argument that "no human being, white or black, has intimated that there ever has existed the least unkind or unfriendly feeling on the part of the prisoner towards Galina."

In fact, he pointed out, "it was understood by both white and black in Mrs. Providence Neely's family" that Temperance liked Galina and favored her among all of her mother's former slaves. This fact, Clement argued, proved that the necessary element to prove murder—malice—didn't exist in the case against his client.

Clement then suggested that this favoritism tainted Sallie, the state's star witness. "So marked was this attachment to Galina, that the colored people who perceived it, even entertained some feelings of envy and jealousy on account of it, as is proven by the testimony of the colored woman fully herself and this feeling may have some influence in warping Sally and making her testify in the extraordinary manner she has done."

Clement claimed "it is immaterial whether the Military Commission believe Sally's testimony or not," because even Sallie admitted that there was no malice between the killer and her victim. In fact, testimony indicated that Temperance had been the champion of Galina and her children, keeping them from eviction. The two women grew up side by side, and "doubtless joined in many a merry romp as girls together."

7

& besides her charac — for truth has been proven, to be very bad. On the other hand, the witness Neely was in a situation, she must she must have heard, & known all that occurred; & she is a lady of good character, her character was never doubted, no one, says the witness, has a better character; so that it seems to me that the commission can have no hesi-tation, in coming to the conclusion, that the transaction occurred as stated by the witness Neely the mother of the prisoner. All must have observed that she is a lady of intelligence & her conduct — that while giving her testimony must have satisfied all that heard her, that she was telling the truth: the witness Sally says, the first fire was in the air over the head of the deceased, as if to frighten & not to shoot her, & that the second fire galance the deceased was on the log leading from the piazza of the mansion-house & five steps from the mansion-house; that Mrs Neely was behind her, & was between her & the mansion-house, but on the ground & that the prisoner ran around & shot her in the breast; ran around how she did not explain. The witness Mrs Neely the mother of the prisoner says Galance was on the log halfway from the mansion house to the cook house, that is 7 steps from the piazza towards the cook-house, at the instant of the last fire — the 1st the first fire she was certain it was upwards in the air & not at Galance

Page from Nathaniel Boyden's closing argument, in which he compares Sallie's credibility with that of Providence Neely, the mother of the accused. NATIONAL ARCHIVES

No, Temperance Neely was no murderess. "On the day of this unfortunate and in every respect deplorable calamity, the prisoner was again interposing in the holy and blessed character of the peace maker," Clement said.

That is, until Temperance shot Galina—but Clement pointed out that it was done without malice, so it wasn't by definition murder. It wasn't manslaughter, either, Clement argued. The shooting didn't occur during a heated argument between Temperance and Galina. "Here was no sudden fighting together of prisoner and deceased. There was neither a fight nor even a quarrel or any bad blood between them"

The shooting, according to Clement, fell into a third category—"homicide by misadventure," when "the best of men and the best of women sometime by some fatal accident slay a friend."

Testimony established that the first bullet was fired into the air away from Galina, intended as a warning shot. Even Sallie admitted this fact. When Temperance saw Galina raise her clenched fists, she fired a second warning shot. This bullet, Clement suggested, ricocheted off something in the piazza and wound up by chance, and chance only, in Galina's chest. "Now suppose that ball had struck the ceiling of the piazza, or a nail, or knot, in the ceiling, and rebounded and killed Galina, Ellen, or Mrs. Neely—would that be sufficient to convict the prisoner of manslaughter?"

Clement carried his argument to the extreme. "The conduct of the prisoner was not culpable, but praiseworthy, if her attention was to frighten Galina and thus stop the difficulty." According to the attorney, not only was Temperance Neely to be congratulated for attempting to keep the peace, she was also a victim of her own apparently itchy trigger finger. "It was an unlucky accident, fatal not only to poor Galina but also it may be, fatal to the peace of mind, to the happiness, and flattering prospects of the future of the unfortunate prisoner."

Clement did acknowledge the political situation, noting that "If crime needs an example of punishment to repress it let the punishment fall upon the guilty and not upon the innocent. It is humbly insisted that this is no case to make an example of—punishment here is not called for"[29]

In his closing salvo, Boyden repeated the assertion that the shooting resulted from a "misadventure," not murder or manslaughter. Boyden noted that Providence was well within her rights "in punishing the girl Ellen," as a schoolmarm has a right to whip a recalcitrant pupil, and "Galina was wrong in interfering to prevent the chastisement. But whether the mother was right or wrong, the daughter had an unquestionable right, when she saw her mother rudely assaulted and thrown upon the floor, to interfere and come to the rescue of her mother, and was guilty of no offence in doing so, and she had a right to resort to such force as was necessary to prevent a repetition of the assault."

Like his partner, Boyden also attacked Sallie's credibility. He empha-sized that according to a professional surveyor, she could not have seen the shooting. Besides, he noted, three "disinterested" witnesses—Arthur Neely, George W. Campbell, and C. W. Pearson—all testified that Sally did not have a good reputation for telling the truth. And he reminded the court that when he brought up the idea that Sallie changed her story, first telling General Schofield a different version altogether, she refused to answer the question.

Like his co-counsel, Nathaniel Boyden was acutely aware of the politi-cal situation outside of the courtroom: Although "crimes are more on the decrease," he noted, "I am sorry to say, there will still be, I feel, enough of which be made examples." The case of Temperance Neely, he suggested, was not the place to set the precedent for future criminals who commit out-rages against freed slaves.[30]

Yet there was one undisputed fact that Boyden could not wipe away with a legal argument. Temperance Neely shot Galina—a fact underscored by Judge Advocate Wood in his written statement. "I think there can be no question in your minds, the evidence of Sallie, combined by the dying dec-larations of Galina, as proven by Henderson, the admission of the prisoner to her uncle Arthur Neely, and the evidence of the prisoner's mother, establishes the fact beyond all doubt in your minds."

Wood argued that even if the crime was committed in the heat of pas-sion, "No provocation whatever can render homicide justifiable or even excusable; the least it can amount to is manslaughter."

Boyden and Clement tried to establish that the four-barrel Sharp's pis-tol could only hurt a fly, and therefore Temperance Neely didn't intend to use it to harm Galina. Any reasonable person, Wood argued, should have realized that any gun is dangerous.

Then Wood went to the heart of the defense's case: the credibility of Sallie's testimony. Wood argued that the witnesses called to discredit Sal-lie's statement did not do the trick. "But how, by introducing a few wit-nesses who testified that her general character for truth among colored people was not good, they assigned no other reason why the witness's testi-mony should not be taken." Wood added that "it requires stronger, much stronger, evidence than this to impeach a witness."

The case, he said, came down to this: only two people—Providence Neely and Sallie Neal—witnessed the shooting. Who would the commis-sion believe? In asking the court to judge both on their respective merits, and not on the color of their skin, he subtly reminded the Hoosier judges about the explosive political climate not just in the Tar Heel State, but throughout the South.

"I will ask you to compare her (Sallie) testimony with that of (you might say an interested witness) the mother of the prisoner. You will see the variance is so slight that it must be taken as corroboration of the testimony of Sallie."

As for the professional surveyor who claimed to have empirical evidence that Sallie couldn't have seen the incident, Wood asserted that Johnson's measurements were not accurate. He "merely stepped the distance—that he took the bearing with his eyes and not by instruments—which could not be done with any degree of accuracy." He also didn't know if he used a "scale of 40 or 80 yards to the inch," too big a variation to render an accurate map of the crime scene.

Wood summed up his argument succinctly. "The evidence of the mother places the matter beyond a doubt that Temperance Neely, the prisoner at the bar, was the person who fired the fatal shot that caused the death of Galina."[31]

After a short period of considering the arguments, the commission rendered its judgment. They found the accused, Temperance Neely, not guilty of murder but guilty of the lesser charge of manslaughter. They fined her $1,000.

It was a major victory for the defense. The affluent Neelys could easily pay the fine. Some, General Ruger among them, felt that Temperance Neely had gotten away with murder. Ruger was concerned about the message the commission's hand slap would send. Instead of rubber stamping their finding, he returned it on August 12, asking them to reconsider. He wanted jail time for Temperance.

"I am clearly of the opinion that the sentence is entirely inadequate for the crime of which the prisoner is found guilty," Ruger wrote. "It is a dangerous precedent to establish, particularly at this time, that a human life can be taken almost entirely without fear of greater punishment than a fine. To a person of property such punishment is the very lightest which could be inflicted and the effect of such an administration of justice is simply to encourage crime."[32]

He also complained about the part of the sentence that ordered Temperance Neely to pay the fine to Rowan County instead of the military and that the court order didn't "impose confinement upon the prisoner until the fine is paid, which is the only means by which the sentence can be effected."

The commission amended their sentence but not their verdict. Temperance Neely would go to jail until she paid the $1,000 fine to an officer of the United States Government. Ruger approved the verdict and sentence on August 29, 1865.

Temperance Neely remained in Davie County following her release. In 1867, she married Gustavus A. Bingham. A few years later, the couple began their family with the birth of Annie, the first of their four children

Headquarters Department No Ca
Raleigh N.C. August 12th 1865

The foregoing record in the case of Temperance Neely is respectfully returned to the court for reconsideration. I am clearly of the opinion that the sentence is entirely inadequate for the crime of which the prisoner is found guilty. It is a dangerous precedent to establish, particularly at this time, that a human life can be taken, almost entirely without provocation or extenuating circumstances, and without fear of greater punishment than a fine. To a person of property such punishment is the very lightest which could be inflicted, and the effect of such an administration of justice is simply to encourage crime. a thorough consideration by the court of these points is earnestly recommended —

as regards the sentence as it stands, the clause directing the fine to be paid over to the trustees of Rowan County N.C. for the use of that county is wholly without precedent and unauthorized. a fine imposed by a military commission can only go to the use of the Government. in addition to this the sentence is inoperative from the fact that it fails to impose confinement upon the prisoner until the fine is paid, which is the only means by which the sentence can be enforced. Attention is invited to G.O. War Dept 61 — enclosed
Nos D Ruger

General Ruger was very disappointed with the light sentence Temperance Neely received for shooting Galina. He calls the sentence "entirely inadequate" and a "dangerous precedent to establish, particularly at this time." Ruger was afraid it would encourage crimes against former slaves. NATIONAL ARCHIVES together. Like her mother before her, Temperance outlived her lifelong mate. The widow Temperance Neely died in 1922 at the age of eighty-six.

While the aspects of her case were unique, Temperance Neely wasn't the only white who stood accused of violent crimes against blacks in North Carolina. Thirteen other cases came to bar in the ensuing months.[33]

Neely also wasn't the only one who got off with a hand slap. One defendant was found guilty of murder and sentenced to hang, but Ruger commuted the crime to manslaughter and ordered the prisoner released. In another case, a defendant was convicted of shooting, but not killing, a freedman. He was fined $500 and thrown in jail for ninety days. Ruger reduced the light sentence further when he cut the fine to $250 and the prison sentence to thirty days.[34]

As for black perpetrators of crimes, even minor ones, the courts meted out draconian punishments, including public humiliation. An indignant reporter from the *New York Tribune* observed that "negroes are receiving treatment at the hands of the Provost-Marshals so inhuman and diabolical that the people of the North would not believe the tale if it were told them. A negro passing through an unfenced and unoccupied lot picks a few peaches, and by order of the Provost-Marshal he is suspended by the thumbs for hours, under the blazing sun, where he may be assailed by the jeers of all loafers of the town."[35]

By the end of the summer, however, the pendulum had swung the other way. While the military courts still tended to go light on white perpetrators, they eased up on black convicts. Ruger even did away with the dreaded ball and chain as a punishment for thieves.[36]

Temperance Neely may have shot Galina by accident, or she may have gotten away with cold-blooded murder; the truth remains obscured by time. One thing, however, is clear: Life was cheap in Davie County on the morning when the military commission rendered its verdict. At $1,000, Temperance paid less for shooting Galina than it would have cost to buy her at auction before the war.

CHAPTER 16

The War Crimes Trial of Andersonville's Controversial Commandant
1865

During the latter years of the Civil War, the mere mention of the name "Andersonville" sent shudders the Union ranks. They heard whispers of unbelievably inhumane treatment at the prison camp in west Georgia: rations cut to mere ounces a day and none at all on some days; men mercilessly gunned down by the camp's sadistic stockade commander, Henry Wirz, who allegedly once claimed his camp did more for the Confederate cause than rebel bullets;[1] escaped prisoners hunted by dogs, their emaciated bodies shredded when the hounds caught up with them; prisoners given inoculations infected with what one doctor called "poisonous matter," leading to the spread of deadly diseases such as syphilis;[2] men falling each day from thirst, starvation, exposure, and disease; emaciated souls, just skeletons covered by a thin coat of skin; corpses lying unburied for days, their swollen, bloated bodies turning hues of blue and green, filling the air with foul, noxious odor.

This was the Andersonville of rumor, whispers, and legend. The Andersonville described in Northern newspapers. But what exactly happened behind the stockade's fences, and was it murder?

✦ ✦ ✦

Just what went on at Andersonville was the central question pondered at the war crimes trial of Henry Wirz, who faced a military tribunal for murder and conspiracy to commit murder. Over the past century and a half, the trial and its aftermath have generated as much controversy as the prison camp itself. Accusations of staged or fabricated testimony, wildly exaggerated claims of abuse, and prejudicial treatment have left some to question whether Andersonville's controversial commandant was a murderer or a martyr.

Henry Wirz was born Heinrich Hartmann Wirz in Geneva, Switzerland, on November 25, 1823. Wirz came to the United States sometime during his twenties. He lived for a while in Kentucky, where he married a widow with two daughters. They eventually settled in Louisiana, and Wirz established a successful medical practice. Although he spoke with a thick German accent, he could converse in three languages: his native German as well as Dutch and English. He described himself as "by profession a physician" and practiced medicine until hostilities erupted in 1861.[3]

"Like a thousand others," Wirz later said, "I had nothing else to do when Louisiana seceded than to join the southern army."[4] According to some reports, Wirz saw action with the Army of Northern Virginia during the 1862 Battle of Seven Pines, where he took a minié ball in the right arm that left him in almost constant pain.

In March 1864, Wirz made the transition from soldier to jailer when Gen. John H. Winder, the commander of all Southern prisons east of the Mississippi River, sent him to a remote railroad depot called Anderson, Georgia. There he was to serve as the stockade commander of a new prison facility being constructed roughly sixty miles southwest of Macon. The camp, originally called Camp Sumter, opened in February 1864. The prisoners called it "Andersonville."

The original compound was a 16.5-acre rectangle surrounded by a wooden stockade fifteen feet high. The camp quickly became overcrowded. By June 1864, the compound had been enlarged by ten acres, but the camp still could not accommodate the sheer mass of Union prisoners sent there. By August 1864, the camp designed to house ten thousand held over thirty thousand, becoming the Confederacy's fifth most populous metropolis.

By 1864, the Federal blockade of Southern seaports had squeezed the lifeblood from the Confederacy. Everyday resources such as coffee and sugar became scarce—valuable commodities that had to be smuggled into the CSA onboard blockade runners. People went without the basics, and Confederate prison officials lacked the necessities to provide for their charges. At Andersonville, prisoners died of starvation, exposure, and disease every day. The death toll was staggering.

Prison records indicate that during the camp's fourteen months of operation between late February 1864 and April 1865, approximately thirteen thousand souls died there. The deadliest month was August 1864—typically one of the hottest months in Georgia. On August 23 alone, 127 men perished in the sweltering heat.[5] In all, about twenty-nine percent of the forty-five thousand prisoners who served time in Andersonville wound up in one of the camp's mass graves—shallow ditches where men were placed next to each other without coffins.

Dr. A. W. Barrows, one of the very few prisoners who managed to escape, later described the conditions at the prison camp. Barrows traveled with the Twenty-Seventh Massachusetts as the company's physician. When captured and sent to Andersonville, he was pressed into service as a camp doctor. For six months, Barrows worked in the camp's hospital until he managed to flee in early October 1864. Dr. Barrows estimated that ninety percent of ill prisoners at the camp lay not in hospital beds but on the ground, many of them partially clothed in rags or naked. At one time, Barrows noted, he saw six hundred to seven hundred such prisoners lying in one fleshy heap, awaiting treatment for severe diarrhea, gangrene, and other life-threatening ailments.[6]

Prisoners who entered one of the camp's two points of entry were immediately met with the sight of the tent community's emaciated prisoners lying around. A foul stench hung in the air—the combination of smells from decaying corpses and the grease-covered creek that ran through Andersonville.

Michael Dougherty, who fought for the Thirteenth Pennsylvania before his capture in 1863, did stints in several Southern prisons before arriving at Andersonville. In his war diary, Dougherty described in graphic detail the scene he witnessed when he arrived at the infamous prison camp: "The cheerless sight near the gate, of a pile of ghastly dead, the eyes of which shone with a stony glitter, the faces black with a smoky grime and pinched with pain and hunger, the long matted hair and almost fleshless frames swarming with vermin—gave us some idea that a like fate awaiting us inside."[7]

There were other life-threatening "ailments" besides disease at Camp Sumter. There was a certain lawless element inside the stockade. One group of thugs, nicknamed the "Raiders," brutalized fellow prisoners, stealing what they could and beating or murdering anyone who attempted to stop them. Charles Curtis, one of their ringleaders, had terrorized inmates of Richmond's Castle Thunder before Confederate authorities moved him to Georgia.

Inside Andersonville, Curtis once again turned on his fellow prisoners, leading the group that is sometimes called "Curtis' Raiders." Their behavior became so flagrant that when Wirz heard about one inmate who was severely beaten by the Raiders, he threatened to withhold rations. The Raiders were eventually rounded up by another group of prisoners—the "Regulators"—and tried in front of a prisoner court with Wirz's blessing. Six of the troublemakers, including Curtis, were then sentenced to death and hanged by the other inmates.

While Curtis's brutality was notorious, some survivors claimed the worst thug in the place was Capt. Henry Wirz. When Michael Dougherty first arrived at Andersonville, he came face-to-face with the infamous overseer. He described the jailer as a "grinning-faced rebel captain on a gray horse" with a quick temper. When Dougherty pleaded for water, the captain brandished his revolver and snapped, "You — — Yankee, you must vait, or you got so much vater wat you drown in putty quick."[8]

Such anecdotes were common among Andersonville survivors. The "grinning-faced" rebel had a notoriously sharp temper, an irritability that some sources attributed to the constant pain in his injured right arm. Wirz would erupt into a tirade with little or no provocation and often swore at prisoners and guards alike.

To keep prisoners inside the camp, Wirz established a "dead line," a boundary line around the compound that prisoners were forbidden to cross, about twenty feet from the stockade fence. The dead line was in most spots a split-rail fence that indicated the outermost perimeter of the prisoners' territory. Prisoners who ventured beyond this fence would be shot by guards posted in wooden towers called "pigeon roosts."

The drawing of a dead line was a common practice in prisons in both the North and the South, but it generated particular controversy at Andersonville. Some inmates later testified that there was no fence all in some spots, making it difficult to determine boundaries. According to others, Wirz didn't wait for prisoners to cross the line. Eyewitnesses later alleged that Wirz transitioned from jailer to criminal when he gunned down prisoners inside the dead line— just one in a litany of allegations of Wirz's criminal behavior at Andersonville.

Another prisoner said that Wirz offered guards a furlough for every prisoner shot crossing the dead line—an incentive which, if true, may have led guards to gun down prisoners inside the boundary. A young private from Maine, Thomas O'Dea, survived Andersonville and drew a map containing panels that supposedly illustrated what he witnessed inside the compound. One panel depicts a guard shooting a helpless inmate who is at the stream filling his canteen with water.

Inside the stockade, Wirz kept strict law and order by meting out corporal punishment when he felt it was necessary. He assembled chain gangs consisting of prisoners chained to each other and anchored down with thirty-two and sixty-eight-pound iron balls. He also bucked (tied a prisoner's arms and legs together, forcing him into a seated, fetal position) and gagged inmates as well locking them in the stocks. Wirz even punished his own men for transgressions; according to one of the camp's doctors, a hospital clerk was bucked for not reporting a missing man.

In another one of his panels, Thomas O'Dea shows prisoners being subjected to all sorts of corporal punishments for breaking the rules: skeletal

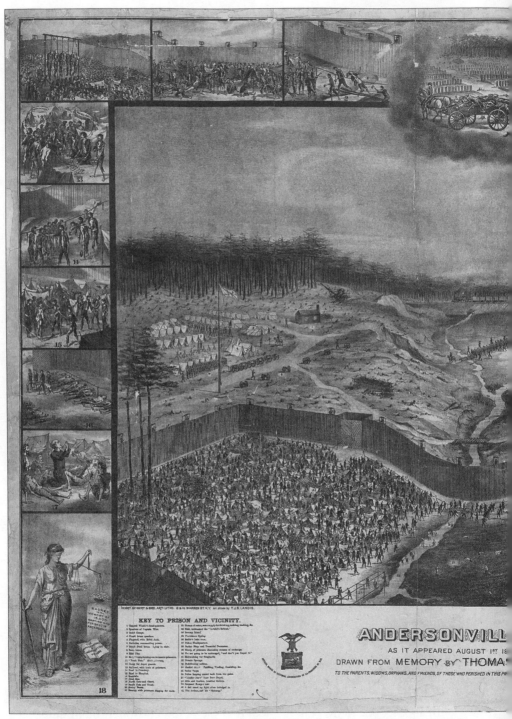

Andersonville, or Camp Sumter, as drawn by Thomas O'Dea, a private from Maine who survived a stint in the notorious prison.

The border of the panorama contains vignettes of atrocities that supposedly occurred at the camp.

inmates "thumbed" (suspended by the thumbs or wrists), bucked and gagged, and shackled to ball and chain.

These types of punishments were consistent with those used in other prisons of the time, both in the North and the South. George Alexander used them at Castle Thunder in Richmond. At Alton Penitentiary, an Illinois state prison that was reopened to accommodate captured Confederates and later gained a reputation as "the Andersonville of the North," prison authorities bucked and gagged inmates as a punishment.

But did Wirz go too far in laying down the law he established inside Camp Sumter? According to some former inmates, he did. They claimed Wirz rode around the compound on a white horse with a bullwhip that he wasn't afraid to use. According to others, this image of Wirz doesn't fit the facts: His battle injury left him without the use of much of his right arm.

Scenes of horror from O'Dea's Andersonville panorama. Above: prisoners enduring corporal punishments, including the "buck and gag" and "thumbing." Facing page, top: Wirz with a bullwhip and the dogs he used to track escaped inmates. Facing page, bottom: the "Raiders," including Charles Curtis, hanged by fellow prisoners with Wirz's blessing. LIBRARY OF CONGRESS

In late summer 1864, Confederate officials moved many of the prisoners to other Southern prisons. The numbers incarcerated at the Georgia stockade remained low throughout the rest of the war, and with less crowding, the conditions improved somewhat, although the mortality rate remained high. Over a hundred prisoners died in March 1865, the prison's last full month of operation.[9] By April, only a skeleton crew remained.

The skeletons that emerged from the infamous stockade were nothing but skin stretched tightly over bones. Their appearance prompted poet Walt Whitman to remark, "The dead there are not to be pitied as much as some of the living that come from there—if they can be call'd living—many of them are mentally imbecile, and will never recuperate."

Gen. John Winder, the officer in charge of Confederate prisons, had died of a massive heart attack in February 1865, leaving the officers below him in rank, including Henry Wirz, to answer for what happened at Andersonville. And there were a lot of questions to answer. For months before the war ended, Northern newspapers carried headline articles detailing the cruelties inside the dead line of Andersonville. The court of public opinion convicted Confederate authorities of purposely neglecting Union prisoners of war. When the war ended, the same court wanted justice for the soldiers who died at Andersonville.

Wirz remained at his post, unaware of what Union officials had in store for him. On May 7, he was arrested by Federal cavalry under Gen. James Wilson. He was taken to Macon, Georgia, and jailed as a criminal without being told why. Wirz maintained his innocence and reminded his captors that when Johnston surrendered to Sherman, Sherman granted "parole" to all under Johnston's command, including him. His pleas fell on deaf ears.

Two weeks after his arrest, Wirz was shipped from Macon to Nashville, Tennessee, and from there to Washington, DC, where he would stand trial for conspiracy to commit murder and thirteen counts of "wanton cruelty." The charges of cruelty included murdering prisoners by shooting them in cold blood as well as other examples of mistreatment that led to the deaths of Andersonville inmates.

In a letter to the superintendent of Carroll Prison—the Washington jail where Wirz awaited trial—Wirz noted that he acted as the officer "in charge of the Interior of the Prison . . . never during the whole time was I in command of the prison, or had any control over Commissary or Quartermaster department, acting myself solely in obedience to orders from my superior officer."[10] Wirz was not, he claimed, the one in charge of the prison or its food supply and was just following orders.

His Union jailors didn't buy either excuse; Henry Wirz was going to court for what he supposedly did at Andersonville. Wirz was charged, along with other Confederates, including Robert E. Lee, of conspiring to murder

Northern soldiers held in Southern prisons. To Southerners and Southern sympathizers, Henry Wirz began to look like a scapegoat. Just before the trial began, James W. Denver, one of Wirz's original attorneys, wrote in a letter to his wife, "I am of the opinion that the intention is hang him and that no stone will be left unturned to effect it."[11]

Captain Wirz wasn't the highest-ranking officer at Andersonville. At war's end, the post commander was Col. George C. Gibbs, who took over as the garrison commander the previous October. Gibbs supervised the soldiers stationed at Camp Sumter, but he had nothing to do with the oversight of the prison facilities—a fact he emphasized in a letter written to Gen. E. M. McCook on May 12, 1865.

Perhaps realizing that someone was going to swing for Andersonville, Gibbs explained his position and pointed the finger of blame at Wirz, essentially throwing him under the carriage. In the letter, Gibbs described the difference between post commander—his job—and prison commander. "I never had anything to do with the prisons," Gibbs said. That responsibility, he pointed out, belonged to Henry Wirz, who was in actual command of the stockade and what happened to it.[12] McCook forwarded Gibbs's note to division headquarters and added, "I think he is the wrong man, and Captain Wirz (that you already have) the guilty party."[13]

Wirz may not have entirely realized the gravity of his situation; in the same letter to his Washington jailer in which he minimized his role at the camp, he asks to be let out of prison. "My humble petition," Wirz said, "is to be released and allowed with my family to leave the United States and return to my native country. I am to [sic] old to start the world anew, all my property is lost and I could not support my family here. In Switzerland I have some property left."[14]

Wirz's "humble petition" was denied. He wasn't headed to the verdant highlands of Switzerland, but instead bound for a packed courtroom a few blocks away where his fate would rest with a military tribunal. He would stand alone in the dock. Just before the trial began, Secretary of War Stanton ordered the charges against Lee and the other Confederates indicted alongside Wirz to be dropped. He would not do the same for Henry Wirz. Although the amended indictment still included the names of others associated with the notorious prison, Wirz would be the only one to face Wallace's military commission.

Wirz had prepared for his defense while in prison. He made a list of thirty-four people he wanted to testify for the defense and requested that they be subpoenaed. The government assured him that it would do whatever necessary to find the witnesses and summon them to court.

While the controversial commander awaited trial, a group convened at Andersonville in order to identify the dead and create a cemetery with proper grave markers. The group owed its existence in part to Dorance

Atwater's "death roll." Atwater did time in Andersonville and lived to tell about it. After spending a few months inside the prison, Atwater went to work as a prison clerk assigned to compile a list who perished at the camp. On the sly, he made a duplicate copy of the "death roll" and hid the list of some 13,000 names inside the lining of his coat. He kept his list secret out of fear that the prison authorities would destroy a document that might potentially implicate them in wrongdoing.

Later, after his release, Atwater's story caught the eye of Clara Barton, the famous nurse who went on to later cofound the American Red Cross. Barton contacted the secretary of war, who organized a party consisting of herself, Atwater, a military quartermaster, and a contingent of forty painters and carpenters.

With Atwater's "death roll" in hand, the group arrived at Andersonville on July 26, 1865. Working amid the scorching summer sun and to the background music of locusts, they unearthed the thousands of bodies of men who died during the camp's fourteen-month lifespan, including four hundred Confederates who died while on duty at Camp Sumter.

By August 24, the group had managed to identify just less than thirteen thousand Union prisoners by name. They laid out a cemetery and prepared wooden markers for each fallen soldier. Eighty thousand board feet of pine were required for the markers in this city of the dead. The group also created a dead line of a different sort for the former POW camp—a wooden fence that enclosed the fifty-acre graveyard.

Back in the nation's capital, on August 21, Andersonville's former stockade commander went before a military tribunal led by Maj. Gen. Lew Wallace, who had just served on a panel that tried the Lincoln conspirators and who would later become famous as the author of *Ben Hur*. Col. N. P. Chipman was selected as the judge advocate, the prosecuting attorney who would question witnesses.

At about 1:30 on the afternoon of August 23, 1865, Wirz made his grand entrance, escorted into the Court of Claims Hall by eight soldiers of the Veteran Reserve Corps. A standing-room only audience, roughly one-third of them women, came to watch the drama unfold. All eyes in the audience followed Wirz as he walked into the room.

Wirz stood about five feet eight, with salt-and-pepper hair and a matching moustache. Slightly hunched with rounded shoulders, Wirz looked like a man worn down by time and the elements. He suffered through constant, agonizing pain in his right arm, and he was emaciated from a long-running illness that began a year earlier. While at Andersonville in August 1864, Wirz had gotten sick and spent much of the month in his cabin about five miles from the stockade.

The *New York Times* described Wirz as having a "cadaverous, sallow face" and "dark blue intelligent eyes." Despite his appearance, Wirz impressed the *Times* correspondent as "a man of iron will, determined in purpose, and heartless in the execution of it."[15]

The ailing former CSA captain listened and occasionally whispered to his counsel as the commission read the long list of charges. Wirz winced when he heard the bit alleging he poisoned vaccinations.

Wirz faced two separate charges. The first alleged that he conspired "Maliciously, willfully and traitorously . . . to injure the health and destroy the lives" of Union solders incarcerated in Camp Sumter. The second charge—"Murder, in the violation of the laws and customs of war"—cited thirteen separate instances of assault and murder that Wirz either ordered or carried out himself. The "specifications" do not list the names of the victims, but allege that Wirz did everything from stomping and kicking an inmate (specification 2) to causing the death of another by chaining him together with others for a protracted period of time and anchoring the group with thirty-two-pound iron balls (specification 7) to using blood-hounds to run down and then "tear in pieces a soldier" (specification 11).

Wirz's defense questioned the military commission's right to try the case, since the defendant didn't serve in the US military. This question of the military's jurisdiction had been argued just a few months earlier during the trial of the Lincoln conspirators with the same result: The military was going to stand in judgment over Henry Wirz. The accused also reiterated his belief that he was covered by the blanket parole extended to Confederates under the terms of Johnston's surrender to Sherman, and then entered a plea of "not guilty."

The trial, which spanned about two months, featured a long line of witnesses that included former camp inmates, guards, and physicians, including two camp doctors.

George C. Gibbs testified for the prosecution. Gibbs, a colonel in the Confederate army, was posted as commander of Camp Sumter but said he played no part "in the police regulations or military discipline" of the prison. His garrison supplied Wirz with prison guards and that was all. "I had no control, whatever, of the prison," Gibbs testified. "Captain Wirz had exclusive control of the prison while I was there." Gibbs went on to describe the stockade when he visited the prison, in August 1864, during its population spike. "It had more the appearance of an anthill," Gibbs said.[16]

Dr. John Bates, a surgeon who worked at Anderson's infirmary from September 19, 1864, to March 29, 1865, also testified. When the war began, Bates was a seasoned doctor. In September 1864, he was detailed to work as an assistant surgeon in the camp's hospital. In his decade of experience, Dr. Bates had seen nothing like Andersonville.

During his testimony, Dr. Bates described the conditions at Camp Sumter, characterizing the inmates as unclothed, unfed wretches who would constantly beg for food, even bones to grind up into meal. Bates's description of the camp's cleanliness caused some in the courtroom to twitch. "Of vermin and lice there was a very prolific crop there," Bates recalled. "I would generally find some upon myself after retiring to my quarters . . . they were so numerous that it was impossible for a surgeon to enter the hospital without having some upon him when he came out, if he touched anybody or anything save the ground, and very often if he merely stood still any considerable length of time he would get them upon him."[17]

Dr. Bates told the story of a fifteen- or sixteen-year-old boy in his ward afflicted with gangrene and scurvy, which affected his digestive system. He gave the boy potatoes and instructed the youth to eat them raw, which would help with the digestion. Nonetheless, the boy became so ill that he could not move. He was bedridden without a bed and developed sores that became gangrenous. "The lice, the want of bed and bedding, of fuel and food, were the cause of his death," Bates concluded.

Bates went on to describe other cases of men afflicted with scurvy—men who couldn't chew anything solid because all of their teeth had become loose, men reduced to crawling on their hands and knees. He also graphically described other maladies suffered by inmates, including gangrene and the amputations that resulted.

During Bates's graphic descriptions, counsel for the defense O. S. Baker objected that Dr. Bates's testimony didn't relate to any of the charges pending against Henry Wirz, but the court overruled Baker's objection, and the doctor continued his testimony.

Bates explained that the epidemic of scurvy, which caused sores that in turn led to gangrene, could have been solved by inserting green corn into the diet. Even though western Georgia was "pretty good corn-growing country," Dr. Bates said, no green corn was issued to sick inmates.

Dr. Bates also testified that it was his belief, and the belief of the other doctors who worked at the hospital, that they could not administer even one dose of medicine without Captain Wirz's approval, indicating that Wirz had oversight over the hospital and what did or did not happen there.

At one point during his tenure at Camp Sumter, Dr. Bates was temporarily assigned to the stockade, which, he testified, was so overrun with disease that if a prisoner "should chance to stump his toe," the minor injury would most likely turn into a life-threatening case of gangrene.[18] The prevalence of gangrene in the camp led to a noxious stench of fetid, rotting flesh. Many of the prisoners fell ill and died due to exposure in the winter-time, Dr. Bates said, but oddly, no one cut timber from the white pine stands surrounding the stockade—an action that he concludes would have likely saved lives.

"From your observation of the condition and surroundings of our pris-oners—their food, their drink, their exposure by day and by night, and all the circumstances you have described—state your professional opinion as to what proportion of deaths occurring there were the result of the cir-cumstances and surroundings which you have narrated," Colonel Chip-man asked.

"I feel myself safe in saying that seventy-five percent of those who died might have been saved, had those unfortunate men been properly cared for as to food, clothing, bedding," Dr. Bates responded.[19]

O. S. Baker cross-examined Dr. Bates.

"Did it ever strike you that anyone about those premises was conspir-ing for the death of Union prisoners there?" Baker asked during his cross.

Colonel Chipman objected to Baker's question. After a short period of discussion, Chipman's objection was overruled.

"It never so impressed me," Dr. Bates responded. "I always objected to the shortness of the allowance, but I never attributed it to a conspiracy."

Baker continued to hammer at Dr. Bates's implication that Wirz was responsible for the general conditions of Camp Sumter. "Were not those prisoners taken care of by the persons there as well as they possibly could be with the means at hand?"

"We took care of them the very best we could, but we always objected to the means furnished."

"To whom did you object?"

"Through the morning report we objected, in the usual course, to the surgeon in charge."

"Do you not know that it was generally complained of up to higher authorities?"

"That was what our intention was."

"You always looked to higher authority for relief from these troubles?"

"Yes, sir."

"Do you know of Captain Wirz doing anything in the way of starving these prisoners any more than the rest of you?"

"Personally I never knew anything about Captain Wirz, whether he ever signed an order to issue anything or not."[20]

The prosecution also called Dr. A. W. Barrows, a physician from Mas-sachusetts who found his way inside Andersonville. Barrows testified about sores caused by vaccinations that "had every symptom of 'sec-ondary' syphilis.'"

Dr. Barrows then implied that someone had poisoned the vaccinations: "a person can be impregnated with that disease by inoculation; it is so put down in medical history. I should say I have seen two or three hundred cases of that description in the course of my stay there . . . In my opinion, the matter used must have been impure. I considered it as poisonous, judging from the effects and results"[21] These sores, another witness later said, were "twice as large as a silver half dollar," and crawling with maggots.[22]

Barrows also described men chained together for as long as a week, and cited specific examples of men he treated who were "mangled" by the hounds used to hunt them when they escaped. In one instance, he recalled, a man had been "torn by the dogs" so badly that he later died from his wounds, which became gangrenous.

The doctor also refuted there even was a dead line at the infirmary. "I have often heard Captain Wirz tell the guard at the hospital," Dr. Barrows testified, "that if any of those 'Yanks' tried to get away to shoot them. We had no dead line established there."[23]

Dr. Barrows seconded Dr. Bates's opinion that the area would have provided enough wood to build shelters and fuel fires during the winter months. He noted that he saw slaves cutting down trees for the garrison, but the Union prisoners were not allowed to leave the camp to do the same.

He also described the stream that flowed through the camp as "perfectly horrible." According to Dr. Barrows, the stream—the chief water supply for the prisoner population—became both the dump and the bathing facility for the thirty thousand men living in Andersonville. "I certainly did not think that anyone could live in the vicinity and enjoy health with even the best of diet."[24]

According to Dr. Barrows, Wirz also curtailed the food supply. He testified that there was an order specifying that Union prisoners could not possess green vegetables and some were even arrested for having them after they bartered with the guards. Dr. Barrows also said that Wirz cut off the rations of all thirty thousand men for twenty-four hours when he caught some of the men attempting to tunnel their way out of the stockade.

Wirz, according to the camp doctor, also beat prisoners. "I could not hear Captain Wirz's language to him, but I saw Captain Wirz knock him down and stamp on him," Barrows said, recalling one particular instance. "I think it was in September, 1864; [Wirz] had a revolver, but I could not say whether he struck him with his revolver or his hand; I was perhaps four rods from him."[25] And Wirz, Dr. Barrows alleged, boasted of his brutality, once remarking that he did more for the Confederacy than four regiments on the front lines.

"Are you prepared to give professional opinion as to the percentage of deaths that might have been averted by proper treatment?" Colonel Chipman asked the former prison-camp surgeon.

"I have talked that matter over frequently, while there and since," Dr. Barrows replied. "It has been my honest opinion that, had we had proper food, clothing, quarters and everything necessary to the sanitary commission of men, probably from seventy-five to eighty per cent might have been saved under favorable circumstances."[26]

Robert K. Kellogg, an Andersonville inmate during the peak of its population, testified for the prosecution. Kellogg recalled a few occasions when inmates were allowed to go foraging in the woods, but for the most part, they relied on roots dug from inside the dead line for fuel.

Another former prisoner named Thomas C. Alcoke testified that Captain Wirz stole from the inmates. During his testimony, he stood and pointed at the stooped figure as the man who, he said, took his money as well as a pocketknife and a gold ring. Alcoke also described an incident when he witnessed Wirz murder a prisoner in cold blood. The prisoner asked Wirz if he could go outside the compound for some fresh air. "Captain Wirz asked him what he meant by that," Alcoke said. "The poor fellow 'wormed' around and said he wanted air. There was something said, when Captain Wirz wheeled again, pulled out a revolver and shot him down."[27] Alcoke went on to say that when he made a comment that Wirz didn't like, he wound up with a ball and chain. He managed to saw his way through the chain, escape the prison, and rejoin his regiment.

Boston Corbett, who had made a name for himself when he gunned down John Wilkes Booth in April, also testified against Wirz. Corbett made it through most of the war until he was captured during the summer of 1864 and sent to Andersonville.

Corbett made a break for it but didn't get as far as Alcoke; he was run to the ground by the dogs. According to Corbett, the guard who caught him said, "The old captain told me to make the dogs tear you, but I have been a prisoner myself and know what it is to be a prisoner, and I would not like to do that."

Baker cross-examined Corbett. "Did you ever yourself see Captain Wirz perpetrate any personal violence on anyone?" he asked.*

"I cannot answer without stating what I heard."

"Answer yes or no, and the circumstances can be stated afterwards."

"I did not see any outrage," Corbett admitted.

"Very well, that is enough." Baker was satisfied with the admission, but Corbett wasn't.

"You said that when I answered I might state the circumstances; I now insist on my right to do so."

---

* Note: the trial transcripts are in a Q and A format. Attribution tags (e.g. "Baker asked") have been added to create a more readable narrative.

General Wallace interrupted the exchange. "State under what circumstances and from whom you heard what you refer to."

"We object," Baker yelled, but Wallace told him to sit down and asked Corbett to continue.

"I was being removed from the stockade to the cars, to be taken to another prison. It was at night. Just back of me some prisoners, who were unable to walk, had fallen. I heard Captain Wirz's voice swearing, and I heard what indicated that blows had been given. I did not see him strike any blows, but I heard something of that going on. I could not swear that I saw it, yet I knew of the occurrence."[28]

The prosecution called witness after witness who told personal anecdotes about Wirz's alleged inhumane and cruel treatment of prisoners. One former inmate even told of watching dogs receive rations, while another said he spent thirty-six hours in the stocks, subsisting on nothing but two sips of dirty creek water as punishment for an escape attempt. Such testimony runs for hundreds of pages in the official trial transcript.

About a week after proceedings began, Wirz's attorneys had had enough of the circus trial. Frustrated by dozens of overturned objections and what they believed was a clearly biased court, they withdrew, leaving Wirz without legal counsel. But they had a change of heart and reentered the case shortly after dropping out.

The testimony continued. Even some former rebel troops testified about Wirz's alleged cruelties. Calvin Huneycutt, a Georgian who was detailed to Camp Sumter during its peak population from May through September 1864, testified that his former boss kicked an inmate when the man, who was ill, didn't stand up straight during muster.

Several former soldiers stationed at Camp Sumter said they heard Wirz claim that he killed more of the enemy than Confederate troops or, as one remembered hearing it, Robert E. Lee. Another remembered an outraged Wirz threatening to fire grapeshot into the compound, and another told of a teenager from Michigan who Wirz pistol-whipped with such force that the prisoner fell to the ground, trembling from a seizure. He died a few days later.

Former inmate Frank Maddox said that on Wirz's orders, a black soldier was whipped, apparently for attempting to forge a pass, a staggering two-hundred and fifty times from head to toe. Maddox also said that he knew of a white man coloring himself and trying to escape" by passing as a black field hand. Wirz sentenced the man to thirty-nine lashes.[29]

Felix de la Baume, a former Andersonville inmate from New York, said that Wirz ordered one man tied up by this thumbs and left to hang for two hours. He testified that on another occasion, he saw Wirz shoot two men without cause. De la Baume recalled specific events and comments that

Wirz allegedly made and even presented the court with renderings of the scenes he witnessed.

As the trial progressed, Wirz's health continued to erode. By mid-September, he had become so ill that a couch was brought in for him. When asked to stand up to be identified, he struggled to pull himself up from the "lounge."

When the prosecution finally ran out of witnesses and rested on September 23, O. S. Baker requested an adjournment for a week so he could prepare his case. He said he was exhausted from the strenuous trial, and described his client Wirz as a man "with a mind so shattered that he is unable even to give his counsel reliable information upon the most vital points of his defence."[30]

The court overruled Baker's request, but "out of courtesy" to Baker and his health, the commission agreed to adjourn until September 26. After the short break, the defense began its case, calling witnesses to testify on Wirz's behalf and recalling prosecution witnesses to quiz them about various facets of their earlier testimony. Baker and co-counsel Louis Schade tried to smash earlier testimony depicting Wirz as a bloodthirsty fiend who preyed on his defenseless charges.

Col. James H. Fannin, an officer stationed at Andersonville from May through September 1864, was recalled to the stand.

"Did you in any way know or hear of furloughs given to the guards for shooting Union prisoners?" Baker asked, referring to claims made during the prosecution's case.

"I am satisfied that it was never done," Fannin said, dismissing one of the rumors circulating about the shooting of prisoners on or near the "dead line."

"Did a guard ever apply to you for a furlough on the ground that he had shot a Union prisoner, or did you ever hear of such a thing while you were there?"

"I heard that such things were spoken of there," Fannin explained, "but they were mere rumor, and there was no truth in them; I cannot say that any soldiers ever applied to me for furloughs on that ground."[31]

The defense also called Augustus Moesner, a Union soldier captured and taken to Andersonville in May 1864. Moesner lived in the stockade for three weeks before Wirz "paroled" him and made him a clerk. "I never saw, knew, or heard about Captain Wirz shooting, beating, or killing men in any way while I was there. I never saw, knew, or heard in any way of Captain Wirz carrying a whip while I was there. He never did," Moesner said.[32]

He also explained that Wirz did have the power to reduce or cut off rations, and he did exercise this power, but not very often and not for the entire prison population. According to his former clerk, Wirz stopped rations to a squad when one of that squad's men was missing. The rations were continued when the man was found.

Moesner also told a story about a group of boys captured and incarcerated at Camp Sumter. Fearing that they would become sick, Wirz sent them to work at the hospital as assistants. Some of them, Moesner noted, were sent out to find blackberries for the infirm in the hospital.

As for the story of dogs mauling an escapee to death, Moesner had heard of no such cases. Even a consummate escape artist with more than a half dozen escape attempts under his belt came back alive after Wirz and the hounds tracked him during his seventh attempt. The man returned with his pants slightly tattered, nothing more, according to Moesner.

As for beating inmates, Wirz was, according to Moesner, incapable of using his right arm for just about anything. "His right arm was crippled; he always had a bandage round it and a blister. He could use it in writing, but I do not think I ever saw him using his right arm in another way. He had pain to go on horseback."[33]

The defense recalled Dr. Bates, who earlier testified that green corn would have alleviated the prison's scurvy epidemic. During his second time on the stand, Bates admitted that the country around Andersonville was very poor and may not have been able to provide the green vegetables that he earlier testified would aid the prisoners suffering from scurvy. He also testified that he had never seen Wirz "shooting, beating, kicking, or otherwise maltreating Union prisoners."[34]

Like Moesner before him, Bates also noted that Wirz didn't look well. "I do not know anything about the sickness of Captain Wirz or his absence. I think that when I saw him in September, he was poorly; he looked feeble."[35]

Dr. Bates and Dr. C. J. Ford—an assistant surgeon for the U.S. army who cared for Wirz during his imprisonment in Washington—examined Henry Wirz on the last day of the trial. They found scars up and down Wirz's legs from scurvy and severe damage to both of his arms. Both of the bones in his right arm, Dr. Ford believed, were dead.

"Would he be capable with that arm of pushing or knocking down a person, or using a heavy or even a light instrument in doing so? Baker asked Dr. Ford.

"I can't answer that question entirely," Dr. Ford answered. "I don't know how much strength has in the arm; but I should think him incapable of knocking a man, or using a very heavy instrument of any kind, without doing great injury to the arm."

Wirz's left arm wasn't in much better shape. Most of his left deltoid muscle was gone. Baker asked Ford what effect such atrophy would have on the strength of the arm.

"It prevents in a great measure the action of the deltoid muscle, the use of which is to elevate the arm," Ford replied.

It appeared that Henry Wirz was physically incapable of lifting a hand against the prisoners. The reality of the man appeared to contradict the image of him presented by the various prosecution witnesses, who depicted Wirz as at various times beating and even horsewhipping inmates. Chipman tried to deflect this testimony during his cross-examination of Dr. Ford, suggesting that Wirz's feeble state was a recent development. Ford did not agree.

"From the symptoms presented, can you reason back and tell us what was his condition in 1864?" Chipman queried.

"I should not think the right arm was any better in 1864 than it is now," Dr. Ford concluded.[36]

Dr. Bates concurred, adding that unlike Dr. Ford, he had seen (but not examined) Wirz at Andersonville and noticed Wirz's "difficulty in using his right arm."[37]

Wirz's trial ended on October 24, 1865; it would take a week for the commission to sift through the various allegations and return its verdict. While the members discussed the testimony, Wirz returned to his cell. The ordeal of the trial had taken a heavy toll on the former jailor, which is evident from his writings. During the trial, Henry Wirz sweated out the time by keeping a diary and writing letters to various acquaintances from his cell at the Old Capitol Prison. In the entry dated October 1, 1865, he characterizes himself as a "beggar, crippled with my health and spirit broken."

In the entry, Wirz notes that he has a constant companion in the cell—a guard stationed there to prevent a jailhouse hanging; "they are afraid I might cheat them and the public at large from having their revenge and giving, at the same time, the masses the benefit of seeing a man hung." It wasn't the first time that authorities intervened to present a possible suicide attempt. In the trial's first week, attorney Baker requested that Wirz spend the night in handcuffs—a painful intervention, given the prisoner's arm injury, but apparently considered a necessary one at the time.

In his diary, Wirz contemplates robbing the hangman but decides against suicide. "I owe it to myself, my family, my relations, even the world at large to prove that there never existed a man so utterly devoid of all humanity, such a fiend incarnate, as it has been attempted to prove me to be."

Wirz ends the entry with a hint of indignation. "I think it is high time to blot out the eagle in the American escutcheon and substitute a buzzard." If the eagle is king of the birds, Wirz says, then "how is it that he stoops so low to tear with his talons an [sic] humble captain"? [38]

As the commission deliberated, Wirz may have had a change of heart about cheating the hangman. One of the more curious stories about Wirz's trial and imprisonment came from Gen. Lafayette C. Baker. According to Baker, Wirz was either the intentional or unintentional victim of a poison plot. During a visit with his wife, they shared a last embrace and a kiss, during which the crafty Mrs. Wirz slipped her husband the tongue, and along with it a piece of silk containing a dose of strychnine (some sources say arsenic, although it doesn't matter much—either one would have been just as effective in cheating the hangman).

General Baker, who watched this tender moment, immediately recognized the mouth-to-mouth ploy and grabbed Wirz by the throat and threw him to the floor, throttling him until he coughed up the poisoned pill. According to Baker, who describes the incident in his book *History of the United States Secret Service*, both Mrs. Wirz and one of Wirz's attorneys, Louis Schade, verified the story, even though the *New York Times* denounced it as a total fabrication and reported that both the wife and the lawyer denied it happened.[39]

On October 31, 1865, a few days after the alleged poison plot failed, the military commission returned its verdict. They found Henry Wirz guilty of both charges: murdering (guilty of ten of the thirteen specifications) and conspiring to murder inmates of Camp Sumter. Wirz was sentenced "to be hanged by the neck till he be dead." The execution would take place in mid-November.

After the verdict and sentence was read, Colonel Chipman added, "And the court also find the prisoner, Henry Wirz, guilty of having caused the death . . . by means of dogs, of three prisoners of war in his custody . . . but which finding as here expressed has not and did not enter into the sentence of the court"[40]

Wirz made one last appeal in a letter to President Johnson, requesting either a pardon or a quick death. At this point, Wirz clearly had no illusions about the public perception of him. "I am considered a monster of cruelty," he said, "a wretch that ought not to pollute the earth any longer. Truly, when I pass in my mind over the testimony given, I sometimes almost doubt my own existence. I doubt that I am the Captain Wirz spoken of . . . GIVE ME LIBERTY OR GIVE ME DEATH."[41]

Wirz, according to some versions of his story, did have a way out of the noose. On the eve of the execution, a person claiming to represent an unnamed, high-ranking official offered to commute Wirz's death sentence if he agreed to testify that Confederate president Jefferson Davis had a hand in the doings at Andersonville. Wirz's attorney, Louis Schade, doubted the veracity of this offer, but it didn't matter. Henry Wirz wasn't going to sell Davis to save himself, even if he could somehow implicate the former rebel president. Wirz rejected the eleventh-hour offer.

On November 10, 1865, at about ten in the morning, Henry Wirz made his way alongside two priests through the prison yard toward the scaffold. He wore a black robe and a sling for his right arm. His head held high and with a slight smile, he climbed the stairs to the scaffold in front of a standing-room-only crowd that had massed outside the prison walls and on the rooftops of nearby houses. Everyone wanted to see Wirz go down, and some men even climbed trees outside the Old Capitol court-yard to watch the proceedings.

When Wirz reached the platform, he remarked to one of the priests that his black robe would soon be white. He sat down on a stool placed over the trapdoor. Maj. George B. Russell, the provost marshal, noted with a tone of sadness in his voice that he was only doing what the military commission ordered him to do. Wirz responded that he was about to swing for follow-ing his orders. Russell read the charges, which took several minutes. Wirz listened, at one point shaking his head in disagreement.

When Major Russell finished, Wirz stood up. A detective bound his arms and legs with leather straps, placed a black hood over his head, and fastened the noose around his neck. During the preparations, voices erupted from the rooftops and tree branches where the curious perched to watch the execution. "Hang the scoundrel," one man jeered; "There's a dead line for you," another shouted. And then the trapdoor was released.

The drop failed to break Wirz's neck; it took several minutes for him to die a slow death by strangulation. As Wirz dangled, the crowd jeered and cheered, chanting "Remember Andersonville." The *New York Times* described Henry Wirz's final moments: "There were a few spasmodic con-vulsions of the chest, a slight movement of the extremities, and all was over."[42] Fifteen minutes later, the body was taken down. Henry Wirz was forty-one-years-old.

"He disappointed all those who expected to see him quiver," the *New York Times* reported. "He met his fate, not with bravado, or defiance, but with a quiet, cheerful indifference."[43] Onlookers rushed to the scaffold and began to take away pieces of wood and the rope as souvenirs of the macabre scene. If the guards hadn't stepped in, the mob would have made away with the entire scaffold one piece at a time.

Wirz's postmortem trial was even more humiliating than his ante-mortem one. He was initially buried in the arsenal grounds next to con-victed Lincoln plotter George Atzerodt, who had been hanged four months earlier. After years of sifting through yards of bureaucratic red tape, Louis Schade finally obtained Wirz's remains from Federal authorities. Well, most of them. To his horror, Wirz's former attorney discovered that his most infamous client's corpse was missing a few body parts, which were on dis-play at the Old Capitol Prison. In early 1869, Wirz's remains were rein-terred at Washington's Mount Olivet Cemetery.

Wirz's case did not die with him; it has been an endless fountain of debate among historians, history buffs, and law students ever since. Critics of the trial contend that many of the witnesses who testified for the prosecution exaggerated or lied outright about their experiences at Andersonville. One witness in particular became controversial in the wake of the guilty verdict.

Felix de la Baume's recollection of events inside the stockade of Camp Sumter was so detailed that it seemed unreal. That's because it apparently was. De la Baume impressed someone, because at about the time he went on the stand against Henry Wirz, he was hired as a clerk at the Department of the Interior.

Just over a week after Wirz's execution, de la Baume was unmasked as Felix Oeser, a Union deserter who had fabricated his entire testimony. When the story broke, he lost his government job, but the revelation was too late to help Wirz. De la Baume's treachery, according to some, raises the specter of suborned perjury and casts a shadow over the other witnesses, such as Thomas Alcoke, who supposedly bragged about lying on the stand. Another witness, Boston Corbett, may have been delusional. Historians have long questioned his sanity. In part, the scandal caused by their dubious testimony kept Stanton from trying others associated with the prison.

Another flaw often cited is the prevalence of hearsay testimony—a problem addressed by Wirz's lawyer, O. S. Baker. In late September 1865, about midway through the trial, Baker asked the court to exclude certain testimony that he believed would be thrown out of a civilian court. When Chipman asked Baker to elaborate on his objection, Baker noted that some witnesses added "rumors and hearsays."[44] Witnesses who testified at Wirz's trial frequently repeated things they heard someone else say they heard or saw the captain doing, not things they witnessed firsthand.

This hearsay may have severely damaged Henry Wirz's chances of an acquittal, but the most damning aspect of the trial may have been what wasn't said. Critics claim that the prosecutors cherry-picked witnesses for their case and intimidated or cajoled witnesses for the defense. When Wirz awaited trial, he made a list of thirty-four names, witnesses whom he wanted the government to subpoena and who would presumably speak in his favor. Of Wirz's list, just eighteen made an appearance during the trial, and of those eighteen, only a dozen testified for the Andersonville stockade commander.

Defense lawyer Baker complained to the court that "witnesses have complained that improper language has been used to them to draw out of them something for the prosecution. I hardly believe that the judge advocate would himself attempt to use the influence of the government to frighten or press out of our witnesses anything for the prosecution, and I will not charge it. But witnesses come here under very peculiar circumstances."[45]

There may have been others whose testimony would have helped Wirz. One of Wirz's original lawyers claimed that "quite a number who were prisoners have come forward and say that they will testify to his good conduct and treatment as far as he had power, and if they prove what they say they will he ought to be acquitted."[46]

These opinions weren't heard during the trial, but they haven't gone unspoken, either. In the years since the Wirz trial and execution, several diaries of Union soldiers who served time in Andersonville have been published. And many of them speak of their jailor as a kind albeit quick-tempered fellow who did his best with what he had, which wasn't much.

The story of a Union officer who was imprisoned at Camp Sumter went public more than forty years after Wirz's execution. James Madison Page's 1908 book was called *The True Story of Andersonville Prison: A Defense of Major Wirz*. "Of course there were suffering, hunger, and misery," Page wrote, and the "hospital was inadequate." There was indeed a dead line and men were shot for crossing it, which Page calls a cruel practice.

But the guards "were respectful, humane, and soldierly,"[47] and according to Page, so was Wirz. Page described a time when he dared approach the captain about the lack of food and fuel for heat. Wirz didn't rant, rave, or foam at the mouth, but, Page said, thanked the soldier for bringing the complaint to him. Then Wirz said that he was doing all he could to better conditions. Page's was one of several accounts authored by both Northern and Southern troops who attempted to exonerate Henry Wirz after the fact.

People in Wirz's corner also point out that conditions in some Northern POW camps, like on the one at Alton, Illinois, were just as bad as those at Andersonville. A former state penitentiary, Alton was reopened to house Confederate prisoners of war. Dank, dark, and dirty, the monolithic building was a roof over the prisoners' heads, but that was about it. The inmates there died of disease, such as smallpox, and exposure. No prison authorities went to trial.

Some historians speculate that the fault for Andersonville may ultimately lie with Union authorities. According to the doctors who testified at the trial, many of the deaths at Andersonville were caused by problems that resulted from overcrowding. The sheer number of soldiers placed critical pressure on already scant resources, such as food, water, and medicine. As a result, disease, thirst, and starvation took control.

This overpopulation was the direct result of the Union's 1863 decision to halt prisoner exchanges. After this point, the Confederacy had to use more of its dwindling resources to care for a greater number of Federal prisoners—part of the Union's war of attrition, some say. They believe that Wirz's trial was a diversionary tactic designed to redirect blame away from Federal authorities for the tragedy that was Andersonville. Wirz, according to this line, died for the sins of Union generals.

In 1905, the United Daughters of the Confederacy in Georgia funded the construction of a memorial to Henry Wirz. The four sides of the needle's base each contain an inscription. The inscription on the pillar's south side pretty much sums up the Wirz-as-martyr argument:

> Discharging his duty with such humanity as the harsh circumstances of the times, and the policy of the foe permitted, Captain Wirz became at last the victim of a misdirected popular clamor. He was arrested in time of peace, while under protection of a parole, tried by a military commission of a service to which he did not belong and condemned to ignominious death on charges of excessive cruelty to Federal prisoners. He indignantly spurned a pardon, proffered on condition that he would incriminate President Davis and thus exonerate himself from charges of which both were innocent.[48]

Felonious or framed? Perpetrator or patsy? Ruthless renegade or railroaded? Murderer or martyr? Or somewhere in between? A hundred and fifty years after his trial and execution, Henry Wirz remains a polarizing figure, although it is widely acknowledged that if Wirz had been given an impartial trial, he probably would have been acquitted. And most agree that at least to some extent, he became a scapegoat for the unfortunate reality of Andersonville prison and the fate of the prisoners confined there.

"To some extent," though, isn't strong enough language for some Wirz supporters and apologists, who believe that Wirz' trial was criminal, and his execution, murder.

Chronology

1862

March	Sam Upham begins mass-producing facsimiles of Confederate banknotes
May 1	Benjamin "Beast" Butler becomes commander of occupied New Orleans
May 2	Federal troops under Col. J. B. Turchin perpetrate the Sack of Athens
July 7	Court-martial of Colonel Turchin begins (ends July 30)
September 29	Gen. Jefferson C. Davis murders Gen. William "Bull" Nelson in Louisville, Kentucky
December 16	Butler ordered out of New Orleans

1863

March 5	Trial of "The Negro Faulkner" in Detroit
March 6	Riot in Detroit following Faulkner trial
April 11	CSA Congress investigates treatment of prisoners at Castle Thunder (ends May 1)
May 7	Dr. Peters murders Gen. Earl Van Dorn in Spring Hill, Tennessee
August 4	The Beckham family is murdered at Compromise Landing, Tennessee
August 17–27	Contraband tried for the slaying of the Beckham family
August 21	Guerrillas under William Quantrill sack Lawrence, Kansas
September 4	Ray, Stevinson, and Webb hanged for the murder of the Beckham family
September 6	CSA generals John Marmaduke and Marsh Walker duel outside of Little Rock, Arkansas
October 9	Cole, Davis, and Dood executed for the murder of the Beckham family

1864

February	Camp Sumter, or Andersonville, opens in Georgia
February 15	Stephen G. Burbridge takes command of the Military District of Kentucky
April 12	Rebels under Nathan Bedford Forrest allegedly perpetrate Fort Pillow Massacre
July 16	Burbridge issues Order No. 59
September 27	"Bloody" Bill Anderson's gang perpetrate the Centralia Massacre
October 11	Sue Mundy makes her first appearance in the *Louisville Daily Journal*
October 26	Federal cavalry gun down "Bloody" Bill Anderson near Albany, Missouri
November 25	Rebel plot to burn down New York's business district fails

1865

January 17	Trial of Robert Cobb Kennedy begins in New York
February 22	Gen. John Palmer takes over as military commander of Kentucky
March 12	Guerrillas Clarke, Magruder, and Metcalf captured in Kentucky
March 14	Trial of Marcellus Jerome Clarke, alias Sue Mundy, begins
March 15	Clarke is hanged in Louisville, Kentucky
March 25	Robert Cobb Kennedy is hanged at Fort Lafayette in New York
April 14	John Wilkes Booth assassinates President Lincoln
May 10	Guerrilla hunter Edwin Terrell ambushes William Quantrill in Kentucky
May 12	Testimony in the trial of the Lincoln assassination conspirators begins (ends June 29)
July 1	Temperance Neely shoots her former slave, Galina
July 7	Convicted Lincoln assassination conspirators hanged in the yard of the Old Arsenal
July 11	Testimony in Champ Ferguson's trial begins in Nashville (ends September 26)
July 31	Murder trial of Temperance Neely takes place in Salisbury, North Carolina (ends August 2)
August 23	Trial of Henry Wirz begins in Washington, DC (ends October 24)
October 20	Ferguson is hanged in Nashville
November 10	Wirz is hanged in the yard of the Old Capitol Prison

Endnotes

1. James J. Williamson, *Prison Life in the Old Capitol and Reminiscences of the Civil War* (West Orange, NJ, 1911), 68.
2. Ibid., 38.
3. Ibid., 42.
4. *Richmond Dispatch*, September 9, 1862.
5. *Richmond Dispatch*, August 23, 1862.
6. *Daily National Republican*, February 4, 1864.
7. *Daily National Republican*, May 25, 1863, Second Edition, Extra.
8. Williamson, *Prison Life*, 47.
9. *Richmond Dispatch*, July 31, 1862.
10. *Daily National Republican*, October 23, 1863.
11. *Richmond Dispatch*, November 11, 1862.
12. *Richmond Dispatch*, August 14, 1862.
13. William E. Doster, *Lincoln and Episodes of the Civil War* (New York: G. P. Putnam's Sons, 1915), 106.
14. Ibid.
15. Williamson, *Prison Life*, 42.
16. *New York Times*, April 15, 1862. N. T. Colby, "The 'Old Capitol' Prison" in Alexander K. McClure, *The Annals of the War Written by Leading Participants North and South* (Philadelphia: Times Publishing Company, 1879), 502–512.
17. Newton T. Colby, *The Civil War Papers of Lt. Newton T. Colby, New York Infantry*. ed. William E. Hughes (Jefferson, NC: McFarland & Company, 2003), 508.
18. Testimony of Sgt. John Maguire, September 28, 1863, *Proceedings of the Trial of Private Thomas Wright*, RG 153, Records of the Office of the Judge Advocate General (Army), Court Martial Case Files, 1809–1894, Textual Archives Services Division, National Archives and Records Administration, Washington, DC.
19. Ibid.
20. Crystal Feimster, "The Threat of Sexual Violence during the American Civil War," *Daedalus* Vol. 38, Issue 2 (Spring 2009): 126–134. According to Feimster, "Most rapes . . . likely went unreported because many women, especially women of the planter elite, considered sexual assault a fate worse than death. Because a white woman's virtue represented her most valuable commodity, much was at stake in making public a crime understood to tarnish that virtue."
21. Michael Kauffman, *American Brutus: John Wilkes Booth and the Lincoln Conspiracies* (New York: Random House, 2005), 332–334.

22. John C. Schneider, "Detroit and the Problem of Disorder: The Riot of 1863." *Michigan History* 58 (Spring 1974): 13.

Inside Castle Thunder, Notorious Richmond Prison

1. Frank B. Doran, "Prison Memories," *National Tribune*, November 16, 1905. Doran was a noncombatant captured while tending to his sick brother, a Union soldier, on December 26, 1862. He was en route to Libby Prison when Confederate authorities discovered he was a civilian, so he was thrown into Castle Thunder in late March 1863 under suspicion of espionage. He spent much of the war in one rebel prison or another, eventually being released on March 4, 1865. After the war, Doran served as mayor of St. Paul, Minnesota, from 1896 to 1898.
2. Ibid. Curtis is a shadowy character whose pre-Andersonville days are murky. According to Doran, he was a two-time deserter: He deserted from a New Orleans-raised Confederate regiment and later from the Union army. Doran said that he later met Curtis at Salisbury, which was in 1864, so it is likely that Doran came across Curtis at Castle Thunder in late March or early April 1863.
3. Testimony of George W. Thomas, contained in United States War Department, *The War of the Rebellion: A Compilation of the Official Records of the Union and Confederate Armies*, 128 vols. (Washington, DC: Government Printing Office, 1880–1901), ser. 2, vol. 5, 882. Hereafter referred to as *O.R.*
4. Frances Casstevens, *George W. Alexander and Castle Thunder: A Confederate Prison and Its Commandant* (Jefferson, NC: McFarland & Company, 2004), 80.
5. Ibid., 81.
6. J. Marshall Hanna, "Castle Thunder in Bellum Days," *Southern Opinion*, November 23, 1867. For contemporary news articles related to Richmond during the Civil War, see Michael D. Gorman's website *Civil War Richmond* (www.mdgorman.com), which contains transcriptions of hundreds of era newspaper articles about all aspects of the rebel capital during the conflict.
7. Testimony of George W. Thomas. *O.R.*, ser. 2, vol. 5, 882.
8. Hanna, "Castle Thunder in Bellum Days."
9. "Old Castle Thunder: Death of Colonel Alexander, Who Was Superintendent of the Prison," *Richmond Dispatch*, March 3, 1895.
10. *Baltimore Sun*, February 22, 1895.
11. Both versions of Alexander's escape are from obituaries lauding Alexander's military career: the *Baltimore Sun* (February 22, 1895) and the *Richmond Dispatch* (March 3, 1895).
12. "Old Castle Thunder," *Richmond Dispatch*, March 3, 1895. According to Speer, the inmates gave the prison its nickname. Lonnie Speer, *Portals to Hell: Military Prisons of the Civil War*, (Mechanicsburg, PA: Stackpole Books, 1997).
13. Testimony of John Caphart in *O.R.*, ser. 2, vol. 5, 875.
14. Ibid.
15. Ibid., 874.
16. Hanna, "Castle Thunder in Bellum Days."
17. Ibid.
18. "Old Castle Thunder," *Richmond Dispatch*, March 3, 1895.
19. Testimony of T. E. Bland in *O.R.* ser. 2, vol. 5, 874.

20. Testimony of James McAlister in *O.R.* ser. 2, vol. 5, 908.
21. Testimony of John Adams in *O.R.* ser. 2, vol. 5, 902.
22. Doran, "Prison Memories." Doran identifies the man as "Webster, the Union Spy," but Timothy Webster was confined to Castle Godwin and executed on April 29, 1862—before Castle Thunder opened. Doran was jailed in Castle Thunder in March 1863, so the man Doran met was probably A. C. Webster, who was put in Castle Thunder on December 17, 1862, and attempted to flee the prison by leaping out of an infirmary window. A. C. Webster was hanged in April 1863.
23. Testimony of Marion C. Riggs, in *O.R.* ser. 2, vol. 5, 899.
24. Testimony of John De Butts, M.D., in *O.R.* ser. 2, vol. 5, 904.
25. Testimony of T. E. Bland, April 11, 1863, in *O.R.* ser. 2, vol. 5, 873.
26. Testimony of Dennis O'Connor, in *O.R.* ser. 2, vol. 5, 896.
27. Testimony of T. E. Bland, in *O.R.* ser. 2, vol. 5, 880–881.
28. Testimony of Stephen B. Childrey, in *O.R.* ser. 2, vol. 5, 885.
29. Testimony of Baldwin Allen, in *O.R.* ser. 2, vol. 5, 889.
30. Testimony of John Caphart, April 13, 1863, in *O.R.* ser. 2, vol. 5, 874.
31. Testimony of Lieutenant Bossieux, in *O.R.* ser. 2, vol. 5, 912.
32. Testimony of J. T. Kirby, in *O.R.* ser. 2, vol. 5, 890, 892.
33. Quoted in *Richmond Dispatch*, March 3, 1895.
34. Letter from John Winder to George Alexander, *O.R.*, ser. 2, vol. 5, 916.
35. *O.R.* ser. 2, vol. 5, 920.
36. Ibid., 919–920.
37. Ibid., 919.
38. Ibid., 920.
39. "An Old Public Functionary Departed," *Richmond Whig*, November 11, 1864; "Death of a Detective," *Richmond Sentinel*, November 11, 1864.

Sam Upham's Counterfeiting Scheme

1. Upham's advertisements are reproduced in Arlie R. Slaubaugh, *Confederate States Paper Money* (Iola, WI: Krause Publications, 1998), 102–104.
2. Letter from Samuel Upham to Dr. William Lee, dated October 12, 1874, and quoted in several sources, including Richard Cecil Todd, *Confederate Finance* (Athens: University of Georgia Press), 100. Dr. Lee, a contemporary researcher interested in Confederate currency, wrote a letter to the infamous facsimile maker. In his response, Upham detailed the history of his operation. Because Upham also counterfeited Confederate postage stamps, philatelists have long taken an interest in the Chestnut Street operation. Upham's letter to Dr. Lee appears in *MeKeel's Weekly Stamp News*, a Boston weekly for stamp enthusiasts. Vol. 28, no. 48 (Nov. 28, 1914).
3. Arlie R. Slaubaugh, *Confederate States Paper Money* (Iola, WI: Krause Publications, 1998), 105.
4. Confederate Secretary of Treasury Christopher G. Memminger to Hon. Thomas S. Bocock, Speaker of the House of Representatives, Confederate States of America, August 18, 1862. *O.R.*, ser. 4, vol. 2, 62.
5. *Harper's Weekly*, January 31, 1863. Curiously, the same edition contains advertisements for both Upham's and Hilton's facsimiles. Hilton's advertisements are reproduced in Slabaugh, 112.

Benjamin Butler, Beast of New Orleans

1. General Orders No. 111, December 24, 1862, *O.R.*, ser. 2, vol. 5, 795–97.
2. Quoted in Benjamin Franklin Butler, *Autobiography and Personal Reminiscences* (Boston: A. A. Thayer and Co., 1892), 375.
3. Quoted in Robert Werlich, *"Beast" Butler: The Incredible Career of Major General Benjamin Franklin Butler* (Washington, DC: Quaker Press, 1962), 34.
4. Julia LeGrand, *The Journal of Julia LeGrand: New Orleans 1862–1863*, ed. Kate Mason Rowland and Mrs. Morris L. Croxall (Richmond: Everett Wadey, 1911), 120.
5. Butler's order, June 30, 1862, quoted in *Life and Public Services of Major-General Butler: the Hero of New Orleans* (Philadelphia: T. B. Peterson and Brothers, 1864), 90.
6. Letter from Benjamin Butler to Secretary of War Edwin M. Stanton, May 16, 1862. Benjamin F. Butler and Jessie A. Marshall, *Private and Official Correspondence of Gen. Benjamin F. Butler: During the Period of the Civil War* (Norwood, MA: Plimpton Press, 1917), 490.
7. Butler, *Autobiography and Personal Reminiscences*, 426.
8. Ibid., 416.
9. Ibid., 417.
10. Quoted in *Butler, Private and Official Correspondence*, 490.
11. Butler, *Autobiography and Personal Reminiscences*, 418.
12. Ibid., 419.
13. Letter from Benjamin Butler to O. C. Gardner, June 10, 1862. *Butler, Private and Official Correspondence Vol. 1*, 582.
14. Letter from Sarah Butler to Harriet Heard, May 15, 1862. *Butler, Private and Official Correspondence Vol. 1*, 486.
15. Letter from Mayor John T. Monroe to Benjamin Butler, May 16, 1862. *Butler, Private and Official Correspondence Vol. 1*, 498.
16. Butler, *Autobiography and Personal Reminiscences*, 419.
17. "Important News from Corinth—Atrocious Manifesto of the Yankee Commander in New Orleans," *Charleston Mercury*, May 21, 1862.
18. Quoted in Werlich, *"Beast" Butler*, 41.
19. Butler, *Autobiography and Personal Reminiscences*, 419.
20. Ibid., 440.
21. Ibid., 441.
22. Ibid., 441.
23. Ibid., 443.
24. General Orders No. 111, December 24, 1862, *O.R.*, ser. 2, vol. 5, 795–97.
25. Butler, *Autobiography and Personal Reminiscences*, 449.
26. Eliza Moore Chinn McHatton Ripley, *Social Life in Old New Orleans: Being Recollections of My Girlhood* (New York: Appleton and Company, 1912), 213.
27. Ibid., 213–214.
28. Order No. 22, May 4, 1862, quoted in *Autobiography and Personal Reminiscences Vol. 1*, 383.
29. Ibid.
30. Benjamin Butler to Secretary of War Stanton, *O.R.*, ser. 1, vol. 15, 423.
31. Werlich, *"Beast" Butler*, 67.

32. Letter from George Dennison to Salmon P. Chase, October 10, 1862. *Annual Report of the American Historical Association for the Year 1902, Vol. 2.* (Washington: Government Printing Office, 1903), 321.
33. Letter from General Benjamin F. Butler to Salmon P. Chase, November 14, 1862. *Private and Official Correspondence of Gen. Benjamin F. Butler, Vol. 2*, 423.
34. Quoted in Werlich, *"Beast" Butler*, 75.
35. Butler, *Autobiography and Personal Reminiscences*, 395.
36. LeGrand, *The Journal of Julia LeGrand*, p. 55.
37. Ibid., 56.
38. Ibid., 59.
39. Quoted in Werlich, *"Beast" Butler*, 60.
40. "Butler—Dead or Alive." *Charleston Mercury*, January 9, 1863.

The Sack of Athens and the Court-Martial of Col. J. B. Turchin

1. At the court-martial on July 12, 1862, Athens citizen W. P. Tanner claimed several men of the Eighteenth Ohio told him that Turchin said he would close his eyes for two hours. Since then, there have been several variants on this alleged statement published in both primary and secondary sources. This one, given in dialect form, is from S. F. Horrall, *History of the 42nd Indiana Volunteer Infantry*, (n.p., published by the author, 1892), 28. Horrall served with the Forty-Second Indiana in northern Alabama. According to Angus Waddle, another soldier who penned his memoirs after the war, Turchin said he would "shut mine eyes for one hour." Angus Waddle, *Three Years with the Armies of the Ohio and the Cumberland* (Chillicothe, OH: Sciotto Gazette and Job Office, 1889), 17. Waddle goes on to say that the people of Bellefonte, Alabama, rejoiced when Waddle's unit left town, but within an hour, they were praying "for our return. The Nineteenth Illinois had relieved us."
2. Diary entry, May 31, 1863, reprinted in Mary Ellen McElligott, ed., "'A Monotony of Sadness': The Diary of Nadine Turchin, May, 1863–April, 1864," *Illinois State Historical Society Journal* 52 (1977): 33. Nadine Turchin recorded her observations in several diaries she kept throughout the war. Only one, written in French, has survived. This diary covers the period from May 1863 to April 1864. A translation of the entire text is presented in McElligott's article.
3. Statement of John Basil Turchin, July 29, 1862, taken from *Proceedings of the Court Martial of Colonel John Basil Turchin*. Record Group 153: Records of the Office of the Judge Advocate General (Army), Court Martial Case Files, 1792–2010, Textual Archives Services Division, National Archives and Records Administration, Washington, DC; also quoted in James Grant Wilson, *Biographical Sketches of Illinois Officers Involved in the War against the Rebellion of 1861* (Chicago: James Barnet, 1863), 70.
4. Wilson, *Biographical Sketches*, 71.
5. Ibid.
6. John Basil Turchin, *Chickamauga* (Chicago: Fergus Printing Company, 1888), 11.
7. Brig. Gen. S. A. Hurlbut to Col. J. B. Turchin, July 16, 1861. *O.R.*, ser. 2, vol. 1, p. 186.
8. Ibid., 187.
9. General Order No. 81, March 15, 1862, *O.R.*, ser. 1, vol. 10, pt. 2, 292.
10. General Order No. 85, March 23, 1862, *O.R.*, ser. 1, vol. 10, pt. 2, 293.

11. The three men were Col. Carter Gazlay of the Thirty-Seventh Indiana and Lt. Knowlton Chandler and Sgt. Daniel Marcy, both from the Nineteenth Illinois.
12. Letter from Maj. Gen. Ormsby Mitchel to Secretary of War Edwin M. Stanton, July 19, 1862. *O.R.*, ser. 1, vol. 10, pt. 2, 291.
13. Horrall, *History*, 28, and Waddle, *Three Years*, 17.
14. *O.R.*, ser. 1, vol. 16, pt. 2, 274.
15. Quoted in Eugene Willard, ed. et al, *A Standard History of The Hanging Rock Iron Region of Ohio, Volume 1* (n.p., The Lewis Publishing Company, 1916), 613.
16. George C. Bradley and Richard L. Dahlen. *From Conciliation to Conquest: the Sack of Athens and the Court-Martial of Col. John B. Turchin* (Tuscaloosa: The University of Alabama Press, 2006), 121.
17. Extract of Orders to Col. J. B. Turchin, May 3, 1862, *O.R.*, ser. 1, vol. 10, pt. 2, 294.
18. Extract of Orders to Col. J. B. Turchin, May 5, 1862, *O.R.*, ser. 1, vol. 10, pt. 2, 294.
19. Extract of Orders to Col. J. B. Turchin, May 7, 1862, *O.R.*, ser. 1, vol. 10, pt. 2, 294.
20. Letter from Maj. Gen. Ormsby Mitchel to J. B. Turchin, May 16, 1862, *O.R.*, ser. 1, vol. 10, pt. 2, 294.
21. Letter from Maj. Gen. Ormsby Mitchel to Secretary of War Edwin M. Stanton, May 19, 1862, *O.R.*, ser. 1, vol. 10, pt. 2, 204.
22. Letter from Maj. Gen. Ormsby Mitchel to Secretary of War Edwin M. Stanton, July 19, 1862. *O.R.*, ser. 1, vol. 10, pt. 2, 290.
23. Maj. Gen. Ormsby Mitchel to Col. J. B. Fry, Jun 30, 1862, in *Index to the Miscellaneous Documents of the House of Representatives for the First Session of the Forty-Ninth Congress, 1885–86* (Washington, DC: Government Printing Office, 1886), 80.
24. Letter from Maj. General Ormsby Mitchel to Secretary of War Edwin M. Stanton, July 19, 1862. *O.R.*, ser. 1, vol. 10, pt. 2, 290.
25. Letter from Maj. Gen. Ormsby Mitchel to George S. Hunter and others, May 24, 1862. *O.R.*, ser. 1, vol. 10, pt. 2, 212–213.
26. Letter from Maj. Gen. Don Carlos Buell to Secretary of War Edwin M. Stanton, June 29, 1862. *O.R.*, ser. 1, vol. 16, pt. 2, 71.
27. Col. J. B. Turchin to Col. J. B. Fry, July 5, 1862. *Index*, 98.
28. General Orders No. 39, August 6, 1862. *O.R.*, ser. 1, vol. 16, pt. 2, 273–78. The order details the charges against Turchin, listing the alleged atrocities committed against the citizens of Athens.
29. General Orders No. 39, *O.R.*, ser. 1, vol. 16, pt. 2, 274.
30. General Orders No. 39, *O.R.*, ser. 1, vol. 16, pt, 2, 273.
31. General Orders No. 39, *O.R.*, ser. 1, vol. 16, pt, 2, 275.
32. General Orders No. 39, *O.R.*, ser. 1, vol. 16, pt, 2, 275.
33. General Orders No. 39, *O.R.*, ser. 1, vol. 16, pt. 2, p. 275.
34. General Orders No. 39, *O.R.*, ser. 1, vol. 16, pt. 2, 274.
35. General Orders No. 39, *O.R.*, ser. 1, vol. 16, pt. 2, 274.
36. Stephen Chicoine, *John Basil Turchin and the Fight to Free the Slaves* (Westport, CT: Praeger, 2003), 90.
37. Testimony of Mildred Anne Clayton, July 11, 1862. *Proceedings of the Court Martial of Colonel J. B. Turchin*.
38. Testimony of Charlotte Hine, July 11, 1862, *Proceedings*.
39. Testimony of W. P. Tanner, July 12, 1862, *Proceedings*.
40. Testimony of Pvt. Joseph Arnold, July 15, 1862; Testimony of Pvt. Joel Stevens, July 15, 1862, both from *Proceedings*.

41. Testimony of Col. Timothy Stanley, July 25, 1862, *Proceedings*.
42. The three men were Col. Carter Gazlay of the Thirty-Seventh Indiana and Lt. Knowlton Chandler and Sgt. Daniel Marcy, both from the Nineteenth Illinois. Gazlay testified on July 25, Chandler on July 23, and Marcy on July 24, 1862.
43. Statement of John Basil Turchin, July 29, 1862, *Proceedings*.
44. Statement of John Basil Turchin, July 29, 1862, *Proceedings*; also quoted in Wilson, *Biographical Sketches*, 70.
45. Statement of John Basil Turchin, July 29, 1862, *Proceedings*.
46. Ibid.
47. General Orders No. 39, *O.R.*, ser. 1, vol. 16, pt. 2, 277.
48. Ibid.
49. Ibid.
50. "Col. J.B. Turchin," *Chicago Daily Tribune,* July 15, 1862.
51. *New York Times*, August 22, 1862.
52. Ibid.
53. Quoted in Wilson, *Biographical Sketches*, 71.

Feuding Generals

1. General W. B. Hazen, *A Narrative of Military Service* (Boston: Ticknor and Company, 1885), 55.
2. Letter from General Stanley Matthews to Mr. A. N. Ellis, quoted in Hazen, *Narrative*, 57–60.
3. Quoted in Hazen, *Narrative*, 60.
4. Quoted in Hazen, *Narrative*, 60.
5. Quoted in Hazen, *Narrative*, 56–57.
6. Howard Peckham, "'I Have Been Basely Murdered,'" *American Heritage*, 14, no. 5 (August 1963).
7. Hazen, *Narrative*, 56.
8. Kirk C. Jenkins, "A Shooting at the Galt House: the Death of General William Nelson," *Civil War History* 43, no. 2 (1997): 105.
9. This account is based on the story told by James Barnet Fry, who knew both Davis and Nelson, in "Article XIII: Killed by a Brother Soldier," contained in Fry, *Military Miscellanies* (New York: Brentano's, 1889). Fry didn't witness the altercation. He heard it secondhand from Dr. Irwin Ellis, whom Davis asked into the room as an eyewitness.
10. Fry, *Military Miscellanies*, 492.
11. Ibid., 489.
12. Ibid, 489.
13. Ibid., 486.
14. Jenkins, "A Shooting at the Galt House," 110.
15. Quoted in Peckham, "'I Have Been Basely Murdered.'"
16. Fry, *Military Miscellanies*, 500.
17. Jenkins, "A Shooting at the Galt House," 115. According to Jenkins, Fry didn't tell Buell about the paper wad. As a result, Buell misrepresented the circumstances of the shooting when he requested that a court-martial take place in Washington. "Buell's call for Davis's trial quickly became lost as the impression that Nelson was at fault took hold," Jenkins notes.

18. Fry, *Military Miscellanies*, 496.
19. Quoted in Peckham, "'I Have Been Basely Murdered.'"
20. Fry's "Killed by a Brother Soldier" originally appeared as a monograph published by Putnam in 1885. The article was reprinted in 1889 as "Article XIII" in *Military Miscellanies*, a memoir of Fry's Civil War experiences. The latter is the work cited throughout this chapter.
21. Fry, *Military Miscellanies*, 492.
22. Fry, *Military Miscellanies*, 500.
23. Ellis, Dr. A. M. "Major General William Nelson," *Kentucky State Historical Society Register* 7 (May 1906): 62.
24. Report of Brig. Gen. Marmaduke, July 25, 1863, *O.R.*, ser. 1, vol. 22, pt. 1, 437.
25. Ibid.
26. Report of Lieut. Gen. Theophilus H. Holmes, August 14, 1863, *O.R.*, ser. 1, vol. 22, pt. 26, 410.
27. Col. John C. Moore, *Missouri. Confederate Military History, Vol. IX* ed. Clement Evans, (Atlanta: Confederate Publishing Company, 1899), 137.
28. Ibid.
29. Ibid. Marmaduke's second, John C. Moore, related the story to a reporter from the *San Francisco Sunday Call*. According to Moore, Walker was old-school and would not answer oral messages. Frank Brooks, "First Full Story of the Civil War's Most Daring Cavalry Raid." *The San Francisco Sunday Call*, July 9, 1911.
30. Gen. Walker to Gen. Marmaduke, Sept. 2, 1863. The *Washington Telegraph* published the notes between the parties and the terms of the duel in its October 21, 1863, edition. Leo E. Huff also reproduces these notes on pp. 455–458 in his article about the duel, "The Marmaduke-Walker Duel: The Last Duel in Arkansas," *Missouri Historical Review* 58 (July 1964). Huff's article is the most thorough treatment of the duel to date.
31. Gen. Marmaduke to Gen. Walker, Sept. 2, 1863. *Washington Telegraph*, October 21, 1863.
32. Gen. Walker to Gen. Marmaduke, Sept. 3, 1863. *Washington Telegraph*, October 21, 1863.
33. Capt. Moore to Col. Crockett, Sept. 4, 1863. *Washington Telegraph*, October 21, 1863.
34. Col. Crockett to Capt. Moore, Sept. 4, 1863. *Washington Telegraph*, October 21, 1863.
35. "Terms of Agreement" from Capt. Moore to Col. Crockett, Sept. 5, 1863, *Washington Telegraph*, October 21, 1863.
36. Ibid.
37. Maj. Gen. Sterling Price to Col. Archibald Dobbin, November 25, 1863, *O.R.*, ser. I, vol. 22, pt. 1, 525.
38. Huff, "The Marmaduke-Walker Duel," 459.
39. Ibid., 460.
40. Thomas Jacob Barb, Civil War diary, 27–28.
41. Maj. Gen. Sterling Price to Col. Archibald Dobbin, November 25, 1863, *O.R.*, ser. 1, vol. 22, pt. 1, 525.
42. Huff, "The Marmaduke-Walker Duel," 461.
43. Col. John M. Harrell. *Arkansas Confederate Military History Vol. X*, ed. Clement Evans, (Atlanta: Confederate Publishing Company, 1899), 222.

44. "Marmaduke's Two Duels—the Dead Governor was a Man of Great Nerve." *St. Paul Daily Globe*, January 11, 1888.
45. Quoted in Harrell, *Arkansas*, 220.

The Faulkner Outrage and Detroit's Draft Riot

1. The author does not condone or promote the use of racially derogatory language. Since it is part of the historical record, however, it is faithfully reproduced here, verbatim.
2. *A Thrilling Narrative From the Lips of the Sufferers of the Late Detroit Riot, March 6, 1863: With the Hair Breadth Escapes of Men, Women And Children, And Destruction of Colored Men's Property, Not Less Than $15,000* (Detroit: printed by the author, 1863), 8–9.
3. "The Faulkner Outrage," The *Detroit Free Press*, March 1, 1863. Sources vary on Faulkner's first name. Contemporary newspaper reports refer to him by his surname. Early Detroit historians call him "William Faulkner," but the primary source for this chapter, *A Thrilling Narrative*, refers to him as "Thomas Faulkner," so that is the name used in this text.
4. Arthur M. Woodford *This is Detroit, 1701–2001* (Detroit: Wayne State University Press, 2001), 63.
5. John C. Schneider, "Detroit and the Problem of Disorder: The Riot of 1863," *Michigan History* 58 (Spring 1974): 11.
6. "An Amalgamation Den Broken Up," *Detroit Free Press*, February 20, 1863.
7. Quoted in Schneider, "Detroit," 13.
8. Schneider, "Detroit," 13.
9. "Horrible Outrage," *Detroit Free Press*, February 27, 1863; *Detroit Advertiser and Tribune*, February 27, 1863
10. "The Faulkner Outrage," *Detroit Free Press*, March 1, 1863.
11. Ibid.
12. Ibid.
13. Ibid.
14. Ibid.
15. Schneider, *Detroit*, 14.
16. "Trial of the Negro Faulkner," *Detroit Free Press*, March 6, 1863.
17. Ibid.
18. "A Bloody Riot," *Detroit Free Press*, March 7, 1863.
19. Ibid.
20. *A Thrilling Narrative*, 3.
21. Ibid., 4.
22. The introduction of *A Thrilling Narrative* notes that five men—Robert Bennette, Joshua Boyd, Lewis Houston, Solomon Houston, and Marcus Dale—were in the cooperage when the mob attacked. But the work also includes the story of Lewis Pearce, who claimed to be in the shop at the time.
23. Ibid., 5.
24. Ibid., 4.
25. Ibid., 2.
26. "A Bloody Riot," *Detroit Free Press*, March 7, 1863.
27. *A Thrilling Narrative*, 8–9.

28. Ibid., 9.

29. Ibid., 7.

30. Ibid., 7.

31. Quoted in *A Thrilling Narrative*, 20.

32. "A Bloody Riot," *Detroit Free Press*, March 7, 1863.

33. Ibid.

34. Schneider, "Detroit," 17.

35. "The Great Riot," *Detroit Free Press*, March 8, 1863.

36. Ibid.

37. *Detroit Advertiser and Tribune*, March 14, 1863; Quoted in *A Thrilling Narrative*, 19.

38. *Detroit Advertiser and Tribune*, March 14, 1863; Quoted in *A Thrilling Narrative*, 20.

39. Schneider, "Detroit," 21–22.

The Slaying of the Beckham Family

1. "What One Woman Has Suffered," *Charleston Mercury,* July 20, 1864; *Daily Constitutionalist* (Augusta, Georgia), July 22, 1864.

2. The official court-martial documents refer to him as Frank A. Beckham; in fact, his name was Alexander Fanning Beckham.

3. Andrew Napolitano. *Dred Scott's Revenge: A Legal History of Race and Freedom in America* (Nashville, TN: Thomas Nelson, 2009), 80–81.

4. Testimony of Jim Webb and William Ray, August 17, 1863, from *Proceedings of the Trial of William Ray*, RG 153, MM-813, Records of the Office of the Judge Advocate General (Army), Court Martial Case Files, 1809–1894, Textual Archives Services Division, National Archives and Records Administration, Washington, DC, and *Proceedings of the Trial of Jim Webb*, RG 153, MM-813, Records of the Office of the Judge Advocate General (Army), Court Martial Case Files, 1809–1894, Textual Archives Services Division, National Archives and Records Administration, Washington, DC.

5. Testimony of Jim Webb, August 17, 1863, *Proceedings of the Trial of Jim Webb*.

6. Testimony of Joshua Everett, *Proceedings of the Trial of George Harris*, RG 153, MM-915, Records of the Office of the Judge Advocate General (Army), Court Martial Case Files, 1800–1894, Textual Archives Services Division, National Archives and Records Administration, Washington, DC.

7. "A Most Horrible tragedy at Compromise Landing, Mo." *Dubuque Herald*, August 22, 1863.

8. The assault on the Beckham family involved at least ten contraband. Lt. Col. William R. Roberts, who dispatched Maj. Peter Dobozy to the Beckham house, said that nine men were brought aboard the steamer *Rob Roy* and delivered to the provost marshal. Contemporary news reports indicate a tenth man, Bradley Jones, took part in the raid; the JAG records indicate that the military commission tried Jones, but the trial transcript has been lost. Records of the Tennessee State Penitentiary state that Bradley Jones was tried for murder by military commission in 1863 and subsequently imprisoned along with Bridgewater and Harris. These facts suggest that the commission sentenced Jones to death, but military authorities later commuted his sentence to five years of hard labor.

9. Testimony of Maj. Peter Dobozy, August 18, 1863, from *Proceedings of the Trial of Lewis Stevinson*, RG 153, MM-813, Records of the Office of the Judge Advocate General (Army), Court Martial Case Files, 1809–1894, Textual Archives

Services Division, National Archives and Records Administration, Washington, DC.

10. Ibid.
11. Ibid.
12. Ibid.
13. Testimony of Lt. Charles Nelson, August 18, 1863, from *Proceedings of the Trial of Lewis Stevenson.*
14. Testimony of Lt. Col. William R. Roberts, from *Proceedings of the Trial of Aaron Bridgewater*, RG 153, MM-931, Records of the Office of the Judge Advocate General (Army), Court Martial Case Files, 1800–1894, Textual Archives Services Division, National Archives and Records Administration, Washington, DC.
15. Testimony of Lt. Charles Nelson, August 18, 1863, from *Proceedings of the Trial of Lewis Stevenson.*
16. Testimony of Mrs. Harriet Hatcher, August 8, 1863, from *Union Provost Marshals' File of Papers Relating to Two or More Civilians*, F1601, War Department Collection of Confederate Records, RG109.14.4, Miscellaneous Records, Microcopy No. 416, Roll 22, No. 6066, August 1863, the Textual Archives Services Division, National Archives and Records Administration, Washington, DC.
17. Ibid.
18. "Murder by Negro Soldiers; A Family Assassinated in Cold Blood," *New York Times*, August 9, 1863.
19. "A Most Horrible tragedy," *Dubuque Herald.*
20. Testimony of Lt. Charles Nelson, August 18, 1863, *Proceedings of the Trial of Lewis Stevenson.*
21. "A Most Horrible tragedy," *Dubuque Herald.*
22. "Retribution upon the Guilty Ones," *Chicago Daily Tribune*, September 7, 1863.
23. Statement of William Ray, August 17, 1863. *Proceedings of the Trial of William Ray*, RG 153, MM-813, Records of the Office of the Judge Advocate General (Army), Court Martial Case Files, 1809–1894, Textual Archives Services Division, National Archives and Records Administration, Washington, DC.
24. Ibid.
25. Testimony of W. E. Jones, August 17, 1863.
26. Statement of Jim Webb, August 17, 1863. *Proceedings of the Trial of William Ray.*
27. Ibid.
28. Testimony of Maj. Peter Dobozy, August 18, 1863. *Proceedings of the Trial of Lewis Stevenson.*
29. Ibid.
30. Testimony of Lieutenant Charles Nelson, August 18, 1863. *Proceedings of the Trial of Lewis Stevenson.*
31. Ibid.
32. Ibid.
33. Testimony of Benjamin Robinson, August 18, 1863. *Proceedings of the Trial of Lewis Stevenson.*
34. Testimony of Emma Beckham, August 21, 1863, *Proceedings of the Trial of Wade Good*, RG 153, MM-915, Records of the Office of the Judge Advocate General (Army), Court Martial Case Files, 1809–1894, Textual Archives Services Division, National Archives and Records Administration, Washington, DC.
35. Testimony of Lt. Col. William R. Roberts, August 21, 1863, *Proceedings of the Trial of Wade Good.*

36. Testimony of Emma Beckham, *Proceedings of the Trial of Joseph Davis*, RG 153, MM-915, Records of the Office of the Judge Advocate General (Army), Court Martial Case Files, 1800–1894, Textual Archives Services Division, National Archives and Records Administration, Washington, DC.

37. *Proceedings of the Trial of Joseph Davis*, August 22, 1863.

38. Statement of Joseph Davis, *Proceedings of the Trial of Joseph Davis*, August 22, 1863.

39. Testimony of Emma Beckham, *Proceedings of the Trial of George Harris*, August 25, 1863.

40. Testimony of Lt. Col. William R. Roberts, *Proceedings of the Trial of George Harris*, August 25, 1863.

41. Testimony of Joshua Everett, *Proceedings of the Trial of George Harris*, August 25, 1863.

42. Statement of George Harris, *Proceedings of the Trial of George Harris*, August 25, 1863.

43. Testimony of Lt. Col. William R. Roberts, *Proceedings of the Trial of Aaron Bridgewater*, August 26, 1863.

44. Statement of Aaron Bridgewater, *Proceedings of the Trial of Aaron Bridgewater*, August 26, 1863.

45. Testimony of Emma Beckham, *Proceedings of the Trial of Abram Cole*, RG 153, MM-915, Records of the Office of the Judge Advocate General (Army), Court Martial Case Files, 1800–1894, Textual Archives Services Division, National Archives and Records Administration, Washington, DC.

46. Testimony of Joshua Everett, *Proceedings of the Trial of Abram Cole*, August 27, 1863.

47. "Retribution," *Chicago Daily Tribune*.

48. Ibid.

49. "Execution of Three of the Beckham Murderers." *Chicago Daily Tribune*, October 10, 1863.

50. "The Beckham Tragedy," *Dubuque Herald*, Sept. 9, 1863.

51. "A Most Horrible tragedy," *Dubuque Herald*, August 22, 1863.

52. "What One Woman Has Suffered," *Charleston Mercury* and *Daily Constitutionalist*.

53. Ibid.

54. Ibid.

55. "A Most Horrible tragedy," *Dubuque Herald*.

56. Testimony of Lt. Col. William R. Roberts, August 21, 1863, *Proceedings of the Trial of Wade Good*. Roberts testified that when he questioned Wade Good aboard the *Rob Roy*, Good said he put the watch in a "bag or a satchel," which he said was later searched before the nine contraband boarded the *Rob Roy*. According to Roberts, Good said that after he put the watch in the satchel, he never saw it again.

57. Joanna Patterson Moore, *"In Christ's Stead": Autobiographical Sketches* (Chicago: the Women's Baptist Home Mission Society, 1902), 26.

58. "A Most Horrible tragedy," *Dubuque Herald*, August 22, 1863.

59. "Murder by Negro Soldiers; A Family Assassinated in Cold Blood," *New York Times*, August 9, 1863.

60. "Retribution," *Chicago Daily Tribune*.

The Lawrence Massacre

1. William Elsey Connelley, *Quantrill and the Border Wars* (Cedar Rapids, IA: The Torch Press, Publishers, 1910), 311. Major Edwards, who was present for the discussion about raiding Lawrence, quotes Bill Anderson in Connelley's seminal work about Quantrill. In producing his account, Connelley interviewed many survivors of the "Lawrence Massacre." Although many historians criticize Connelley's book as highly biased against Quantrill, he did include many first-person accounts of people from both sides of the conflict.
2. Connelley describes several hair-raising incidents of violence from "Bleeding Kansas" in *Quantrill*, 286–290.
3. Ibid., 294.
4. Ibid., 352. The March 27, 1898, edition of the *Morning Herald* (Lexington, Kentucky) ran an article about Quantrill containing quotes from a conversation Quantrill had with W. L. Davis, based on Davis's memory. According to Davis, Quantrill said he went to Lawrence to look for Lane.
5. Ibid., 308.
6. Charles F. Harris, "Catalyst for Terror: The Collapse of the Women's Prison in Kansas City." *Missouri Historical Review* 89 (April 1995): 300.
7. Ibid., 297.
8. Ibid., 300.
9. Quoted in Connelley, *Quantrill*, 343. The quote comes from "The Gregg Manuscript," a document written by Bushwhacker captain Edward Gregg and acquired by Connelley.
10. Letter from Sophia Bissell to her "Dear Cousin," September 8, 1863. Quoted in Fred N. Six, ed., "Eyewitness Reports of Quantrill's Raid: Letters of Sophia Bissell & Sidney Clarke." *Kansas History* 28 (Summer 2005): 97. Original letter is in the collection of the Chicago Historical Society.
11. Connelley, *Quantrill*, 349; Edward E. Leslie *The Devil Knows How to Ride: The True Story of William Clarke Quantrill and His Confederate Raiders* (New York: Random House, 1996), 219.
12. Quoted in Connelley, *Quantrill*, 365. Grovenor gave a lengthy statement in an interview with Connelley.
13. Connelley, *Quantrill*, 363.
14. Ibid., 383.
15. Quoted in Ibid., 382.
16. Connelley, *Quantrill*, 419.
17. Letter from Sidney Clarke to "My dear friends," August 26, 1863, quoted in Six, "Eyewitness Reports," 101–102.
18. Quoted in Thomas S. Duke, *Celebrated Criminal Cases of America* (San Francisco: The James H. Berry Company, 1910), 371.
19. Quoted in Connelley, *Quantrill*, 365.
20. *O.R.*, ser. 2, vol. 22, pt. 2, 472.
21. Harris, "Catalyst," 305.
22. *O.R.*, ser. 2, vol. 22, pt. 2, 713.
23. The number of soldiers aboard the train varies. Some sources place the number at twenty-three. Goodman, however, states that there were twenty-seven soldiers on the train, including himself. There are various versions of who did what during this

phase of the Centralia incident. Unknown are the exact roles played by Frank and Jesse James. Most accounts have Frank James boarding the train and rifling through the baggage car; it is likely, but unproven, that Jesse also went aboard. It is generally agreed that both Frank and Jesse were there when the train pulled into Centralia.

24. Thomas M. Goodman, *A Thrilling Record: Founded on Facts and Observations Obtained during Ten Days' Experience with Colonel William T. Anderson (the Notorious Guerrilla Chieftain); Edited and Prepared for the Press by Harry A. Houston* (Des Moines, IA: Mills & Co., 1868), 35.

25. Lt. Colonel Dan. M. Draper to Brig. Gen. Fish, September 29, 1864; *O.R.* ser. 1, vol. 41, pt. 1, 440.

26. Darryl Wilkinson, "Samuel Cox—A Daviess County Hero." The Daviess County Historical Society. Available http://www.daviesscountyhistoricalsociety.com.

27. Quoted in Wilkinson, "Samuel Cox." In his official report, Cox said that two men, "charged through our lines," and he identifies this second man as Captain Rains. Also Albert Castel and Thomas Goodrich, *Bloody Bill Anderson: The Short, Savage Life of a Civil War Guerrilla* (Mechanicsburg, PA: Stackpole Books, 1998) and "Report of Lieut. Col. Samuel P. Cox, Thirty-third Infantry Enrolled Missouri Militia," September 27, 1864. *O.R.* ser. 1, vol. 41, pt. 1, p. 442.

28. John N. Edwards, *Noted Guerrillas, or the Warfare of the Border* (St. Louis, MO: Bryan, Brand & Co, 1877), 443–446. This version is also recounted in John Palmer, *Personal Recollections of John M. Palmer: the Story of an Earnest Life* (Cincinnati: The Robert Clarke Company, 1901), 269–72.

29. Edwards, *Noted Guerrillas*, 444.

30. Edwards, *Noted Guerrillas*, 446.

31. Duke, *Celebrated*, 371.

The Murder of Gen. Earl Van Dorn

1. Quoted in *A Soldier's Honor, with Reminiscences of Major-General Earl Van Dorn by His Comrades* (New York: Abbey Press, 1902), 59–60.

2. Letter to sister Octavia, January 13, 1848, quoted in *A Soldier's Honor*, 26.

3. Letter to sister Octavia, July 28, 1846, quoted in *A Soldier's Honor*, 23.

4. Ibid.

5. Arthur B. Carter, *The Tarnished Cavalier: Major General Earl Van Dorn, C.S.A.* (Knoxville: University of Tennessee Press, 1999), 32–33.

6. *A Soldier's Honor*, 278–79

7. Ibid.

8. *Mobile Advertiser and Register*, March 22, 1863.

9. Ibid.

10. Letter from Lt. William L. Nugent to his wife, Nellie, March 24, 1863. Quoted in William Lewis Nugent and Eleanor Smith Nugent, *My Dear Nellie: the Civil War Letters of William L. Nugent to Eleanor Smith Nugent* (Oxford, MS: University of Mississippi, 1977), 80.

11. Carter, *Tarnished*, 186.

12. *Mobile Advertiser and Register*, May 15, 1863; also reproduced in *A Soldier's Honor*, 254–55

13. Quoted in Carter, *Tarnished*, 184.

14. The appendix of *A Soldier's Honor* contains the full account from an unnamed officer of Van Dorn's staff, including diagrams of the crime scene. The officer is referred to as "an anonymous, unauthenticated source" Robert G. Hartje, *Van Dorn: the Life and Times of a Confederate General* (Nashville, TN: Vanderbilt University Press, 1967), 315.
15. *A Soldier's Honor*, 351.
16. Ibid.
17. *A Soldier's Honor*, 352.
18. Quoted in Hartje, *Van Dorn*, 315.
19. Dr. Peters's statement quoted in John Fitch, *Annals of the Army of the Cumberland: Comprising Biographies, Descriptions of Departments, Accounts of Expeditions, Skirmishes, and Battles; Also Its Police Record of Spies, Smugglers, and Prominent Rebel Emissaries Together with Anecdotes, Incidents, Poetry, Reminiscences, etc. and Official Reports of the Battle of Stone River and of the Chickamauga Campaign*, Fifth Ed. (Philadelphia: J. B. Lippincott, 1864), 618.
20. Ibid, 619.
21. Ibid.
22. Ibid.
23. Ibid.
24. Ibid.
25. The appendix of *A Soldier's Honor* contains a letter, dated October 25, 1901, from Peters's roommate at the Nashville boardinghouse just after the murder, pp. 349–350.
26. Ibid., 350.
27. *Mobile Advertiser and Register*, May 7, 1863.
28. Quoted in *Fayetteville (Tennessee) Observer*, June 4, 1863.
29. *Fayetteville Observer*, June 4, 1863.
30. *Mobile Advertiser and Register*, May 16, 1863.
31. Quoted in *A Soldier's Honor*, 250.
32. *A Soldier's Honor*, 250.
33. *Mobile Advertiser and Register*, May 16, 1863.
34. *Mobile Advertiser and Register*, May 16, 1863.
35. Carter, *Tarnished*, 191.
36. Medora's marker in Shelby County, Tennessee's Elmwood Cemetery lists a birthday of January 26, 1865, which if accurate would make it impossible for her to be Van Dorn's child. The 1900 Federal census, however, lists Medora's date of birth as January 1864. Her 1931 death record also lists an estimated age of sixty-seven, indicating a birth date in 1864.
37. *A Soldier's Honor*, 256.

No Quarter: Bedford Forrest and the Fort Pillow Massacre

1. Testimony of Woodford Cooksey, Mound City, Illinois, April 22, 1864. United States Joint Committee on the Conduct of the War. *Reports: Fort Pillow Massacre; Returned Prisoners*. 38th Congress, 1st Session. House of Representatives. Report No. 65, 67. Washington, 1864, p. 36.
2. John Allan Wyeth. *Life of Lieutenant-General Nathan Bedford Forrest* (New York: Harper and Brothers, 1908), 13. Wyeth's biography of Forrest is particularly inter-

esting as a Southern perspective not just on Forrest, but on Fort Pillow. Although clearly biased, Wyeth did what Gooch and Wade didn't: he interviewed Confederate eyewitnesses. The accounts most cited for the Southern perspective of the Fort Pillow battle are early Forrest biographies by Wyeth and an 1868 book by Thomas Jordan and J. P. Pryor. While both condemn the Congressional Report on the "Fort Pillow Massacre" and both include eyewitness accounts from the Confederate army to substantiate their claims, Wyeth's chapter on Fort Pillow provides the more thorough deconstruction of the "massacre" allegations.

3. Ibid., 15.
4. Quoted in Wyeth, *Life*, 20.
5. Ibid, 21.
6. "Fort Pillow: General Forrest's Responsibility for the Slaughter in 1864—the Testimony of Eye Witnesses and His Own Account," *New York Times*, September 13, 1868.
7. *O.R.*, vol. 32, pt. 1, 592.
8. United States Joint Committee on the Conduct of the War, *Reports*, 98.
9. "Extracts from the report of Captain Anderson." *O.R.* ser. 1, vol. 32, pt. 1, p. 596. The text of this note differs according to the source. In his report, Capt. Charles Anderson, who claimed he was in possession of the original note, said Forrest's surrender demand included the final line, "Should my demand be refused, I cannot be responsible for the fate of your command." Lt. Mack Leaming, who was one of the Union officers sent out to receive the surrender note, recalled ("As nearly as I can remember," were his words) a slightly different version of the last line in a report he wrote in January 1865: "I have received a new supply of ammunition and can take your works by assault, and if compelled to do so you must take the consequences" (*O.R.* ser. 1, vol. 32, pt. 1, p. 560). The version of the note given in Jordan and Pryor is similar to that in Leaming and Wyeth, except it does not contain Forrest's ultimatum. While most sources agree about the gist of Forrest's note, they disagree about its spirit. Was his ultimatum merely an intimidation tactic, or a viable threat? In this context, it is interesting to note that during his assault of the earthworks at Paducah, Forrest allegedly sent a similar ultimatum: "If you surrender you shall be treated as prisoners of war, but if I have to storm your works you may expect no quarter" (*O.R.* ser. 1, vol. 32, pt. 1, p. 547). In their report, Gooch and Wade used this statement as evidence of a deliberate black-flag policy, but early Forrest biographers, such as Wyeth, suggest that the general used this threat to intimidate his enemies into surrendering to avoid further bloodshed (Wyeth, *Life*, 329).
10. "Fort Pillow," *New York Times*.
11. Wyeth, *Life*, 346.
12. "Fort Pillow," *New York Times*.
13. Wyeth, *Life*, 350.
14. Testimony of Captain James Marshall, Fort Pillow, Tennessee, April 25, 1864. *Reports: Fort Pillow Massacre; Returned Prisoners*, 86.
15. Ibid.
16. Testimony of Major Williams, Mound City, Illinois, April 22, 1864, in United States Joint Committee on the Conduct of the War, *Reports*, 27.
17. Testimony of Daniel Tyler, Mound City, Illinois, April 22, 1864, in United States Joint Committee on the Conduct of the War, *Reports*, 19.

18. Quoted in numerous sources, notably Eddy W. Davison and Daniel Foxx, *Nathan Bedford Forrest: In Search of the Enigma* (Gretna, LA: Pelican, 2007), 246.

19. General Nathan Bedford Forrest report on battle of Ft. Pillow, April 15, 1864, in *O.R.,* ser. 1, vol. 32, pt. 1, 610.

20. Testimony of Eli Bangs, Fort Pillow, Tennessee, April 25, 1864, in United States Joint Committee on the Conduct of the War, *Reports,* 91.

21. Ibid., 91.

22. Nathan Bedford Forrest to Maj. C. C. Washburn, June 23, 1864, *O.R.,* ser. 1, vol. 32, pt. 1, 592.

23. "The Black Flag; Horrible Massacre by the Rebels," *New York Times,* April 16, 1864.

24. United States Joint Committee on the Conduct of the War, *Reports,* 13.

25. Testimony of Horace Wardner, Mound City, Illinois, April 22, 1864, United States Joint Committee on the Conduct of the War, *Reports,* 13.

26. Testimony of Daniel Tyler, Mound City, Illinois, April 22, 1864. United States Joint Committee on the Conduct of the War, *Reports,* 18.

27. Ibid.

28. Testimony of George Shaw, Mound City, Illinois, April 22, 1864, United States Joint Committee on the Conduct of the War, *Reports,* 25–26.

29. Statement of Dr. M. Black, United States Joint Committee on the Conduct of the War, *Reports,* 58.

30. Testimony of John Penwell, Mound City, Illinois, April 23, 1864, United States Joint Committee on the Conduct of the War, *Reports,* 82.

31. United States Joint Committee on the Conduct of the War, *Reports,* 4.

32. United States Joint Committee on the Conduct of the War, *Reports,* 5.

33. Quoted in Wyeth, *Life,* 384.

34. Quoted in Wyeth, *Life,* 385.

35. Wyeth, *Life,* 355.

36. Testimony of Daniel Stamps, Mound City, Illinois, April 23, 1864, United States Joint Committee on the Conduct of the War, *Reports,* 45.

37. Testimony of James Stamps, United States Joint Committee on the Conduct of the War, *Reports,* 47.

38. Testimony of Major Williams, Mound City, Illinois, April 22, 1864. United States Joint Committee on the Conduct of the War, *Reports,* 27.

39. Wyeth, *Life,* 389.

40. Testimony of William Clary, Mound City, Illinois, April 23, 1864, United States Joint Committee on the Conduct of the War, *Reports,* 52.

41. Wyeth, *Life,* 356.

42. Ibid., 381.

43. Ibid., 379.

44. Ibid., 381.

45. Quoted in Thomas Jordan and J. P. Pryor. *The Campaigns of Lieut.-Gen. N.B. Forrest, and of Forrest's Cavalry* (New York: Blelock & Co., 1868), 443.

46. Wyeth, *Life,* 357.

47. "Fort Pillow," *New York Times.*

Manhattan Burning: The Rebel Arson Plot

1. John W. Headley, *Confederate Operations in Canada and New York* (The Neale Publishing Company, 1906), 273.
2. Headley, *Confederate*, 268.
3. Excerpts of confession from Benn Pitman, *The Assassination of President Lincoln and the Trial of the Conspirators* (New York: Moore, Wistach, and Baldwin, 1865), 28; and ed. Ben Perley Poore, *The Conspiracy Trial for the Murder of the President, and the Attempt to Overthrow the Government by the Assassination of Its Principal Officers* Vols. 1–3 (Boston: J. E. Tilton and Company, 1865), 403–405.
4. Headley, *Confederate*, 271.
5. Headley, *Confederate*, 272.
6. Ibid., 274–275.
7. Ibid., 275.
8. Ibid.
9. Ibid.
10. Ibid., 275–276.
11. Ibid., 276.
12. Ibid.
13. Ibid., 277.
14. Ibid.
15. Ibid.
16. Ibid., 272.
17. "The Rebel Plot," *New York Times*, November 26, 1864.
18. Quoted in "The Rebel Plot," *New York Times*.
19. Ibid.
20. Ibid.
21. Quoted in "The Rebel Plot," *New York Times*.
22. Excerpts of confession from Pitman, *Assassination*, 28; and Purley Poore, *Conspiracy*, 403–405.
23. Lt. T. E. Fell, quoted in "Escape of Prisoners from Johnson's Island," *Southern Historical Society Papers, Vol. 28* (Richmond, VA: Southern Historical Society, January–December, 1890), 428–431.
24. Quoted in "The Rebel Plot," *New York Times*.
25. "The Hotel Burning Plot," *New York Times*, February 28, 1865
26. Quoted in "Kennedy's Execution," The *New York Times*, March 26, 1865.
27. Ibid.
28. Ibid.
29. Ibid.
30. Ibid.
31. Excerpts of confession from Pitman, *Assassination*, 28; and Purley Poore, *Conspiracy*, 403–405.
32. Ibid.
33. Kennedy was hanged on the same scaffold used in the execution of John Yates Beall, who was convicted of violating the laws of war and acting as a spy and hanged at Governor's Island on February 24, 1865. The *New York Times* of February 25 described the scaffold as "not built with a drop, but furnished with weights and pulleys, by means of which the condemned man is jerked into the air with a sudden motion which instantly dislocates the vertebrae of the neck."

34. Quoted in "Kennedy's Execution," *New York Times*.
35. Ibid.
36. Ibid.
37. Headley, *Confederate*, 280.

Sue Mundy, Terror of Kentucky

1. L. L. Valentine, "Sue Mundy of Kentucky: Part 1," *Register of the Kentucky Historical Society* 62, no. 3 (July 1964): 179.
2. Ibid., 182.
3. Ibid., 185.
4. General Order No. 59, July 16, 1864. *O.R.*, ser. 1, vol. 39, pt. 2, 174.
5. Ibid.
6. Ibid.
7. Valentine, "Sue Mundy: Part 1," 185.
8. Betty Carolyn Congleton, "George D. Prentice: Nineteenth Century Southern Editor," *Register of the Kentucky Historical Society* 65, no. 2 (April 1967): 110.
9. Ibid., 111.
10. Clarke's status during this phase of the war is debatable. According to some sources, Clarke continued to fight for the cause as a "partisan ranger" or a "detached" soldier. According to others, he became a guerrilla and fought under no particular flag.
11. There are various theories about where Prentice got the name for his paper bandit. Some sources say he named Sue after a notorious whorehouse madam, Susannah Mundy. Thomas Watson and Perry Brantley suggest that he borrowed the surname of Union colonel Marcellus Mundy, the one-time Louisville provost marshal and a Prentice critic. Colonel Mundy was also connected to a story about women who enlisted in the Federal army disguised as men. Watson and Brantley, *Confederate Guerrilla Sue Mundy: A Biography of Kentucky Soldier Jerome Clarke* (Jefferson, NC: McFarland, 2008), 14–15.
12. Prentice's motive remains elusive. Valentine suggests that the elderly editor wanted to needle authorities into doing something about the guerrilla menace but went too far with "Sue Mundy." Prentice may also have had a more personal reason for attacking Federal officials. Their laxity left Kentucky open to assault from Morgan and his men, and as numerous writers have pointed out, Prentice may have harbored a grudge against Morgan because his son Courtland died while fighting for him. In this light, it is interesting to note that Marcellus Jerome Clarke also served under Morgan. The timing of Sue Mundy's appearance—just weeks from the November presidential election—presents another possible motive. Prentice, who was by October 1864 a Democrat supporting George B. McClellan for president, may have wanted to use Sue Mundy to discredit Federal authorities and turn Kentucky voters away from Lincoln. Or, Prentice may have just been an angry man, irked by what he perceived as a repressive regime.
13. *Louisville Daily Journal*, October 11, 1864.
14. Prentice later changed the spelling to "Mundy." Union officers frequently spelled her name "Munday." The spelling of the name is given exactly as it appears in the original source. According to some versions of the story, the driver of a stagecoach robbed by Clarke's gang mistook the long-haired rebel for a woman. It is possible

that Prentice heard this version and jumped to the conclusion that Clarke was a female bandit, applied the name "Sue Mundy" to Clarke, and let his imagination do the rest.

15. *Louisville Daily Journal*, October 11, 1864.
16. *Louisville Daily Journal*, October 11, 1864.
17. *Louisville Daily Journal*, October 17, 1864.
18. General Order No. 8, October 26, 1864. *O.R.*, ser. 1, vol. 39, pt. 3, 457.
19. Maj. Samuel Martin to Capt. J. S. Butler, November 7, 1864. *O.R.*, ser. 1, vol. 39, pt. 1, 899.
20. Valentine, "Sue Mundy of Kentucky: Part 1," 197.
21. *Louisville Daily Journal*, November 9, 1864. Early historians often depicted Clarke as effeminate, which fit the theme of a man dressed as a woman. Photographs of Clarke show a man with boyish features, but "womanly" doesn't really describe Clarke in either appearance or action.
22. Ibid.; Valentine, "Sue Mundy of Kentucky: Part 1," 197.
23. *Louisville Daily Journal*, December 8, 1864.
24. Valentine, "Sue Mundy of Kentucky: Part 1," 198.
25. Watson and Brantley, *Confederate Guerrilla*, 118.
26. *Louisville Daily Journal, January 10, 1865; New York Times*, January 15, 1865.
27. *Louisville Daily Journal*, January 26, 1865.
28. *Louisville Daily Journal*, January 27, 1865.
29. Valentine, "Sue Mundy of Kentucky: Part 1," 201.
30. *Louisville Daily Journal*, February 1, 1865.
31. Watson and Brantley, *Confederate Guerrilla*, 124.
32. Capt. E. W. Easley to Brig. Gen. E. H. Hobson, February 2, 1865. *O.R.*, ser. 1, vol. 49, pt. 1, 633.
33. Lt. Thomas A. Howes to Lt. Col. Rogers, February 2, 1865. *O.R.*, ser. 1. vol. 49, pt. 1, 634.
34. Valentine, "Sue Mundy of Kentucky: Part 1," 202.
35. *Louisville Daily Journal*, February 3, 1865.
36. *Louisville Daily Journal*, February 10, 1865.
37. John M. Palmer, *Personal Recollections of John M. Palmer: The Story of an Earnest Life* (Cincinnati: The Robert Clarke Company, 1901), 267.
38. Ibid., 267.
39. *Louisville Daily Journal*, March 7, 1865.
40. Testimony of Major Cyrus J. Wilson, March 14, 1865, *Proceedings of the Trial of Jerome Clark, alias Sue Munday*, RG 153, MM-1732, Records of the Office of the Judge Advocate General (Army), Court Martial Case Files, 1800–1894, Textual Archives Services Division, National Archives and Records Administration, Washington, DC; Valentine, "Sue Mundy of Kentucky: Part 2," 283; Edward E. Leslie, *The Devil Knows How to Ride: The True Story of William Clarke Quantrill and His Confederate Raiders* (New York: Random House, 1996), 360. Both Wilson and Captain Marshall testified that they agreed to treat the captives as POWs only until the party reached Louisville; both also testified that they believed Clarke would be hanged there as a criminal.
41. *Louisville Daily Journal*, March 15, 1865.
42. Valentine, "Sue Mundy of Kentucky: Part 2," 285.
43. Ibid.

44. Ibid, 287.
45. *Proceedings of the Trial of Jerome Clark*; Valentine, "Sue Mundy of Kentucky: Part 2," 286.
46. It has been widely published that Clarke himself told this story about how he acquired the name "Sue Mundy," but this is not true. Captain Marshall testified that Clarke told the story, but when quizzed about Clarke pointing the finger at Prentice for coining the name, the captain stumbled and admitted that the accused may have said something of the sort to another officer. Marshall's testimony is dubious. It is possible that Clarke referred to himself as Mundy as a type of "saddle cred" among bandits, or that others referred to him as Mundy, but the only documentary evidence that someone other than Prentice gave the name "Sue Mundy" to Clarke comes from questionable testimony during the trial.
47. Testimony of Major Cyrus Wilson, March 14, 1865; testimony of Captain Lewis Marshall, March 14, 1865; *Proceedings*; Valentine, "Sue Mundy of Kentucky: Part 2," 293–94.
48. Valentine, "Sue Mundy of Kentucky: Part 2," 294.
49. Watson and Brantley, *Confederate Guerrilla*, 172.
50. Quoted in Lewis Franklin Johnson, *Famous Kentucky Tragedies and Trials: A Collection of Important and Interesting Tragedies and Criminal Trials which have Taken Place in Kentucky* (Louisville, KY: Baldwin Law Book Company, 1916), 186.
51. Valentine, "Sue Mundy of Kentucky: Part 2," 303.
52. Quoted in Johnson, *Famous Kentucky Tragedies and Trials*, 185.
53. *New York Times*, March 26, 1865.
54. *New York Times*, March 26, 1865.
55. Palmer, *Personal Recollections*, 268.
56. Watson and Brantley, *Confederate Guerrilla*, 12.
57. E. Polk Johnson, *A History of Kentucky and Kentuckians: The Leaders and Representative Men in Commerce, Industry and Modern Activities, Vol. 1* (Chicago: The Lewis Publishing Company, 1912), 370.
58. *Charleston Daily News*, May 17, 1869.
59. This story, "A Girl's Apron," appeared in numerous newspapers in 1898, including the (Cincinnati) *Democratic Standard*, August 12, 1898.

The Trial of the Lincoln Assassination Conspirators

1. Lewis Payne was born Lewis Powell. When he signed the Union's Oath of Allegiance, Payne inked the name "Paine." The official court record refers to him as "Lewis Payne," so that is the name used in this text.
2. The official trial record refers to "Edman" Spangler as "Edward" Spangler.
3. Testimony of Lt. Alexander Lovett, May 16, 1865, from Benn Pitman, *The Assassination of President Lincoln and the Trial of the Conspirators* (New York: Moore, Wistach, and Baldwin, 1865), 87.
4. Testimony of Everton Conger, in Pitman, *The Assassination*, 92. Pitman compiled the official trial record, so most of the quotes used here are from his account, which is put into narrative form and categorized by topic. In this chapter, testimony is presented in dialogue form to create the tone and atmosphere of a courtroom drama.

5. La Fayette Curry Baker, *History of the United States Secret Service* (Philadelphia: LC Baker, 1867), 507–508. Modern historians have discounted Baker's book as highly sensationalized, exaggerated, and inaccurate.

6. "Opinion on the Constitutional Power of the Military to Try and Execute the Assassins of the President, by Attorney General James Speed," July 1865, from Pitman, *The Assassination*, 409.

7. Ben Perley Poore, ed., *The Conspiracy Trial for the Murder of the President, and the Attempt to Overthrow the Government by the Assassination of Its Principal Officers* Vol. 1 (Boston: J. E. Tilton and Company, 1865), 11–13. Ben Perley Poore's record of the trial was published in three volumes and, unlike the Pitman version, is presented in a Q & A format more consistent with the back-and-forth of a typical trial. The three volumes were published in very limited quantities and are very rare. As a result, most accounts about the Lincoln conspiracy trial cite Pitman's official record.

8. Testimony of Major August Seward, May 26, 1865. Pitman, *The Assassination*, 156.

9. Testimony of Colonel H. H. Wells, May 19, 1865. Pitman, *The Assassination*, 158; Poore, *The Conspiracy*, Vol. 2, 45.

10. Testimony of Spencer Clark, May 19, 1865. Pitman, *The Assassination*, 159; Poore, *The Conspiracy* Vol. 2, 25.

11. Testimony of Spencer Clark, May 19, 1865. Poore, *The Conspiracy* Vol. 2, 27.

12. Statement of William Doster, June 2, 1865. Pitman, *The Assassination*, 161.

13. Testimony of Dr. James C. Hall, June 13, 1865. Pitman, *The Assassination*, 165.

14. Testimony of Dr. James C. Hall, June 14, 1865. Pitman, *The Assassination*, 167.

15. Testimony of Willie S. Jett, May 17, 1865. Pitman, *The Assassination*, 90. Jett, a Confederate soldier, testified that he ran into Booth and Herold in Virginia. This is when Herold bragged about Lincoln's murder.

16. Testimony of Francis Walsh, May 30, 1865. Pitman, *The Assassination*, 96.

17. Testimony of Dr. Samuel A. H. McKim, May 31, 1865. Pitman, *The Assassination*, 97.

18. "Argument in Defense of David E. Herold by Frederick Stone, Esq." Pitman, *The Assassination*, 274.

19. Testimony of John Fletcher, May 17, 1865. Pitman, *The Assassination*, 145.

20. Text of Atzerodt's confession reproduced in several sources, notably Edward Steers Jr., ed., *The Trial: the Assassination of President Lincoln and the Trial of the Conspirators: A Special Edition of the Trial Transcript as Compiled and Arranged in 1865 by Benn Pitman* (Lexington: The University Press of Kentucky, 2003).

21. "Argument in Defense of George A. Atzerodt, by W. W. Doster, Esq." Pitman, *The Assassination*, 306–307.

22. "Argument in Defense of Mary E. Surratt, by Frederick A. Aiken, Esq." Pitman, *The Assassination*, 293.

23. Ibid., 296

24. "Argument of the Law and Evidence in the Case of Dr. Sam'l A. Mudd by Thomas Ewing, Jr." Pitman, *The Assassination*, 319.

25. Testimony of Colonel H. H. Wells, May 16, 1865. Pitman, *The Assassination*, 169.

26. Ibid.

27. Ibid.

28. Testimony of William Evans, June 5, 1865. Pitman, *The Assassination*, 175.

29. "Argument of the Law and Evidence in the Case of Dr. Sam'l A. Mudd by Thomas Ewing, Jr." Pitman, *The Assassination*, 318.

30. Ibid., 328.

31. "Argument in Defense of Michael O'Laughlin and Sam'l Arnold, by Walter S. Cox, Esq." Pitman, *The Assassination*, 344.
32. Ibid., 344.
33. Testimony of John T. Ford, May 31, 1865. Pitman, *The Assassination*, 103.
34. Testimony of Joseph Burroughs, Alias "Peanuts," May 16, 1865. Pitman, *The Assassination*, 74.
35. Testimony of Joseph Ritterspaugh, May 19, 1865. Pitman, *The Assassination*, 97.
36. "Argument in Defense of Edward Spangler, by Thomas Ewing, Jr." Pitman, *The Assassination*, 286.
37. Quoted in Clara Elizabeth Laughlin, *The Death of Lincoln: The Story of Booth's Plot, His Deed and the Penalty* (New York: Doubleday, Page & Co., 1909), 333.
38. *The New York Herald*, July 8, 1865.
39. Ibid.
40. Ibid.
41. Edward Steers Jr., *Blood on the Moon: The Assassination of Abraham Lincoln* (Lexington: University Press of Kentucky, 2001), 211.

Fifty-Three Counts of Murder: Champ Ferguson's Private War

1. Testimony of John Huff, August 10, 1865, *Proceedings of the Trial of Champ Ferguson*, RG 153, MM-2297, Records of the Office of the Judge Advocate General (Army), Court-Martial Case Files, 1800–1894, Textual Archives Services Division, National Archives and Records Administration, Washington, D.C.
2. Ibid.
3. Testimony of Lucinda Hatfield, August 10, 1865, *Proceedings*.
4. Major J. A. Brents. *The Patriots and Guerillas of East Tennessee and Kentucky*, 37.
5. Ibid.
6. Basil Wilson Duke, *Reminiscences of General Basil W. Duke* (New York: Doubleday, Page, & Co., 1911), 124.
7. Brian McKnight, *Confederate Outlaw: Champ Ferguson and the Civil War in Appalachia* (Baton Rouge: Louisiana State University Press, 2011), 24.
8. Duke, *Reminiscences*, 123.
9. Duke, *Reminiscences*, 125.
10. Quoted in Duke, *Reminiscences*, 124.
11. *O.R.*, ser. I, vol. 20, pt. 2, 185.
12. *O.R.*, ser. I, vol. 23, pt. 1, 307.
13. Report of Thomas J. Harrison, January 14, 1864, *O.R.*, ser. I, vol. 32, pt. 1, 65–66.
14. Ibid.
15. "Champ Ferguson's Full Confession," *Louisville Daily Journal*, October 24, 1865.
16. *O.R.*, ser. I, vol. 49, pt. 1, 765.
17. Order of Major General Thomas, May 1, 1865, *O.R.*, ser. 1, vol. 49, pt. 2, 552–553.
18. H. C. Wittemore to Major General Milroy by Order of Major General Rousseau, May 16, 1865, *O.R.*, ser. 1, vol. 49, pt. 2, 806.
19. "The Trial of Champ Ferguson; Details of Atrocious Barbarities," *New York Times*, August 15, 1865.
20. Testimony of Esther Ann Frogg, August 2, 1865, *Proceedings*.
21. Testimony of Elizabeth Wood, August 4, 1865, *Proceedings*.
22. Ibid.

23. Testimony of Orange Sells, August 12, 1865, *Proceedings*.
24. "Ferguson's Last Speech." *New York Herald*, October 29, 1865.
25. Quoted in *New York Herald*, October 29, 1865
26. Quoted in Bromfield Lewis Ridley, *Battles and Sketches of the Army of Tennessee* (Mexico, MO: Missouri Printing & Publishing Company, 1906), 526.
27. "The Execution of Champ Ferguson, the Guerilla: His Last Speech." *New York Herald*, October 29, 1865.
28. "Champ Ferguson; Confession of the Culprit," *New York Times*, October 29, 1865; "Champ Ferguson's Full Confession," *Louisville Daily Journal*, October 24, 1865.
29. Ibid.
30. Ibid.
31. Ibid.
32. Ibid.
33. Ibid.
34. Ibid.
35. Ibid.
36. Ibid.

Murder of Misadventure? Temperance Neely Kills Her Former Slave

1. The 1850 slave schedule lists twenty slaves from ages one to thirty-eight as the property of Providence Neely. Fifteen of the slaves were fifteen years old or younger, which suggests that the widow Neely owned two or three families.
2. Testimony of Sallie Neal, July 31, 1865. *Proceedings of the Trial of Temperance Neely*, RG 153, MM-2968, Records of the Office of the Judge Advocate General (Army), Court Martial Case Files, 1809–1894, Textual Archives Services Division, National Archives and Records Administration, Washington, DC.
3. Testimony of Henderson, July 31, 1865, *Proceedings*.
4. *Raleigh Daily Standard*, July 18, 1865; Kenneth E. St. Clair, "Military Justice in North Carolina, 1865: A Microcosm of Reconstruction," *Civil War History*, vol. 11, no. 4 (December 1965), 346.
5. *Proceedings*
6. Ibid.
7. Ibid.
8. The official trial transcript is in Q & A form. While the testimony is presented here as dialogue, the wording remains unaltered. The transcript does not record which defense counselor questioned which witness; for the purpose of this narrative, senior counsel Nathaniel Boyden is depicted as the one asking the questions, although it is likely that both attorneys played a role in examining witnesses.
9. Testimony of Sallie Neal, July 31, 1865, *Proceedings*.
10. Ibid.
11. Testimony of Sallie Neal, July 31, 1865.
12. Ibid.
13. Ibid.
14. Ibid.
15. Ibid.
16. Testimony of Henderson, July 31, 1865, *Proceedings*.
17. Testimony of Cassandra, July 31, 1865, *Proceedings*.
18. Ibid.

19. Testimony of Providence Neely, August 1, 1865, *Proceedings*.
20. Ibid.
21. Ibid.
22. Testimony of Arthur Neely, August 1, 1865, *Proceedings*.
23. Testimony of John D. Johnson, August 1, 1865, *Proceedings*. Johnson's plat is marked Defense Exhibit "A."
24. Testimony of John D. Johnson, August 1, 1865, *Proceedings*.
25. Testimony of Meek Neely, August 1, 1865, *Proceedings*.
26. Testimony of George W. Campbell, August 1, 1865, *Proceedings*.
27. Testimony of C. W. Pearson, August 1, 1865, *Proceedings*.
28. Testimony of Alexander S. Nail, August 1, 1865, *Proceedings*.
29. Argument in the Defense of Temperance Neely by J. M. Clement, August 2, 1865, *Proceedings*.
30. Argument in the Defense of Temperance Neely by Nathaniel Boyden, August 2, 1865, *Proceedings*.
31. Argument for the Prosecution, by J. G. Wood, August 2, 1865, *Proceedings*.
32. Letter from General Thomas H. Ruger to Military Commission, August 12, 1865. *Proceedings*.
33. St. Clair, *Military Justice*, 347.
34. St. Clair, *Military Justice*, 348.
35. *New York Tribune*, August 15, 1865; St. Clair, *Military Justice*, 347.
36. St. Clair, *Military Justice*, 349.

The War Crimes Trial of Andersonville's Controversial Commandant

1. Testimony of Dr. Barrows, United States Congress, House, *The Trial of Henry Wirz*, 40th Cong., 2nd sess., 1867–1868. H. Doc. 1331, 51.
2. Ibid., 46.
3. Letter from Henry Wirz to W. P. Wood, superintendent of Caroll Prison, July 6, 1865.
4. Ibid.
5. The superintendent of the camp's cemetery, J. M. Bryant, kept an approximate tally of deaths by day, month, and year. According to Bryant's bottom line, 12,920 prisoners died at the camp. Official camp records suggest that Bryant's estimate was a lowball and indicate that 13,171 prisoners died at Andersonville. The total number varies depending on source. Bryant's records are presented in Norton Parker Chipman, *The Tragedy at Andersonville: The Trial of Captain Wirz, the Prison Keeper* (Sacramento: printed by author, 1911), 375.
6. Testimony of Dr. Barrows, *The Trial of Henry Wirz*, 44.
7. Michael Dougherty, *Prison Diary of Michael Dougherty* (Bristol, PA: Chas. A. Dougherty, 1908), 28.
8. Ibid. In deference to the reader, Dougherty replaces Wirz's expletive with dashes. Trial transcripts and contemporary news items indicate that Wirz often referred to prisoners as "God damned Yankees." This was likely the phrase that Dougherty omitted.
9. Bryant records 108 deaths for this month.
10. Letter from Henry Wirz to W. P. Wood, superintendent of Caroll Prison, July 6, 1865.
11. James William Denver, letter to his wife, August 13, 1865.
12. Letter from Col. George C. Gibbs to Gen. E. M. McCook, May 12, 1865. *O. R.* ser. 2, vol. 8, p. 552–553.

13. Letter from Gen. E. M. McCook to Headquarters First Division, May 18, 1865. *O.R.* ser. 2, vol. 8, p. 553.
14. The "Andersonville/Wirz Collection" at the University of Notre Dame includes Wirz' handwritten list of witnesses. The list contains thirty-four entries, including Colonel Gibbs. Gibbs, however, would testify for the prosecution.
15. "The Rebel Assassins: Trial of Henry Wirz, the Andersonville Jailor. *New York Times*, August 21, 1865.
16. Testimony of George C. Gibbs, *The Trial of Henry Wirz*, 21.
17. Testimony of Dr. John Bates, *The Trial of Henry Wirz*, 28.
18. Ibid., 33.
19. Ibid., 38.
20. Ibid., 42.
21. Testimony of Dr. A.V. Barrows, *The Trial of Henry Wirz*, 45.
22. *The Trial of Henry Wirz*, 149.
23. Testimony of Dr. A. V. Barrows, *The Trial of Henry Wirz*, 47.
24. Ibid., 49.
25. Ibid., 51.
26. Ibid., 61.
27. Testimony of Thomas C. Alcoke, *The Trial of Henry Wirz*, 67.
28. Testimony of Boston Corbett, *The Trial of Henry Wirz*, 72.
29. Testimony of Frank Maddox, *The Trial of Henry Wirz*, 177.
30. *The Trial of Henry Wirz*, 415.
31. Testimony of Col. James H. Fannin, *The Trial of Henry Wirz*, 433.
32. Testimony of Augustus Moesner, *The Trial of Henry Wirz*, 544.
33. Ibid.
34. Testimony of Dr. John Bates, *The Trial of Henry Wirz*, 663.
35. Ibid.
36. Testimony of Dr. C. J. Ford, *The Trial of Henry Wirz*, 804.
37. Testimony of Dr. John Bates, *The Trial of Henry Wirz*, 805.
38. Henry Wirz. Diary entry for October 1, 1865. Quoted in *New York Times*, "The Diary of Wirz," November 15, 1865.
39. Baker, *History*, 580. "The Alleged Attempt to Poison Wirz," *New York Times*, November 13, 1865. If the story was a tall tale, it wouldn't be the only time that Baker stretched the truth. His memoirs have not stood up to scrutiny over the years; some of Baker's facts have turned out to be half-truths, exaggerations, or outright fabrications.
40. *The Trial of Henry Wirz*, 846.
41. Letter from Henry Wirz to President Andrew Johnson, November 6, 1865, quoted in James Madison Page, *The True Story of Andersonville Prison* (New York: Neale Publishing Company, 1908), 62–63 and 226.
42. "Execution of Wirz," *New York Times*, November 11, 1865.
43. Ibid.
44. *The Trial of Henry Wirz*, 181.
45. *The Trial of Henry Wirz*, 266.
46. James William Denver, letter to his wife, August 13, 1865.
47. Page, *The True Story*, 62–63.
48. James Joseph Williamson, *Prison Life in the Old Capital and Reminiscences of the Civil War* (West Orange, NJ: n.p., 1911), 152.

Bibliography

Andersonville/Wirz Collection. *Manuscripts of the American Civil War.* Department of Special Collections, Hesburgh Libraries of Notre Dame, University of Notre Dame, Notre Dame, Indiana. Available online at http://www.rarebooks.nd.edu/digital/civil-war/topical_collections/andersonville.

Baker, La Fayette Curry. *History of the United States Secret Service.* Philadelphia: LC Baker, 1867.

The Baltimore Sun, February 22, 1895.

Barb, Thomas Jacob. Civil War Diary. Department of Special Collections, University of Notre Dame.

Beard, William Ewing. *It Happened in Nashville, Tennessee.* Nashville, TN: Nashville Industrial Bureau, 1912.

Bradley, George C., and Richard L. Dahlen. *From Conciliation to Conquest: The Sack of Athens and the Court-Martial of Colonel John B. Turchin.* Tuscaloosa: University of Alabama Press, 2006.

Brents, Major J. A. *The Patriots and Guerillas of East Tennessee and Kentucky: The Sufferings of the Patriots, Also the Experience of the Author as an Officer in the Union Army, Including Sketches of Noted Guerillas and Distinguished Patriots.* New York: J. A. Brents, 1863.

Brooks, Frank. "First Full Story of the Civil War's Most Daring Cavalry Raid." *San Francisco Sunday Call*, July 9, 1911.

Burnett, Alfred. *Incidents of the War: Humorous, Pathetic, and Descriptive.* Cincinnati: Rickey & Carroll Publishers, 1863.

Butler, Benjamin Franklin. *Autobiography and Personal Reminiscences of Major General Benjamin F. Butler: Butler's Book.* Boston: A. A. Thayer and Co., 1892.

Butler, Benjamin F., and Jessie A. Marshall. *Private and Official Correspondence of Gen. Benjamin F. Butler: During the Period of the Civil War.* Norwood, MA: Plimpton Press, 1917.

Carter, Arthur B. *The Tarnished Cavalier: Major General Earl Van Dorn, C.S.A.* Knoxville: University of Tennessee Press, 1999.

Casstevens, Frances. *George W. Alexander and Castle Thunder: A Confederate Prison and Its Commandant.* Jefferson, NC: McFarland & Company, 2004.

Castel, Albert, and Thomas Goodrich. *Bloody Bill Anderson: The Short, Savage Life of a Civil War Guerrilla.* Mechanicsburg, PA: Stackpole Books, 1998.

Castel, Howard. "Quantrill's Bushwhackers: A Case Study in Partisan Warfare." *Civil War History* 13, no. 1 (March 1967): 40–50.

Charleston Daily News, May 17, 1869.

The Charleston Mercury, May 21, 1862; January 9, 1863; July 20, 1864.

Chicago Daily Tribune, July 15, 1862; September 6, 1863; October 10, 1863.

Chicoine, Stephen. *John Basil Turchin and the Fight to Free the Slaves*. Westport, CT: Praeger, 2003.

Chipman, Norton Parker. *The Tragedy at Andersonville: The Trial of Captain Wirz, the Prison Keeper*. Sacramento: printed by author, 1911.

Colby, Newton T. *The Civil War Papers of Lt. Newton T. Colby, New York Infantry*. Edited by William E. Hughes. Jefferson, NC: McFarland & Company, 2003.

Congleton, Betty Carolyn. "George D. Prentice: Nineteenth Century Southern Editor." *Register of the Kentucky Historical Society* 65, no. 2 (April 1967): 94–119.

Connelley, William Elsey. *Quantrill and the Border Wars*. Cedar Rapids, IA: The Torch Press, 1910.

———. *The Life of Preston B. Plumb, 1837–1891*. Chicago: Browne & Howell, 1913.

Cunningham, O. Edward. "'In Violation of the Laws of War': The Execution of Robert Cobb Kennedy." *The Journal of the Louisiana Historical Association* 18, no. 2 (Spring 1977): 189–201.

Davison, Eddy W., and Daniel Foxx. *Nathan Bedford Forrest: In Search of the Enigma*. Gretna, LA: Pelican, 2007.

"Death of a Detective." *The Richmond Sentinel*. November 11, 1864.

Democratic Standard (Cincinnati), August 12, 1898.

Denver, James William. Letter to his wife, August 13, 1865. Andersonville/Wirz Collection. Manuscripts of the American Civil War. Department of Special Collections, Hesburgh Libraries of Notre Dame, University of Notre Dame, Notre Dame, Indiana.

Detroit Advertiser and Tribune, March 14, 1863 and February 27, 1863.

The Detroit Free Press, March 1, 1863; March 6, 1863; March 7, 1863; March 8, 1863; March 27, 1863.

Doran, Frank B. "Prison Memories." *The National Tribune*, November 16, 1905.

Doster, William E. *Lincoln and Episodes of the Civil War*. New York: G. P. Putnam's Sons, 1915.

Dougherty, Michael. *Prison Diary of Michael Dougherty*. Bristol, PA: Chas. A. Dougherty, 1908.

Dubuque Herald, August 22, 1863; September 9, 1863.

Duke, Basil Wilson. *History of Morgan's Cavalry*. Cincinnati: Miami Printing and Publishing Company, 1867.

———. *Reminiscences of General Basil W. Duke*. New York: Doubleday, Page, & Co., 1911.

Duke, Thomas S. *Celebrated Criminal Cases of America*. San Francisco: The James H. Berry Company, 1910.

Edwards, John N. *Noted Guerrillas, or the Warfare of the Border*. St. Louis: Bryan, Brand & Co, 1877.

Ellis, Dr. A. M. "Major General William Nelson." *Kentucky State Historical Society Register* 7 (May 1906): 56–64.

Ellis, John B. *The Sights and Secrets of the National Capital: A Work Descriptive of Washington City in all its Various Phases*. New York: United States Publishing Co., 1869.

"Escape of Prisoners from Johnson's Island," *Southern Historical Society Papers, Vol. XVIII*. Richmond, VA: Jan.–Dec, 1890, pages 428–431.

Fayetteville (Tennessee) Observer, March 22, May 15, June 4, 1863.

Feimster, Crystal. "The Threat of Sexual Violence During the American Civil War," *Daedalus* 38, no. 2 (Spring 2009): 126–134.

Fitch, John. *Annals of the Army of the Cumberland: Comprising Biographies, Descriptions of Departments, Accounts of Expeditions, Skirmishes, and Battles; Also Its Police Record of Spies, Smugglers, and Prominent Rebel Emissaries Together with Anecdotes, Incidents, Poetry, Reminiscences, etc. and Official Reports of the Battle of Stone River and of the Chickamauga Campaign*, Fifth Ed. Philadelphia: J. B. Lippincott, 1864.

Fry, James Barnet. "Article XIII: Killed by a Brother Soldier." *Military Miscellanies*. New York: Brentano's, 1889.

Goodman, Thomas M. *A Thrilling Record: Founded on Facts and Observations Obtained during Ten Days' Experience with Colonel William T. Anderson (the Notorious Guerrilla Chieftain); Edited and Prepared for the Press by Harry A. Houston*. Des Moines, IA: Mills & Co., 1868.

Gorman, Michael D. *Civil War Richmond*. www.mdgorman.com.

Harrell, Col. John M. *Arkansas. Confederate Military History, Vol. X*. Edited by Clement Evans. Atlanta: Confederate Publishing Company, 1899.

Hanna, J. Marshall. "Castle Thunder in Bellum Days," *Southern Opinion*, November 23, 1867.

Harris, Charles F. "Catalyst for Terror: The Collapse of the Women's Prison in Kansas City." *Missouri Historical Review* 89 (April 1995): 290–306.

Hartje, Robert G. *Van Dorn: the Life and Times of a Confederate General*. Nashville, TN: Vanderbilt University Press, 1967.

Hazen, General W. B. *A Narrative of Military Service*. Boston: Ticknor and Company, 1885.

Headley, John W. *Confederate Operations in Canada and New York*. The Neale Publishing Company, 1906.

Hogue, Albert Ross. *History of Fentress County, Tennessee*. Nashville, TN: Williams Printing Company, 1916.

Horrall, S. F. *History of the 42nd Indiana Volunteer Infantry*. N.p.: printed by author, 1892.

Huff, Leo E. "The Marmaduke-Walker Duel: The Last Duel in Arkansas." *Missouri Historical Review* 58 (July 1964): 452–463.

Jenkins, Kirk C. "A Shooting at the Galt House: the Death of General William Nelson." *Civil War History* 43, no. 2 (1997): 101–118.

Johnson, E. Polk. *A History of Kentucky and Kentuckians: The Leaders and Representative Men in Commerce, Industry and Modern Activities, Vol. 1*. Chicago: The Lewis Publishing Company, 1912.

Johnson, Lewis Franklin. *Famous Kentucky Tragedies and Trials: A Collection of Important and Interesting Tragedies and Criminal Trials which have Taken Place in Kentucky*. Louisville, KY: Baldwin Law Book Company, 1916.

Jordan, Thomas, and J. P. Pryor. *The Campaigns of Lieut.-Gen. N. B. Forrest, and of Forrest's Cavalry*. New York: Blelock & Co., 1868.

Kauffman, Michael. *American Brutus: John Wilkes Booth and the Lincoln Conspiracies*. New York: Random House, 2005.

Kundinger, Matt. "Racial Rhetoric: The *Detroit Free Press* and Its Part in the Detroit Race Riot of 1863." *Michigan Journal of History* (Winter 2006). Available: http://www.umich.edu/~historyj/pages_folder/articles/Racial_Rhetoric.pdf

Laughlin, Clara Elizabeth. *The Death of Lincoln: The Story of Booth's Plot, His Deed and the Penalty*. New York: Doubleday, Page & Co., 1909.

LeGrand, Julia. *The Journal of Julia LeGrand: New Orleans 1862—1863*. Edited by Kate Mason Rowland and Mrs. Morris L. Croxall. Richmond: Everett Wadey, 1911.

Leslie, Edward E. *The Devil Knows How to Ride: The True Story of William Clarke Quantrill and His Confederate Raiders*. New York: Random House, 1996.

Life and Public Services of Major-General Butler: the Hero of New Orleans. Philadelphia: T. B. Peterson and Brothers, 1864.

Lomax, Virginia. *The Old Capitol and Its Inmates, By a Lady, Who Enjoyed the Hospitalities of the Government for a "Season."* New York: E. J. Hale & Son, 1867.

Louisville Daily Journal, October 11, October 17, November 9, 1864; January 26, January 31, February 2, February 3, March 7, March 15, 1865.

McElligott, Mary Ellen, ed. "'A Monotony of Sadness:' The Diary of Nadine Turchin, May, 1863—April, 1864." *Illinois State Historical Society Journal* 52 (1977): 27–89.

McKnight, Brian. *Confederate Outlaw: Champ Ferguson and the Civil War in Appalachia*. Baton Rouge: Louisiana State University Press, 2011

Mobile Advertiser and Register, March 22, 1863; May 7, 1863; May 15, 1863.

Moore, Joanna Patterson. *"In Christ's Stead": Autobiographical Sketches*. Chicago: Women's Baptist Home Mission Society, 1902.

Moore, Col. John C. *Missouri. Confederate Military History, Vol. IX*. Edited by Clement Evans. Atlanta: Confederate Publishing Company, 1899.

"The Murder of Gen. Nelson." *Harper's Weekly*, October 18, 1862.

Napolitano, Andrew. *Dred Scott's Revenge: A Legal History of Race and Freedom in America*. Nashville, TN: Thomas Nelson, 2009.

The New York Herald, July 8, 1865; October 29, 1865.

The New York Times, August 11, 1862; September 30, 1862; August 9, 1863; April 16, 1864; November 26, 1864; November 27, 1864; January 15, 1865; February 28, 1865; March 14, 1865; March 26, 1865; March 27, 1865; August 16, 1865; August 21, 1865; October 29, 1865; November 11, 1865; November 15, 1868; September 13, 1868.

New York Tribune, August 15, 1865.

Nugent, William Lewis, and Eleanor Smith Nugent. *My Dear Nellie: the Civil War Letters of William L. Nugent to Eleanor Smith Nugent*. Oxford: University of Mississippi, 1977.

Page, James Madison. *The True Story of Andersonville Prison*. New York: Neale Publishing Company, 1908.

Palmer, John M. *Personal Recollections of John M. Palmer: the Story of an Earnest Life*. Cincinnati: The Robert Clarke Company, 1901.

Parton, James. *General Butler in New Orleans*. New York: Mason Brothers, 1864.

Peckham, Howard. "'I Have Been Basely Murdered.'" *American Heritage Magazine* 14, no. 5 (August 1963).

Pitman, Benn. *The Assassination of President Lincoln and the Trial of the Conspirators*. New York: Moore, Wistach, and Baldwin, 1865.

Poore, Ben Perley, ed. *The Conspiracy Trial for the Murder of the President, and the Attempt to Overthrow the Government by the Assassination of Its Principal Officers*. Vols. 1–3. Boston: J. E. Tilton and Company, 1865.

The Portrait Monthly: Containing Sketches of Departed Heroes, and Prominent Personages of the Present Time, Interesting Stories, Etc. Volume 1. New York: T. B. Leggett & Co., 1864.

Proceedings of the Court Martial of Colonel J.B. Turchin. RG 153, KK-122, Records of the Office of the Judge Advocate General (Army), Court Martial Case Files, 1800–1894, Textual Archives Services Division, National Archives and Records Administration, Washington, DC.

Proceedings of the Court Martial of Private Thomas Wright. RG 153, Records of the Office of the Judge Advocate General (Army), Court Martial Case Files, 1809–1894, Textual Archives Services Division, National Archives and Records Administration, Washington, DC.

Proceedings of the Trial of Aaron Bridgewater. RG 153, MM-931, Records of the Office of the Judge Advocate General (Army), Court Martial Case Files, 1800–1894, Textual Archives Services Division, National Archives and Records Administration, Washington, DC.

Proceedings of the Trial of Abram Cole. RG 153, MM-915, Records of the Office of the Judge Advocate General (Army), Court Martial Case Files, 1800–1894, Textual Archives Services Division, National Archives and Records Administration, Washington, DC.

Proceedings of the Trial of Benjamin Robinson. RG 153, NN-328, Records of the Office of the Judge Advocate General (Army), Court Martial Case Files, 1800–1894, Textual Archives Services Division, National Archives and Records Administration, Washington, DC.

Proceedings of the Trial of Champ Ferguson. RG 153, MM-2297, Records of the Office of the Judge Advocate General (Army), Court Martial Case Files, 1800–1894, Textual Archives Services Division, National Archives and Records Administration, Washington, DC.

Proceedings of the Trial of George Harris. RG 153, MM-915, Records of the Office of the Judge Advocate General (Army), Court Martial Case Files, 1800–1894, Textual Archives Services Division, National Archives and Records Administration, Washington, DC.

Proceedings of the Trial of Jerome Clark. RG 153, MM-1732, Records of the Office of the Judge Advocate General (Army), Court Martial Case Files, 1800–1894, Textual Archives Services Division, National Archives and Records Administration, Washington, DC.

Proceedings of the Trial of Jim Webb. RG 153, MM-813, Records of the Office of the Judge Advocate General (Army), Court Martial Case Files, 1809–1894, Textual Archives Services Division, National Archives and Records Administration, Washington, DC.

Proceedings of the Trial of Joseph Davis. RG 153, MM-915, Records of the Office of the Judge Advocate General (Army), Court Martial Case Files, 1800–1894, Textual Archives Services Division, National Archives and Records Administration, Washington, DC.

Proceedings of the Trial of Lewis Stevinson. RG 153, MM-813, Records of the Office of the Judge Advocate General (Army), Court Martial Case Files, 1809–1894, Textual Archives Services Division, National Archives and Records Administration, Washington, DC.

Proceedings of the Trial of Temperance Neely. RG 153, MM-2968, Records of the Office of the Judge Advocate General (Army), Court Martial Case Files, 1809–1894, Textual Archives Services Division, National Archives and Records Administration, Washington, DC.

Proceedings of the Trial of Wade Good. RG 153, MM-915, Records of the Office of the Judge Advocate General (Army), Court Martial Case Files, 1800–1894, Textual Archives Services Division, National Archives and Records Administration, Washington, DC.

Proceedings of the Trial of William Ray. RG 153, MM-813, Records of the Office of the Judge Advocate General (Army), Court Martial Case Files, 1809–1894, Textual Archives Services Division, National Archives and Records Administration, Washington, DC.

Raleigh Daily Standard, July 18, 1865.

The Richmond Dispatch, March 3, 1895.

Richmond Shield and Banner, August 30, 1898.

The Richmond Whig, November 11, 1864.

Ridley, Bromfield Lewis. *Battles and Sketches of the Army of Tennessee.* Mexico, MO: Missouri Printing & Publishing Company, 1906.

Ripley, Eliza Moore Chinn McHatton. *Social Life in Old New Orleans: Being Recollections of My Girlhood.* New York: Appleton and Company, 1912.

Robbins, William. "Guerilla's Bones Get a Confederate Soldier's Funeral." *The New York Times,* October 25, 1992.

St. Clair, Kenneth E. "Military Justice in North Carolina, 1865: A Microcosm of Reconstruction." *Civil War History* 11, no. 4 (December 1965): 341–350.

St. Paul Daily Globe, January 11, 1888.

Sanders, Stuart. "Bloody Bill's Centralia Massacre." *America's Civil War* 12, no. 6 (March 2000): 34–41.

"Schedule 2—Slave Inhabitants in the County of Davie, State of North Carolina," August 31, 1850.

Schneider, John C. "Detroit and the Problem of Disorder: The Riot of 1863." *Michigan History* 58 (Spring 1974): 4–24.

Sheridan, Richard B. "A Most Unusual Gathering: The 1913 Semi-Centennial Memorial Reunion of he Survivors of Quantrill's Raid on Lawrence." *Kansas History* 20 (Autumn 1997): 176–191.

Six, Fred N., ed. "Eyewitness Reports of Quantrill's Raid: Letters of Sophia Bissell & Sidney Clarke." *Kansas History* 28 (Summer 2005): 94–103.

Slaubaugh, Arlie R. *Confederate States Paper Money.* Iola, WI: Krause Publications, 1998.

A Soldier's Honor, with Reminiscences of Major-General Earl Van Dorn by His Comrades. New York: Abbey Press, 1902.

Speer, Lonnie. *Portals of Hell: Military Prisons of the Civil War.* Mechanicsburg, PA: Stackpole Books, 1997.

Steers, Edward Jr. *Blood on the Moon: The Assassination of Abraham Lincoln.* Lexington: University Press of Kentucky, 2001.

Steers, Edward, Jr., ed. *The Trial: The Assassination of President Lincoln and the Trial of the Conspirators: A Special Edition of the Trial Transcript as Compiled and Arranged in 1865 by Benn Pitman.* Lexington: The University Press of Kentucky, 2003.

A Thrilling Narrative From the Lips of the Sufferers of the Late Detroit Riot, March 6, 1863: With the Hair Breadth Escapes of Men, Women And Children, And Destruction of Colored Men's Property, Not Less Than $15,000. Detroit: printed by the author, 1863.

Todd, Richard Cecil. *Confederate Finance*. Athens: University of Georgia Press, 1954.

Turchin, John Basil. *Chickamauga*. Chicago: Fergus Printing Company, 1888.

United States Congress, House, The Trial of Henry Wirz, 40th Cong., 2d sess, 1867–1868. H. Doc. 1331.

United States Joint Committee on the Conduct of the War. Reports: Fort Pillow Massacre; Returned Prisoners. 38th Congress, 1st Session. House of Representatives. Report No. 65, 67. Washington, 1864.

United States War Department. *The War of the Rebellion: A Compilation of the Official Records of the Union and Confederate Armies*, 128 vols. Washington, D.C.: Government Printing Office, 1880–1901.

Valentine, L. L. "Sue Mundy of Kentucky: Part 1." *Register of the Kentucky Historical Society* 62, no. 3 (July 1964): 175–205.

———. "Sue Mundy of Kentucky: Part 2." *Register of the Kentucky Historical Society* 62, no. 4 (October 1964): 278–306.

Waddle, Angus. *Three Years with the Armies of the Ohio and the Cumberland*. Chillicothe, OH: Sciotto Gazette and Job Office, 1889.

Washington Telegraph, October 21, 1863.

Watson, Thomas Shelby with Perry A. Brantley. *Confederate Guerrilla Sue Mundy: A Biography of Jerome Clarke*. Jefferson, NC: McFarland & Company, 2008.

Werlich, Robert. *"Beast" Butler: The Incredible Career of Major General Benjamin Franklin Butler*. Washington, DC: Quaker Press, 1962.

Wilkinson, Darryl. "Samuel Cox—a Daviess County Hero." *The Daviess County Historical Society*. Available http://www.daviesscountyhistoricalsociety.com.

Willard, Eugene, and Hon. Daniel W. Williams, George O. Newman, and Charles B. Taylor, eds. *A Standard History of The Hanging Rock Iron Region of Ohio, Volume 1*. Chicago: The Lewis Publishing Company, 1916.

Williamson, James Joseph. *Prison Life in the Old Capital and Reminiscences of the Civil War*. West Orange, NJ, 1911.

Williamson, James J. *Prison life in the Old Capitol and reminiscences of the Civil War*. Illustrations by B F Williamson. West Orange, NJ: [no publisher], 1911.

Wilson, James Grant. *Biographical Sketches of Illinois Officers Involved in the War against the Rebellion of 1861*. Chicago: James Barnet, 1863.

Wirz, Henry. Letter from Carroll Prison to W. P. Wood, Superintendent of Carroll Prison, Washington, DC, July 6, 1865. Andersonville/Wirz Collection. Manuscripts of the American Civil War. Department of Special Collections, Hesburgh Libraries of Notre Dame, University of Notre Dame, Notre Dame, Indiana.

Woodford, Arthur M. *This is Detroit, 1701–2001*. Detroit: Wayne State University Press, 2001.

Wyeth, John Allan. *Life of Lieutenant-General Nathan Bedford Forrest*. New York: Harper and Brothers, 1908.

Index